The Politics of (M)Otherin

"The editor's introduction is a well-informed overview of the major themes and trends in the subject . . . This is a book that will not be ignored in any serious study of African literature."

Isidore Okpewho, *SUNY, Binghamton*

"Nnaemeka's introduction is a brilliant critique of current scholarship and represents an ingenious use of orality in literary criticism as she sets the framework of the volume by highlighting the complexities and contradictions in defining 'woman.'"

Helen N. Mugambi, *California State University*

Over the last decade, post-colonial studies have become a defining feature in critical thought, but until very recently attention has been focused on areas other than Africa and its wealth of literatures. The arrival of *The Politics of (M)Othering* signals an important shift of focus. African Studies will certainly be setting the agenda in the future.

This study of African literature examines the paradoxical location of (m)other as both central and marginal and is framed by the idea of "mother"—motherland, mothertongue, motherwit, motherhood, and mothering. Whilst the volume stands as a sustained feminist analysis, it engages feminist theory itself by showing how issues in feminism are, in African literature, recast in different and complex ways. The core arguments in the volume foreground epistemological questions—the construction, containment, and dissemination of knowledge—and the role that gender politics plays in them. Even more significantly, *The Politics of (M)Othering* insists on the importance of cultural literacy to an effective analysis of cultural productions such as African literary texts. The volume is unique in its extensive territorial claims, in terms of genre (orature, fiction, theater, and autobiography) and geography (from all regions of Africa to the African Diaspora).

This collection brings together critics at the forefront of African literatures—Trinh T. Minh-ha, Françoise Lionnet, Obioma Nnaemeka, Huma Ibrahim, Peter Hitchcock, Charles Sugnet, Uzo Esonwanne, Renée Larrier, Celeste Fraser Delgado, Ousseynou B. Traoré, Juliana Makuchi Nfah-Abbenyi, and Cynthia Ward.

The Editor: **Obioma Nnaemeka** is Associate Professor of French, Women's Studies, and African American Studies at Indiana University, Indianapolis.

Feminism for Today
General Editor: Teresa Brennan

The Politics of (M)Othering

Womanhood, identity, and resistance in
African literature

Edited by Obioma Nnaemeka

London and New York

First published 1997
by Routledge
11 New Fetter Lane, London EC4P 4EE

Simultaneously published in the USA and Canada
by Routledge
29 West 35th Street, New York, NY 10001

Typeset in Times by
Ponting–Green Publishing Services, Chesham, Buckinghamshire
Printed and bound in Great Britain by
Mackays of Chatham PLC, Chatham, Kent

British Library Cataloguing in Publication Data
A catalogue record for this book is available from the
British Library

Library of Congress Cataloguing in Publication Data
The politics of (m)othering: womanhood, identity, and resistance in
African literature / edited by Obioma Nnaemeka.
    p.   cm.—(Opening out)
    Includes bibliographical references and index.
    1. Mothers in literature.   2. African literature—History and
criticism.   3. Femininity (Psychology) in literature.   4. Feminism
and literature—Africa.   5. Politics and literature—Africa.
6. Gender identity in literature.   7. Women and
literature—Africa.   8. Motherhood in literature.
I. Nnaemeka, Obioma, 1948–   .   II. Series.
PL8010.P57   1996
809'.8896—dc20   96–20491
                            CIP

ISBN 0–415–13789–6 (hbk)
ISBN 0–415–13790–X (pbk)

To my mother,
Jessie Obidiegwu
(a.k.a. Lawyer),
with love and gratitude

"Nothing comes close in individual or collective engagement to demonstrate that feminist discourse has a vital role in African literary or cultural processes. This volume is authoritative, bold and incisive and delivered with the suavity and confidence that can only come from a keen knowledge of Africa with all its intrinsic paradoxes and the sundry cultural complexities exacerbated by the encounter with the West."

Chimalum Nwankwo, *North Carolina State University*

"Amidst all the anomy of interpretative grids, and vulgarisation of African cultures and peoples, *The Politics of (M)Othering* emerges as a breath of fresh air. The collection is indeed a 'tour de force' and an excellent contribution to the ongoing debate about feminism and African literature."

Michael Mbabuike, *City University of New York*

Contents

Contributors

Uzo Esonwanne is Assistant Professor of English at Saint Mary's University, Halifax, Canada. A graduate of the University of Nigeria, Nsukka, and the University of New Brunswick, Fredericton, he is an alumnus of the Michigan Society of Fellows, University of Michigan, Ann Arbor. His essays have appeared in books and journals, including *ReImaging Women: Representations of Women in Culture, African-American Review, Cultural Critique*, and *Research in African Literatures*. Dr Esonwanne is currently editing a collection of critical essays on Christopher Okigbo.

Celeste Fraser Delgado is Assistant Professor of English at the Pennsylvania State University, University Park. She has published in *Cultural Critique* and the *Latin American Literary Review*. She co-edited with José Muñoz a collection of essays titled *Politics in Motion: Culture and Dance in Latin/o America* (forthcoming, Duke University Press). She is completing a book titled *Global Economies, Local Sexualities: The Structural Adjustment of Gender.*

Peter Hitchcock is Associate Professor of English and Cultural Studies at Baruch College, CUNY. He is the author of *Working Class Fiction in Theory and Practice* (1989) and *Dialogics of the Oppressed* (1993). He has also published articles on international fiction, cultural studies, materialism, feminist theory, and film in journals such as *Research in African Literatures, Cultural Studies, Critical Texts, Transition, Third Text*, and *Modern Fiction Studies*. He is currently writing a book on millennial materialism.

Huma Ibrahim is Assistant Professor of Literature at the American University. As a DuBois-Mandela-Rodney Post-Doctoral Fellow at the Center for AfroAmerican and African Studies, University of Michigan, she completed a full-length study of Bessie Head, titled *Bessie Head: Subversive Identities in Exile*, that is being published in Fall 1996 by The University Press of Virginia. Under the auspices of the Zora Neale Hurston Fellowship at Northwestern University, Dr Ibrahim is working on a second book, titled *The Other Body: From Spectacle to Sexuality.*

Renée Larrier, a Columbia University Ph.D., is Associate Professor of French at Rutgers University where she won the Faculty of Arts and Sciences Distinguished Contributor to Undergraduate Education Award in 1991. She has published numerous articles in edited volumes and scholarly journals such as *French Review, CLA Journal, Studies in Twentieth Century Literature, Présence francophone*, and *World Literature Today*. She is currently working on a book-length manuscript on women writers from Africa and the Caribbean.

Françoise Lionnet teaches French and Comparative Literature at Northwestern University. During 1991–92, she was a Rockefeller Fellow at the Center for Advanced Feminist Studies, University of Minnesota. She is the author of *Autobiographical Voices: Race, Gender, and Self-Portraiture* (Cornell, 1989), *Postcolonial Representations: Women, Literature, Identity* (Cornell, 1995), is co-editor of *Post/Colonial Conditions: Exiles, Migrations and Normadism, Yale French Studies*, 1993, and has written the article "Postcolonial, Emergent, and Indigenous Feminisms," *Signs*, 1995.

Juliana Makuchi Nfah-Abbenyi, a McGill University Ph.D., is Assistant Professor of English and Postcolonial Literatures at the University of Southern Mississippi, Hattiesburg. She has conducted extensive research on African oral tradition, particularly the study of women in Beba folktales. Her other interests include feminist and post-colonial theories. Her publications on orature, autobiography, and literatures of Africa and the African diaspora appear in edited volumes and scholarly journals. Her book titled *Gender in African Women's Writing* is forthcoming from Indiana University Press.

Obioma Nnaemeka is Associate Professor of French, Women's Studies, and African-American Studies at Indiana University, Indianapolis, and a 1991–92 Rockefeller Humanist-in-Residence at the Center for Advanced Feminist Studies, University of Minnesota, Minneapolis. Her publications have appeared in edited volumes and scholarly journals, including *Signs, Feminist Issues, Research in African Literatures, The Western Journal of Black Studies*, and *International Third World Studies Journal and Review*. Her book titled *Marginality: Orality, Writing, and the African Woman Writer* will be published by Routledge.

Charles Sugnet is Associate Professor of English at the University of Minnesota and a literary journalist. He has published on Shakespeare, William Blake, and various aspects of contemporary fiction. He co-edited *The Imagination on Trial* with Alan Burns. His reviews and cultural journalism have appeared in a variety of publications, including *The Utne Reader, The Nation, The Village Voice, In These Times* and *d'Art*. He has written on Chinua Achebe and Tsitsi Dangarembga, and the first issue of the newly revived *Transition Magazine* contains his essay on travel writing and the post-colonial situation.

Ousseynou B. Traoré is the Chairperson of the Department of African, African-American and Caribbean Studies at the William Paterson College of New Jersey. He holds an M.Phil. in African-American Studies from the Sorbonne, and an M.A. and a Ph.D. in African Languages and Literature from the University of Madison-Wisconsin. Some of his work is published in *Approaches to Teaching Achebe's Things Fall Apart, Beloved She's Mine*, and *The Langston Hughes Review*. He is the founding editor of *The Literary Griot: International Journal of Black Expressive Culture Studies*.

Trinh T. Minh-ha is a writer, filmmaker, and composer. Her more recent works include the books: *Framer Framed* (1992), *When the Moon Waxes Red* (1991), *Woman, Native, Other* (1989), *En minuscules* (book of poems, 1987); and films: *A Tale of Love* (1995), *Shoot for the Contents* (1991), *Surname Viet Given Name Nam* (1989), *Naked Spaces* (1985), *and Reassemblage* (1982). She taught at the Dakar Conservatory of Music in Senegal, and at universities such as Cornell, San Francisco State, Smith College, and Harvard. She is presently Professor of Women's Studies and Film at the University of California, Berkeley.

Cynthia Ward, a Stanford University Ph.D., is Assistant Professor of English at the University of Hawai'i, Manoa, and the (m)other of four white males. Her publications have appeared in scholarly journals such as *PMLA, Modern Fiction Studies*, and *Text and Performance Quarterly*. She is currently researching working-class perceptions of "home."

Series preface

Feminist theory is the most innovative and truly living theory in today's academies, but the struggle between the living and the dead extends beyond feminism and far beyond institutions. *Opening Out* will apply the living insights of feminist critical theory in current social and political contexts. It will also use feminist theory to analyze the historical and cultural genealogies that shaped those contexts.

While feminist insights on modernity and postmodernity have become increasingly sophisticated, they have also become more distant from the *realpolitik* that made feminism a force in the first instance. This distance is apparent in three growing divisions. One is an evident division between feminist theory and feminist popular culture and politics. Another division is that between feminism and other social movements. Of course this second division is not new, but it has been exacerbated by the issue of whether the theoretical insights of feminism can be used to analyze current conflicts that extend beyond feminism's "proper" field. In the postmodern theory he has helped build, the white male middle-class universal subject has had to relinquish his right to speak for all. By the same theoretical logic, he has also taken out a philosophical insurance policy against any voice uniting the different movements that oppose him, which means his power persists *de facto*, if not *de jure*. Currently, there are no theoretical means, except for fine sentiments and good will, that enable feminism to ally itself with other social movements that oppose the power networks that sustain the white, masculine universal subject. *Opening Out* aims at finding those means.

Of course, the analysis of the division between feminist and other social movements is a theoretical question in itself. It cannot be considered outside of the process whereby feminist theory and women's studies have become institutionalized, which returns us to the first division, between feminist practice and feminism in the academy. Is it simply the case that as women's studies becomes more institutionalized, feminist scholars are defining their concerns in relation to those of their colleagues in the existing disciplines? This could account both for an often uncritical adherence to a postmodernism that negates the right to act, if not speak, and to the distance between feminism in the institution and outside it. But if this is the case, not only do the political concerns of feminism have to be reconsidered, but the disciplinary boundaries that restrict political thinking have to be crossed.

Disciplinary specialization might also be held accountable for a third growing division within feminism, between theoretical skills on the one hand, and literary analysis and socio-economic empirical research on the other. Poststructuralist or postmodern feminism is identified with the theoretical avant-garde, while historical, cultural feminism is associated with the study of how women are culturally represented, or what women are meant to have really done.

Opening Out is based on the belief that such divisions are unhelpful. There is small advantage in uncritical cultural descriptions, or an unreflective politics of experience; without the theoretical tools found in poststructuralist, psychoanalytical and other contemporary critical theories, our social and cultural analyses, and perhaps our political activity, may be severely curtailed. On the other hand, unless these theoretical tools are applied to present conflicts and the histories that shaped them, feminist theory itself may become moribund. Not only that, but the opportunity feminist theories afford for reworking the theories currently available for understanding the world (such as they are) may be bypassed.

None of this means that *Opening Out* will always be easy reading in the first instance; the distance between developed theory and practical feminism is too great for that at present. But it does mean that *Opening Out* is committed to returning theory to present political questions, and this just might make the value of theoretical pursuits for feminism plainer in the long term.

Opening Out will develop feminist theories that bear on the social construction of the body, environmental degradation, ethnocentrism, neocolonialism, and the fall of socialism. *Opening Out* will draw freely on various contemporary critical theories in these analyses, and on social as well as literary material. *Opening Out* will try to cross disciplinary boundaries, and subordinate the institutionalized concerns of particular disciplines to the political concerns of the times.

Teresa Brennan

Acknowledgments

I am most grateful to the contributors—Françoise, Minh-ha, Uzo, Charlie, Peter, Juliana, Huma, Ousseynou, Celeste, Renée, and Cindy—for their longstanding friendship and intellectual support, and for their scholarship that continues to illuminate my path. In some respect, this volume is a tribute to mothers in their daily experiencing of motherhood. In this regard, my profound gratitude goes to my two wonderful sons and best friends, Ike and Uche, who have survived because, unlike the proverbial little crocodiles, they take "mother's talk" very seriously. I thank them (my sons, not the little crocodiles!) for making mothering extremely easy for me and motherhood the best and most rewarding experience of my life.

Thoughts of my sons lead to warm thoughts of some extraordinary women and outstanding mothers who have over the years hugged and loved my kids like their own: Caroline Obetta, Amaka Ndukwe, Idah Obidiegwu (*Mama Nnukwu*/Big Mother), Ezihe Afigbo, Florence Achonu, Utonwa Analike, Rose Okonkwo (a. k. a. White House), Joy Maduka, Opportune Zongo, Susan Geiger, Gloria Obidiegwu, Charity Oju, Janet Spector, Abike Eyo, Chinwe Achebe, Lesley Obiora, Marie Umeh, Lehn Benjamin, Jane Lommel, Carolann Dickinson, Donna Blaker, Pat Nwoga, Obiageli Obikwelu, Uka Obidiegwu, Chinye Amankwe, Pat Orisakwe, Violet Ehilegbu, Maria Ijeoma, Tola Mosadomi, Ada Obidiegwu, Sarah Obidiegwu, Uche Amazigo, Alice Chukwujekwu, Egondu Onyejekwe, Julie Okpala, Udo Obidiegwu, Agnes Akandu, Doris Egonu, Patience Obidiegwu, Ada Udechukwu, Joy Ijomah, Gladys Akobundu, Christie Obidiegwu, Ijele Anozie, Pamela Smith, Pat Jemie, Cecilia Anuforo, Bertha Obi, Ada Oziri, Bessie Obidiegwu, Yvonne Williams, Annetta Jefferson, Martha Banks, Anabel Blaker, Penny Dollens Smith, Abrefi Saaka, Ngozi Okose, Chinwe Obi, Mansah Prah, Florence Asobie, Joy Orah, Joe Idigo, Betty Owsley, Kate Oradubanya, Helen Mugambi, Esther Uchendu, Grace Offorma, Patience Onokala, Takyiwaa Manuh, Tess Onwueme, Beatrice Okonkwor, Massa Udeozo, Melissa Smith, May Okolie, Lou Burdick, Ada Okoye, Kate Onyenehu, Rita Oriji, Veronica Okeke, Rosalie Ackerman, and Laurie Kienke; I thank them very much for their kindness.

Much of the work on this volume was completed last summer with a generous faculty development grant from my home institution, the Indiana University–Purdue University at Indianapolis. The institutional and individual support that I have received from IUPUI has nourished me in many ways. Special thanks to Vice-Chancellor Herman Blake for his strong support and encouragement; to Chancellor Gerald Bepko, Dean Bill Platter, and Dean John Barlow for their encouragement and leadership; to Ann Donchin, Amanda Porterfield, Barbara Jackson, Jane Schultz, Ed Byrne, Rosalie Vermette, Missy Kubitschek, Larbi Oukada, David Hoegberg, Susan Sheperd, Didier Bertrand, and Stan Denski for their friendship, laughter, and intellectual support. Amy Jones always goes beyond the call of duty to make life less complicated for me and I am indebted to her. I thank my research assistant, Uzoamaka Maduka, for her patience, understanding and loyalty.

I thank *Callallo* for the permission to republish Françoise Lionnet's essay, "Geographies of Pain: Captive Bodies and Violent Acts in the Fictions of Gayle Jones, Bessie Head and Myriam Warner-Vieyra." Many thanks to my editors at Routledge who have been most gracious and understanding: Teresa Brennan of Cambridge University who heard me speak at a conference and believed I could write a good book—not only did she back up her faith in me with two book contracts from Routledge but she has continued to be most generous with her encouragement and professional advice; and Emma Davis whose prodding and kind words have helped to bring this second project to a conclusion.

Introduction

Imag(in)ing knowledge, power, and subversion in the margins

Obioma Nnaemeka

Nwanyibuife[1]

Unable to produce its own history in response to its inner sense of identity, nationalist ideology sets up Woman as victim and goddess simultaneously. Woman becomes the allegorical name for a specific historical failure: the failure to coordinate the political or ontological with the epistemological within an undivided agency.

R. Radhakrishnan, "Nationalism, Gender, and the Narrative of Identity"

(85)

Les chants nostalgiques dédiés à la mère africaine confondue dans les angoisses à la Mère Afrique ne nous suffisent pas.

[The nostalgic songs to the African mother that, in moments of anguish, conflate her with Mother Africa are no longer adequate.][2]

Mariama Bâ, "La Fonction politique des littératures françaises écrites"

(7)

In its narration of woman, identity, and nation, this book navigates the contours of the category woman/mother as the "other" in past and current debates in the orature, literatures, and mother tongues of Africa. In its articulation of the many faces of "(m)other"—motherland, mother tongue, motherwit, motherhood, mothering—the volume goes beyond ontological questions in order to address broader issues such as the use and abuse of gender in knowledge legitimation as well as the place of feminist theory in the study of African literature. As a sustained feminist analysis of African literature, the volume engages feminist theory itself by showing how issues in feminism—voice, victimhood, agency, subjectivity, sisterhood, etc.—are recast in different, complex, and interesting ways in African literature, in general, and works by African women writers, in particular. By being very mindful of cultural imperatives and shifts, these essays emphasize the importance of cultural literacy to any valid feminist theorizing of African literature.

As a critique of the inventors and inventions of the margin, the volume urges the reader to rethink marginality by insisting that he/she listen carefully to "marginal discourses" as manifested by the silences and other patterns of articulation of the marginalized. To see knowledge, power, and agency in the margins is to wrestle with contradictions, and some essays in this volume articulate the possibilities of contradictions by recognizing the dilemma inherent in the weaving of individual histories and collective allegories/ mythologies and casting it within the context of the nation as "imagined community" (in the Andersonian context).[3] More importantly, the essays examine how these "imaginings" are located, gendered, and politicized and, in addition, assess the potency of linguistic identity in defining the contours of the "imagined community." R. Radhakrishnan forcefully argues for a rethinking of the complex relationship between women's politics and nation-alist politics, particularly the nature of "nationalist totality" and the legitim-acy of its representation. Citing Partha Chatterjee, Radhakrishnan asserts that in "the ideology of nationalist politics ... the women's question ... is constrained to take on a nationalist expression as a prerequisite for being considered "political" (78). But the truth of the matter is that most of the time (on the African continent, for example), nationalist politics depoliticizes women's politics, forcing the repoliticization of women's politics back on the national agenda only as an aftermath of nationalist struggles. Nonetheless, some of the essays in this volume echo the main arguments of Radhakrishnan's essay in their examination of the centrality of women to the dilemma of identity formation in nationalist struggles (Charles Sugnet, Celeste Fraser Delgado, Uzo Esonwanne, and Cynthia Ward). The essays focus on, among other issues, what Radhakrishnan calls the "schizophrenic vision" of the rhetoric of nationalism in which "[w]oman becomes the allegorical name for a specific historical failure: the failure to coordinate the political or the ontological with the epistemological within an undivided agency" (85). In an earlier work, Trinh Minh-ha identifies this "schizophrenia" as the "obsess-ive *fear* of *losing connection*" in the search for and assertion of "*authen-ticity*" that relies on "undisputed origin" (*Woman* 94, emphasis in the original). Essays by Renée Larrier, Celeste Fraser Delgado, and Cynthia Ward locate this search for "undisputed origin" in identity formation in the *mère-terre*/Mother Africa/Motherland/Mother Tongue tropes that pervade the literature, language question, and nationalist discourse in Africa.

Furthermore, the essays speak eloquently to the complexities and ambigu-ities of African literature, in general, and creative writing by African women, in particular, thereby calling into question some of the existing feminist studies of African literature that insist on straitjacketing the complex web of issues raised in the literary works into *oppositional* binaries, such as traditional/modern, male/female, agent/victim, when the works themselves and the reality from which they evolve disrupt such binaries; when the central arguments of the works and their appeal (very instructive, I might add) rest on the authors' insistence on border crossings, gray areas and the ambiguous interstices of the binaries where woman is both benevolent *and* malevolent with powers that are healing *and* lethal (Trinh Minh-ha), both traditional *and* modern (Uzo Esonwanne), both victim *and* agent (Françoise Lionnet, Peter

Hitchcock, Huma Ibrahim, Charles Sugnet, Renée Larrier, and Cynthia Ward), both goddess *and* whore (Juliana Nfah-Abbenyi and Celeste Fraser Delgado), "soft but stern" (Morrison 11); in short, just human. In my view, what much of the existing feminist analyses of African literatures designate as irreconcilable, "unfeminist," contradictions are actually the tensions of mutuality, not antagonism, (*complementary* not *oppositional*) that give life, vibrancy, and meaning to the African environment (Ousseynou Traoré).[4] The fact that the essays in this volume engage in a feminist analysis of African literature underscores the complexities and heterogeneity of feminist scholarship itself and points to its possibilities. It seems to me that the paradox of feminist theorizing stems from its failure to articulate the ideals of fairness, power-sharing, etc., that gave impetus to feminism itself. Like new wine in old skin, feminist theorizing is sometimes paralyzed by its tortuous attempt to cast complementarity, relatedness, and, to some extent, relativism in the context of the absolutism, separatism, and the winner take all mentality of the patriarchal culture against which it argues. The paradox of some of the existing feminist analyses of African literature is that they ignore the elaboration of the feminist ideals in the African texts and choose instead to force them (the texts) into absolutist, either/or molds. African literature's engagement with feminist issues is very instructive. For example, the essays in this volume disrupt the oppressor/victim dichotomy to demonstrate that agency and victimhood are not mutually exclusive, to show that victims are also agents who can change their lives and affect other lives in radical ways. In many respects, this complexity is captured by the title of a seminal work in the study of women in African literature—*Ngambika* (a Tshiluba phrase that means "help me balance this load"). *Ngambika* delinks victimhood and powerlessness. This forceful articulation of agency in victimhood asks for assistance, not the removal of the load. *Ngambika* reveals not the absence but the limitation of agency; it says in effect that "I can carry this load only if you can balance it for me." On the one hand, *Ngambika* speaks against debilitating excess and unevenness and, on the other hand, it argues for balance and fair share. I will discuss later the importance and centrality of "balance" in African literature and cosmology.

I will focus on the ways in which these essays wrestle with African literature's reimag(in)ing of certain central issues in feminism—victimhood, motherhood, subjectivity, speech, silence, agency, power, gaze, knowledge, and nation. To a great extent, works by women of African descent underscore the ways in which space constructs gender identities, as evidenced in the feminization of restricted spaces—Dikeledi in "The Collectors of Treasures" (prison), Juletane in *Juletane* (hospital room), Firdaus in *Woman at Point Zero* (prison), Tanga in *Tu t'appelleras Tanga* (prison), Eva in *Eva's Man* (hotel room), Ramatoulaye in *So Long a Letter* (unidentified, restricted, cultural space). In their studies of female victims who act in resistance against their victimization, Lionnet, Ibrahim, and Nfah-Abbenyi bring to the discussion an interrogation of the victim/victimhood issue in feminist discourse. They recast the victim status that is fundamental to feminist scholarship by foregrounding agents of insurrection and change operating within an oppressive situation. What is important is not whether these agents survive their insurrection or are crushed by it; what is crucial is the fact that they *choose* to act.

Feminist notions of agency draw the line between feminist interpretations of the situation of women in African novels and African women's perceptions of their own situations. For example, while some feminist analyses of the African novel conflate silence (the noun) and silence (the verb), the novels themselves make a distinction between "to be silenced" and "to be silent" (the former as imposition and the latter as choice). One exercises agency when one *chooses* not to speak; the refusal to speak is also an act of resistance that signals the unwillingness to participate. Juletane (*Juletane*), Eva (*Eva's Man*), Tanga (*Tanga*), Firdaus (*Woman at Point Zero*), Ramatoulaye (*So Long a Letter*), and many other female characters are silenced but at certain moments, they reclaim agency by *choosing* to remain silent and thereby gain the attention that initiates talk. Silence can, therefore, mean both a refusal to talk and an invitation for talk.

Through a reading of Linda Alcoff's essay, "The Problem of Speaking for Others," Obioma Nnaemeka's chapter examines the intersection of the issues of choice and voice as they are argued in current feminist debates about involvement or non-involvement in speaking other people's problems. Nnaemeka sees the feminist dilemma as an issue of extremes—to be involved or not to be involved—but also argues for the possibility and necessity of devising ways in which "involvement (proximity) and withdrawal (distance) can evolve into a workable symbiosis that is fashioned in the crucible of mutually determined temperance" (163). Such a strategy will require that we focus our attention more on issues by *speaking up against/for issues* with others without necessarily *speaking for them*. On another level, Nnaemeka's paper looks at the specific dilemma that faces legitimized "authentic" feminist voices from the so-called Third World in their attempt to produce a counterdiscourse to hegemonic Eurocentric discourse without monopolizing the discursive field of their own sisters. Above all, Nnaemeka argues that Western feminism's search and legitimation of "authentic" voices from the "Third World" sets such voices up for ridicule and resistance on two fronts: "if they accord their traditional culture some modicum of respect, they are dismissed by feminists as apologists for oppressive and outdated customs; if they critique their culture, they are faced with put-downs and ridicule from members of their own society as having sold out" (164). In inscribing the practice of polygamy in contemporary urban Africa as a sign of post-colonial dislocations and cultural hemorrhage in an environment where internal systems are undergoing self-induced and externally enforced rearticulation, Nnaemeka shows how simplistic analytical paradigms oversimplify and distort the complex issues in African literary texts and short-circuit any meaningful engagement with the central feminist issue of *choice*.

The other area of conflict is the different perceptions of motherhood. Two decades ago, Adrienne Rich's path-breaking book, *Of Woman Born*, made an interesting distinction between motherhood as an institution and motherhood as experience, arguing that patriarchy constructs the institution of motherhood while women experience it. It seems to me that the strident feminist arguments of the 1970s and 1980s against motherhood are based on motherhood as institution:

> Motherhood is dangerous to women because it continues the structure within which females must be women and mothers and, conversely, because it denies to females the creation of a subjectivity and world that is open and free. An active rejection of motherhood entails the development and enactment of a *philosophy of evacuation*. Identification and analysis of the multiple aspects of motherhood not only show what is wrong with motherhood, but also the way out. A philosophy of evacuation proposes women's collective removal of themselves from all forms of motherhood. Freedom is never achieved by the mere inversion of an oppressive construct, that is, by seeing motherhood in a "new" light. Freedom is achieved when an oppressive construct, motherhood, is vacated by its members and thereby rendered null and void. (Allen 315, emphasis in the original)[5]

Although feminist theorizing of motherhood has shifted in the past decade in terms of articulating the affirming aspect of motherhood, the earlier stridency against motherhood has not quite subsided. The yoking of motherhood and victimhood continues to be a feature of feminist discourse on motherhood. On the contrary, African women writers attempt most of the time to delink motherhood and victimhood the way they separate wifehood and motherhood (Adaku in *The Joys of Motherhood* and Aïssatou in *So Long a Letter* reject wifehood not motherhood),[6] although feminist readings of the African texts have a tendency to conflate wifehood pains and motherhood pains. The arguments that are made for motherhood in the African texts are based not on motherhood as a patriarchal institution but motherhood as an experience ("mothering") with its pains and rewards. Consequently, motherhood is discussed in relative terms that reflect different personal histories. As it were, the African texts give a human face to motherhood. It is not surprising then that in spite of the pains of motherhood, most mothers in the texts are not prepared to evacuate it *à la* Allen because they know that they are also the beneficiaries of the rewards of mothering. In some of the literary texts under study, adoption is indicative of the women's eagerness to "mother" while rejecting the abuses (physical, sexual, emotional, etc.) of the institution of motherhood under patriarchy. As mother to four non-biological children, Mira Masi rejects exploitation by men while defining and participating in motherhood as mothering on her own term (Ibrahim). Renée Larrier notes that although Aoua Kéita did not have her own biological children, her choice of career—midwifery—made it possible for motherhood to provide the context for a fruitful professional life for her in the same way that it provided

Andrée Blouin a space for political activism. Tanga asserts her freedom by rejecting motherhood and abandoning prostitution, and embraces motherhood as mothering by adopting Mala, a disabled child (Nfah-Abbenyi).

Peter Hitchcock's chapter problematizes and reframes another central issue in feminist discourse—the gaze. Hitchcock's critique of Malek Alloula's *The Colonial Harem*—"[it] places too much emphasis on the 'eye of the beholder' rather than the looking of the seen"(70)—can also be leveled against the feminist discourse on the gaze. Through a reading of Blanchot (*The Gaze of Orpheus*), Lacan (*The Four Fundamentals of Psycho-Analysis*), and Malek Alloula (*The Colonial Harem*), Hitchcock also looks at the potential of the critic's complicity in "othering" women in other cultures or as he puts it "reobjectifying the voices of African womanhood." Hitchcock's chapter and other contributions in the volume (Nfah-Abbenyi, Lionnet, Sugnet, Ibrahim, Esonwanne, Delgado, and Traoré) raise issues of subjugation and dominance *in tandem* with questions of complementarity, empowerment, and solidarity. These two visions are captured in the distinction that Hitchcock makes between the gaze (dominance) and the look (solidarity). His chapter opens with the story of daughters and mothers (look) and unfolds into the story of daughters and sons/lovers (gaze). The epigraph to his essay charts the look as an organizing principle in the mother–daughter relationship. In describing her relationship with her mother, Firdaus brings eyes ("I"s) to her discussion of subjectivity and the subject-in-relation: "They were eyes that I watched. They were eyes that watched me. Even if disappeared from their view, they could see me, and follow me wherever I went, so that if I faltered while learning to walk they would hold me up" (69). In this instance, the eyes ("I"s) that "hold me up" are the eyes that support me; the "eyes that watch me" are the eyes that *watch over*, protect and empower me; they are not the eyes that gaze at me in dominance. In addition to the reciprocity that the look connotes, it points to agency in the sense that looking is also a form of speech and a precondition for action. The look is a response in the sense of "looking back," challenge, response, and counterdiscourse. Ways of seeing/looking are also ways of knowing (Esonwanne) as is demonstrated in the connection Hitchcock makes between visual and cognitive questions.

To the feminist question "Is the Gaze Male?" Hitchcock's chapter seems to respond "yes, but much more." By framing his arguments in a broader context of orientalism and unequal power relations, the gender politics of gazing is placed in the context of the West and the Rest of Us ("Other") model that is embedded in imperial fictions. In this power game, Hitchcock takes an unusual perspectivist stance; he takes a look with the "Other" eye. It is from the margins that his chapter speaks. For Egyptian women writers under study, the "Orpheus' Gaze" is both patriarchal/cultural (internal) and Western/imperial (external), and like Eurydice, Egyptian women are "seen" in their distant nocturnal darkness (the margin), but unlike Eurydice, they speak from the dark thereby keeping "Orpheus" alive to face his scopic dance of power. Hitchcock notes that Nawaal el Saadawi's work is a two-pronged attack on the "masculinist gaze in Egyptian culture" and the imperialist gaze in imperial mythologies. Saadawi's remark points feminist discourse to the complexity of the gaze and its own complicity in (imperialist) gazing. Furthermore, by placing the look in the field of the gaze, Hitchcock demystifies the omnipotent, omniscient status of the gaze in feminist and imperialist discourses.

This volume centers ontological and epistemological questions in its theorizing and analysis. Aware that gender construction is part of the processes of knowledge construction, many of the essays locate storytelling at the heart of knowledge construction while recognizing the gender politics that often banishes storytelling to the periphery of "real knowledge." To a great extent, critics as knowledge producers and disseminators are also storytellers who are capable of creating not only new meanings but also new mythologies as noted by Hitchcock with regard to Western (cross)cultural critics reappropriating and "reobjectifying the voices of African womanhood (or, in this case, the eyes of Egyptian womanhood)" (79). Furthermore, as Lionnet and Trinh argue, the storyteller's ability to refashion and shift social contexts by tinkering with the limits of our notions of what is "ordinary" and "believable" resides in the nature and potential of storytelling itself: "Talking therefore brings the impossible within reach" (Trinh 28). Above all, storytelling is about survival (to live beyond/after the event)- —"survivre" (*sur*/over, above; *vivre*/to live); one must outlive/survive the event in order to engage in its telling. It is in this regard that I find most appropriate and compelling the metaphor, "anthills of the savannah,"[7] chosen by Chinua Achebe, to describe storytellers:

> If you look at the world in terms of storytelling, you have, first of all, the man who agitates, the man who drums up the people—I call him the drummer. Then you have the warrior, who goes forward and fights. But you also have the storyteller who recounts the event—and this is one who survives, who outlives all the others. It is the storyteller, in fact, who makes us what we are, who creates history. The storyteller creates the memory that the survivors must have—otherwise their surviving would have no meaning . . . [The anthill survives] so that the new grass will have memory of the fire that devastated the savannah in the previous dry season. (*A World of Ideas* 337)

Storytelling registers survival on two scores—the survival of the storyteller and that of his/her listeners. The storyteller survives to tell the story and his/her listeners survive because they learned from the story; those that fail to learn do so at their own peril as demonstrated in the story of Mother Crocodile (Trinh), the story of the Snake-Lizard and that of Okonkwo in *Things Fall Apart* (Traoré). Coincidentally but appropriately, this volume starts with storytelling and it is with storytelling that I proceed.

In summer 1992, I convened the first international conference on "Women in Africa and the African Diaspora: Bridges across Activism and the

Academy" that was held in Nsukka, Nigeria. Early in the previous year, I commissioned a well-known Nigerian artist, an Igboman, to design a logo that would capture the spirit, scope, and focus of the conference, and he produced nine beautiful logos for the organizing committee to select from. Many members of the organizing committee were impressed by the artist's extraordinary gift but reacted negatively to the four logos that depicted a woman carrying a load on her head or a baby on her back. Personally, I liked the baby but hated the load. To some extent, I saw the merit in my colleagues' position that we demand an image of the woman without the "encumbrances." We sent the artist back to the drawing board with one request: "give us the woman in all her elegance, take off the load." The four logos that we rejected tell the artist's story of womanhood.

But in its search for the origin of the word *nwanyi* (woman), Igbo folklore tells the story of womanhood differently. Once upon a time, there lived a couple whose marriage would have been perfect if only they had been blessed with children. Fortunately, after many years of childlessness, they had a child. This child was remarkable; it had something dangling between its legs.[8] The couple was very pleased because this baby was very malleable, and did as it was told. If it was told to sleep, it would sleep; if it was told to keep quiet, it acted accordingly. A couple of years later, the couple had another child that was different from the first; it did not have the dangling thing. Furthermore, the second baby was not as docile as the first; it had a mind of its own and acted independently. If it was told to sleep but did not want to do so, it would keep awake; if it was told to keep quiet but wanted to cry, it would scream for the whole village to hear. The couple got tired of the child and decided to give it away. Midway through a long journey, they arrived at a crossroads where they met a man to whom they gave the child because it was *nwa nyiri anyi* (a child that cannot be controlled)—a phrase from which *nwanyi* (woman) derives. The man was named *di* (husband)—a word that is derived from *dibe* (be patient or long-suffering) or *ndidi* (patience).

From these two "stories" of womanhood, it is clear that where the artist saw limitations, my ancestors envisaged possibilities; where the artist enunciated encumbrances, my forebears articulated freedom. The artist and my ancestors are right. These paradoxes and opposing views expose the complexities of womanhood in African literature. While recognizing the contradictions inherent in the images of women in African literature (idealized/objectified, central/marginal, powerful/powerless, passive/active, victim/agent), the essays in this volume draw theoretical conclusions from ontological issues ("womanbeing"/the being of womanhood, motherhood or woman/motherhood), and raise epistemological questions ("the coming into being" of womanhood or the construction of knowledge about woman/motherhood) with particular attention paid to the sexual and cultural politics that construct the institution of motherhood in patriarchy as opposed to the actual experiencing of motherhood (mothering) by women. At the center of the myriad of issues thus raised—history, memory, wisdom, knowledge,

etc.—is the old woman (mother/grandmother); the old woman as storyteller/
historian. Because gendered knowledges are also located knowledges, the old
woman's interlocutors (the males, in particular) hear not the knowledge-in-
wisdom in her narrative but the silly and nonsensical sounds of the periphery.
And for a most illuminating story of the old woman, I turn to one of the
greatest storytellers of all times—Toni Morrison:

> "Once upon a time there was an old woman. Blind. Wise."
> In the version I know the woman is the daughter of slaves, black, American,
> and lives alone in a small house outside of town. Her reputation for wisdom
> is without peer and without question. Among her people she is both the
> law and its transgression. The honor she is paid and the awe in which she
> is held reach beyond her neighborhood to places far away; to the city where
> the intelligence of rural prophets is the source of much amusement. One
> day the old woman is visited by some young people who seem to be bent
> on disproving her clairvoyance and showing her up for the fraud they
> believe she is. Their plan is simple: they enter her house and ask the one
> question the answer to which rides solely on her difference from them, a
> difference they regard as profound disability: her blindness. They stood
> before her and one of them says, "Old woman, I hold in my hand a bird.
> Tell me whether it is living or dead." She does not answer . . . The
> old woman's silence is so long, the young people have trouble holding their
> laughter. Finally she speaks, and her voice is soft but stern. "I don't
> know," she says. "I don't know whether the bird you are holding is dead
> or alive, but what I do know is that it is in your hands. It is in your hands."
> Her answer can be taken to mean: if it is dead, you have either found
> it that way or you have killed it. If it is alive, you can still kill it.
> Whether it is to stay alive is your decision. Whatever the case, it is your
> responsibility. (9–12)

The old woman in this story tests the limits of marginality ("the [blind]
woman is the daughter of slaves, black, American, and lives alone in a small
house outside town") and is subject to most of the prejudicial "isms" that
afflict marginalized people—sexism, ageism, racism, ablism; the prejudice
that initiates the young people's visit to her house; the prejudice that explodes
in stupid laughter as it fails to recognize knowledge-in-wisdom; the prejudice
that denies itself the key to unlock the old woman's enigmatic response. But
Toni Morrison—*daughter* of slaves, black, American—understands; she
unravels the enigma. The story of knowledge as told in this volume is also
the story of mothers and sons. While Morrison identifies generational (old
vs. young) and locational (rural vs. urban) differences as indices of knowledge legitimation, many essays in this collection, through a sustained
feminist analysis, broaden the knowledge/wisdom debate by exposing the
sexual politics that govern knowledge construction and legitimation.

V.Y. Mudimbe's study of the authority and (male) power of the French
language, and the silencing of the African woman locates the grandmother at

the center of an important debate on the hierarchy and valorization of knowledge:

> She is, in fact, the mother of mother and, based on that, the grandest, that is to say, the grand mother who can within herself reunite positive knowledge (wisdom) and negative knowledge (sorcery). ("Letters of Reference" 77)

Trinh Minh-ha's chapter echoes Mudimbe's views by showing how the grandmother is epistemologically located in the ambiguous interstices of good and evil but some of the chapters (Trinh's included) go further to interrogate Mudimbe's positive/negative binary by arguing that, for sons, mother's/grandmother's "positive knowledge (wisdom)" is not even "knowledge" and as such not taken seriously. The children of Mother Crocodile Diassigue ignored their mother's talk/wisdom and chose instead to listen to Golo-the-*He*-Monkey (my emphasis) who left them believing that "their mother really did sometimes talk a lot of nonsense" (Trinh). Of course, mother is not talking nonsense; the little crocodiles and their He-Monkey fail to grasp what Traoré calls "motherwit (womanish wisdom)." Even in its articulation of "wisdom," folklore as we now hear it (note that Mother Crocodile's story is told by a lineage of *male* voices) foregrounds age not gender. In other words, the woman is wise because she is old, not necessarily because she is a woman. Not surprisingly, "wisdom" always emanates from "the old woman" (often cast in the figure of the grandmother); it is not associated with "young woman" or simply "woman." But that is the story of sons. Trinh Minh-ha's chapter, "Mother's Talk," is about mother but it is also the story of sons; it is the story of memory and stupidity in the battleground of knowledge and survival. Stylistically and thematically, Trinh's essay creates the space for a conversation; it announces a *palava* to which the other contributors are invited. The essay announces both an end and a beginning; behind its final proclamation, "[s]o my story ends," lurks an unvoiced reminder of the beginning of other stories into which the first story is projected; and the story goes on.

Based on an African folk tale, Trinh Minh-ha's chapter, "Mother's Talk," exposes, through a gendered reading of wisdom and knowledge, motherhood in all its ambivalences. "Mother's Talk" does not only reveal the sexual politics that is at the heart of the struggle between memory and forgetting but also delineates the ontological, epistemological, and pedagogical issues that undergird its telling. Before noting the impact of mother's talk, I shall examine its nature and purpose and possibly explain why it is prone to resistance and/or dismissal. Mother's talk is not usually about violence or national exploits. Sugnet's chapter notes the conspicuous absence of the *chimurenga* war in Tsitsi Dangarembga's *Nervous Conditions*. In her study of African women autobiographers, Larrier looks at their autobiographies as history that does not document national heroics and historical moments but focuses instead on the gender issues that shape women's daily lives. Lionnet notes that in the works she studied, the violence of slavery and colonialism is invoked but hovers on the periphery while the text's "principal focus remains sexual, familial, and domestic" (207). Buchi Emecheta's disingenuous disclaimer—"I chronicle the little happenings in the lives of the African women that I know. I did not know that by doing so I was going to be called a feminist. But if I am now a feminist then I am an African feminist with a small f" ("Feminism" 175)—falls under this category.

In fact, the centrality of motherhood in African literature peripherizes violence. Violent acts by women do not take the form of infanticide or matricide; they are willful acts of resistance against abusive husbands and lovers (Lionnet, Nfah-Abbenyi, Ibrahim, and Hitchcock). The few occasions when a mother engages in telling stories of violence, she uses them as cautionary tales for her children to learn from but not necessarily to live by (Trinh). In contrast, the stories of and by men ("father's talk") are stories of violence: "[t]he division set up between the world of crocodiles and the world of men is one that differentiates not only animals from humans, but also mothertellers from fathertellers, warfleers from warmakers, sapience from stupidity" (Trinh). In *Things Fall Apart*, for example, Okonkwo tells the boys, Nwoye and Ikemefuna, "stories of violence and bloodshed . . . tribal wars, or how, years ago, he had stalked his victim, overpowered him and obtained his first human head" (52–53). In contrast to Mother Crocodile Diassigue who tells her children tales of violence in order to warn them against violence, brute force, and bloodshed, Okonkwo tells his tales of violence in order to indoctrinate the boys and inculcate in them the need to aspire to the perceived "virtue" of brute force and violence. Okonkwo uses violence as a pedagogical tool both in theory and practice (he beats his son, Nwoye, into compliance):

> That [his mother's stories] was the kind of story that Nwoye loved. But he knew that they were for *foolish women* and children, and he knew that his father wanted him to be a man. And so he feigned that he no longer cared for *women's stories*. And when he did this he saw that his father was pleased, and no longer rebuked him or beat him. (53, my emphasis)

But the story of Mother Crocodile tries to explain why the crocodiles are the most stupid of all animals but have the best memory in the world. The little son crocodile is stupid because he fails, at his own peril, to take advantage of his mother's memory. What is at issue here is the memory of mother and the stupidity of sons. The little crocodiles are stupid on two scores: too stupid (unintelligent) to grasp the meaning behind mother's talk ("[m]y child, the dry grass can set fire to the green grass"), and too stupid (unwise) to dismiss mother's talk. Sandwiched between these two types of stupidity is male arrogance; in fact, the dismissal of mother's talk appears to be a "male thing." Such dismissiveness has tragic consequences; the son crocodile lost his brain, although mother got blamed for it.

In this regard, the story of Okonkwo *vis-à-vis* the tale of Mosquito and the ear is very revealing:

> Another one was wailing near his right ear. He slapped the ear and hoped he had killed it. Why do they always go for one's ear? When he was a child his mother had told him a story about it. *But it was as all women's stories.* Mosquito, she had said, had asked Ear to marry him, whereupon Ear fell on the floor in uncontrollable laughter. "How much longer do you think you will live? she asked. "You are already a skeleton." Mosquito went away humiliated, and any time he passed her way he told Ear that he was still alive. (72, my emphasis)

Like the little crocodiles, Okonkwo does not take mother's talk seriously. Okonkwo is plagued in adulthood by ignorance due to a childhood in-discretion—his habitual dismissal of mother's talk. Consequently, he loses sleep, literally and metaphorically, over his indiscretion. Okonkwo did not listen carefully to his own mother's story because if he had done so, the mosquito's persistence would not have been that puzzling after all; his mother's story told him why and counseled him against the ear's arrogance and insensitivity (traits that Okonkwo has in high dosage). If he had taken mother's talk seriously, he would have taken measures to protect his ears. Okonkwo's problem is not his ear but himself; he should have slapped himself, not his ear. This disturbance and concomitant self-inflicted wound (slap) during one night's sleep is very ominous; Okonkwo's life ended tragically with a final, suicidal slap (another self-inflicted wound). Mother's talk is simultaneously constructive and destructive depending on whether one wants to listen and act upon it or not.

How does one explain the male dismissal of mother's talk in the face of the persistent inscription of the power, knowledge (to concoct healing medicine, for example), and centrality of woman in the texts themselves? The old woman is invited as a healer in Mother Crocodile's story. In *Things Fall Apart*,

> Umuofia was feared by all its neighbours. It was powerful in war and magic, and its priests and medicine men were feared in all the surrounding country. Its most potent war-medicine was as old as the clan itself . . . the *active principle* in that medicine had been an old woman with one leg. In fact, the medicine itself was called *agadi-nwanyi*, or old woman. It had its shrine in the *center* of Umuofia. . . . "The people of Umuike wanted their market to grow and swallow up the markets of their neighbors. So they made a powerful medicine . . . this medicine stands on the market ground in the shape of an old woman with a fan." (15, 107, my emphasis)

The dismissal of mother's talk as silly women's stories or "womanish wisdom" (Trinh and Traoré), is often registered in the arrogant laughter (Morrison 11) that hides stupidity and ignorance. Trinh Minh-ha argues that because mother's wisdom presents itself through indirection, the crocodiles failed to catch the meaning behind the "screen of the real." As complex and ambiguous as the Sphinx (in Greek mythology, a winged creature that has the body of a lion and the head of a woman), mother also frames her wisdom/knowledge in sphinxlike enigma with similar dire consequences (the Sphinx was notorious for killing those who could not answer its riddle). But unlike the Sphinx, mother interweaves useful clues and warnings in her telling. However, the dilemma faced by mother is that she is blamed for the consequences of her children's failure to heed her warning and advice; for example, Mother Crocodile is blamed for the brainlessness of crocodiles.

From the foregoing, one can surmise that male dismissal of mother's talk is not unaware of the power, and knowledge-in-wisdom of mother's talk. The male arrogantly dismisses mother's talk as nonsensical when, in fact, he is incapable of grasping the meaning behind the "screen of the real"; his dismissal of mother's talk reveals not his superiority but his inadequacy, incompetence, and lack of intelligence.[9] Fortunately, mother's talk is not doomed to total dismissal; often, daughters in the texts, Ezinma in *Things Fall Apart* and Tambudzai in *Nervous Conditions*, survive because they listen to, remember, and learn from mother's talk. In her long journey from her village to the mission and on to the boarding school, Tambudzai survives because she never quite left home as it is symbolized in the person of her grandmother. On numerous occasions, African *women* writers, from Flora Nwapa and Grace Ogot to Mariama Bâ and Buchi Emecheta, have made it known that they listened to and learned from their foremothers' storytelling. Grace Ogot credits her grandmother ("Interview" 57), while Buchi Emecheta pays homage to her aunt, "Big Mother" ("Feminism" 173).

Closely related to the issue of gender politics in knowledge legitimation is the gender politics of knowledge articulation—language. The colonialist/ imperialist enterprise is first and foremost an epistemic violence (Esonwanne, Sugnet, and Ward), particularly in view of the ways in which the "other" and "other places" are invented, controlled, and acted upon through the "instrumentalities of pedagogy" (Appiah 155) mediated by the colonial language—"the false father" (Mudimbe 77). Cynthia Ward's study of the relationship between orality (mother tongue) and literacy (father's pen) goes beyond the debate in the 1970s and 1980s about the use or non-use of mother tongues as literary languages in Africa to compare the role played by European languages in Africa today with that played by Learned Latin in Europe for many centuries and examine the processes through which indigenous languages (mother tongues) are embodied, naturalized, feminized, and *mater*(ial)ized (motherized), and subsequently appropriated by the pen of the father (authentic and/or false) to marginalize and silence the mother. Furthermore, the colonial deindigenization and homogenization (standardization) of mother tongues in its invention of a homogenized orality that stands as the "other" of literacy is more in the service of colonial administrative convenience than a fundamental difference between orality and literacy.

The "othering" through language is complex in the sense that the "other" can assume the "objective" position in Europe-defined monoglossia (particularized by each colony's unique experience with a given "false father") but the "othered" space (the ex-colony, for example) is a heterogeneous space prone to sexual/patriarchal and imperialist/feminist politics that places "Third World" women in an inferior position *vis-à-vis* their Euro-American counterparts and elevates Western-induced "authentic" voices from "Third World" nations whose representativeness marks both hierarchy and alienation. Hitchcock's chapter also evokes this Western search for "an authentic voice" among the heterogeneous voices of women in Egypt and its reification as the "other" in orientalist discourse. The inscription and legitimation of such representative "authentic" voices create dilemmas because such female "authentic" voices (African women writers, for example) risk being harassed and silenced by internal patriarchal forces for not being "traditional" enough and by external imperialist forces for being apologists for primitive, oppressive, and moribund "traditions." Ward sees the persistence of vernaculars in Africa as a sign of resistance to linguistic imposition from the outside. Even the technologizing of the word and creation of national (literary) languages are fraught with the danger of erecting other levels of "othering" (political, social, and economic) that could potentially cause the flaring up of ethnic fears and antagonisms. Apart from the ethnic division, the gender hierarchy that is instituted could be equally daunting: "Even if the material hindrances to widespread literacy are overcome, however, success in transforming African vernaculars into literary languages risks institutionalizing a monoglossia that will not decolonize the mind so much as patriarchize it" (125). One of the ways to make mother tongue/mother (*mater*) matter is to absorb "non-reading" practices in national discourses.

   The way that mother tongue is naturalized in the fight for appropriation by the father's pen mimics the way that motherhood is naturalized and idealized in what Larrier calls "master texts" (the works of male writers such as Léopold Sédar Senghor and Camara Laye), that differs markedly from its inscription in the works of women writers where the focus is on motherhood as experience (mothering). Delgado's elaboration of the search for the originary in nationalist discourse points to the same strategy that motherizes/*mater*izes and naturalizes mother-tongues as discussed in Ward's chapter. In this regard, Trinh Minh-ha's "search for *authenticity*" and Radhakrishnan's "schizophrenia of nationalist ideology" have profound implications for understanding the positioning of mother/woman in the literature of nostalgia (Négritude literature, for example) and nationalist discourses. The Motherland or *mère/terre* trope in individual, national and nationalist mythologies hide the traumas, disruptions, and ambivalences of personal and collective histories. Chapters by Sugnet, Delgado, and Esonwanne examine these disruptions in the context of gender and colonial/imperialist politics. The "medicalization" of these traumas in both colonialist and anti-colonialist discourses are apparent in Sugnet's and Delgado's discussions of the colonial and post-colonial dilemma.

Like mother's talk that registers its meaning by "indirection" (Trinh), Delgado's essay on the problematic of the categories "nation" and "woman" constructs a critic of imperial fictions through a discourse on "Kenyan womanhood": "[t]his is not a story of Kenya. This is the story of the stories of Kenya, as I have heard them from the outside, from the so-called 'developed' world" (Delgado 31). In many respects, Delgado's essay echoes Betsy Hartman's brilliant book, *Reproductive Rights and Wrongs*, which critiques global population policies and interventions as a site for the interconnection of global politics, economy, and other related issues such as imperialism, racism, and sexism. Delgado's chapter opens with an epigraph in which a former colonial officer, the Right Honorable McDonald, echoes the "medicalization" of the colonial discourse in his sigh of relief for the "unexpected" survival of *infant* Kenya after one year of independence, in defiance of the naysayers who thought "that within a few months of its emergence from the womb of Mother Africa it would die from chronic internal disorders" (130). The presence of "woman as mother" in McDonald's discussion of "Africa the child" is maintained in his entire speech cast in metaphors of childbirth: "many others who supposed that its birth soon afterwards was inevitable assumed it would be stillborn" (130). Some of the arguments of Delgado's chapter anchor on this speech in which fertility, maternity, and infantilism resonate in order to show how technology and global politics of population control are the weapon and motherhood (as metaphor and practice) the theater (as battleground, playground, and/or medical site) on which are assembled different actors with competing interests: "international donors who promote population planning; the political regimes who mandate an officially delimited Motherland; revolutionaries who reconstruct the Motherland as a point of origin before colonial and post-colonial domination; women for whom these preceding discourses, whether or not they participate in them" (131), will have far-reaching consequences in terms of reproductive rights and choice.

Like most of the essays in this volume (Lionnet, Ibrahim, Hitchcock, Nfah-Abbenyi, Esonwanne, and Sugnet), Delgado's chapter writes domination and resistance simultaneously. It uses Rebeka Njau's *Ripples in the Pool* and *Maitu, Njugira (Mother, Sing for Me)*, produced by Ngũgĩ wa Thiong'o and the Kamiriithu Community Center in 1982, to produce a counterdiscourse to the imperial fiction that governs global population control. The active participation of women and the centrality of their voices in the *Maitu, Njugira* project show another face of Kenyan womanhood that is different from the womanhood construction in imperial fiction of global population control and nationalist discourse (chapters by Nfah-Abbenyi and Nnaemeka elaborate on this discussion of voice and speech). Women's resistance to this assault from a combination of internal and external forces is well documented in Stephanie Urdang's work on women in Guinea-Bissau, *Fighting Two Colonialisms*, where women hope that through participation in revolutionary struggles they can challenge, disrupt, and transform oppressive imperialist and patriarchal forces from without and from within. Unfortunately, the aftermath of revolutionary/nationalist struggles is notorious for the marginalization of women from active participation in the political and economic life of newly liberated nations. What was significant in the collaboration between Ngũgĩ and the Kamiriithu community was the people's participation in producing and articulating a counterdiscourse in their own language. But what was truly radical in that collaboration was the women's reworking of the end of the original text. The women reconstructed Ngũgĩ's script in order to position women as active participants in nation building. In Ngũgĩ's original script, Mwendanda rapes Nyathira who goes back into prostitution. In the version reworked by the women, agency is reinvested in Nyathira who, although raped, is not destroyed or paralyzed by it.

While the Right Honorable McDonald articulates colonial disorders in the context of the "nation" as country (Kenya), Charles Sugnet's chapter individualizes such traumas in the context of personal dilemma and gender politics. Sugnet continues Delgado's argument about the inscription of women during and their marginalization after nationalist struggles. By linking feminist and nationalist discourses, Sugnet's essay reads *Nervous Conditions* as a feminist reworking of Frantz Fanon's "Colonial Wars and Mental Disorders." Both Dangarembga's novel (*Nervous Conditions*) and Fanon's work (*Wretched of the Earth*) that provides the title of the novel "medicalize" the colonial condition and discourse. Sugnet identifies the pervasive inscription of eating disorders (bulimia, anorexia nervosa) and other related manifestations (vomiting, [in]digestion, and excretion) as both a symptom of colonial domination and a sign of resistance. The persistence or absence of these bodily dysfunctions is indicative of resistance to (Nyasa and Tambu) or incorporation into (Babamukuru) the colonial system. Females suffer these disorders more than the men, implying that the men are more comfortable with/in the colonial system. As demonstrated in the chapters by Lionnet, Ibrahim, Hitchcock, and Nfah-Abbenyi, domination is violence that breeds violence (resistance). The women in *Nervous Condition* fight back in different ways and from different locations. But *Nervous Condition* is, above all, a story of survival. Again, at the center of survival and storytelling is the grandmother, Tambu's grandmother, whose brief but "complete" analysis of colonization and its impact is most compelling. Tambu survives because, unlike the little crocodiles, she does not dismiss mother's talk.

Colonial disorders come in various forms. Unlike the psychosomatic manifestations noted above, colonial disorders in Mariama Bâ's *Une si longue lettre* (*So Long a Letter*) are manifested at the cultural and cognitive levels. Before examining the ways in which colonialist/imperialist politics and Enlightenment epistemology fashion the cognitive field (ways of seeing/knowing) of the post-colonial subject, Uzo Esonwanne's chapter calls into question the linear notion of history and progress that informs the tradition/modernity debate. Esonwanne situates his reading of Mariama Bâ's work at the interstice of Afro-Islamic cultural politics and Enlightenment epistemology in order to show how the collision of world-views is at the core of colonial disorders. A gender analysis of patriarchal and imperialist structure shows how women simultaneously affirm and disrupt such structures. Ramatoulaye, for example, appropriates and disrupts culturally designated Islamic space of silence and exclusion in order to "speak" (write). Furthermore, colonial disorders are manifested in her assessment of polygamy that is influenced by the Enlightenment epistemology in which is rooted her education at Ponty-ville. *So Long a Letter* and Esonwanne's reading of it call into question the validity of the pervasive binaries, such as tradition/modern, that color some of the existing analyses of Bâ's novel.

Essays by Lionnet, Ibrahim, and Nfah-Abbenyi examine the relationships between victimhood, agency, madness, and solidarity. Ibrahim interrogates, on the one hand, the feminist imperialist construction of the "generic victim" as a "Third World woman" and, on the other, the feminist universalizing notion of victim as "female" that fails to account for the impact of difference—race, class, ethnicity, etc.—in constructing the subject position of victimhood.[10] In her studies of the works of Bessie Head (*Question of Power* and *A Gesture of Belongings*), Nawal el Saadawi (*Woman at Point Zero*), Anita Desai (*A Clear Light of Day*), and Buchi Emecheta (*The Joys of Motherhood* and *In the Ditch*), Ibrahim examines the different factors that structure women's victimization, but also shows women looking for and discovering a way out. Even the women who are driven to madness and exile by oppressive situations use madness and exile as weapons against victimization. By tearing off the covering her captors and tormentors place on her, Dopdi, the radical peasant leader, shows the capacity of a downtrodden victim to burst forth like Phoenix from the ashes of oppression in order to challenge her oppressors by throwing the ugly image of victimization back in their faces.

Nfah-Abbenyi frames her reading of Calixthe Beyala's *Tu t'appelleras Tanga* in the context of self/other, agency/lack of agency, speech/silence that is at the core of feminist debates about voice. More importantly, she focuses on the female body as the site for the conflict between different forms and levels of violence, and foregrounds women's struggles to reclaim their bodies. Tanga is raped and impregnated by her father and forced into prostitution by her mother but she gets out of prostitution and seals off her vagina with clay as a sign of self-defining freedom in its resistance to patriarchal violence, just like her mother who, at thirteen, stuffs palmnuts into her vagina to avoid the sexual violence and exploitation to which her own mother was subjected. Nfah-Abbenyi goes further to examine how Calixthe Beyala takes steps to reframe the woman question both in patriarchal and feminist discourses. Through a process of hyphenated (re)namings of "woman" ("*femme-fillette*/woman-young girl," "*femme-enfant*/woman-child," "*femme-mère*/woman-mother/wife-mother," "*femme-maîtresse*/woman-mistress," "*pute-enfant*/prostitute-child," etc.) Beyala challenges the yoking of womanhood and motherhood in Iningué society by delinking and problematizing the woman/mother twin. Beyala's strategy reinscribes the many faces of womanhood. Unlike most African women writers in whose works the abandonment of motherhood is unthinkable and unpardonable (Emecheta, Bâ, Nwapa), Beyala's novel makes the abandonment of motherhood as an institution both a possibility and an act of freedom/self-definition. Like her grandmother, Tanga rejects motherhood as a patriarchal institution, and chooses instead motherhood as an experience (mothering) by adopting a child. Beyala also subverts the ever-pervasive racial hierarchy in feminist discourse. In the show-and-tell scenario that opens the book, the black woman (Tanga) "shows and tells" and the white Jewish-French woman (Anna-Claude) listens.[11] The meeting of Tanga and Anna-Claude foregrounds the complexity of "womanbeing"—the control and oppression of women (symbolized by the prison cell) but also the possibility of solidarity under such circumstances. Nfah-Abbenyi's chapter argues that marginalized women have often struggled to reject "otherness" as constructed by others and in the process recreate themselves in a gesture of resistance. One cannot say the same thing for Anna-Claude's "recreation" of herself as a questionable clone of Tanga. It is not surprising that Tanga's mother, Taba, neither sees nor accepts Anna-Claude (cloned as Tanga) as her daughter. Anna-Claude's simplistic, "multiculturalist" insurgency against difference is what is being rejected here. Multiculturalism should concern itself more with the respect for difference and less with the impossible (and unnecessary, I might add) task of annihilating difference.

Françoise Lionnet lends a diasporic dimension to the volume with her study of the gendered reworkings of familiar cultural scripts and collective mythologies by black women writers from Africa (Bessie Head, *The Collectors of Treasures*) and the African diaspora (Gayl Jones, *Eva's Man* and Myriam Warner-Vieyra, *Juletane*). In this diasporic context, Lionnet demonstrates that women writers from Africa and the African diaspora show a cross-fertilization that is evidenced by their use of themes, particularly "the negative mythic images of women—such as Medusa, Jezebel, Salome, the Furies, the Amazon, the mad woman, the hysteric, etc.—which they exploit and translate into powerfully subversive fictions" (209). Her chapter focuses on feminized spaces ("geographies of pain") where pain and the desire for its articulation are intensely felt; where the explosive language of pain erupts tragically. The works of black women writers from the nineteenth century to the present index these eruptions as women's desire for freedom. By bringing under strict scrutiny the pains of gender relations in marriage and sexual relationships, Head, Jones, and Warner-Vieyra show to what extent men are implicated in and accountable for women's pains. The texts join feminist scholarship and activism to debunk the myth of home as a place of safety and protection from the wild world out there.[12] The thread that runs through the texts under study is the desire and ability of women to respond to violence with violence: "[t]hough victimized by patriarchal social structures that perpetuate their invisibility and dehumanization, black female characters actively resist their objectification, to the point of committing murder" (Lionnet 206). Recall that Mother Crocodile's story is about the violence of men, warmongering men; that the story of Okonkwo (*Things Fall Apart*) is the story of violence, male violence. In telling the story of female violence, these novels by black women are in effect telling the story of male violence; female violence is a symptom of (reaction to) male violence. The concern for freedom and survival is the impetus for the actions of these desperate women for whom the end justifies the means and for whom extreme situation demands extreme measure.

However, works by black women writers also show that there are other channels, such as writing and solidarity/sisterhood, through which women survive and gain freedom. Extreme pain and suffering push women victims to the brink of madness, but as indicated by some women writers themselves, such as Buchi Emecheta and Mariama Bâ,[13] writing pulls them away from that precipice. Larrier notes in her chapter that black women autobiographers see writing as therapy; a view also echoed by Juletane (Lionnet). The texts discuss women's solidarity as an issue of survival; solidarity among women offers a safety net and a breath of fresh air in a suffocating, constraining environment. Bâ, Beyala, Saadawi, Jones, and Head demonstrate that in confining and painful marriages and sexual relationships, solidarity and friendship among women mitigate pain and suffering. In the works under study, restricted feminized spaces are simultaneously sites of exclusion and inclusion, oppression and solidarity, speech and silence, abuse and respect, neglect and friendship (Eva, Firdaus, Tanga, Ramatoulaye, Dikeledi, etc.). Women appropriate and refashion oppressive spaces through friendship, sisterhood, and solidarity and in the process reinvent themselves.

In exposing the insidiousness of male violence and abuse, the chapters in this volume do not fail to stress the pain and betrayal of woman-on-woman abuse. They show how the oppression of women is not simply a masculinist flaw as some feminist analyses claim but that it also entails woman-on-woman violence that is often the outcome of institutionalized, hierarchical female spaces that make women victims and collaborators in patriarchal violence. African women writers—such as Bâ, Emecheta, Beyala, Dangarembga, and Nwapa—overwhelmingly agree on this issue (Lionnet, Nfah-Abbenyi, Larrier) although feminist criticism of African literature often remains silent on the issue.[14]

The violent acts of the female characters provide a context for examining the relationship between madness, murder, and knowledge. What is radical in the female characters' violent acts is not so much what they did (murder) but how it was done (intentionally). What is interesting is not so much the fact that the female characters are mad but how they use their madness. Here, the question of agency is linked to *intentionality*. Recall that in Chinua Achebe's *Things Fall Apart*, Okonkwo's accidental manslaughter is called *ochu* ("*female* murder," my emphasis). What undergirds Eva's action, for example, is the way that intentionality links knowledge and action: "When Eva bites off Davis's penis after poisoning him, she explicitly relates the event to Eve's biting into the apple of knowledge: 'I got back on the bed and squeezed his dick hard in my teeth. I bit down hard. My teeth in an apple' (128)" (Lionnet 218). These mad (in the sense of angry/incensed, *not* crazy/mentally ill) women *know* how to use their "madness" to bring their suffering to a *logical* conclusion.

Let me end this discussion of victimhood and agency with a few remarks on Simone Schwarz-Bart's extraordinary novel about powerful female "victims" of rural Guadeloupe, *Pluie et vent sur Télumée Miracle (The Bridge of Beyond)*. Like many texts that are discussed in this volume, Télumée's story is also the story of mother and grandmother. Télumée is the scion of a long lineage of women who "rise over the earth like a cathedral" (35), who in the face of suffering and victimhood claim agency by accepting their condition philosophically: "No matter how heavy your breasts you'll always be strong enough to support them" (42), who speak pain but refuse to be crushed by it: "[b]ehind one pain there is another. Sorrow is a wave without end. But the horse mustn't ride you, you must ride it" (51), who speak for balance and against excess: "there are paths that are bad for a man to take: to see the beauty of the world and call it ugly, to get up early to do what is impossible, and let oneself carried away by dreams—for whoever dreams becomes the victim of the dream" (30). The linkage between obsession and victimhood is an interesting one in light of the fact that it complicates the oppressor/victim binary by showing that oppressors are also victims of their obsession/extremism as, for example, in the case of Okonkwo in Chinua Achebe's *Things Fall Apart*.

By culturally contextualizing his reading of Chinua Achebe's *Things Fall Apart*, Ousseynous Traoré emphasizes the importance of cultural literacy in the analysis of creative works from Africa. We, as critics, must always remind ourselves that literary texts evolve from specific cultural contexts to which they refer. Through a reading of the Igbo world-view as it is elaborated in *Things Fall Apart*, Traoré demonstrates that Okonkwo's tragic end is an outcome of his attempt to decenter the woman/mother principle as it is encoded in Igbo myths and names like Nneka ("Mother is supreme"). Basing his arguments on Chinua Achebe's essay, "Chi," that examines the story of Eri in Nri oral tradition, Traoré evokes the pervasive inscription of complementary dualities that speak to the importance of balance in Igbo cosmology: Chukwu/Ani, Chukwuka/Nneka, male/female, yam and palm tree/cocoyam and vegetables, etc. The problematic of womanhood and motherhood as encoded in the myths of "Mosquito and the Ear" and "Why the Snake-Lizard killed his Mother," speaks for gender balance and against its disruption. Okonkwo failed because his excesses created a disruption that his environment could not absorb. Like the sons of Mother Crocodile, Okonkwo dismisses "womanish wisdom"—"Okonkwo and the Snake-Lizard fail to understand the centrality of woman's wisdom and the earth force in the epistemological and ontological systems of their culture" (Traoré 64)—and like the little male crocodile, Okonkwo came to a tragic end. Okonkwo's mission early in the novel is very instructive but unfortunately he fails to learn. When a daughter of Mbaino is murdered, Okonkwo is chosen by his people as *mediator* and *negotiator* for their demand of a virgin and a young man. One should ask why it is necessary to replace a female with a male and a female. It seems to me that the demand for the virgin and young man is a symbolic gesture of complementary duality intended to restore the cosmic balance that has been disrupted by violence (murder). Okonkwo's mission evokes the importance of middle-ground and balance. As E.N. Njaka aptly notes, "[t]he Igbo believes he can negotiate anything . . . how to negotiate with Chukwu puzzled him and he created intermediaries . . . go-betweens" (14). As he grew older, Okonkwo became impatient with and rejected his people's valorization of moderation and balance: "Okonkwo was not the man to stop beating somebody half-way through, not even for fear of a goddess" (*Things Fall Apart* 21). As I have noted elsewhere, "Okonkwo is simultaneously normative and marginal (in the sense of excess/excessive). He is for excess and against "half-way"; his people are for balance and against excess . . . Okonkwo would not survive; his fatal flaw is his excess" ("Feminism" 99).

The essays in this volume speak to the complexities, ambiguities, gray areas, and interstices in the literary texts in the belief that it is in those "this *and* that" locations that the meanings are. As the essays themselves admit, the question of women's subordination and oppression is a reality that faces women in their quotidian lives. The female characters are victims of multiple oppressions that are internally generated by oppressive customs and practices and externally induced by an equally oppressive, inegaliterian world order. As noted in the paper by Delgado, gender differentiation and hierarchy are inscribed in the title of the production by Ngũgĩ wa Thiong'o, *Maitu, Njugira* (literally translated as "Mother, trill *ngemi* for me), that is taken from a joyful song announcing the birth of a baby—five trills for boys and four trills for girls.[15] But as noted above, we see women who faced discrimination even at birth rework Ngũgĩ's original script to show women as agents of change; beaten down but not out, and actively participating in nation building. Sugnet notes the discrimination young Tambudzai faces as a girl; for example, her brother, Nhamo, is sent to school while she is left at home. But Tambudzai does not stay home as mandated, she grows maize in order to send herself to school. The important lesson here is not that women should accept the status quo without question but rather that they should equip themselves for *effective* resistance and participation in societal transformation. Tambudzai is the notable survivor in the novel.

The chapters in this volume recognize the marginalization of women; however, they urge readers and critics to take an "other" look at the texts in order to see the ways in which they complicate the issues that are often discussed in feminist scholarship and in existing criticism of literature by African women. This volume shows how victims are equally agents, and oppressors are also victims; how violence is not a male but a human problem, how woman-on-woman violence and abuse show women as a group suffering from self-inflicted wounds; how the broader issue of globality and imperialism intensifies gender politics in nationalist discourses. Unlike some feminist analyses of African literature that are entrenched in the inflexible notion of women's permanent victim status, these essays show that the African literary texts themselves speak simultaneously about the victimhood and power of women; a position that feminist analysis can learn from. It is paradoxical that feminism, as a philosophy and a pedagogy of social change, is sometimes mired in the paralysis of pessimistic theorizing.

This volume is a provocative study in similarities and contrasts. In this regard, it can be said that one of its unique features is the extensive territorial claims (in terms of genre and geography) it makes in grounding its arguments. In terms of genre, it moves from orature and fiction to theater and autobiography; in terms of geography, it stretches from all regions of Africa (east, west, north, and south) to the African diaspora (USA and the Caribbean). Above all, the essays constitute a powerful articulation of theoretical frameworks that are informed and nourished by a profound understanding of cultural shifts and imperatives. While not dismissing the relevance of theory to the analysis of the literary texts, the essays argue forcefully that the African texts, as cultural productions, must not be decontextualized from the cultural contexts that gave them life and to which they refer. Any epistemology or theory that is alien to the African environment must be used guardedly as a frame of reference, at best, and not as a substitute for the literary texts themselves.

POSTSCRIPT

During the process of spellchecking the entire volume, my computer repeatedly informed me that "foremother" is not in the dictionary and suggested that I use "forefathers" instead. Those dictionaries, that's another story of sons! Like the grandmother whose truth is marked by indirection, I sound a cautionary note: *"onye akpakwana agu aka nodu ma odi ndu, ma onwulu anwu"* (Igbo phrase that means "do not touch the tail of the tiger whether it is dead or alive"). And the story goes on!

NOTES

1 *Nwanyibuife*, one of the female given-names in Igboland, means "woman is something," but, if written without a subscript dot under the "u" the word is pronounced differently and means "woman is carrying something" (*nwanyibuife*). It is true that *nwanyibuife* (woman is something) posits the valorization of woman. However, it seems to me that the phrase could be understood as a response to an unarticulated doubt; an affirmation that says in effect "woman is something regardless of your thinking otherwise." Or as Chimalum Nwankwo told me in a conversation, "women have their spaces and even if you do not see them, they are there." But I also know that in Igboland, *nwokebuife* (man is something) is not articulated, it is assumed. Rather, what I have heard is *nwokenife* (man and something) that designates "man engaged in activity" (agency).

2 My translation.

3 See Benedict Anderson. *Imagined Communities*.

4 I have raised similar concerns in an earlier essay titled "Feminism, Rebellious Women."

5 Allen credits "Julie Murphy for suggesting the phrase 'philosophy of evacuation'" (328).

6 See my comments in "From Orality to Writing."

7 *Anthills of the Savannah* is the title of Chinua Achebe's latest novel.

8 When I heard this story as a child, I was told that dangling things happen exclusively to male babies. In fact, the beauty and power of the oral tradition (folktales, proverbs, etc.) lie in the indirection of its telling and its capacity to generate multiple interpretations/versions in which meaning is deferred *à la* Derrida. I was recently informed by a *male* Igbo scholar that *nwanyi* can also be interpreted as a combination of two words "*nwa anyi*" (our child).

9 This recalls the politics that undergirds the opposition to "minority studies" (women's studies, black studies, and ethnic studies) in the US academy by those who declare these areas as "unintellectual" at best and totally irrelevant at worst, simply because they are ignorant of the issues therein and are unwilling to learn or retool themselves professionally. I agree with Stanley Fish that although the controversy and debates over "minority studies" are couched in philosophical and intellectual terms, the real issue is energy, physical and intellectual, to retool oneself: "I don't think it has that much to do with philosophy, although philosophical terms are often used to characterize it. It's more generational. It has to do with a shift that has occurred within the memory of practitioners who bought their ticket many years ago and find that they're on a different train" quoted in Peter Prescott, "Learning to Love the PC Canon."

10 The feminization of "victim" is inscribed in the French language, for example. It is very interesting to note that in a dual-gendered language such as French the word "victim" (la victime) is feminine, even when the victim is male. The implications are many among which are the following: that victims are supposed to be female; or that to reduce the male to the level of victim is to feminize him.

11 The innocence of childhood that provides the context for "show and tell" couches the power game that undergirds the exercise through its demarcation of *active* speaker and *passive* listener. Black women have usually been pushed to the listener end of the continuum from where they are expected to listen to the racially defined speaking subjects ("the showers and tellers"). Black women's frustration with and resistance to this state of affairs is captured in the title of Hazel Carby's essay, "White Woman Listen!"

12 Particularly in the wake of the O.J. Simpson criminal trial that has placed wife-battering on the national agenda.

13 See Nnaemeka, "From Orality to Writing."

14 See also Nnaemeka, "Feminism."

15 This hierarchical gender differentiation cuts across cultures. For example, a film about women in rural China, titled *Small Happiness*, claims that a baby girl is welcomed into the world as "small happiness." The implication is that the baby boy is "big happiness;" a discriminatory thinking that is initiated and sustained throughout life by a complex naming system.

WORKS CITED

Achebe, Chinua. *Things Fall Apart*. London: Heinemann, 1958.

——. "Chi in Igbo Cosmology." *Morning Yet on Creation Day*. New York: Doubleday, 1976, 131–45.

——. *Anthills of the Savannah*. New York: Doubleday, 1987.

Alcoff, Linda. "The Problem of Speaking for Others." *Who Can Speak?* Ed. Judith Roof and Robyn Wiegman. Urbana: University of Illinois Press, 1995.

Allen, Jeffner. "Motherhood: The Annihilation of Women." *Mothering: Essays in Feminist Theory*. Ed. Joyce Trebilcot. Totowa, NJ: Rowman & Allanhead, 1984.

Alloula, Malek. *The Colonial Harem*. Trans. Myrna Godzich and Wlad Godzich. Intro. Barbara Harlow. Minneapolis: University of Minnesota Press, 1986.

Anderson, Benedict. *Imagined Communities: Reflections on the Origins and Spread of Nationalism*. London: Verso, 1984.

Appiah, Kwame Anthony. "Out of Africa: Topologies of Nativism." *Yale Journal of Criticism* 2.1 (1988): 153–178.

Bâ, Mariama. "La Fonction politique des littératures africaines écrites." *Écriture française* 3.5 (1981): 4–7.

——. *Une si longue lettre*. Dakar: Nouvelles Éditions Africaines, 1986.

——. *So Long A Letter*. Trans. Modupé Bodé-Thomas. London: Heinemann, 1989.

Barry, Kesso. *Kesso, princesse peuhle*. Paris: Seghers, 1988.

Beyala, Calixthe. *Tu t'appelleras Tanga*. Paris: Éditions Stock, 1988.

Blanchot, Maurice. *The Gaze of Orpheus*. Trans. Lydia Davis. New York: Station Hill Press, 1981.

Blouin, Andrée. *My Country, Africa*. With Jean MacKellar. New York: Praeger, 1983.

Bugul, Ken. *Le Baobab fou*. Dakar: Nouvelles Éditions Africaines, 1984.

Carby, Hazel. "White Woman Listen! Black Feminism and the Boundaries of Sisterhood." *The Empire Strikes Back: Race and Racism in 1970s Britain*. Birmingham University Centre for Contemporary Cultural Studies. London: Hutchinson, 1982.

Chinweizu. *The West and the Rest of Us*. New York: Random House, 1975.

Dangarembga, Tsitsi. *Nervous Conditions*. Seattle: The Seal Press, 1988.

Desai, Anita. *Clear Light of Day*. New York: Harper & Row, 1980.

Diallo, Nafissatou. *De Tilène au plateau*. Dakar: Nouvelles Éditions Africaines, 1975.

Diop, Birago. "Maman-caïman." *Les Contes d'Amadou Koumba*. Paris: Présence africaine, 1961. 49–57.

——. "Mother Crocodile." *Tales of Amadou Koumba*. Trans. Dorothy S. Blair. Oxford: Oxford University Press, 1966. 45–51.

Emecheta, Buchi. *In the Ditch*. London: Barrie & Jenkins, 1972.

——. *The Joys of Motherhood*. New York: George Braziller, 1979.

——. "Feminism with a Small 'f!' *Criticism and Ideology*." Ed. Kirsten Holst Petersen. Uppsala: Scandinavian Institute of African Studies, 1988. 173–177.

Fanon, Frantz. *The Wretched of the Earth*. Trans. Constance Farrington. New York: Grove Press, 1963.

Hartman, Betsy. *Reproductive Rights and Wrongs: The Global Politics of Population Control and Contraceptive Choice*. New York: Harper & Row, 1987.

Head, Bessie. *A Question of Power*. London: Heinemann, 1973.

——. *The Collector of Treasures*. London: Heinemann, 1977.

Jones, Gayl. *Eva's Man*. Boston: Beacon Press, 1977.

Kéita, Aoua. *Femme d'Afrique: La Vie d'Aoua Kéita racontée par elle-même*. Paris: Présence africaine, 1975.

Kenyatta, Jomo. *Harambee: Speeches 1962–1963*. Nairobi: Oxford University Press, 1964.

Lacan, Jacques. *The Four Fundamental Concepts of Psycho-Analysis*. Trans. Alan Sheridan. New York: Norton, 1977.

Moyers, Bill. *A World of Ideas*. New York: Doubleday, 1989.

Mudimbe, V.Y. "Letters of Reference." *Transition* 53 (1991): 62–78.

Njaka, E.N. *Igbo Political Culture*. Evanston: Northwestern University Press, 1974.

Njau, Rebeka. *Ripples in the Pool*. Nairobi: Heinemann: 1975.

Nnaemeka, Obioma. "From Orality to Writing: African Women Writers and the (Re)Inscription of Womanhood." *Research in African Literatures* 25.4 (1994): 137–157.

——. "Feminism, Rebellious Women and Cultural Boundaries: Rereading Flora Nwapa and Her Compatriots." *Research in African Literatures*. 26.2 (1995): 80–113.

Ogot, Grace. "Interview with Grace Ogot." With Bernth Lindfors. 13 Aug. 1976. *World Literature Written in English* 18 (1979): 56–68.

Prescott, Peter. "Learning to Love the PC Canon," *Newsweek* (December 24, 1990): 50–51.

Radhakrishnan, R. "Nationalism, Gender, and the Narrative of Identity." *Nationalisms and Sexualities*. Ed. Andrew Parker, Mary Russo, Doris Sommer, and Patricia Yaeger. New York: Routledge, 1992, 77–95.

Rich, Adrienne. *Of Woman Born: Motherhood as Experience and Institution*. New York: W.W. Norton, 1986.

Saadawi, Nawal El. *Woman at Point Zero*. London: Zed Books, 1983.

Schwarz-Bart, Simone. *The Bridge of Beyond*. Trans. Barbara Bray. London: Heinemann, 1982.

Trinh Minh-ha. *Woman, Native, Other*. Bloomington: Indiana University Press, 1989.

——. "Not You/ Like You: Post-Colonial Women and the Interlocking Questions of Identity and Difference," *Inscriptions* 3/4 (1988): 71–77.

Warner-Vieyra, Myriam. *Juletane*. Paris: Présence africaine, 1982.

——. *Juletane*. Trans. Betty Wilson. Oxford: Heinemann, 1987.

1   Mother's talk

Trinh T. Minh-ha

When memory goes a-gathering firewood, it brings back the sticks that strike its fancy.

Birago Diop

"The most stupid of all animals that fly, walk and swim, that live beneath the ground, in water, or in the air, are undoubtedly crocodiles, which crawl on land and walk at the bottom of the water . . . And this, for no other reason than that they have the best memories in the world." This is how Senegalese poet and storyteller Birago Diop begins the tale of Mother Crocodile.[1] This is how he recounts a narrative of his elders, which he ascribes to another teller—the *griot* (storyteller, singer, and genealogist) Amadou Koumba. And, to complicate matters further, this is also what Amadou Koumba said he remembered from another teller yet, for "that is not my opinion, said Amadou Koumba. That is what Golo the monkey says. And although everyone agrees that Golo is the most coarsely spoken of all the creatures, since he is their *griot*, he sometimes manages to make the most sensible remarks, so some say; or at least to make us believe he has made them, according to others."

Stupidity and memory. Talking brought three male-identified voices together while deferring their unity. The story presents itself as a piece of gossip that circulates from teller to teller. The man who narrates (Diop) implicitly warns the reader that he is quoting Amadou Koumba who actually got it from Golo-the-He-Monkey. Right at the outset, the question is raised as to the real source of such a gossip: if the reader can't really tell whether Golo makes "sensible remarks" or whether he simply takes the lead in making people believe that he is the one to have made them, then whose opinion is it exactly? As the tale progresses, storytelling becomes increasingly reflexive and the reader is further led to ask: Who among the tellers is the real monkey? Whose stupidity is it finally? Here lies the power of indirection in which the tale weavers excel. Through the spell of words the latter must both resonate the comments passed on and fullfill the function of the tale, which is not merely to deliver a message, but rather to invite talk around it.

The postponed subject of the tale, the loved-hated figure that elicits mockery from the male tellers but is talked about only with much caution, is here the most persevering storyteller of all: Mother Crocodile Diassigue. A tale's resonance lies in its ability to proceed by indirection and by sharp digressions. Nobody understood this better than Diassigue who educated her children with his/stories of men—"not of Crocodiles, for crocodiles have no his/stories." Mother always remembers. And what she remembers, she never forgets to weave with what her mother, her grandmother, her great-grandmother remembered. Diassigue, the mother of crocodiles, was thus reputed for her very good memory. "And much as he deplored this, in his heart of hearts Golo had to admit it," wrote Diop. As for her being stupid, "it was difficult to tell whether Golo's statement was intended to be praise or blame." The saddest part of the whole business, however, was that Diassigue's own children, the little crocodiles, began to share the monkeys' opinion of their mother and to think that Golo spoke the truth. "They thought that perhaps their mother really did sometimes talk a lot of nonsense." So goes the tale, which proceeds to tell us how Diassigue, the all-absorbing spectator, remembered best because she spent her time, from her lair in the mud or under the sunny banks of the river, watching the movements of life, lending a patient ear to the chatter of women and of other living creatures, and thus collecting all the news and noises of her talkative environment.

> —*Here is a story!*
> —*A story it is.*
> —*It has happened.*
> —*It has already been told.*

When Mother gathered her children around her and told them what she and her foremothers had seen, they yawned and yawned. For while they dreamt of great crocodile exploits, all they could hear were stories of black men and white men. Having witnessed "empires born and kingdoms die," the mothers were only eager to recount the times when the river turned red with corpses after the coming and going of men. And what they remembered of places, events, and passers-by was, in fact, no more and no less relevant to the crocodiles than the history of men, of wars, of massacres of men by other men. One day, it was said, alerted three times by the disturbing messages of the crows, Diassigue hurriedly collected her children to urge them to leave their home, for "the Emir of Tzara has declared war on the Wolofs." To her youngest son's question, "What difference does it make to us crocodiles if the Wolofs of Wolo fight against the Moors of Tzara?" she then replied, "My child, the dry grass can set fire to the green grass. Let us go." But the little ones would not follow their mother. To shorten Diop's tale, at the end of seven days of terrible fighting, the Moors lost and the Wolofs won, taking with them the heir to the Moorish kingdom who bore a wound in his right side. All the priests and medicine-men were summoned to care for the young captive prince, but to no avail. Finally, there came to the court an old, old woman who prescribed the effective remedy, which was: "to apply, three times a day, to the sore place, the fresh brain of a young crocodile."

"The tale is of all countries," wrote literary critic Mohamadou Kane.[2] Referred to as "the loyal mirror of African sensibility and wisdom," it is, of all literary genres, the one to circulate the most, and its extreme mobility has led literary critics to proclaim it not only the best genre to depict rural life, but also one whose continuity and variety cuts across cultural and ethnic boundaries. While remaining specific to local events, customs, and land-scapes, the tale also functions as a depersonalizing, hence a generalizing tool for initiating talk around a moral instruction. Each society has its own treasure-house from which its culture draws in order to live, and it is precisely through storytelling that one is said to encounter the genius of a people. To (re)tell stories is "to enter into the constant recreation of the world, of community, of mankind."[3] Talking therefore brings the impossible within reach. It contributes to widening the horizon of one's imagination; to constantly shifting the frontier between reality and fantasy; and to question-ing, through the gifts of the so-called supernatural and the unusual, the limits of all that is thought to be "ordinary" and "believable."

Nothing seems more ordinary in the tale of Mother Crocodile than the gendered construction of wisdom. Diassigue is here presented both as a palaverer and a wise matron. Typically, Mother's talk is exasperating, nonsensical, at the same time as it is perilously clairvoyant and caringly farsighted. By persisting in remembering, it tends to overplay and to reiterate the immorality of men's his/stories. The division set up between the worlds of crocodiles and of men is one that differentiates not only animals from humans, but also mothertellers from fathertellers, warfleers from warmakers, sapience from stupidity. African folklore abounds with stories and proverbs whose moral is to caution men against women's supposedly most treacherous shortcoming: their indiscretion. "Give your love to the woman, but do not trust her" remains, for example, one of the best advice a man can give another man.[4] Utterly incapable of holding their tongues when they are asked to keep a secret (in a male-is-norm world), women are repeatedly depicted as those who "work their tongues so much harder than their hands," and they are always seen chattering away nineteen to the dozen.

Wisdom is here at the heart of the struggle of memory against forgetting. Without it, history is bound to repeat itself blindly; and access to the forces of the surreal is impossible, for the surreal universe is hidden from men by the screen of the real. To be able to see beyond sensible manifestations is to understand that "A thing is always itself and more than itself."[5] Mother's prosy knowledge of men's his/stories is, in fact, no ordinary gossip. In the village environment, idle talk may contribute to the communal mapping of the social terrain, while ill-considered talk is likely to sow dissension in the group. As the result of the compilation work of several generations of mothers, Diassigue's history-informed accounts could neither be reduced to trivial interpersonal reactions among women, nor can they be attributed to any malevolently divisive intent. On the contrary, if these accounts recalled the deeds of the great men of Black Africa, it was mainly to display the continuity of violence and of wars in men's world; wars which had already forced her grandmother to leave her home, the Senegal River, only to encounter everywhere else, in her search for peaceful waters, more killings and more corpses.

Commonly enough, however, Mother's dignified speeches failed to command (men's) respect. (It is, indeed, significant that the child who questioned Diassigue's decision to leave home at the outbreak of war, was her *youngest son*.) What was believable from mothers to daughters may become (temporarily) unbelievable in the process of transmitting men's his/stories (to crocodiles). "A woman will find ninety-nine lies, but she will betray herself with the hundredth," says a Hausa proverb;[6] while a multitude of Fulani sayings warn: "If your mother has prepared food, eat; if she has concocted [a plan for you], refuse;" because "He who follows a woman's plan, is bound to drown." Or else: "One does not confide in a woman," for "[a] woman is the fresh water that kills, the shallow water that drowns."[7] In many African folktales, male wisdom thus departs markedly from female wisdom. The wisdom attributed to men is one that generally works at conserving the social group, while the wisdom attributed to women is consistently equated with a supernatural malefic power. She who appears in almost every tale in the form of "an old, old woman" often holds powers that are both maleficent and beneficent, black and white magic. She can operate wonders, she can heal and make dreams come true at will; but she can also kill, punish, and prompt irrevocable losses. As she names death, Death appears.

> —*A story is coming!*
> —*A story.*
> —*Let it go, let it come.*
>   . . . .
> —*Call it back!*
> —*It has already started. It cannot be called back.*

Destructive wisdom remains the prerogative of women. Such a clear (unacknowledged) moral implication is likely to be divisive, but even in its divisiveness it should remain open to talk, if the function of storytelling in African contexts is to be respected. The moral retrieved from the tale of Mother Crocodile can easily be: "Always listen to the wisdom of the elders." But a gendered reading of this same tale can hardly be content with such a genderless generalization. The reader remembers, instead, that it was through a deferred male voice that we were told the story of a female character who failed to spellbind her children with tales of wondrous men (she equally failed to indulge in tales of crocodile exploits). And as the story drew to its "last word," the reader is again abruptly faced with another female character—albeit "an old, old woman"—who succeeded in healing the young captive prince by dooming the destiny of the young crocodiles. Once the healing words of malediction are let out, they cannot be taken back. Thus, She warns first, then She acts accordingly: for whoever remembers her words with good intent, She cures; while for those who neglect, forget, or use them with ill intent, her punishment is irrepealable. If the crocodiles had disobeyed their mother, it was largely due to the fact that they trusted the immediate *believability* of Golo-the-He-Monkey's words and their vision stopped at the *screen of the real* (the illusory separation of the animals's world from that of the humans). They had, in other words, sided with the men (whether the latter praise or blame) in judging mother, and had thus failed to recognize that mother's talk was talk but also more than talk.

> *Ho! call the women*
> *call the women*
> *I didn't know what it means*
> *to be a woman*
> *if I knew*
> *I would have changed into a bird*
> *in the bush*
> *if I could not change into a bird*
> *in the bush*
> *I would have changed into a hind*
> *in the bush*
> *to be married*
> *is a misfortune*
> *not to be married*
> *is a misfortune*
> *I would have changed into a bird*
> *in the bush*
> *to have a child*
> *is a misfortune*
> *not to have a child*
> *is a misfortune*
> *I would have changed into a hind*
> *in the bush*
> *call the women*
> *call the women*
> *I didn't know what it means*
> *to be a woman*
>   (A song by women in Mali)[8]

Talk is what it takes to expose motherhood in all its ambivalences. Mothering is exalted only so long as women either conscientiously conform to their role as guardians of the status quo and protectors of the established order, or they perform a fairygodmother's task of fulfilling harmless wishes, dreams, and desire. Since wisdom may be defined as a form of knowledge based on *discretion*, it is not readily perceived as knowledge by the unwise, and cannot be measured or controlled in a system of power relations dependent on accumulative, factual knowledge. The need to contain and restrict women's wisdom within the mothering role is therefore a constant in social institutions across cultures; and women's status as childbearer continues in many African contexts to be the test of their womanhood. From one generation to another, mothers are called upon to perfect their duty as the killjoy keepers of tradition—especially in matters that concern their gender. As is well-known, a woman's lot is to conceive, bear, feed, and, above all, indoctrinate her children. The tale of Mother Crocodile revolves, typically enough, round Diassigue's role as educator. In the process of transmitting knowledge, women are held solely responsible for their children's errors. No matter how unfailing Diassigue's memory was when it recounted the historical deeds of great men, because she failed to convince her own offspring of the value of Mother's words, the entire crocodile species would have to suffer the die-hard reputation of being . . . brainless.

Mother's knowledge is always discreet in its indiscretion. She may fail in speech (as women often do when speaking means inserting themselves into the patriarchal socio-symbolic order), and she may be so "indiscreet" as to compel her male companions to arm themselves with thousand strategies to defend the "men's secrets." (Unless a man wishes to bring about his own downfall, affirms a Senegalese man, he should not confide in women for "they don't know what is essential.") But her word is paradoxically kept as the word of truth—of what has been, what is, and what will be. Says a Fulani proverb, "The speech [that stays] in the belly is the child of your mother, the speech [that springs] from your mouth is the child of your father."[9] What marks Mother's talk, therefore, is a practice of indirection that is at times overt and other times secret. Like a historian, Diassigue filled her stories with factual names, places, and events, and the indirect took shelter under the figures of the direct and of verifiable accounts about great men. But when the time came to warn her children of the imminent danger of men's war, Mother's wisdom preferred the secret of truth in this overtly indirect reply: "My child, the dry grass can set fire to the green grass."

In the politics of remembering, public opinion maintains a reduced conception of memory. It is apparently always opposed to obliviousness and identified with the power to recall what has been learned . Thus, says the tale, the neglect of memory leads to the loss of brain—hence the notoriously unequaled stupidity of those who dare to defy memory, the family of crocodile. Reverse this logic *à la* monkey, and the talk will continue. If crocodiles are stupid for no other reason than that they have the best memories, then whoever remembers the story of crocodiles' memories and carries it on must be . . . abysmally stupid. These are, for example, the storytellers and storycommentators who praise and blame, who talk to initiate talk, who write to invite writing, and who can only laugh at mother-memory by laughing at themselves and their function—as repositories of creative tradition and as transmitters of the genius of a people. Once set in motion, the story that strikes their fancy is both irreversible and infinitely shifting. An assertion of gentleness, Mother's talk does not let itself be caught, for kindness belongs to no system; it stands at the limit of the tale's moral. As she speaks, she crosses limits, she remembers the texture of memory and if she loses, she loses without losing. The loss of brain, for some, is the healing of an open wound, for others. After all, it is said with much insight that "Poetry has to be a bit stupid" (Pushkin).

So my story ends

NOTES

1 "Maman-caïman," in Birago Diop, *Les Contes d'Amadou Koumba*, pp. 49–57. Translations from the French are largely taken from the English version "Mother Crocodile," in *Tales of Amadou Koumba*, pp. 45–51.
2 Mohamadou Kane, *Birago Diop. L'Homme et l'œuvre*, p. 37. My translation.
3 Roger D. Abrahams, *African Folktales* p. 22.
4 *Les Contes d'Amadou Koumba*, p. 47.
5 Quoted as a representative statement of the African conception of the supernatural in Mohamadou Kane, *Birago Diop*, p. 68.
6 In Alta Jablow, *Yes and No. The Intimate Folklore of Africa*, p. 127.
7 In Henri Gaden, *Proverbes et Maximes Peuls et Toucouleurs*, pp. 15–16. My translations.
8 Collected in René Luneau, *Chants de femmes au Mali*, p. 156. My translation.
9 In Henri Gaden. p. 148.

WORKS CITED

Abrahams, Roger D. *African Folktales*. New York: Pantheon, 1983.
Diop, Birago. "Maman-caïman." *Les Contes d'Amadou Koumba*. Paris: Présence africaine, 1961, 49–57.
——. "Mother Crocodile." *Tales of Amadou Koumba*. Trans. Dorothy S. Blair. London: Oxford University Press, 1966, 45–51.
Gaden, Henri. *Proverbes et Maximes Peuls et Toucouleurs*. Paris: Institut d'Ethnologie, 1931.
Jablow, Alta. *Yes and No. The Intimate Folklore of Africa*. New York: Horizon Press, 1961.
Kane, Mohamadou. *Birago Diop. L'Homme et l'œuvre*. Paris: Présence africaine, 1971.
Luneau, René. *Chants de femmes au Mali*. Paris: Luneau Ascot Éditeurs, 1981.
Tarkovsky, Andrey. *Sculpting in Time. Reflections on the Cinema*. Trans. K. Hunter-Blair. New York: Alfred A. Knopf, 1987.

2 *Nervous Conditions*

Dangarembga's feminist reinvention of Fanon

Charles Sugnet

NATIONALISM AND FEMINISM: "EQUAL AND DIALOGIC"?

From Kumari Jayawardena's historical survey of *Feminism and Nationalism in the the Third World* (1986) to more specific articles like Anne McClintock's "Women and Nationalism in South Africa" (1991),[1] nationalism and national liberation movements continue to be criticized for their failure to serve women's needs. In his contribution to the recent collection *Nationalisms and Sexualities* (1992), R. Radakrishnan puts a series of theoretical questions that flow from this failure:

> Why is it that the advent of the politics of nationalism signals the subordination if not the demise of women's politics? . . . Why could not the two be coordinated in an equal and dialogic relationship of mutual accountability? What factors constitute the normative criteria by which a question or issue is deemed "political"? . . . Is it inevitable that one of these politics must form the horizon for the other, or is it possible that the very notion of a containing horizon is quite beside the point?[2]

In light of Radakrishnan's questions, Tsitsi Dangarembga's 1988 novel, *Nervous Conditions*, constitutes an interesting and successful effort to redefine the "political" and rearticulate the relationship between feminism and anti-colonial nationalism.

While other Zimbabwean novels published by male authors in the late 1980s, such as Shimmer Chinyoda's *Harvest of Thorns* and Chenjerai Hove's *Bones*, foreground the *chimurenga* struggle for national liberation, *Nervous Conditions* barely mentions it, foregrounding instead the struggles of two young women against the simultaneous double oppression of sexism and colonialism. The book is a first-person account of a young Shona woman named Tambudzai coming of age in the 1960s and 1970s, as she moves from her father, Jeremiah's, impoverished farm to the mission school where her uncle Babamukuru is headmaster, and on to the exclusive Sacred Heart convent school, where most of the students are white.

Tambudzai appears destined for co-optation into the educated elite of colonized Rhodesia, but her rising consciousness averts this, and the novel offers sophisticated answers to questions of post-colonial identity and resistance. Her remarkable and tormented cousin Nyasha, raised partly in England, is her companion, double, and sometime guide on this journey. By taking us inside Tambudzai's consciousness, the novel makes us *feel* the injustice when her brother is sent to school and she is left at home, or when her powerful uncle tries to silence all the women in the family, and this strength of feeling is matched with lucid analysis.

Tambudzai's peril is as complex and multiple as her identity: she might, for example, free herself from the sexism that denies her an education only to educate herself into perfect complicity with the Rhodesian colonial elite. Chantal Mouffe characterizes such multiplicity this way: "How can we grasp the multiplicity of relations of subordination that can affect an individual if we envisage social agents as homogeneous and unified entities? What characterizes the struggles of these new social movements is precisely the multiplicity of subject-positions which constitutes a single agent, and the possibility for this multiplicity to become the site of an antagonism and thereby politicized."[3] Tambudzai's narrative is the story of such multiple subordination, antagonism, and politicization; it also narrates the slow unfolding of the many defenses against this process, the hesitations, the fragmentary realizations.

Right from the opening pages of description, as the narrator tells how precolonial patterns of commerce and travel reorganized themselves around the British Council houses, or how the lyrics of Rhodesian pop songs body forth the distressing social conditions, the reader is in the hands of a politically conscious novelist who understands the reach of colonialism into the texture of daily life. And *Nervous Conditions* contains enough chronological specifics so a reader familiar with Zimbabwean history will know that the novel's period encompasses such landmark events in the national narrative as the founding of ZAPU and ZANU, the ten-year detention of Robert Mugabe and Joshua Nkomo, Ian Smith's Unilateral Declaration of Independence, and the officially celebrated "first battle" of the *chimurenga* war on April 28, 1966. There appear, however, to be only three direct references to these events in the novel, and they are brief and passing ones: one place where the narrator is "not concerned that freedom fighters were referred to as terrorists" (155);[4] a second passage where the narrator is "beginning to understand that our Government was not a good one" (101) and a third passage where the narrator's friend Nyasha wants to know "exactly why UDI was declared and what it meant" (93). The national liberation struggle is conspicuous by its absence in this novel, and yet I think there may be a complex, partly subterranean relationship between it and the struggles of the young Tambudzai against the immediate manifestations of patriarchy in her life.

COLONIAL PSYCHOLOGY AS "HINGE"

I want to try to describe that relationship in the spirit of Radakrishanan's questions, without subordinating either politics to the other. Perhaps the best way to begin this delicate task is to consider the quotation which gives the novel both its title and its epigraph, since the quote has considerable explanatory power and may provide a sort of hinge between the novel's feminism and the discourse of nationalism: "The condition of native is a nervous condition." The flyleaf of *Nervous Conditions* identifies this passage as coming "From an introduction to Fanon's *The Wretched of the Earth*." Though Dangarembga chooses not to advertise the fact, these words are a translation of Sartre, rather than of Fanon himself.

Dangarembga says she had not read Fanon until the novel was completed and she was searching for an appropriate title; a friend referred her to *The Wretched of the Earth*.[5] The friend's advice was astute, because there are amazing areas of overlap (and important areas of difference) between Fanon's theory and Dangarembga's novel, especially with regard to colonial psychology and the manifestation of resistance through physical symptoms. It must have been an immediate fit, a "Eureka!" I think Dangarembga seized on this particular phrase for her title because her novel redefines Fanon's insights, and because she wanted the slight double meaning in "nervous conditions" —"nervous" in the ordinary sense of anxious, uneasy, or worried, but also in the formal medical or psychiatric sense of "so-and-so suffers from a nervous condition." Dangarembga studied medicine and psychology before taking up writing full time. Psychiatry, of course, was Fanon's profession, and the "nervous conditions" he describes in "Colonial War and Mental Disorders" are very relevant to Dangarembga's concerns. Note also that the epigraph from Sartre/Fanon, because it describes a point of contact between individual psychology and colonial politics, offers an opening for an experientially based feminism to insist that it be "deemed political" (in Radakrishnan's phrase), an opening Dangarembga makes full use of.

The most obvious and quintessential "nervous condition" in the novel is the startling bulimia/anorexia nervosa of Tambudzai's cousin, Nyasha. Other characters also have trouble eating, and the imagery of eating, digestion, nutrition, vomiting, and excretion provides crucial metaphors for domination and resistance in the novel. If one rereads *The Wretched of the Earth* after having read *Nervous Conditions*, one is struck by how many of the cases Fanon describes in "Colonial War and Mental Disorders" involve eating disturbances. One patient "could no longer swallow a bite," and began to waste away; five torture victims suffer "loss of appetite arising from mental causes." Fanon describes patients who will not eat and explode with hostility when touched, which is more or less what happens with Nyasha in the critical stage of her disease, and he uses the term "anorexia" to describe these cases.

In addition to these eating disorders, Fanon describes other kinds of quasi-voluntary bodily resistance to colonialism, such as excessive muscular rigidity. And beyond Nyasha's striking case, virtually everyone in Dangarembga's portrait of colonial Rhodesia shows some symptoms of nervous illness (as the epigraph from Fanon via Sartre implies). In the course of the novel, she uses the word "nervous" to describe each African character in turn, though her novel suggests significant gender difference in the ways these "nervous" responses to colonialism are expressed.

THE COLONIAL MALE AS "HISTORICAL ARTEFACT"

Without suppressing an ounce of its legitimate anger at the misogyny of the African men who mistreat the female characters, *Nervous Conditions* nevertheless shows clearly how those men are themselves products of the colonial system. Dangarembga explores the specifics of Fanon's insight (formulated in opposition to D.O. Mannoni and other theorists) that the "native" does not preexist colonization, but is artificially produced by it. Tambudzai's father, Jeremiah, deprived by the British of his ancestral lands, becomes the stereotype of the shiftless "native," spending his children's school fees on beer, letting his homestead run down, enthusing about traditional ceremonies while lacking the money to carry them out, critical of the whites but secretly admiring them. Brandishing an imaginary spear and leaping around his powerful brother's automobile, Jeremiah embodies a parodic debasement of "traditional" values.[6] Tambudzai says: "It was fortunate that my father was so obviously impossible, otherwise I would have been confused" (33). So much for nativism. Her father and brother always look to her as though they are cringing; using her grandmother's description of colonialism as a kind of bewitchment, she understands that her "father and brother had suffered painfully under the evil wizards' [the British] spell." And she connects that suffering with their impulse to bully others, including the women in their family (50).

African men higher on the ladder of colonial education have also learned to negotiate the precarious position of the "native." Mr. Matimba, Tambu's sympathetic teacher, speaks in a special way to white people, and she notices it: "'Excuse me, Madam,' Mr. Matimba said in English, in the softest, slipperiest voice I had ever heard him use" (27). The young Tambu at first thinks her uncle Babamukuru, the family patriarch, is different, has not cringed, and has broken the spell of the British wizards. But the events of the novel reveal that with all of his advanced degrees and Christian ways, Babamukuru the schoolmaster is a more impressive kind of "native," created by the British colonial system to serve its purposes. Moving to the mission to go to school, Tambu is disappointed in Babamukuru: "My uncle's identity was elusive. I had thought it would be like the good old days . . . with Babamukuru throwing us up in the air and giving us sweets" (102). Instead, we are told "his nerves were bad. His nerves were bad because he was so busy." And indeed he is caught between the demands of his life as a surrogate

Englishman and his obligations as the head of a large African family. He's also terribly alienated from his body and has "an inbred aversion to . . . biological detail" (131). One of the few moments in the novel when he is spontaneously happy is when he starts to hum an old song on his way back to the countryside: "Unaccountably, unusually, Babamukuru was happy. Free of tensions and in the best of spirits, he looked younger and more lovable than he ever did at the mission" (122–23). The farther he gets from his English-made job and personality, the farther he gets from his nervous condition.

Babamukuru treats his daughter Nyasha atrociously, trying to control her sexuality and even her food intake. In one critical scene where he strikes her and calls her a whore because she is late coming home from a school dance, his motives are clear: "How can you go about disgracing me? Me! Like that! No, you cannot do it. I am respected at this mission" (114). Her behavior threatens his anxious status as a "good African." Later, Nyasha, half-dead with anorexia, offers Tambudzai her desperate insight:

> Then she sat on her bed and looked at me out of her sunken eyes, her bony knees pressed together so that her nightdress fell through the space where her thighs had been, agitated and nervous and picking her skin. "I don't want to do it Tambu, really I don't, but it's coming, I feel it coming." Her eyes dilated. "They've done it to me," she accused, whispering still. "Really, they have." And then she became stern. "It's not their [her parents'] fault. They [the British] did it to them. You know they did," she whispered. "To both of them, but especially to him."

Even in her extreme circumstances (perhaps by virtue of them), Nyasha sees the whole chain of causality that oppresses her, and sarcastically imagines how the white Rhodesians speak of her father: "He's a good boy, a good munt. A bloody good kaffir" (200). Her desperate analysis offers a paradigm for the whole social structure in this book. (Note the phrase "especially to him," since it implies that women may paradoxically be better off because less assimilated to the hegemonic system.)

On the first page of the novel, the socialization that created Babamukuru is already working effectively on Tambudzai's brother Nhamo, who hates riding the bus home from mission school because it's slow and "Moreover, the women smelt of unhealthy reproductive odors, the children were inclined to relieve their upset bowels on the floor, and the men gave off strong aromas of productive labour." Nhamo doesn't like to walk, or to work on the family farm either. He wants his status as an educated person to be marked by a special vehicle, and insists that his sisters should carry his bags. Later, he shows that he's willing to guard his male privilege by directly thwarting his sister's attempt to go to school.

Nhamo seeks elevation to the elite at the cost of his connection with the body, and with communal life, which will certainly make him "nervous" and may be what kills him. His mother believes so and uses the word "bewitched" to describe his death; the same word Tambu's grandmother uses to describe the effects of colonialism on earlier generations of African men. The socialization process that destroys Babamukuru and Nhamo is at work later when Babamukuru's son Chido, also described as "nervous," gets a scholarship to a white school. Nyasha sums up this Fanonian point by arguing that Babamukuru, her father, "was a historical artefact" (160).

When Babamukuru returns from studying in England, his brother Jeremiah greets him with that warrior's spearing gesture and says: "Our father and benefactor has returned appeased, having devoured English letters with a ferocious appetite! Did you think degrees were indigestible? If so, look at my brother. He has digested them" (36). Jeremiah's metaphor, connecting food and digestion with colonialism and "English letters," is threaded through the whole novel. Later, for example, when Tambudzai is preparing to go to Sacred Heart convent school, her mother warns her not to expect the ancestors "to stomach so much Englishness" (203).

Jeremiah is wrong about everything else, so he's probably wrong here too. The fact that Babamukuru has bad nerves and beats his daughter, or the fact that his wife leaves him, indicate that he may have indigestion after all. The novel does not give us full access to his interior, but he seems unable to mobilize his discontent for any act of resistance to "Englishness," or even to raise his own consciousness. Compared to the women characters, he is of course much closer to the colonial system, much more a material beneficiary of it, and this is one reason why he's less likely to fully express his indigestion. Another reason may be that his "inbred aversion to biological detail," probably induced both by masculine socialization and by Victorian class training, leaves him with less access to messages from his own body.

If we go back to Sartre/Fanon to locate the epigraph, we find there is another clause to the sentence, a clause Dangarembga chose not to quote: "The status of 'native' is a nervous condition introduced and maintained by the settler among colonized people *with their consent*." Certainly Baba-mukuru, Nhamo, and Chido give a sort of coerced consent to their status as agents of colonial hegemony. That status may ultimately be bad for them, but they seek it out because it offers privilege, material reward, and apparent security. And they in turn participate in the double colonization of the women nearest them. The colonial system makes education scarce; sexism deter-mines that boys shall have first access to it.

COLONIZED WOMEN: ACCOMMODATION AND THE SOURCES OF RESISTANCE

Dangarembga redeploys Fanon's concept to show that "woman," like "native," is not natural but is a "historical artefact" constructed by an oppressive social situation. In order to clarify its feminist analysis, the novel systematically compares several African female characters of different temperaments, ages, and social stations to show the outcomes of their different responses to sexism in the Rhodesia of the 1970s. Babamukuru's wife, Maiguru, with her Masters' degree from London and her own job, is analogous to the "Superwoman" created by mass media interpretations of Western feminism. But the novel shows over and over how powerless she still is to stand up to her husband or protect her daughter. Tambu's aunt Lucia, who defies the men and uses her sexuality as she sees fit, is eventually forced to beg Babamukuru for a job so she can support her child. Tambu's mother, trapped in the role of Jeremiah's wife and able to resist only passively, reaches a point of total paralysis. Anna, the servant girl, learns to kneel before her master.

Even along the Nyamarira river, which sometimes functions as a utopian spring of communal and sexual life, the young Tambu quickly learns the gender rules that govern who swims where, and learns that as a woman (when "my breasts grew too large") she should be afraid to swim naked (4). Babamukuru is explicit that child discipline and habit formation are important, "especially in the case of girls" (171). When Babamukuru disciplines Nyasha, he aims directly at her femaleness, calling her a whore, and Tambudzai gets the point: "What I didn't like was the way all of the conflicts came back to this question of femaleness. Femaleness as opposed to and inferior to maleness" (116). The clarity of this insight does not, of course, protect her from the effects of systematic conditioning; quite late in the novel, she says "There was definitely something wrong with me" (164) because she cannot stand up to Babamukuru.

But this is only half the story, for the women resist as well. One other element of Fanon's argument was his celebrated emphasis on violence as the decisive rupture in the colonial situation. The women in this book violently resist patriarchal domination on several occasions. In the scene where Babamukuru slaps his daughter Nyasha, she gives him a murderous look, punches him in the eye, and continues "doing what damage she could" (114–15) as they roll on the floor in struggle. Lucia twists her shiftless lover Takesure's ears to make him submit to a humbling interrogation. Tambu fights back against her brother's bullying by pushing a log from the fire in his face; when she finds out he's been stealing the maize she grew to put herself through school, she goes straight to him and physically attacks him. Perhaps the most important instance of such an overt rupture, though, is Tambudzai's acknowledgment in the very first sentence of the novel that "I was not sorry when my brother died." Their home, she says, was healthier when Nhamo was not there, and she's better off for his death, able to feel more, not less. In a way, the whole novel is the story of how Tambudzai came to be capable of writing this sentence, and Dangarembga has taken some pains to wrench the novel's structure around so that it can begin with this declaration. Tambudzai has not literally killed Nhamo, but she harbored murderous impulses toward him, and she is willing to accept his death as the price of her own freedom.

The novel suggests several reservoirs of strength for this resistance;

women's solidarity with each other is one of the most obvious. Tambudzai is explicit about the fact that without Nyasha's friendship and restless example, she would not have gotten free of Babamukuru's colonial ideology (151–152). Tambudzai's mother, Aunt Lucia, and Maiguru all offer sympathy, advice, and example. Tambudzai's grandmother gives her, through oral storytelling, a more accurate and useful history of colonization than can be found in any book; it is, moreover, a *woman's* history, told by a grandmother who is proud to have been "pretty and plump," with "heavy, strong hips." The grandmother conveys a very different female aesthetic than the one that leads the bulimic Nyasha to tell Tambudzai "Pity about the backside . . . It's rather large" (91). And by her wonderful rule of alternating stories with weeding rows of maize, she teaches Tambu the relations between history, imagination, and work, suggesting that productive labor can itself be a kind of resistance. This teaching leads directly to Tambu's growing maize to send herself to school; in fact, she grows the crop literally as well as figuratively on her grandmother's ground—on land that used to be her grandmother's garden.[7]

Tambudzai gets much that is useful from her mother and grandmother, but it is a mixed inheritance. The line between resistance and accommodation is sometimes a difficult one to draw; indeed the grandmother's story suggests that surviving by accommodation may sometimes be the only mode of resistance available. It is the grandmother who brought Babamukuru to the mission and asked that he be educated, to prepare him for life under the colonizers. After one of her grandmother's stories, Tambu notes that it had a "tantalising moral that increased your aspirations, but not beyond a manageable level" (19). Her mother's dire warnings are often right; as Tambudzai says: "Mother knew a lot of things and I had regard for her knowledge" (203). But she also passes on to her daughter her history of compromise and her tendency toward passivity and paralysis. And the mother thinks in terms of binary oppositions (good vs. evil, indigenousness vs. "Englishness") that Tambudzai will have to outgrow if she is to cope with her complex historical situation and her own complex identity.

In addition to the solidarity of women, another obvious source of strength for Tambudzai is her rootedness in childhood, the Zimbabwean landscape, and her own female body. Much of the early narrative captures the felt immediacy of the presocialized child; these memories provide Tambuzai with a position from which to judge the adult world. In an Edenic early passage, Tambudzai plunges into the Nyamarira river, deep enough, she says, "to engulf me to my nipples." At this point, she seems to own her own body, and says "We could play where we pleased" (3). Gender differences quickly enter the picture, as the children learn that the men and women have different bathing areas, and as the colonial commercial system overruns their favorite swimming spots. But Tambudzai can occasionally still recover Eden: "Nevertheless, when I was feeling brave, which was before my breasts grew too large, I would listen from the top of the ravine and when I was sure I had felt no one coming, run down to the river, slip off my frock [which marks both gender difference and British colonialism] . . . and swim blissfully for as long as I dared in the old deep places" (4).

As a child, Tambu loves "music and movement pulsing through the night to make your armpits prickle, your body up and impatient to be concerned with the beat" (42). Fanon seems to have been a terrible rationalist about dancing and traditional ceremonies, which he usually could read only as irrational symptoms; this is one place where Dangarembga diverges sharply from his position. Tambudzai quits dancing for a while at the mission school, but takes it up again as she comes out from under Babamukuru's spell.

This direct, innocent contact with the spiritual life of the landscape and the body does get occluded as Tambudzai learns modesty, absorbs Christian messages about the body being dirty, and embraces the upwardly mobile trajectory that will lead her away from the family's farm. Yet I'm convinced that "the old deep places" remain available to Tambudzai as sources of strength and points of orientation; the poetry with which she can describe them in her written account proves they are still available. One way to read the difference between Tambu and Nyasha is to note that Nyasha, for all her sophistication, does not have such "old deep places" to orient herself. Dangarembga is passionate about the work of recovering and preserving cultural roots, about the impossible archaeology of recovering/reinventing what colonialism destroyed. But this is not a straighforward or simple project: it may require writing a novel in English or even learning how to make films in Berlin (as Dangarembga is currently doing). Relying only on the "old deep places" as touchstones of identity would be problematic because it repeats the reductive pattern of identifying woman's body with the landscape, her spirit with the nation's soul, etc. As Annette Kolodny and others have shown, this trope is often an opening move in the exploitation of both woman and land.

Starting from Partha Chatterjee's discussion of gender and nationalism in India in *Nationalist Thought and the Colonial World*, Radakrishnan states the problem this way:

> questions of change and progress posed in Western attire were conceived as an outer and epiphenomenal aspect of Indian identity, whereas the inner and inviolable sanctum of Indian identity had to do with home, spirituality, and the figure of Woman as representative of the true self . . . The locus of the true self, the inner/traditional/spiritual sense of place, is exiled from processes of history, while the locus of historical knowledge fails to speak for the true identity of the nationalist subject.[8]

Newly emerging nations, Radikrishnan suggests, find such a gendered schizophrenia convenient, because it enables them to selectively appropriate the West, while preserving an essential identity; but it also locks them into what he calls an "essentialist indigeny," cutting off the deep places from historical knowledge and agency. "Nationalist ideology," he says, "sets up

Woman as victim and goddess simultaneously. Woman becomes the allegorical name for a specific historical failure: the failure to coordinate the political or the ontological with the epistemological within an undivided agency."

By refusing the usual terms of heroic, masculine, national narrative, *Nervous Conditions* avoids this schizophrenia to a remarkable degree. Because it is centered on a particular, dynamic woman, and because it describes so many different kinds of women, *Nervous Conditions* is in no danger of producing a univocal Woman, who can be allegorized to serve the national purpose. And because the narrator is the writer of her own account and therefore in some senses a maker of history and a producer of knowledge, the novel connects the "old deep places" of childhood, homestead, and inner self with history, change, and agency, rather than isolating them in some eternal essence of Woman/Landscape/Nation.

Tambudzai's mother would like her children to survive by remaining uncontaminated, to stomach no Englishness; she is often right in warning of dangers to her children, but her advice flows from a binary view that the novel ultimately finds inadequate. At the opposite pole of this duality is the imperative to Westernize completely. Both poles, both simple choices, are foreclosed by the way Dangarembga constucts her novel. Nyasha, the English educated anorexic/bulimic, and Maiguru the unhappy "Superwoman" demonstrate that Western feminism cannot provide a simple "liberation" for Tambuzai. At the other pole is her mother, uncontaminated in some sense, but paralyzed, deprived of agency, and exiled from history in a way that Tambu could never find satisfactory. Lindsay Pentolfe-Aegerter expresses this dilemma very well: "No simple retrieval of an identity as 'African' or 'woman' is possible, because both are contested terms undergoing continuous revision in the colonial and post-colonial context."[9] Poor Nyasha! The psychiatrist tells her parents that she cannot be bulimic/anorexic, because the disease is not one that Africans get! In her anguish, she perceptively tells her family: "I'm not one of them, but I'm not one of you" (201).

On questions of identity, then, Dangarembga's novel moves beyond choices framed between binary opposites. For both Tambu and Nyasha, identity will be a shifting third term, composed and recomposed from an overlay of culturally various sources: Shona language and ritual, trashy romance novels, stories told by grandmother, *Lady Chatterley's Lover*, the Bible, advertisements for liberated women's cigarettes, Louisa May Alcott's *Little Women*, histories of Africa's colonization, novels by the Brontës, etc. All of these are texts that Tambudzai alludes to in the course of composing herself in *Nervous Conditions*, and it's clear that she will continue to reinvent herself.

One of the most important questions in this novel is how Tambudzai can pursue her dream of education and upward mobility without becoming an agent of colonial hegemony and suffering losses similar to those suffered by Nhamo and Babamukuru.[10] As Anthony Appiah puts it: "When the colonialists attempted to tame the threatening cultural alterity of the African (whether through what the French call *assimilation* or through the agency of 'missionary conversion'), the instrumentalities of pedagogy were their most formidable weapon."[11] At first Tambu's project is a very naive one of succeeding within the colonial system, of imitating (not to say worshipping) Babamukuru. Her education does indeed teach her racist "facts" such as that "sin is black," and she does accept them. But Tambudzai's subject-position as a woman makes her much less assimilable than the men. Even as she consciously embraces the Babamukuru's version of culture and progress, her body and her psyche are preparing underground rebellion.

Dangarembga is brilliant in presenting the specifics of how the dream's very success undermines its assumptions. Living at her father's farm, Tambudzai is very aware of dirt and smells, including that of the outdoor latrine. So when she moves to the mission, the toilet seems the very essence of progress. She's not sure how one uses it, and tries sitting facing the tank, before deciding that the other way is more comfortable. But progress and modernization seem less attractive when Nyasha is constantly gagging and puking in the bathroom, or when we hear Nyasha is "grotesquely unhealthy" because of "the vital juices she flushed down the toilet" (199). The modern convenience turns out to be a life-sucking parasite. Clearly, Nyasha's anorexia/bulimia is a self-destructive form of resistance to her father's will and, less directly, to the will of the colonizers as well. In the grotesque theater of their middle-class dining room, her father (described only by his gender as "the man") forces her to eat, she complies with an eerie cheerfulness, and then goes into the bathroom to throw up the food.

Nyasha has picked up Western notions about the ideal female form; she praises Tambu's looks, but finishes with "Pity about the backside," which she finds too large (91). She stays away from jams and sweets because she prefers angles to curves. Well into her disease, she tells Tambu to expect "a svelte, sensuous me" because she's on a diet! The phrase, terribly grotesque in the context, could be a quote from a television advertisement. I suspect ultimately, though, that her diet internalizes what she feels as a social will to annihilate the female altogether, not just to trim it a bit. Thus, besides being a way to resist her father's will, Nyasha's anorexia is a way of refusing her femaleness, stopping menstruation, reducing female curves (recall that grim descriptive phrase: "where her thighs used to be"). Tambudzai, on the other hand, grows plump at her uncle's house and begins to menstruate, but she too runs afoul of the toilet and the inhuman standard of cleanliness it represents: "Conferences with older cousins and younger aunts, and the questions of older aunts and grandmothers had prepared me for the event . . . the onset of my menses, then, should have been placid, but when it came to washing those rags in Maiguru's white bathroom, to making a mess in the toilet bowl before I flushed it away, the business became nasty and nauseating. I became morose and moody about it" (95). (Note the rich network of female conversation implied in the passage, and also the descent, yet again, into "nervous conditions.")

The discourse of hygiene imposed by colonial conditions in the novel seems clearly arranged at first: Africanness is related to dirtiness (bad smells on the bus, maggots in the latrine) and English-inspired progress is related to cleanliness (Maiguru's kitchen, the white porcelain of the toilet). But the terms reverse as the white porcelain makes normal bodily functions seem "disgusting and nauseating." Moreover, Dangarembga is clever enough to see that what this discourse defines as "African" is really the debased form of indigenous ways left *after* colonialism has disrupted them. In Tambudzai's carefully written description of the family latrine, Dangarembga is insisting on a third possibility: "In the early days, when my mother had insisted I wash it down daily . . . it had never smelt and its pink plaster walls had remained a healthy pink" (123). The dirt on the bus, the maggots in the latrine, and the loss of that "healthy pink" are all related to the disturbances in eating and nutrition caused by colonialism and its attendant "nervous conditions."

Recall that Nyasha is not the only woman in *Nervous Conditions* who has trouble eating. Tambudzai's mother can hardly eat anything for a week before her daughter's departure for the mission school, because she is so anxious. Later, pregnant again and left alone by her husband, she develops "unlocalised aches all over her body" and stops eating, washing, or taking care of herself altogether after the baby is born. Only a forced immersion in the very special Nyamarira brings her back to some semblance of life. If the conditions of the colonized are indeed nervous conditions, Tambudzai as narrator can hardly claim exemption from the general condition. As we might expect, she too experiences times when "the food would not go down" (91) and has uncomfortable symptoms such as "a horrible crawling over my skin, my chest contracted in a breathless tension, and even my bowels threatened to let me know their opinion" (149). But her main symptom appears to be a kind of paralysis that follows from repression. Early in the novel (39), she senses "how unwise it was to think too deeply" about sexism, and busies herself with housework instead. Just a bit later, she explains how she handles preferential treatment given to her brother: "It cost me a lot of energy to bury that incident with Nhamo so deeply that it would not interfere with the business of living." The consequence of this deep burial: "I could no longer bring myself to speak to my brother" (50).

Disturbed that "all the conflicts come back to this question of femaleness," the young Tambudzai finds it "easy to leave tangled thoughts knotted . . . I didn't want to reach the end of those mazes, because there I would find myself" (116). When her uncle insists on a ridiculous Christian wedding to legitimize her parents' long union (thus implying that her existence has been "illegitimate" up this point), Tambudzai is so upset she has physical symptoms, but she still is not able to speak up about it. There is, she says, "definitely something wrong with me, otherwise I would have had something to say for myself" (164). On the morning of the wedding, however, "I found I could not get out of bed" (166).

I think it's generally accurate to say that the more Tambudzai and Nyasha attempt to comply with their own oppression, the more nervous their condition gets, and the more pronounced their symptoms become. So each of these women has a kind of disease, and if they can stop collaborating in their own oppression, they can get better. But the subtlety of Dangarembga's analysis suggests that it may be better to have symptoms than to digest your Englishness too easily; that the symptom is itself a kind of resistance, an involuntary inability to succumb completely to oppression. The symptom is a curse, but it is also a blessing. And the novel suggests that because women are farther from the center of colonial power, their symptoms are likely to be expressed more fully and disruptively.

In an otherwise excellent article[12] that discusses the roots of these symptoms, Sally McWilliams repeatedly calls Nyasha's bulimia "an act of self-control," and says that both young women's "bodies 'talk' in that they are physical disturbances to the status quo of that society's cultural codes." Certainly Nyasha does say after vomiting: "I did it myself. With my toothbrush." (Another instrument of hygiene turned dangerous!) And certainly Nyasha's bulimia and Tambu's inability to get out of bed are forms of resistance. But I think it oversimplifies what is known about bulimia/anorexia, a disorder often treated on the addiction model, to call it purely voluntary. And I think it oversimplifies the politics of the novel to see these forms of resistance as consciously controlled heroics. Nyasha may well die of her bulimia, and the terrible fate of Tambudzai's mother has already shown where Tambudzai's paralytic symptoms lead. Dangarembga ended the novel with Nyasha still alive and struggling; I don't think she's advocating the romance of self-destruction.

Certainly for Tambudzai, the narrative she's producing is part of a major effort to make herself healthy by becoming more and more aware of her oppression and more consciously resistant to it. The decision to compose her own account of herself, although it involves stomaching some "Englishness," is ultimately an empowering one. Nyasha, by contrast, knows more and is more expressive in her defiance, but is still very confused because she loves her father, and is utterly cut off from any practical means of achieving full independence. She wouldn't know how to grow maize to pay her school fees, and depends on the books, cigarettes, and tampons of the very colonial system she condemns.

Even after exploring the sources of Tambudzai's strength in women's solidarity and childhood's "deep places," I still feel that there's something about the level of consciousness she achieves that's unaccounted for in the text of her narrative. Jill Fritz-Pigott, who gave *Nervous Conditions* a very favorable review in *The Women's Review of Books*[13] felt so too, and put it this way: "*Nervous Conditions* ends without explaining how the compromised character Tambudzai becomes the novel's highly conscious narrator." We could rephrase this in lots of ways: How does the character Tambudzai, who thinks the mission living room is heaven, become the narrator Tambudzai who sees that that house is hell? How does the character Tambudzai, who believes that sin is black, become the narrator Tambudzai who can show us the subtleties of racism in the Christian school system? How does the character Tambudzai, who worships Babamukuru, become the narrator Tambudzai, who analyzes the sources of his viciousness? How does the character Tambudzai, who's dying to go to Sacred Heart convent school, become the narrator Tambudzai, who shows how shabbily the school treats its few black students?

The way I'd like to put it is to suggest that the narrator's coming to consciousness parallels the suppressed developments of the *chimurenga* struggle, and there are times when the hidden connection nearly pops through the surface of the text. One night Nyasha is in a rage, tearing up, among other things, her history book. "The next morning she was calm, but she assured me it was an illusion, the eye of a storm. 'There's a whole lot more,' she said. 'I've tried to keep it in but it's powerful. It ought to be. There's nearly a century of it'" (201). Certainly Nyasha is puking up colonialism itself. Her rage, I think, expresses the revolution in a different key. Allegory seekers might note that Tambudzai starts her maize project in 1962, just as ZAPU and ZANU are coming into being. Or that Bishop Abel Muzorewa, who played his own peculiar and finally obstructive part in the liberation struggle, was proud of his education at Old Methodist Mission near Umtali, right where Babamukuru runs his mission school. Allegorizing the women's struggle in terms of the national struggle seems to me a serious mistake, because it does just what Radakrishnan lamented, subordinates women's politics to a masculine, national master narrative. But I do think that for well-informed readers, *Nervous Conditions* will suggest various hazy parallels between the two struggles. And, as practitioners of repression unfortunately know very well, any struggle for freedom is likely to have an inspirational atmospheric effect on other such struggles.

If we are trying to understand, then, how Tambudzai the "compromised" character becomes (and it takes place somewhere off the page) Tambudzai the perceptive narrator, we might take into account such atmospheric effects of the national struggle. Tambudzai's narrative comes up to the early or mid-1970s, up to just before Samora Machel becomes President of Mozambique and the struggle in Zimbabwe moves to its final stages. But her narrative was not published until 1988. Some have suggested that Dangarembga deliberately set the novel back in history in order to blame the colonizers, rather than Mugabe's government, for the plight of women in Zimbabwe. But in a recent *Women's Review of Books* article,[14] Dangarembga explained that the novel was completed by 1984; publishing difficulties, which she attributed to sexism in newly liberated Zimbabwe, kept it from appearing until 1988. Even then, it had to rely on the international network of women's institutions for its publication, appearing first through the Women's Press in London, and only later in Harare.

There is then, a gap of some ten years between Tambudzai's entry (in the imaginary time of the novel) into Sacred Heart school, and the completion (in real time) of the manuscript of *Nervous Conditions*. And what has happened in those ten years? Tambudzai the "compromised" character has become Tambudzai the conscious narrator, and Rhodesia has, through a prolonged and violent educational process called *chimurenga*, become Zimbabwe. One reason I find the novel's title, *Nervous Conditions*, and the epigraph from Fanon/Sartre so important is that they offer a possible point of connection between these two sets of events. They have the odd status of being part of the novel's text, but not part of Tambudzai's first-person narrative. They imply, of course, the various distances and differences between Dangarembga the author and Tambudzai the character. They imply also leverage from the outside, connection with a kind of discourse available to Dangarembga in 1984 (but not to Tambudzai in 1974) partly because of the national struggle.

The fact that Dangarembga read Fanon and found the phrase for her title only *after* her manuscript was complete seems to fulfill Radakrishnan's request for an "equal and dialogic" relationship between women's politics and the politics of nationalism. The phrase from Sartre/Fanon stands as an indicator that the two discourses are in relation, a relation that flows from the body's symptomatic resistance to two different but related forms of domination. But the relation is not predetermined, as Dangarembga's novel has not been produced by relying on a nationalist master narrative. The novel, in fact, does not have a proper ending; as Tambudzai puts it, "Nyasha's progress was still in the balance, and so, as a result, was mine" (202). If the book ends without fully resolving the women's "nervous conditions," what does this say about the nervous conditions of those other "natives"? Can there be a master narrative without closure? Is it possible that "independence" is not an adequate closure for the narrative of anti-colonial liberation? If the two discourses are dialogic and equal, they can each interrogate the other, and national liberation itself be called in question.

One thing that is certain at the end of *Nervous Conditions* is that the story is not finished, that Tambudzai will continue to grow and reinvent herself. This reinvention will doubtless include the "old deep places," but will also continue to reach beyond her mother's binary oppositions to employ "Englishness" (the language itself,[15] ideas from the Brontës, feminism from London, etc.) where it serves her. The crucial move she has made is to use the tools given by colonial education to make her own account of herself. By becoming narrator, teller, writer, finding the language to nudge her symptoms toward articulate consciousness and resistance, she breaks out of those discourses where she would remain perpetually as goddess/victim, and reclaims agency for herself.

NOTES

1 Kumari Jayawardena, *Feminism and Nationalism in the Third World*. Anne McClintock, "'No Longer in a Future Heaven'."

2 R. Radakrishnan, "Nationalism, Gender, and the Narrative of Identity," p. 78.

3 Chantal Mouffe, "Radical Democracy," pp. 34–35.

4 This and all subsequent page numbers refer to the American edition of *Nervous Conditions* (Seattle: Seal Press, 1988).

5 Statement made in answer to a question asked at a public reading at the University of Minnesota, November 10, 1991. Dangarembga offhandedly explained resemblances between her analysis and Fanon's as the result of commonsense response to similar colonial data.

6 For a thorough and brilliant discussion of such flawed appeals to the indigenous, see Kwame Anthony Appiah, "Out of Africa," pp. 153–178.

7 Note Dangarembga's honesty about the limits of self-help in a colonial or neo-colonial situation. Tambudzai does not succeed by selling her crop for a fair price; instead, her serious economic effort becomes an occasion for colonialist charity. The economic game is rigged, and Tambudzai cannot simply work her way or produce her way out of oppression.

8 Radakrishnan, "Nationalism, Gender, and the Narrative of Identity," pp. 84–85.

9 Lindsay Pentolfe-Aegerter, unpublished paper read at the 14th annual West Virginia Symposium on Literature and Film, October 1990.

10 There's much in this novel that reminds me of those nineteenth-century novels Raymond Williams discussed, the fictional territory framed between *Great Expectations* and *Lost Illusions*. Tambu's ambition and education move her painfully away from her origins in a way that resembles the trajectory of such nineteenth-century protagonists as Pip and Rastignac, where gains and losses of upward movement cannot be disentangled from each other. One major difference, of course, is that the African situation makes it much harder to recuperate the pains and losses into a narrative of successful upward class mobility; and the sentimental solution available to Dickens, in which the oppressed protagonist (for example, Oliver Twist) discovers he was part of the bourgeoisie all along, is not available to Dangarembga. Tambudzai's gender, her race, the constraints of (neo)colonialism, and Dangarembga's own honesty make such slippery resolutions impossible. Tambudzai specifically mentions the Brontës, and *Nervous Conditions* contains a fair number of textual echoes of nineteenth-century English fiction. There are, for example, times when this narrative reminds me of *Wuthering Heights*, with the conventional Nelly Dean observing the mercurial Catherine, and with lots of suppressed motive in the telling.

11 Appiah, "Out of Africa," p. 155.

12 Sally McWilliams, "Tsitsi Dangarembga's *Nervous Conditions*," pp. 103–112.

13 Jill Fritz-Pigott, "Surviving Political Abuse."

14 Tsitsi Dangarembga, "This Year, Next Year," pp. 43–44.

15 The decision to write does not, of course, necessitate the use of English, especially in Zimbabwe, where there is a flourishing written literature in Shona. But I think that it does involve some "Englishness" (in the sense that Tambudzai's mother uses the word) in its presumption of literacy, colonial education, etc. Perhaps the important point here is the one made by Appiah: "So that the problem is not only, or not so much, the English or the French or the Portuguese language as the cultural hegemony that it represents" ("Out of Africa," p. 155). And Tambudzai's narrative is certainly an effort to break up English cultural hegemony.

WORKS CITED

Alcott, Louisa May. *Little Women*. New York: Grosset & Dunlap, 1947.

Appiah, Kwame Anthony. "Out of Africa: Topologies of Nativism." *The Yale Journal of Criticism* 2.1 (Fall 1988): 153–178.

Dangarembga, Tsitsi. *Nervous Conditions*. Seattle: Seal Press, 1989.

——. "This Year, Next Year." *Women's Review of Books* 8.10/11 (July 1991): 43–44.

Fanon, Frantz. *The Wretched of the Earth*. Trans. Constance Farrington. New York: Grove Press, 1963.

Fritz-Pigott, Jill. "Surviving Political Abuse." *Women's Review of Books* 6.10/11 (July 1989).

Hove, Chenjerai. *Bones*. Cape Town: David Philip, 1988.

Jayawardena, Kumari. *Feminism and Nationalism in the Third World*. The Hague: Institute of Social Studies, 1982.

Lawrence, D. H. *Lady Chatterley's Lover*. London: Heinemann, 1981.

McClintock, Anne. "No Longer in a Future Heaven: Women and Nationalism in South Africa." *Transition* 51 (Spring 1991): 104–123.

McWilliams, Sally. "Tsitsi Dangarembga's *Nervous Conditions*: At the Crossroads of Feminism and Post-colonialism." *World Literature Written in English* 31.1 (1991): 103–112.

Mouffe, Chantal. "Radical Democracy: Modern or Postmodern?" *Universal Abandon? The Politics of Postmodernism*. Ed. Andrew Ross. Trans. Paul Holden-graber. Minneapolis: University of Minnesota Press, 1988.

Radhakrishnan R. "Nationalism, Gender, and the Narrative of Identity." *Nationalisms and Sexualities*. Ed. Andrew Parker, Mary Russo, Doris Sommer, and Patricia Yaeger. New York: Routledge, 1992, 77–95.

3   Why the Snake-Lizard killed his mother

Inscribing and decentering "Nneka" in *Things Fall Apart*

Ousseynou B. Traoré

Okonkwo's suicide, the closing event of Chinua Achebe's *Things Fall Apart*, is in many ways a direct result of the hero's attempt to displace or decenter the *Nneka* principle in his private and public life. *Nneka*, or "mother is supreme," is an ideal clearly inscribed at the center of the symbolic universe of Okonkwo's people. Achebe's fictional explorations of this and other key epistemological and ontological concepts are much influenced by what he calls his people's "philosophy of life" (Duerden and Peterse 10), which is expressed in several types of Igbo oral tradition. Achebe writes:

> Since the Igbo people did not construct a rigid and closely argued system of thought to explain the universe and the place of man in it, preferring the metaphor of myth and poetry, anyone seeking an insight into their world must seek it along their own way. Some of these ways are folktales, proverbs, proper names, rituals and festivals. ("Chi" 132)

Folktales, proverbs, proper names, rituals, and festivals saturate the narrative of *Things Fall Apart* and suggest the best way to gain insight into the world of the novel.

Proverbs and myths are oral formulations of philosophical debates and verities about essential norms that govern humankind's social and spiritual activities. Commenting on the meaning of his own name as an example, Achebe argues that proper names are "in the manner of my people . . . full-length philosophical statement[s]" ("Named for Victoria" 98). Names are rooted in ontological matrices and have their own narratives of origination and mytho-poetics. The gender ideals and conflicts that structure many of the thematic and formal features of *Things Fall Apart* are codified in names like Nneka (Mother is Supreme) and Chukwuka (Chukwu/God is Supreme) and imbedded in myths such as "Mosquito and Ear," "Why the Snake-Lizard killed his Mother" and a significant number of related proverbs. In the two myths, the *Nneka* principle is embodied by Ear and Snake-Lizard's mother, two central figures of womanhood. Ear is repeatedly assaulted by Mosquito, the rejected would-be-husband, while mother Snake-Lizard is killed by her demanding son. In both myths, the violence of the male figures of the husband

and son is motivated by problematic gender ideals rooted in their own psychological and ontological dysfunction.

From this angle, the problematic of womanhood and motherhood in *Things Fall Apart*, and especially in Okonkwo's tragedy, is paradigmatically inscribed in the gender debates surrounding Ear (a wife figure) and the female Snake-Lizard (a figure of motherhood). Okonkwo's story shares the thematic features of the two myths and is, in fact, structurally modeled on the oral forms. Nneka and Chukwuka function as towering gender-specific tropes and pivotal philosophical statements that complement the debates of the Mosquito and Snake-Lizard myths. The myths function as ontological vehicles through which the ideals of gender balance and the crises caused by its absence or subversion are normatively posited in succinct metaphorical form. The themes and structures of the names, proverbs and myths are then fruitfully explored in the extensive narrative spaces. Through the complex network of formal replications and thematic repetitions, myth and fiction merge and illuminate each other, thereby projecting Okonkwo's suicidal assaults on the *Nneka* principle more essentially through the figural acts of Mosquito and Snake-Lizard, among other paradigms.

The analytical sections of this essay focus on the thematic and structural functions of the tale explaining why the Snake-Lizard killed his Mother. The tale projects the problematic of motherhood or womanhood in general, but can also be read as "Why the Snake-Lizard killed Himself," which conversely foregrounds the problematic of warped ideals of manhood or gender concepts. The thesis advanced here and the need to ground the analysis in the suggested myth matrices necessitate a theoretical and critical context.

THEORY OF GENDER BALANCE: NNEKA AND CHUKWUKA

Nneka ["Mother is Supreme"] and Chukwuka ["Chukwu is Supreme"] are two proper names which, taken together, most succinctly express the philosophical notions of duality and gender balance in *Things Fall Apart*. These names claim the supremacy of one gender principle, either male or female, to inscribe its crucial function in the architecture of the universe of the novel. The tragedy of Okonkwo's life lies in his failure to recognize this gendered architecture in his excessively warped expression of the male principle. This leads him to antagonize and repress the female principle embodied at the spiritual level by *Ani*, the earth goddess, and by woman at the social level.

One of the first questions Okonkwo is asked by Uchendu, his maternal uncle, at the beginning of his seven-year exile from his fatherland to his motherland, centers around the significance of "Nneka." Uchendu's question must be viewed in the context of the series of offenses committed by Okonkwo against *Ani*, his impatience with men without titles referred to metaphorically as *agbala* (woman) and his violence against his wives. Uchendu's question reads as follows:

> Why is it that one of the commonest names we give our children is Nneka, or "Mother is Supreme?" We all know that a man is the head of the family and his wives do his bidding. A child belongs to its father and his family and not to its mother and her family. A man belongs to his fatherland and not to his motherland. And yet we say Nneka—"Mother is Supreme." Why is that? (123)

On the surface, Uchendu's explanation suggests the supremacy of the female principle embodied by the figure of the mother. But, simultaneously and at a different level, the wife/mother does the husband/father's bidding, which suggests the supremacy of "man," "father," and "fatherland" (metaphors of the male principle) over "wife," "mother," and "motherland" (figures of the female principle). Uchendu's question is, therefore, not a simple one, and requires a great deal of philosophical maturity and the ability to balance the seemingly contradictory terms of two vital essences. Significantly, Okonkwo, the great warrior who metaphorically eats with kings and elders (12), can only say to Uchendu, "I do not know the answer" (123). The problematic of motherhood and womanhood in Okonkwo's life, therefore, lies in this epistemological deficit.

The centrality and supremacy of *Nneka* are not challenged but balanced by the male counterpart of the name and concept in the ontological realm mapped out by Akunna, the Umuofian who debates Mr. Brown the missionary over the merits of Christianity and his ancestral Igbo religion. In his theological interpretation of Chukwu's supremacy in the pantheon of the Igbo gods, Akunna says to Mr. Brown:

> "Our fathers knew that Chukwu was the Overlord and that is why many of them gave their children the name Chukwuka—'Chukwu is Supreme' . . ." "But we must fear Him when we are not doing His will," said Akunna. (165)

In seeming opposition to Uchendu's explication of the *Nneka* principle, Akunna's statement foregrounds figures of maleness that suggest dominance through Chukwu's fear-inspiring presence and will. But Chukwu's will is not inflexible because "at crucial cosmological moments [He] will discuss His universe with man" ("Chi" 144). The central philosophical question framed in the reciprocal illumination of *Nneka* and *Chukwuka* in the novel is whether the supremacy of Chukwu, as a male principle embodied at the social level by the father, the husband and the son, contradicts or balances out that of the female principle symbolized by the mother figure and the cluster of female symbols and metaphors vested in women, wives and Ani, the earth goddess, "owner of the land" (20), "the source of all fertility" and "the ultimate judge of morality and conduct" (37).

Rather than conflict, the moral universe of *Things Fall Apart*, "the frame of reference by which we may judge the actions and opinions of [the] characters" ("Image" 10), prioritizes balance, or what Achebe calls "the central place in Igbo thought of the notion of duality." As Achebe explains, "[w]herever Something stands, Something Else will stand beside it. Nothing is absolute" ("Chi" 133). In terms of the gender issues in *Things Fall Apart*, the two essence ideals Achebe refers to as "Something" and "Something Else"—here, male and female principles—are bound by an operative notion of balance and complementarity.

After illustrating the principle of duality through an examination of proper names and different referents for the Igbo concept of God, Achebe reaches a conclusion about the dialectical bond or seeming conflict between *chi* and *eke* which is useful in our theory of the male–female balance and complementarity. He writes:

> From the foregoing it would appear that chi and eke are very closely related deities, *perhaps the same god in a twofold manifestation, such as male and female*; or the duality may have come into being for the purpose of bringing two dialectical tributaries of Igbo into liturgical unity. ("Chi" 142, my emphasis)

There exist a dialectic, a duality and an element of totality through interdependence and interconnection among the male and female clusters of relationship in *Things Fall Apart*: Ezeani, a male character, is the chief priest or "priest/king" of *Ani*, the earth goddess; and Chielo, the priestess, whose name means "the mind of god," is the human interpreter of Agbala, the god of the Oracle of the Hills and the Caves. These balanced relationships, reaching back to the centrality of *Nneka* and *Chukwuka*, suggest that the male and female principles are equally centered in the socio-philosophical concepts of the novel.

The complementarity of *Chukwuka* and *Nneka*, as philosophical expressions of vital life essences, is scripted in a myth of cosmic and social origination which, even though not quoted in the novel, informs the world of *Things Fall Apart*. In his essay on *chi*, Achebe relies heavily on the Nri oral tradition, and points clearly in this direction when he mentions the "story about Ezenri, that fascinating king/priest whose spiritual preeminence was acknowledged over considerable parts of Igbo land" ("Chi" 144). The oral sources, which Achebe is creatively aware of, tell us that

> The father of all Nri was Eri. No one knows where he came from. Tradition (*òdìnàànì*) says that he came from God [*Chukwu*]. He was a great man sent by God to rule all the people of the Anambra. Before he came to the Anambra the people were living in scattered huts. They had no king. It is said that the earth was not firm, as it is today, when he was on earth. He got Akwa smiths to use bellows to dry the flooded land. The Anambra at times floods its banks. When he came there was no food for the people. He prayed God [*Chukwu*] to send food to his people. God demanded that he

should sacrifice his first son and daughter to him. He did the sacrifice
and buried his children. Yam and a palm tree grew out of the spot where
he buried his son and vegetables and cocoyam grew out of the spot where
he buried his daughter . . . Eri brought yam and all the food. The earth
produces it. The "earth force" is great. Thus there was a covenant between
earth and man. The earth produces the food that man eats. The earth
becomes the greatest supernatural force [*alusi*]. Eri controlled yam and
other food and the earth that grows them. No person should defile the earth
by spilling human blood in violence on it. This is the covenant. It must be
kept. We Nri people keep it. We told other Igbo people to whom we gave
yam to keep it. (Isichei 22–23)

The *Nneka* principle is scripted in this variant of the myth of origin as great
"earth force." The earth is figured as mother of all crops, since she produces
all the food that humankind eats. As "the greatest supernatural force," the
supremacy of the cosmic figure of woman is the working principle of the
covenant between humankind and the earth goddess. If Eri, the primal king,
"controls yam and other food and the earth that grows them," his kingship
and supremacy are merely ritual.

Eri is a facilitator of social construction, a connecting human presence and
ritual go-between that links Chukwu (the sun/sky) and Earth in creative and
ontological harmony. His function is concretely symbolized by his archetypal
figure as the agent of sacrifice, not a material creator of yam and other crops
or even an active transformer of human flesh into crops. The creation of
materiality in terms of crops is achieved through Chukwu's creative Word,
his infinite creative Knowledge and the equally infinite and creative Essences
of the female Body of Earth, more significantly referred to as "earth force."
The two gendered principles, *Chukwu* (the sky god) and *Alà* or *Anì* (the earth
goddess) are therefore complementary.

At a divine level, Eri, or Ezenri, who came from Chukwu, is a manifestation
of the *Chukwuka* principle. But, *Alà* or *Anì* (the earth) is more powerful than
Eri in the political and social realm of existence. Tradition tells us that "*Alà*
is the greatest *alusi* [or supernatural power] because other *alusi* are enclosed
in it or are on it" (Isichei 17). In the social and material life of humankind,
therefore, the earth is the ultimate locus of fulfillment. The social organization credited to Eri the great priest/king, unifier of "the people who once
lived in scattered huts and had no king," is built on earth. Yam, closely
associated with Eri, the mythical bringer of the crop, metaphorically referred
to in *Things Fall Apart* as "the king of crops" and a "man's crop," grows
out of the womb of the earth. But without earth the dead bodies of Eri's first
son and daughter would not have been recreated as *male* and *female* crops.
Though earth, as mythical mother of the first son and daughter of Eri, is
supreme, the myth does not marginalize either the son or the daughter. Nor
does the myth establish any hierarchy among the symbolic crops that embody
their vital forces.

OKONKWO AND SNAKE-LIZARD: MALE TROPES AS ABSOLUTE STANDARDS

The Snake-Lizard tale is one of those gender-specific narratives of the oral canon that Okonkwo rejects as inferior to the "masculine stories of violence and bloodshed" he tells Nwoye and Ikemefuna and through which he confirms his warped sense of manhood (52). By opposition, the Snake-Lizard tale co-narrated by Ezinma and Ekwefi refigures the violence and bloodshed of Okonkwo's masculine stories as a violation of humankind's covenant with the "earth force," through the shedding of kindred blood and, perhaps even more atrociously, the ultimate crime of matricide. In Okonkwo's "masculine stories of bloodshed," the *agbala* image of his father, "who was a coward and could not stand the sight of blood" (10), and the *Nneka* principle are effectively decentered and excluded. It is this tragic decentering through matricide that the Snake-Lizard story dramatizes by way of cautionary instruction.

Okonkwo's negative memory of his mother's narrative legacy, as the Mosquito and Ear myth filters through his mind in the three-day period of what he calls his own "womanish" weakness following his murder of Ikemefuna is extremely important: "when he was a child his mother had told him a story about it. But it was as silly as all women's stories" (72). The Snake-Lizard myth, co-narrated by Ekwefi and her daughter Ezinma, is part of woman's expressive culture rejected by Okonkwo. In the telling of the Snake-Lizard myth, which significantly takes place during Okonkwo's absence from the house and his brief journey into the bush, Ekwefi and Ezinma revive the narrative legacy of Okonkwo's mother in the female private space of their own shared hut, diametrically opposed to the male space of Okonkwo's *obi*. The women's tale of decentered motherhood is indeed metaphorically intended for Okonkwo who is not there to hear the mother's wisdom that might have saved his life at the end of the novel.

At the structural level, the Snake-Lizard story is framed by the fictional account of Okonkwo's trip. This strategy creates a link between the fictional and mythic structures by supplying the narrative components which are missing from the tale but implicit in it, especially Snake-Lizard's trips to and from the bush. The myth in turn symbolically completes the fictional scene of the preparation of the *iba* medicine and projects the themes and structures of the ends of Part One and Part Three of the novel, namely Okonkwo's female *ochu* (unintentional manslaughter) and suicide. Much of the formal fusion of myth and fiction depends on the explicit and implicit connections built in the text. Okonkwo's trip into the bush to collect the leaves, grasses, and barks that go into the making of the *iba* medicine (73) is directly related to the context in which Ezinma and Ekwefi co-narrate the Snake-Lizard tale since the occasion concerns the ritual breaking of Ezinma's *ogbanje* cycle of life and death:

> Ekwefi went into her hut to cook yams. Her husband had brought out more yams than usual because the medicine man had to be fed.

Ezinma went with her and helped in preparing the vegetables.

"There is too much green vegetable," she said.

"Don't you see the pot is full of yams?" Ekwefi asked. "And you know how leaves become smaller after cooking."

"Yes," said Ezinma, "that was why the snake-lizard killed his mother."

"Very true," said Ekwefi.

"He gave his mother seven baskets of vegetables to cook and in the end there were only three. And so he killed her," said Ezinma.

"That is not the end of the story."

"Oho," said Ezinma. "I remember now. He brought another seven baskets and cooked them himself. And there were again only three. So he killed himself too." (79–80)

The imagery of the "leaves," "grasses" (green herb images), and "barks" (hard substance) Okonkwo brings parallels the symbolic structure of "female" crops (green vegetables) and "male" crops (yams) cooking in Ekwefi's pot. The debate over the coexistence and complementarity of green vegetables and yams in Ekwefi's pot is initiated by Ezinma's observation that "[t]here is too much green vegetable"—an overabundance of the female crop—and her mother's response that expresses the predominant presence of the crop of manliness: "Don't you see the pot is full of yams? . . . And you know how leaves become smaller after cooking." The complementary expressions of mother and daughter signal the quantitative and qualitative balance of two gendered material principles.

Snake-Lizard "[gives] his mother seven baskets of vegetables," images that mirror the same "leaves" of "green vegetables" Ekwefi puts in her pot with the large quantity of yams—"more yams than usual"—that Okonkwo gives her to cook. Even though the green leaves and vegetables fall into the category of female crops and symbolize the female body of Eri's first daughter, the male–female balance or complementarity is built into the tale through the metaphorical use of the numerology of seven and three established in the fictional components of Okonkwo's story.

METAPHOR AND NUMEROLOGY: THE SYMBOLIC SEVENS AND THREES

In the fiction, Okonkwo's male strength is measured symbolically and mythically in terms of the numerology of seven when he defeats Amalinze, the Cat. The Cat is "the great wrestler who for seven years was unbeaten" until Okonkwo measures his raw eighteen-year-old's strength against the older and more seasoned champion and is transformed into a man. Amalinze is already mythicized as the Cat whose "back would never touch the earth," a trope of absolutely unbeatable standard of manhood. The mythical language of the fiction is extended and heightened by metaphorical association with a masculine narrative legacy, the mythico-historical foundation of Okonkwo's fatherland through the central image of the numerology of seven:

> It was this man [Amalinze] that Okonkwo threw in a fight which the old men agreed was one of the fiercest since the founder of their town engaged a spirit of the wild for seven days and seven nights. (7)

The founder's manly strength and kingly rule over the conquered wild space that becomes Umuofia (Children of the Bush) are measured by his epic victory over the mythical and awesome spirit of the wild. Okonkwo earns his manhood by flooring Amalinze, a mirror-image of the spirit of the wild, in the major wrestling match of the second day of the New Yam Festival that yearly commemorates or reenacts the epic feat of the founder and bringer of yam. The New Yam Festival is, in this regard, a celebration of male achievement.

Within the myth, the symbolic equation of seven and three with manhood and womanhood, respectively, is based on a subtle and complex process of association and typology: Snake-Lizard is associated with the original acquisition of seven baskets, which he measures normatively against the three baskets his mother produces and is associated with. The complexity of the formal interaction between the myth and the fiction is also evident in the fact that Okonkwo's three-day weakness that follows his murder of Ikemefuna, a figural character whose name means "let my strength not become lost" (Shelton 91), is, through structural parallelism and metaphorical transfer, symbolically equated with the three baskets of shrunken vegetables. Okonkwo's realization of the meaning of his change of state on the third day after Ikemefuna's death is revealing, and must be related to the symbolic measure of the three baskets:

> "When did you become a shivering old woman," Okonkwo asked himself, "you, who are known in all the nine villages for your valor in war? How can a man who has killed five men in battle fall to pieces because he has added a boy to their number? Okonkwo, you are a woman indeed." (62–63)

The symbolic and metaphorical operation of the numerology of seven and three in the fiction and in the myth becomes clearer when we juxtapose and merge Okonkwo's reading of his female transformation with Snake-Lizard's association of the three baskets with inferior quantity and his mother's gender through the cooking process.

The Snake-Lizard's killing of his mother is metaphorically identical to Okonkwo's psychological and symbolic murder of the *agbala* figure of his father: "This meeting is for men," Okonkwo said to a man who had no title (*agbala*/woman) for he "knew how to kill a man's spirit" (28). The scene in which Okonkwo shoots at his wife Ekwefi (in the context of the New Yam Festival) for "killing" his banana tree, a figure of his manhood, parallels Snake-Lizard's literal killing of his mother for shrinking his vegetables, which he symbolically perceives as a loss of strength. On the verbal level, Ekwefi actually strips Okonkwo of his male pride or manhood, as she strips the old banana of few leaves, after he "gave her a sound beating and left her and her only daughter crying" (39). The parallels between this fictional event and Snake-Lizard's matricidal act are significant:

> His anger thus satisfied, Okonkwo decided to go hunting. He had an old rusty gun. . . . But although Okonkwo was a great man whose prowess was universally acknowledged, he was not a hunter. In fact he had not killed a rat with his gun. *And so when he called Ikemefuna to fetch his gun the wife who had just been beaten murmured something about guns that never shot.* Unfortunately for her, Okonkwo heard it and ran madly into his room for the loaded gun, ran out again and aimed at her as she clambered over the dwarf wall of the barn. He pressed the trigger and there was a loud report accompanied by the wail of his wives and children. (39, my emphasis)

Chielo's question to Ekwefi, later, brings this incident in line with the theme of the killing of woman and mother: "Is it true that Okonkwo nearly killed you with his gun?" she asks (48).

On the fictional level, Okonkwo's return from the bush reflects Snake-Lizard's return from his two excursions. Snake-Lizard and his mother are mirrored in this fictional image sequence through Okonkwo and Ekwefi:

> Okonkwo returned from the bush carrying on his left shoulder a large bundle of grasses and leaves, roots and barks of medicinal trees and shrubs. He went to Ekwefi's hut, put down his load and sat down. (81)

The boiling of Okonkwo's harvest dramatizes in discursive terms the unspoken gender conflicts and debates inherent in the Snake-Lizard myth. The drama acted out by Okonkwo and Ekwefi significantly helps interpret the symbolic structure of the Snake-Lizard story:

> "Give me a pot," [Okonkwo] said, "and leave the child alone."
>
> Ekwefi went to bring the pot and Okonkwo selected the best from his bundle, in their due proportions, and cut them up. He put them in the pot and Ekwefi poured in some water.
>
> "Is that enough?" she asked when she had poured in about half of the water into the bowl.
>
> "A little more . . . I said *little*. Are you deaf?" Okonkwo roared at her.
>
> She set the pot on the fire and Okonkwo took up his machete to return to his *obi*.
>
> "You must watch the pot carefully," he said as he went, "and don't allow it to boil over. If it does its power will be gone." He went away to his hut and Ekwefi began to tend the medicine pot almost as if it was the sick child. Her eyes went constantly from Ezinma to the boiling pot and back to Ezinma.
>
> Okonkwo returned when he felt the medicine had cooked long enough. He looked it over and said it was done. (81–82)

Like Snake-Lizard, Okonkwo sets the success criteria for the cooking of the herbs. He selects "the best from his bundle," and decides "their due proportions." Ekwefi's function, which reflects the role of the Snake-Lizard's mother, is limited by such controlling phrases as, "don't let it boil over," which recalls Snake-Lizard's concern for his shrunken vegetables; "watch the pot carefully"; "[a] little more . . . I said a *little*"; "leave the child alone"; and "[g]ive me the pot." In addition to setting the criteria, Okonkwo is the judge: he "returned when he felt the medicine had cooked long enough. He looked it over and said it was done." In a parallel way, reflecting the metaphorical relationship between myth and fiction, Snake-Lizard looks over the three baskets of cooked vegetables, which he suspects to be an overcooked and thus a weakened and diminished form of his original seven baskets shrunk by his mother. This is precisely Okonkwo's concern as he rebukes Ekwefi in the cooking process: "Don't allow it to boil over. If it does its power will be gone."

In the myth woman/mother fails, according to rigid and illogical "male" criteria that are contradictory to the law of nature that leaves get smaller after cooking, which Ezinma, Ekwefi and mother Snake-Lizard know. Matricide is thus metaphorical in Okonkwo's case and realized only in the mythic form. The suicidal result of matricide, however, is a consistent element in the myth and the fiction.

THE KILLING OF WOMAN: FOR WHOM IS IT GOOD?

The murder of mother Snake-Lizard is the highest form of the violation of the covenant with earth and leads to disaster. Parallel to this idea, Okonkwo's abominations against Ani the earth goddess (breaking the week of peace, killing Ikemefuna and his accidentally killing Ezeudu's son) have the same implications. As Obierika, another center of cultural authority and literacy, tells Okonkwo, "What you have done will not please the earth. It is the kind of action for which the goddess wipes out whole families" (64).

This catastrophic consequence obtains in the case of Snake-Lizard's matricidal act too, which yokes Snake-Lizard and Okonkwo as mytho-fictional and metaphorical doubles. Uchendu, who poses the question regarding the name "Mother is Supreme" to Okonkwo, amplifies Obierika's statement and places it in a context that speaks more immediately to Okonkwo about the death of his own mother, which mirrors metaphorically the murder or death of Snake-Lizard's mother. Uchendu asks Okonkwo, "Have you not heard the song they sing when a woman dies?" Uchendu does not wait for Okonkwo's answer but sings, foregrounding the catastrophic decentering of the *Nneka* principle:

> For whom is it well, for whom is it well?
> There is no one for whom it is well. (125)

Uchendu's song underscores the significance of Okonkwo's mother and her death in relation to Snake-Lizard's ignorance of the meaning of the name Nneka and of the tragic result of matricide. Uchendu's song points out Okonkwo's lack of memory of his mother's death and his ignorance of the importance of mother's symbolic space, "the earth force" embodied by his motherland. This lack of knowledge and memory is of great thematic relevance, especially in light of the fact that Okonkwo does not share Uchendu's knowledge and memory:

> [It] was [Uchendu] who had received Okonkwo's mother twenty and ten years before when she had been brought home to be buried with his people. Okonkwo was only a boy then and Uchendu still remembered him crying the traditional funeral farewell: "Mother is going, mother is going." (119)

"Mother is going, mother is going," as a lament of the death of mother/ woman and a tribute to the *Nneka* principle, does not cross the mind of the banished hero cast upon the motherland. Okonkwo the man in fact not only does not mourn the death of his mother but rejects her legacy symbolized by what he calls "silly women stories" (72).

This dismissal of the mother and her rhetorical and epistemological legacy is comparable to Snake-Lizard's violent rejection of his mother's culinary legacy. While Snake-Lizard kills his mother, Okonkwo gets rid of his mother and his *agbala* (female) father psychologically, which is a deep form of murder. Even Okonkwo's forced tribute to his mother's memory reveals his inability to reconcile with the *Nneka* principle when he is exiled from his fatherland to his motherland:

> He had called his first child born to him in exile Nneka—"Mother is Supreme"—out of politeness for his mother's kinsmen. But two years later when a son was born he called him Nwofia—"Begotten in the Wilderness." (151)

As philosophical statements, the names Okonkwo gives to his first female and male children born on the earth where his mother is buried suggest very strongly his rejection or psychic murder of the "earth force." Okonkwo's "polite" use of the name Nneka does not signal respect or acceptance. The name Nwofia, on the other hand, is an embodiment or figure of disgruntled and displaced manhood that recalls Okonkwo's fatherland, Umuofia, which means "Children of the Bush," as a norm. "Begotten in the Wilderness," as a figure of displaced or reduced maleness, is Okonkwo's ultimate rhetorical rejection of "Mother is Supreme," a concept to which he merely pays lip service. The name Nwofia redefines the symbolic space of Okonkwo's mother as a "wilderness" on which his manhood is wasted, contrary to the fertile "earth force" which gives constructive direction to his maleness. The seven years Okonkwo spends in the wilderness tie in with the seven baskets of raw vegetable as a negative mirror-image, signifying the loss of male status for Okonkwo. Viewed from an opposing angle, the image assumes the numerological figure for the establishment of the white man's force or rule, which takes place during Okonkwo's seven-year exile. The white man is thus a conflated refiguring of two male historical and mythical forces Okonkwo had to confront at the historical and mythical levels at the beginning of the novel: the new Amalinze (who reigned undefeated for seven years before Okonkwo's heroic victory) and the new "spirit of the wild," the encroaching power of the white man's church and courthouse located in the "evil forest," that recalls the founder's formidable opponent in that seven-day-and-seven-night fight at the beginning of Umuofia's history.

Significantly, and in binding opposition to the name Nwofia, the white man prospers and builds his strength in the "evil forests" of Mbanta and Umuofia. The numerology of seven years means the ascendance of the white man in Umuofia (Okonkwo's fatherland) and in Mbanta (Okonkwo's motherland). Given this symbolic structure, the white man's seven-year reign during which Okonkwo has no political or military mandate in the two symbolic realms of manhood and womanhood is comparable to Amalinze's seven-year reign as a champion wrestler during which Okonkwo's manhood is untested and unproven while his father's *agbala* figure haunts him. The seven years of the white man's military power (manhood) contrast with the seven years of Okonkwo's weakness (womanhood).

Okonkwo's return is thus structurally and thematically modeled on Snake-Lizard's own attempt to measure up against the seven-basket criterion his mother did not meet. This is particularly relevant when viewed in the context of Okonkwo's sense that his mother's people failed to confront and physically remove the white man during these seven years. After his militarist argument failed to move the Mbantans to war against the white man, "Okonkwo made a sound full of disgust. This was a womanly clan, he thought. Such a thing could never happen in his fatherland, Umuofia" (148).

The trope of the test or measurement of manhood central to Snake-Lizard's suicide is further intimated in the fiction, where the language of manly confrontation is very clear and is rooted in the numerology of seven and the metaphor of the lizard's lost tail:

> Seven years was a long time to be away from one's clan. A man's place was not always there, waiting for him. As soon as he left, someone else rose and filled it. The clan was like a lizard; if it lost its tail it soon grew another. Okonkwo knew these things. He knew that he had lost his place among the nine masked spirits who administered justice in the clan. He had lost the chance to lead his warlike clan against the new religion, which, he was told had gained ground. He had lost the years in which he might have taken the highest titles in the clan. But some of these things were not irreparable. He was determined that his return should be marked by his people. He would return with a flourish, and regain the seven wasted years. (157)

Okonkwo's return to Umuofia follows the same pattern established by Snake-Lizard who tries to regain his seven wasted baskets of vegetables by cooking them himself. The reference to the lizard that loses and regains his tail, which prefaces Okonkwo's return to his fatherland, provides a crucial interlocking image that facilitates the metaphorical function of the myth. This hinge image also recalls and reactivates Okonkwo's own self-identification with the lizard that jumps from the high *iroko* tree and lives to brag about it. Okonkwo's loss of his "man's place"—now filled by "someone else"—and the opportunity to take "the highest titles," "lead his warlike clan against the new religion" suggest his status of an *agbala* now ready to earn his manhood.

The Snake-Lizard kills himself after failing to produce seven baskets of cooked vegetables. Okonkwo kills himself because he discerns his inability to measure up against the white man, the new Cat and the new spirit of the wild. The imprisonment and humiliating beating Okonkwo the warrior and producer of yam receives in the white man's colonial system of law are clearly a reduction of Okonkwo's manhood. It is also significant that Okonkwo dies within less than three years after his return, a symbolic numerology that is patterned after that of the Snake-Lizard's three baskets of cooked vegetables, which entails death. The challenge to Okonkwo's manhood within the framework of the fictional three years is conveyed by the court messenger, an extension of the white man's authoritarian rule that displaces Okonkwo's symbolic status of a king.

As an extension of the white man, the messenger comes to break up the meeting of Umuofia's men as they debate a line of liberating action against the colonial government. This recalls the men's meeting at which Okonkwo calls Osugo a woman. The untitled messenger thus reverses Okonkwo's position in the gender scheme, which complicates the issues since the *agbala* messenger is authorized by white male power. He, an untitled outcast, brings the white man's challenge to Okonkwo. Okonkwo's reaction to this symbolic male/female presence dramatizes Snake-Lizard's reaction to his mother's "failure" and his own:

> [Okonkwo] sprang to his feet as soon as he saw who it was. He confronted the head messenger, trembling with hate, unable to utter a word. The man stood his ground, his four men lined up behind him . . ."The white man whose power you know too well has ordered this meeting to stop." In a flash Okonkwo drew his machete. The messenger crouched to avoid the blow. It was useless. Okonkwo's machete descended twice and the man's head lay beside his uniformed body. (187–188)

Okonkwo's violence is motivated by the verbal insult to his manhood, "the white man whose power you know well." Okonkwo remembers the symbols of his "feminization," the welts scripted on his back, his shaven head and the fine paid to bail him out of the white man's jail. The *agbala* figure of Okonkwo is further inscribed in the context of the three-year time structure (three baskets) governing his return:

> It was the wrong year too. If Okonkwo had immediately initiated his two

sons into the *ozo* society as he had planned he would have caused a stir. But *the initiation rite was performed once in three years in Umuofia* [my emphasis], and he had to wait for nearly two years for the next round of ceremonies. (167–168)

Even though the three-year time structure contains the promise of a ritual celebration of manhood, figured in the *ozo* initiation rite, it denies Okonkwo's dream of regained manhood. The fictional three years are metaphorically equivalent to the three mythic baskets of green vegetables and do not measure up to the white man's seven-year reign or that of Amalinze. Okonkwo's murder of the *agbala* messenger, which governs his suicide, is symbolic of matricide since it follows the murder/suicide model established in the Snake-Lizard story: Snake-Lizard kills his mother, then kills himself; Okonkwo kills *agbala* messenger, then kills himself, which recalls the rhetorical question of the woman's funeral song Uchendu quotes: "For whom is it good when a woman dies, for whom is it good?"

Okonkwo's "evil body" is carried away to the "evil forest" by the white man's messengers, since his people cannot touch it and the earth will not receive it in her womb. The rejection of Okonkwo's body by the earth force, which also symbolizes the earth's rejection of Snake-Lizard's evil body, contrasts clearly with the recreative reception of Eri's son and daughter in the womb of earth. Ani's ultimate rejection of Okonkwo evil male body is a strong condemnation of warped or imbalanced gender ideals.

WOMANBEING: BEGINNINGS AND ENDINGS

The art and ideology of *Things Fall Apart* are systematically determined by the aesthetic and valuative configurations through which myth and fiction, oral and written forms, are interfaced and yoked by metaphor and the language of poetry. The *Nneka* principle is centered in the gender debates of the novel set in motion by the murder of an unnamed woman that brings Umuofia and Mabino to the brink of war. "Those sons of wild beasts dared to murder a daughter of Umuofia," Ogbuefi Ezeugo the powerful orator declares, pointing in the direction of Mbaino (15). At this early stage in the novel, Okonkwo, whose acts are in line with the model symbolic kingship and manhood of the founder, is chosen as a spokesperson for Umuofia to demand a young virgin and a young man called Ikemefuna. The sacrificial virgin and young man are not only two ritual symbols of atonement for woman's death, they also recall Eri's mythical first son and daughter. Here Okonkwo's male strength and the righteousness of his warlike act are mandated not only by Umuofia, but by his entire clan, unlike his selfish murders of Ikemefuna and the messenger to prove his manhood. More importantly, "their *agadi-nwayi* [or old woman]" who "would never fight a war of blame," intimates that the war that now threatens between Umuofia

and Mbaino is "a just war" (16). Okonkwo has the signal heroic honor of
mediating that crisis of decentered motherhood "when a woman dies."

In contrast to the war with Mbaino, when Okonkwo kills the messenger,
no one supports him, including the *agadi-nwayi*, and every one asks, "Why
did he do it?" Okonkwo's reasoning, consistent with the gender debates
inscribed in the proverbs and the Snake-Lizard myth, reveals his typical
disregard for the *agadi-nwayi*, a figure of the *Nneka* principle:

> "The greatest obstacle in Umuofia," Okonkwo thought bitterly, "is that
> coward, Egonwanne. His sweet tongue can change fire into cold ash. When
> he speaks he moves men to impotence. If they had ignored *his womanish
> wisdom* five years ago, we would not have come to this." He ground his
> teeth. "Tomorrow he will tell them that our fathers never fought a 'war of
> blame' ... Let Egonwanne talk about a 'war of blame' tomorrow and
> I shall show him my back and head." (184, my emphasis)

The transformations of fire into cold ash and of men into impotence are quite
clearly indexed at the mythic level on the transformation from seven to three
baskets of vegetables. Okonkwo's dismissal of the *agadi-nwayi* and Egon-
wanne's "womanish wisdom" in connection with his view of the concept of
"war of blame" recalls his dismissal of his mother's "womanish wisdom"
as "silly women's stories."

Okonkwo and the Snake-Lizard fail to understand the centrality of
woman's wisdom and the earth force in the epistemological and ontological
systems of their culture. The legacy of the mother is as important and as
central as the legacy of the father and this idea of duality is crucially inscribed
in the mythic origin of male and female crops in which Eri's first son and
first daughter stand together to receive the chopping blows of the father's
machete and lie next to each other in their mother's recreative womb only to
rise again together.

The philosophical crux of Okonkwo's psychology has its roots in his
deviation from the structured truth of the myth of duality. Okonkwo's name
itself expresses his maleness as warrior and master of the economics of yam
farming. *Okonkwo*, a name given to a male child born on the market day of
Nkwo, signals a male achiever in the economic realm. The strong-man idea
built into Okonkwo's name incorporates his physical warlike prowess. The
narrator foregrounds the philosophical debates of names and myth matrices
by establishing early in the text the fact that the material manifestations of
economics and warfare are rooted in an ontologically centered figure of
womanhood and the *Nneka* principle. Umuofia's dreaded war machine is
qualified in the following words:

> Its most potent war-medicine was as old as the clan itself. Nobody knew
> how old. But on one point there was general agreement—the active
> principle in that medicine had been an old woman with one leg. In fact the
> medicine was called *agadi-nwayi*, or old woman. It had its shrine in the
> center of Umuofia, in a cleared spot. (15)

The foundation of the clan itself is co-terminous with the unknowable emergence of the one-legged woman figure of the *Nneka* principle. It is on the strength of this active and centered female principle that Okonkwo is recognized in Mbaino as a descendent of the founder of the clan, whose male and warlike strength is rooted in the active essence or "earth force" of the one-legged woman. Okonkwo is thus "treated . . . like a king" in Mbaino (29). Likewise, Okonkwo's strength as a successful farmer of yam, the king-of-crops and crop-of-manliness, rests on the *agadi-nwayi* principle figured in the old woman with the fan. Obierika reminds us too that economic power is based on the materially productive working principle of womanbeing. He tells us that

> The people of Umuike wanted their market to grow and swallow up the markets of their neighbors. So they made a powerful medicine. Every market, before the first cock-crow, this medicine stands on the market ground in the shape of an old woman with a fan. With this magic fan she beckons to the market all the neighboring clans. She beckons in front of her and behind her, to her right and her left. (107)

This market-economy figure of womanbeing, like the earth force of the war medicine vested in the form of the old woman hopping on one leg, is also centered through the cardinal imagery of her gesture. Okonkwo forgets that his heroic and economic success depends on the earth force of womanbeing (old woman as war medicine and market medicine) that governs his birth as a male child born on the market day of Nkwo. In complementary relationship with the founding father who wrestled the spirit of the wild at the undatable beginning of Umuofia's history and myth of origin, the figure of woman as founding mother is not just centered, but also critically placed at the beginning of beginnings. Of the *agadi-nwayi*, the female force of the war medicine (old woman) that empowers and authorizes the founding father and Okonkwo the emissary of war and peace, we are told: "[It] was as old as the clan itself. Nobody knows how old." It is out of this body of woman, whose womb and breasts are crucial elements of the earth force, that the Children of the Bush are born and mothered.

CONCLUSION

In order to contextualize the arguments of the preceding analysis, it may be useful to point out that Achebe critics have generally been incapable of theorizing or analyzing the reciprocal illumination between oral forms and the fictional structures of *Things fall Apart*. Two major related themes Achebe explores through the metaphorical process that binds together myth, history, philosophy, and fiction in *Things Fall Apart* are precisely the ideal of gender balance, on the one hand, and, on the other, the deadly consequences of gender conflicts at the cosmic and social levels. Here, too, Achebe critics have gloriously failed because their critical theory and cultural assumptions about gender are borrowed from alien epistemological systems that have very little connection with the ideology or construction of *Things Fall Apart*.

Gikandi, who thinks that "'femininity' . . . is marginalized" in Achebe's novel (45), argues that "[o]ften, meanings evolved in one mode of discourse have more power than those developed in another: In the culture represented in *Things Fall Apart*, the proverb and the masculine stories have more authority than songs and feminine stories" (47–48). If anyone is guilty of marginalizing femininity, womanhood or motherhood, it is Gikandi himself. Okonkwo alone is associated with the telling of "masculine stories of violence and bloodshed" in the novel (52). Even then, Okonkwo's audience is restricted to Ikemefuna and Nwoye, two adolescent captive listeners. Okonkwo's narrative space and "masculine authority" are severely limited by the confines of his *obi*. Consequently, Okonkwo's "stories about tribal wars" (53) have no narrative authority and govern no fictional components in the way that "women's stories" like "Tortoise and the Birds," "The Quarrel between Earth and Sky," "Mosquito and Ear," and "Why the Snake-Lizard killed his Mother" are crucial thematic and structural paradigms for significant parts of the novel. In fact, Nwoye "feigned," in listening to Okonkwo's masculine stories of violence and bloodshed, "that he no longer cared for women's stories" (53), but he "still preferred the stories that his mother used to tell" (52); "Ikemefuna's favorite story" (36) is not only one of those women's stories but also provides the cautionary song that warns Okonkwo in the metaphorical terms of poetry not to eat/kill him (*Eze elina, elina!* [king don't eat it, don't eat it!]) (58). What about the story that Uchendu, Okonkwo's maternal uncle, tells to illustrate the motherwit of the tale of Mother Kite, which serves as a philosophical mapping of the Abame massacre? Nwoye, Ikemefuna, and Uchendu have no problem telling or appreciating "women's stories" or motherwit, which wield as much authority as the proverbs. From a more strident angle, Rose Ure Mezu declares: "Achebe's sexist attitude is unabashed and without apology. Unoka, Okonkwo's father is considered an untitled man, connoting femininity" (16). In the context of the foregoing analysis, Mezu's culturally illiterate reading must not be confused with feminist or womanist criticism and certainly does not prove, as she argues, "the absence of a moderating female principle" in *Things Fall Apart* (16). Would-be feminist or womanist positions like those of Mezu and Gikandi falsify and oversimplify the cardinal issue of the politics of gender and the balancing presence of womanhood and motherhood in *Things Fall Apart* where, "wherever Something stands, Something Else stands next to it. Nothing is absolute," as Achebe puts it outside of his fictional work ("Chi" 133). Mezu's pseudo-feminist posture leads her to argue absolutely that "Nigeria and Africa [are] oppressively masculinist" (16) and that "The world in *Things Fall Apart* is one in which patriarchy intrudes oppressively into every sphere of existence" (16).

Speaking of the moderating presence of the other, Achebe himself counsels: "we had better learn to appreciate one another's presence and to accord to every people their due of human respect" ("African Literature as Restoration" 10). Far from being sexist, Achebe's politics of othering applies not only to womanhood, but also to mothering, as celebrated in Igbo culture and "in the culture represented in *Things Fall Apart*," to quote Gikandi again, or in "[t]he world in *Things Fall Apart*," as Mezu puts it. Achebe writes:

> *Mbari* was a celebration through art of the world and of the life lived in it. It was performed by the community on command by its presiding deity, usually the Earth goddess, Ana. Ana combined two formidable roles in the Igbo pantheon as fountain of creativity in the world and custodian of the moral order of human society. . . . The sculptures were arranged carefully on the steps. *At the center of the front row sat the earth goddess herself*, a child on her knee and a raised sword in her right hand. *She is mother and judge*. ("African Literature" 2, my emphasis)

The feminine principle is not only centered in Achebe's art and philosophy of life, but is quite clearly the paragon of proactive mothering, a child on her knee and a sword in her hand: Nneka, indeed! Motherhood and womanhood are only a problem to the pathological sexist that Okonkwo is. When Okonkwo calls the untitled Osugo a woman (*agbala*) at a kindred meeting, Achebe's narrator reports the verbal assault swiftly leveled at Okonkwo in terms of his rejection of woman and mother: "Looking at a king's mouth," said an old man, "one would think he never sucked at his mother's breast" (28). The proverb is not a glorification of masculinist or patriarchal oppression but, rather, a castigation of arrogant royal manhood, a figure of Okonkwo's sexist oppression. The text very clearly foregrounds a male verdict against Okonkwo's warped masculinism through the lips of the old man, a figure of patriarchy (!?): "Everybody at the [male] kindred meeting took sides with Osugo when Okonkwo called him a woman . . . Okonkwo said he was sorry and the meeting continued" (28). In his search for yam, the king of crops that also stands for manliness, Okonkwo appropriates the proverbial king's arrogance and suicidal rejection of vital presence of mother/woman *at the center of the front row:* " I began to fend for myself," Okonkwo brags to Nwakibie the owner of yams seeds, "at an age when most people still suck at their mothers' breasts" (24).

Okonkwo's masculinist rejection of life-giving motherwit (womanish wisdom) and mothermilk symbolized the "mother's breasts" is clearly rooted in the suicidal arrogance of the proverbial king and his own quest for "yamness" (male crop/king of crops), a pursuit that recalls the Snake-Lizard's rigid seven-basket standard. Prefiguring his own Snake-Lizardry, Okonkwo brags to Nwakibie the owner of yams: "The lizard that jumped from the high *iroko* tree to the ground said he would praise himself if no one else did" (24). The figure of the lizard in Okonkwo's proverbial masculinist ("yamly") measurement of manhood is a veiled reference to the Snake-

Lizard story, which underscores the vital centrality of the moderating presence mother and woman. Okonkwo, the lizard and Snake-Lizard set an inflexible standard that "no one else" accepts entirely or praises uncritically. The proverbs and the Snake-Lizard story place Okonkwo's suicide in its proper ontological and literary matrix, the culture's "own way," and not Durkheim's theory of "egotistical suicide," "a distinctively European disease," as Fraser proposes (35). Okonkwo's metaphorical jump from the high *iroko* tree to the ground, which parallels the proverbial lizard's jump, is not broken by the saving presence of the mother/woman in the same way that the Snake-Lizard's suicide is a direct result of the absence of his murdered mother and the male child's rejection of her culinary, womanish, wisdom and life-giving breasts.

WORKS CITED

"Achebe: Interviewed by Dennis Duerden." *African Writers Talking.* Ed. D. Duerden and C. Peterse. New York: Africana Publishing Company, 1972, 9–11.

Achebe, Chinua. "African Literature as Restoration of Celebration." *Chinua Achebe: A Celebration.* Heinemann and Dangaroo Press: London, 1991, 1–10.

——. *Things Fall Apart.* 1958. Greenwich, CT: Fawcett Crest Publications, 1959.

——. "Chi in Igbo Cosmology." *Morning Yet on Creation Day.* New York: Doubleday, 1976, 131–45.

——. "An Image of Africa: Racism in Conrad's *Heart of Darkness.*" *Hopes and Impediments: Selected Essays.* New York: Doubleday, 1989, 1–20.

——. "Named for Victoria, Queen of England." *Morning Yet on Creation Day.* New York: Doubleday: New York, 1976, 95–103.

Amadiume, Ifi. *Male Daughters, Female Husbands.* London: Zed Books, 1987.

Fraser, Robert. "A Note on Okonkwo's Suicide." *Obsidian* 6.1–2 (1980): 33–37.

Gikandi, Simon. *Reading Chinua Achebe.* London: Heinemann, 1991.

Harlow, Barbara. "'The Tortoise and Birds': Strategy of Resistance in *Things Fall Apart.*" *Approaches to Teaching Achebe's* Things Fall Apart. Ed. Bernth Lindfors. New York: MLA, 1991.

Innes, Catherine L. *Chinua Achebe.* Cambridge: Cambridge University Press, 1990.

Isichei, Elizabeth. *Igbo Worlds: An Anthology of Oral Histories and Historical Descriptions.* Philadelphia: Institute for the Study of Human Issues, 1978.

JanMohammed, Abdul. "Sophisticated Primitivism: The Syncretism of Oral and Literate Modes in Achebe's *Things Fall Apart.*" *Ariel* 15.4 (1984): 19–39.

Mezu, Rose Ure. "Women in Achebe's World." *The Womanist* 1.2 (Summer 1995): 15–19.

Ngubane, Jordan K. Foreword. *Ushaba.* Washington, DC: Three Continents Press, 1974, 1–8.

Shelton, Austin J. "The 'Palm-Wine' of Language: Proverbs in Chinua Achebe's Novels." *Modern Language Quarterly* 30 (1969): 86–111.

Soyinka, Wole. *Myth, Literature and the African World.* Cambridge: Cambridge University Press, 1976.

Weinstock, Donald J. and Cathy Ramadan. "Symbolic Structure in *Things Fall Apart.*" *Critical Perspectives on Chinua Achebe.* Ed. Catherine L. Innes and Bernth Lindfors. Washington, DC: Three Continents, 1978, 126–134.

4 The Eye and the Other

The gaze and the look in Egyptian feminist fiction

Peter Hitchcock

> I tried to recall what my mother had looked like the first time I saw her. I can remember two eyes. I can remember her eyes in particular. I cannot describe their colour, or their shape. They were eyes that I watched. They were eyes that watched me. Even if disappeared from their view, they could see me, and follow me wherever I went, so that if I faltered while learning to walk they would hold me up.
>
> Nawal El Saadawi, *Woman at Point Zero*

In a brief but salient essay, "The Gaze of Orpheus," Maurice Blanchot recounts that pivotal moment in Greek mythology when Orpheus, having descended to Hell, looks at Eurydice and ensures his doom. Blanchot, never a doyen of understatement, maintains that "the act of writing begins with Orpheus' gaze," and there are several feminist implications around this notion that are, perhaps, more progressive than this categorical assertion. One emerges in Blanchot's comment that Orpheus' "impulse" is to see Eurydice "in her nocturnal darkness, in her distance, her body closed, her face sealed, which wants to see her not when she is visible, but when she is invisible, and not as the intimacy of a familiar life, but as the strangeness of that which excludes all intimacy; it does not want to make her live, but to have the fullness of her death living in her" (100). Here, Blanchot names a condition of what he calls "inspiration" without exploring the problem of seeing itself in Western discourse, indeed without contemplating what this might mean for women's subjectivity. While much critical work has supported the idea that there is some form of scopic drive which impels the gaze of man I want to consider what this might look like from, as it were, the Other end of the eyeball; in particular, for "acts of writing" which, in their attempts to answer the gaze, produce not only a trenchant epistemology of womanhood in Egyptian fiction. but also a feminist riposte to those Eurocentric eyes that would have woman in the dark, in the distance, invisible.

The Eye of the West is inscrutable, but while there is something axiomatic about the objectification by the gaze in orientalist discourse it is not always clear what forms a counterdiscourse or disruptive logic may take.[1] Certainly such strategies are diverse and conjunctural, and one would not wish to homogenize their respective efficacy the way orientalism itself has been mythologized and to some degree codified. Nevertheless, if one can now state that much post-colonial criticism has moved beyond the binary banalities of logocentric thought the problem of how to specify cultural dissidence remains, just as the long shadow of Western epistemic violence (and violence pure and simple—Iraq?) continues to cast its pall over the various peoples of the Arab world. Theory's role in this is itself problematic for the Western academies in which much of this theory is generated have not been widely known for their activism in attenuating Western hegemony. Some critics, including most notably Marnia Lazreg, have quite rightly challenged the authority of Western progressive critical discourse to take up questions of, for instance, "Arab feminism" precisely because it too readily assumes a collective identity in the face of Western and indeed Arab formations of patriarchy. Although this is not the occasion to negotiate all of the shifting borders of this debate, the following discussion is informed by it even as it uses theory itself to denature certain necessities of "white mythology."[2]

Again, the importance of the gaze to such mythologies is too easily assumed, like the function of the veil for Islamic women, without articulating those symptomatic instances in which the structural logic of the gaze itself is called into question. While I do not intend to sketch the process of this instantiation in detail, I want at least to suggest the contours of a counterlogic in some examples by two Egyptian feminist writers, Nawal el Saadawi and Alifa Rifaat. I will argue that what is held to be the provenance of a psychosexual paradigm, principally that which links the gaze to the drive, has a perplexing aesthetic correlative in fiction, one which poses a significant "twist in the return" and an/other (a different) answer to the question, "What is the voyeur (West, male) gazing at?" We will see (a desire at once in question) that even when the subaltern subject cannot speak or is not speaking she is always looking.

In Malek Alloula's study of Algerian postcards sent by the occupying French earlier this century one is invited to peruse the collective phantasm of a colonial unconscious, the veiled/unveiled Algerian woman. As such, *The Colonial Harem* tracks the process of colonial representation in the absence of an opposing "gaze of the colonized upon the colonizer" and therefore attempts to "return this immense postcard to its sender" (5). I wonder, however, whether this comment accurately describes the effect of imaging colonial desire for a Western audience and, indeed, whether the gaze of the colonized has been sent before the perquisites of structuralist/poststructuralist theory? True, where photography is concerned there has been an unequal development at the technological level but the cultural logic of looking is not the monopoly of colonialism even if power relations bequeath to it the appearance of such domination. Thus, while Alloula's critique is a provocative intervention, it places too much emphasis on the "eye of the beholder" rather than the looking of the seen.[3] While the notes I offer are similarly bound by the possibilities of a certain theoreticism they are underscored if not struck out by an interest in the agency of the seen, by the look as a form of cultural resistance (in opposing the gaze) and solidarity (in an exchange of looks).

Nevertheless, Alloula's analysis of the Western gaze does provide some pointers on which one can build particularly with regard to the veil, simultaneously the mark of a putatively Muslim prohibition (the veil and veiling predate Islam, a fact that has important repercussions for the construction of femininity under Islam) and the ground for the most intense form of Western fetishism. As Alloula notes:

> . . . the eye cannot catch hold of her. The opaque veil that covers her intimates clearly and simply to the photographer a refusal. Turned back upon himself, upon his own impotence in the situation, the photographer undergoes an initial experience of disappointment and rejection . . . She is the concrete negation of this scopic desire and thus brings to the photographer confirmation of a triple rejection: the rejection of his desire, of the practice of his "art," and of his place in a milieu that is not his own. (7)

The argument about the representation of "veiled women," then, turns on a particular reading of Lacan's theorization of the gaze, a detour of theory with some relevance to the scopic drive that extends the field of the colonizing mind. Lacan's conceptualization is not about vision as such, but about how one represents the process of seeing; how, indeed, in this case one can account for the production of the eyes behind the veil *in the absence of* their perceived subjectivity. This, of course, is the provenance of the Other, the object as absence. What is interesting here is that the gaze takes as its object the very organ of its own activity. The singular importance of the veil is that it defamiliarizes the function of the gaze at the very moment that it instantiates the drive as desire. It allows the watcher to be seen watching. Since, as Lacan argues, the privilege of the gaze derives from its structure, this example will require further comment. If one suggests that the veil itself is a cause of desire, it is only as an imaginary object, not the cloth of which it is made. To this degree the veil would seem an *objet a*, somewhere between the subject and the other. But this does not go far enough because, crucially, the veil accentuates the eyes: the eye is the organ that the subject has separated off from itself in order to make itself. For orientalism, it is not the enigma of the veil that conditions the phallogocentrism of Western desire but the eyes that look behind it. As Lacan comments: "Generally speaking, the relation between the gaze and what one wishes to see involves a lure. The subject is presented as other than he is, and what one shows him is not what he wants to see. It is in this way that the eye may function as *objet a*, that is to say, at the level of the lack."(FF 104)[4] In the modern period, whenever one confronts the question of the veil in Egyptian cultural and political life it is girded by the complicity of the West in its reinscription. The veil as *objet a* is simultaneously a signifier and lack of signification; it is the cause of desire and management of women's subjectivity. As such, the gaze may be assessed in direct proportion to the effacement of the female voice and functions as both symbolic and systemic violence. If the gaze allows the seer to be seen as a mark of scopic domination, however, this "inevitability" is not reproduced without psychic cost, nor indeed does it enable the smooth perfection of masculinist identity.

The history of the veil in Egypt is beyond summary here but some elements of it are relevant in clarifying the above. It is over seventy years since three founding mothers of Egyptian feminism, Huda Shaarawi, Saiza Nabarawi, and Nabawiya Musa, represented Egypt at an international women's confer- ence in Rome. After the conference they reappeared in Cairo unveiled, an act that has taken on the aura of popular legend but is, nevertheless, a key moment in Egyptian women's history with repercussions throughout the Arab and Islamic worlds. True, there had been significant critiques of veiling beforehand, most notably those of Rifa'a al-Tahtawi and Qasim Amin, but the *sufur* of 1923 remains a symbolic watershed.[5] Several implications may be drawn from this moment, including the rejection by Egyptian feminists of the elitism associated with the veil (particularly in the class distinction drawn between veiled urban women and their unveiled rural sisters), a recognition that the veil had become a tool of patriarchal control within Islamic customs, and that the veil effectively isolated Egyptian feminists from the broader international feminist movement as an emblem of that control. Given the original institutionalization of the veil by Christianity in Byzantine Egypt the unveiling at issue may appear ironic, as if the wheel had finally come full circle, but it is more accurately described as invoking a revolution in the first sense, a transformation of being. There were detractors of course, and with good reason. For instance, the great advocate of women's rights, Malak Hifny Nassif, argued a more cautious approach to unveiling and suggested that there was a danger that it could infer a capitulation to Westernization and a loss of an independent Egyptian woman's identity. This not only explains the sometimes ambiguous relationship of women's rights to Egyptian nation- alism but also a concomitant antagonism over the role of Islamic fundament- alism in contemporary Egyptian life. Thus, although the *al-burqu'* may have been thrown off in 1923, the veil itself remains an arena of contestation about the roles of women with regard to men, Islam, and the international public sphere.

In more recent times, several developments have accentuated the struggle over the veil, as sign. In an article, "Veiled Activism" Fadwa El Guindi recounts the reappearance of a formal headdress among educated urban women of Egypt including, on occasion, a face veil (*al-niqab*) after the Arab– Israeli war of 1973. In part this is attributed to a conservative sense of community in the face of a national defeat (a secular nationalism was therefore sacrificed for an Islamic version, although in the past, as el Guindi points out, even secular forces in Egypt had espoused the veil). Despite the benevolence el Guindi accords the veil (it is seen as "egalitarian" in character as if it is unrelated to the scene of a certain gender inequality), "Veiled Activism" is an excellent example of how the veil is continually being repoliticized in the Egyptian public sphere. Obviously, it is not a simple barometer of the social condition of women in Egypt but nevertheless it signifies a discursive field of some importance. This field is characterized by insistent dualisms, as Fouad Zakaria has pointed out, particularly that of spirit and body. In this interpretation, either wearing the veil or displaying the unveiled body in a suggestive manner are considered equivalent:

> They both place great emphasis on the importance of the body and the insistence that it is a perennial object of desire and constant source of temptation. From this perspective, the veiled woman conceals her body to render it unattractive, and from the same perspective, the unveiled woman seeks to expose her body to render it more attractive. Despite the seeming contradiction between the two types of women, their behavior asserts that for both the body is the most important thing about a woman and that man's perception of a woman's body is the basic reality in her life. (31–32)

The dualistic investment in the woman's body that Zakaria describes is not unknown to Western patriarchal ideology (indeed, the congruence between this dualism and the madonna/whore split is underlined by Zakaria quoting a Muslim fundamentalist exhorting a group of veiled women to "Be whores to your husbands"). Zakaria is primarily interested in the psychic debilitations evolving from the double think inscribed upon the veiled woman's body, but this logic needs further critique not just within the psychosocial import of Islam but also in the complex ambivalence that riddles the ideological production of the "East" as Other, or "the colonial harem" in Alloula's terminology. Of course, the dualism that makes a fetish of the woman's body within the discursive field of veiling *shares a structural logic* with the disfigurations of orientalist desire. Both are forms of social evaluation and as such may require much more than tinkering with interpretations of the *hadith* and koranic *sura* or challenging individual instances of the nefarious objectification of African and Asian peoples. A revolution in perception, or more specifically the symbolic, maintains a social imperative of the highest order. It is in this light that I wish to consider some examples of feminist interventions over the order of the eye in Egyptian fiction.

The translation of Alifa Rifaat's stories presents an immediate problem to the Western eye that would incorporate all He surveys. Rifaat, a devout Muslim, seems relatively unencumbered by Western influences, particularly those that would impinge upon her Islamic consciousness. She wears the veil and has undertaken the *Hajj* to Mecca. Arab critics have described her life as "conventional" and "everyday," which in the West has immediately granted her the allure of authenticity. Yet, whether or not Rifaat has been influenced by the West (through reading and education) her work contradicts a Western will to enlist her as a native informant, to assimilate her as a pristine example of the subaltern victim (her subalternity, I would argue, denies the victimization that such a will confers). Much of her early stories were written in secret since her husband had forbidden her to write in light of the publication of her provocative fantasy, "My Secret World" (or "My World of the Unknown").[6] For fifteen years she maintained the appearance of dutiful motherhood but in fact continued to write in the privacy of her bathroom. She did not publish again until the death of her husband in 1974. Rifaat's "act of writing" begins in the gaze of that very invisibility accorded the *object* of inspiration. It is therefore somewhat unfortunate yet indicative of the logic at issue that in introducing his translation of Alifa Rifaat's first collection of short stories in English, Denys Johnson-Davies maintains that Rifaat "lifts the veil on what it means to be a woman living within a traditional Muslim society" (vii). For the Western reader, as always, the Arab woman is revealed with the veil itself becoming the fetishistic mark of that desire. The *objet a* (in Lacanian terms, the cause of desire) is here the eye, split off as the gaze elides that the West has eyes that it might not see "that things are looking at it" (FF 109). In what ways does Rifaat disrupt this scene of writing the (in)visible?

Leila Ahmed has suggested several possibilities in this regard, including a historical critique about how Rifaat is writing the body through "the shape and content . . . of the central Islamic written heritage" (54). Ahmed argues that what at first might seem conventional Western representations of sexuality, including homosexuality, owe their frankness to discussions within Islam and in a vibrant oral culture going back at least to medieval times. Ahmed's point is that Rifaat's criticisms from within Islam are consonant with a traditional respect for the contributions of women to cultural debates about the woman's body (including those of sex, contraception, and abortion). According to this argument, therefore, what Rifaat disrupts is the logic of expectation that would assume silence from women within Islamic culture. Given the circumstances of Rifaat's writing career, however, perhaps more needs to be said about how Rifaat articulates the constraints as well as the freedoms of her consciousness. In one story, "Bahiyya's Eyes," Rifaat recounts the tale of an old woman who, before she goes blind, asks that her daughter visit her so that she might see her one last time. The story is written in the first person and is directly addressed to the daughter throughout. Even as Islam informs this story it stands as a poignant vignette of motherhood in contemporary Egypt.

"Bahiyya's Eyes" is named after a traditional song about a peasant woman's beautiful eyes but here the title accentuates that what is lost is their capacity to see. The failing of sight is the occasion for the meeting between Bahiyya and her daughter, a meeting which is ostensibly recounted in monologue and yet articulates a strong sense of the addressee at every moment. Bahiyya tells her daughter of her visit to the doctor. Interestingly, she veils herself for the journey but must be unveiled by the doctor in order for him to perform the examination. Although the doctor provides a diagnosis, Bahiyya is unequivocal about what has caused her blindness: "the tears I shed since my mother first bore me and they held me up by the leg and found I was a girl. The whole of my life I went on crying and how often my mother'd tell me not to but it wasn't any use" (7). The simplicity of Bahiyya's story belies its subjective import, for its organizing principle, the very tenor of Bahiyya's existence, is the eyes. Significantly, just as Bahiyya's mother was the only one to appreciate this in her early life, so now, in old age, this matrilineal knowledge is shared with her daughter. She notes, for instance, that because of her beauty the "evil eye" was upon her and although this may have several connotations they include the idea that a woman's allure is dangerous and must be managed. Not that Bahiyya assumes that that management is purely masculine but it is clear that the gaze is informed by masculinist precepts as interpreted through Islam. There is only one period in her life when Bahiyya experiences a mutual looking with anyone except her women family members. This is with the boy Hamdan who sings a *mawwal* about Bahiyya's eyes and they look at one another with "different eyes." Their love, like much of the companionship between the women in the story, is largely unspoken: "He would follow me about wherever I went, keeping at a distance, and we never had the courage to speak to each other. Only the way he looked at me told me of his love for me" (10). This is the only time when the male look does not objectify Bahiyya; indeed, we might say that the look, in contradistinction to the gaze, is the only medium for a non-hierarchical relationship. It is notable, therefore, that Bahiyya is denied her relationship with Hamdan and, at her father's request, is married off to Dahshan, a man she did not know and never loved. As Bahiyya comments, "All my life I'd been ruled by a man, first my father and then my husband" (11). This knowledge is told by her eyes but, of course, it is the last thing that anybody, apart from her mother and her daughter, expects to see. And so as her sight finally fails, Bahiyya opines "Daughter, I'm not crying now because I'm fed up or regret that the Lord created me a woman. No, it's not that. It's just that I'm sad about my life and my youth that have come and gone without my knowing how to live them really and truly as a woman" (11).

While I would not argue that "Bahiyya's Eyes" is a strong condemnation of the patriarchal values that obtain in a particular interpretation of Islam, it does offer a significant critique by suggesting that the rule of the gaze leaves Bahiyya little more than the order of looking in the conduct of her life. That the latter may be read as a positive activity is chiefly because it is associated with intrafamily bonding between women and non-hierarchical relationships with men: it is a love/friendship nexus opposed to the more nefarious manifestations of power in everyday life. The sadness of the story emerges precisely from the recognition that even the order of looking will be denied Bahiyya in the future. The veil which has highlighted eyes that are not seen, except as a function of scopic desire, will now demarcate eyes that cannot see. But, of course, she will continue to cry. Most of Rifaat's stories are not preoccupied with the eyes and I do not mean to suggest otherwise but

"Bahiyya's Eyes" nicely allegorizes the problem at issue about how fiction might intervene against a certain logic of objectification which would see the veil while denying the eyes the right to look in any other way.

Unlike Rifaat, Nawal el Saadawi has little respect for the veil and has specifically argued against it. She too is a writer who has much to offer in critiquing the seemingly omnipresent masculine gaze in Egyptian culture, while also offering an internationalist perspective on the objectification of Arab women in "white mythologies." Like Rifaat, el Saadawi is also extremely interested in the psychosexual states of being in Egyptian woman-hood, including the "psychic veils" that persist for women even when they do not take the veil (the motto of the Arab Women's Solidarity Association, of which el Saadawi is president, is "The power of women—solidarity—lifting the veil from the mind").[7] I have written elsewhere about some of the problems emerging from the interpellation of el Saadawi as the leading Egyptian feminist in the international public sphere,[8] but here I want to stress that this by no means ameliorates her importance to Egyptian feminism or culture; in fact, it throws into sharp relief some of the more salient characteristics of the logic at issue. Many of her stories highlight the psychic repercussions of objectification even as they show the other lives that women may construct for themselves. *Woman at Point Zero* is a novel which continually stresses the will of Firdaus, the main character, in redefining her life beyond the machinations of the manipulative males whom she often encounters. Eventually, Firdaus becomes a prostitute but even then it is an attempt to articulate a sense of self that is not governed by the watchful eye of masculine authority. Although Firdaus ultimately fails to escape (she is tried and executed for killing her pimp) there are several moments in the book, like the one which begins this essay, when she "lifts the veil from the mind" and recognizes the crucial importance of mother/daughter solidarity in the face of oppression.

El Saadawi's *Two Women in One* is another novel which dramatizes the intense struggles of its woman protagonist, Bahiah Shaheen, who, like Rifaat's Bahiyya, attempts to live her life and youth really and truly as a woman. Educated and more cosmopolitan than Rifaat's character, Bahiah is yet tormented by a conflictual consciousness which tells her, on the one hand, to enjoy the fruits of her privileged upbringing and assume the role that has been decreed for her (principally by her father) and, on the other hand, to be a rebellious spirit by arguing that women can not only liberate themselves but have the potential to transform society as a whole. The double think that splits her sense of self is underlined when her father realizes that Bahiah is a sexual being very different from his image:

Bahiah! . . . Her father's voice rang in her ear like a shot, like the sole voice of truth. It made her realize that she was Bahiah Shaheen, hard-working, well-behaved medical student, the pure virgin, untouched by human hands and born without sex organs . . . She pulled the bedclothes over her head and feigned sleep as she heard her father's footsteps coming toward the bed. His big fingers lifted the blankets and he stared at her and discovered, thunderstruck, that she was not Bahiah Shaheen after all: she was not his daughter, nor was she polite, obedient or a virgin; she had actually been born with sex organs, not only clearly visible through the bedclothes but moving as well, like the very heartbeat of life. By moving, she had removed the barrier in her way. She had torn away the membrane separating her from life. It was a thin membrane, intangible and invisible. like a transparent glass panel dividing her from her body, standing between herself and her reality. She could see herself through it but could not touch it or feel it, for it was like glass; the slightest movement and it would shatter. (75)

Here we have an answer to the gaze of Orpheus in which the masculine look itself is confronted with the limits of its "objectivity." Bahiah is not Bahiah anymore in her father's eyes: he experiences in this moment of Bahiah's visibility the double think that has dislocated her subjectivity. But, more importantly, by moving she promises to shatter an illusion, the "membrane" or veil that stands in for the woman she might be. For the father, this veil has functioned as the *objet a*: it is, as it were, what made him look in the first place. In contrast, Bahiah sees the membrane as something which she has had to look through in order to see herself (seeing). The difference here is crucial: indeed, one might venture that veiling itself may be defined as what man separates off on the one hand, and what woman has to see through on the other. The significance of Bahiah's story is that she comes to realize that her womanhood is precisely *constructed* by such hierarchizing logic. Her realization does not save her but el Saadawi's point is that such consciousness is the degree zero of formidable social activism.

El Saadawi has written other stories about how veiling may function as a symptom of scopic desire (most notably in "The Veil") but there are also narratives in which she specifically explores the contours of the woman's look, not as a consequence of the gaze so much as an alternative to it. Chief among these is "Eyes," a story based upon the experiences of a woman who came to el Saadawi in 1988 for psychiatric help (el Saadawi is a practicing psychiatrist as well as writer and social activist). The woman is referred to throughout the tale as "she" and the story proceeds as an in-depth account of what She sees through the two openings of her veil. Although the woman is educated, her father makes certain that her professional career will keep her isolated from men, so she works in the basement of a museum cataloguing mummies. The latter, of course, allows el Saadawi to draw a correlation between the dead preserved as if in life and the living wrapped as if in death. Again, what is separated off for man is the veil but what this leaves for woman is the eyes: "She was a creature from whose being nothing appears except two small holes in a black cloth" (209). The questions that the narrative considers are how might these eyes look and what are they seeing? The answers suggest that, although she may be a "dutiful daughter" she offers an/other way of seeing.

To say that her life has been restricted would be an understatement: the name-of-the-father and his law (as interpreted through the Koran) are not just the primary, but the only conditions of her existence. Not surprisingly, "since she was born she has gone to bed hearing the voice of her father reciting the Koran. Since infancy her face has not been seen by a stranger. During her student years she never talked to anyone" (205). What is surprising is not that she denies the law of the father, but that she overinvests it by denying a desire for a husband and following the rules of seclusion to the utmost. The story figures the excess of Her seeing by her being overly dutiful. This excess is what produces a statue in the basement that had not been there before: the statue functions as her *objet a*, as the cause of her desire, but it is also the object of it (desire) and there, perhaps, lies the danger of psychosis. There is nothing particularly distinctive about the statue except, of course, for the eyes which "were looking at her with a movement in the pupils that she had never seen before in any other statue" (206). From the appearance of these eyes a tension develops in the story between her eyes on the lines of "God's book" and the exchange of looks with the statue. Nobody else notices the eyes except her and they become her obsession: "He doesn't look anywhere with these eyes except at her. Since seeing it for the first time, she never stops looking at it. If she turns her head away or leaves the office his eyes are always before her continually looking at her with same expression as if he were alive now, not several thousand years ago" (207). She explains that she is overcome by the desire to know what is in his gaze and when she sees movement in his eyes "her closed lips underneath the black cloth part with a faint sigh" (207). She has taken the logic of seeing being seen and located it in eyes that only see her. From being reduced to her scopic drive she now demands that her look be answered and finds that answer in the eyes of a statue that predates the introduction of the veil in Egypt, and indeed the spread of Islam. She takes him home from work and "sleeps with her eyes fixed on his eyes." She has a recurring dream in which the man with these eyes drowns in the flood that Noah escapes. He keeps looking at her right up to the time that he is covered with water, and his eyes are the last thing to disappear. She is thunderstruck by the dream because it suggests that the man is a follower of the devil (he does not survive, unlike Noah).

Her fantasy extends ever further into her waking hours such that she starts to see his eyes in the eyes of other men on their way to work. And each time this occurs she learns something new about the nature of her subjectivity: first, by recognizing her own body and, second, by realizing that there is another kind of body, "male" (a realization that causes her to raise her hand to cover the two small holes in her veil). Even though her father "sees her the same way he sees her every day, modestly veiled going to her office and returning home on time" she has changed. Eventually she throws away the statue because she has become afraid of seeing the statue's eyes; she is scared of the implication this has for her way of seeing. "Eyes" is a brilliant evocation of the psychic trauma that may result from cultural forms of masculine surveillance. The statue is a product of the woman's desire to be looked at the way she looks. There is a reciprocity in this that she does not otherwise see through the two holes in her veil. Whereas her father's gaze is a means of subjugation, the look that enthralls her is a measure of subjectivity. The twist in this tale is that her consciousness ultimately rejects the knowledge of womanhood that her unconscious has discovered; namely, that the gaze is diabolical and the look is dialogical.[9]

The invocation of the dialogic is important because it is a principle which connotes both an insistence on reciprocity and a condition of agency. In this way, it recalls the thoughts of Firdaus which begin this essay where she remembers the look of her mother as a focus of mutual sustenance and active support. Indeed, the look as an *activity* is crucial to an understanding of the examples I have provided for they all, in various ways, counter the logic of objectification (of masculinism, of orientalism) in the gaze that assumes or promotes a passivity in its field of vision. There are, of course, many other implications to the stories considered here and some that would certainly extend the argument about the gaze. These notes are offered, however, as a preliminary attempt to think through some thematic problems where there is a danger of reobjectifying the voices of African womanhood (or, in this case, the eyes of Egyptian womanhood) in crosscultural analysis. The epistemological question here is how to counteract the "all-seeing I" of Eurocentric discourse without assuming the position, as guarantor, of the alternative knowledge that may be at issue (the Western critic, unlike Alloula, is not the person to return the postcard of colonialism to its sender). Here, the possibilities are not simply through a rereading of Lacan but through ways of accounting for the ambivalent narratives of those who might naturally be considered the authentic voices of dissent. My point here has been that unless we can read against the grain of the dislocating logics of the gaze, criticism will continue to be complicit in the othering of women in crosscultural discourse. These logics cannot simply be wished away, as I hope the above examples have underlined, but the materiality of these discourses will ever be the key to their transformation. Only by continually politicizing the gaze will these eyes be made anew, an impulse very much to the fore in Egyptian feminist fiction which, as I have suggested, has the benefit of looking very differently from Orpheus.

NOTES

1 I note this ambivalence not just out of convenience but also to flag how metaphors of sight inform the very analysis of the Western gaze and thus may be "seen" as complicit with the logic of its objectification.

2 For a polemical and insightful critique of current debates on colonial discourse, including the contributions of Edward Said and Homi Bhabha, see Parry.

3   For a detailed review essay of Alloula's book, as well as informed discussion of representation, colonial discourse, and gender, see Schick.

4   Lacan provides an extensive elaboration on the gaze and the *objet a* in *The Four Fundamental Concepts of Psycho-Analysis* (hereafter FF), but see also *Feminine Sexuality*. While there is no happy or exact correspondence between these principles and the fiction to be discussed they do interanimate each other in provocative ways.

5   This is underscored by Amina Said's editorial "Feast of Unveiling, Feast of Renaissance" on the fiftieth anniversay of the unveiling in 1923 translated by Ali Badran and Margot Badran in Badran and Cooke, pp. 359–362. Both the Badran/Cooke and Toubia anthologies contain useful essays on the history and diversity of Arab feminist thought.

6   This story is available in the Johnson-Davies translation and is a fantastic (literally) exploration of one woman's desire. The main character, largely ignored by her husband, has an intimate relationship with a djinn, a spirit in the form of a female snake, which keeps appearing through a hole in the wall. She not only shares ecstasy with the snake, but confides in her "all her longings." Desire is here writ large in the woman's dreams allowing her a fulfillment that she does not find in her everyday married life. The psychosocial implications of this bear on the present discussion although this story demands more analysis in its own right.

7   The Toubia anthology is a collection of papers from an AWSA conference and also contains the AWSA constitution. See also the IFAA collection, to which el Saadawi is a contributor.

8   See, "Firdaus, or the Politics of Positioning" in Peter Hitchcock, *Dialogics of the Oppressed.*

9   A dialogic exchange of looks provides both a visual and a verbal dimension to narratives of the veil. Note, however, that the logic of dialogism does not simply erase the hierarchies issue, it contests them.

WORKS CITED

Ahmed, Leila. "Arab Culture and Writing Women's Bodies." *Feminist Issues* 9.1 (Spring 1989): 41–55.

Alloula, Malek. *The Colonial Harem*. Trans. Myrna Godzich and Wlad Godzich. Intro. Barbara Harlow. Minneapolis: University of Minnesota Press, 1986.

Badran, Margot and Miriam Cooke, eds. *Opening The Gates: A Century of Arab Feminist Writing*. Bloomington: Indiana University Press, 1990.

Blanchot, Maurice. *The Gaze of Orpheus*. Trans. Lydia Davis. Barrytown, New York: Station Hill Press, 1981.

El Guindi, Fadwa. "Veiled Activism: Egyptian Women in the Contemporary Islamic Movement." *Peuples Mediterraneens* 22–23 (Janv.–Juin 1983): 79–89.

El Saadawi, Nawal. *Woman at Point Zero*. Trans. Sherif Hetata. London: Zed Press, 1983.

——. *Two Women in One*. Trans. Osman Nusairi and Jane Gough. Seattle: Seal Press, 1986.

——. "The Veil" in *Death of an Ex-Minister*. Trans. Shirley Eber. London: Methuen, 1987.

——. "Eyes." *Opening the Gates: A Century of Arab Feminist Writing*. Ed. Margot Badran and Miriam Cooke. Trans. Ali Badran and Margot Badran. Bloomington: Indiana University Press, 1990.

Hitchcock, Peter. *Dialogics of the Oppressed*. Minneapolis: Minnesota University Press, 1993.

Institute for African Alternatives. *Islamic Fundamentalism*. London: IFAA Publications, 1990.

Lacan, Jacques. *The Four Fundamental Concepts of Psycho-Analysis*. Trans. Alan Sheridan. New York: Norton, 1977.

——. *Feminine Sexuality*. Ed. Juliet Mitchell and Jacqueline Rose. Trans. Jacqueline Rose. New York: Norton, 1982.

Lazreg, Marnia. "Feminism and Difference: The Perils of Writing as a Woman on Women in Algeria." *Feminist Studies* 14.1 (Spring, 1988): 81–107.

Parry, Benita. "Problems in Current Theories of Colonial Discourse." *Oxford Literary Review* 9.1–2 (1987): 27–58.

Rifaat, Alifa. "Bahiyya's Eyes" *Distant View of a Minaret*. Trans. Denys Johnson-Davies. London: Heinemann, 1985.

Schick, Irvin Cemil. "Representing Middle Eastern Women: Feminism and Colonial Discourse." *Feminist Studies* 16.2 (Summer 1990): 345–380.

Toubia, Nahid, ed. *Women of the Arab World*. Trans. Nahed El Gamal. London: Zed Press, 1988.

5 Enlightenment epistemology and "aesthetic cognition"

Mariama Bâ's *So Long a Letter*

Uzo Esonwanne

To find an acceptable and viable *modus vivendi* between the *forces* of tradition and the *realities* of the present is almost a *tour de force*.

Irène Assiba d'Almeida, *Ngambika*

Mariama Bâ did not attack tradition and custom blatantly, but she expressed her disapproval of certain glaring abuses of *tradition* which impede *progress*.

Edris Makward, *Ngambika*[1]

"AESTHETIC COGNITION" AS A DIMENSION OF LITERARY CRITICISM

So Long a Letter has become one of the most widely read African novels in the American academy.[2] Taken up by critics of diverse interpretive and ideological affiliations, it has been adjudged "the best-known epistolary novel" in African literature and the first "explicit, self-conscious meditation on gender difference written by a woman in francophone sub-Saharan Africa."[3]

These comments suggest that critical opinion about the novel is unanimous and positive. Nothing could be further from the truth. Among African critics the verdict is mixed. Perhaps Femi Ojo-Ade, whose "Still a Victim? Mariama Bâ's *Une si longue lettre*" shares with the epigraphic comments above the view that the novel dramatizes the conflict of cultures, is exemplary of a dissenting view. For him, the novel is an autobiographical text which traces the life of the heroine "in a society caught between the established order of the past and the exigencies of the present." Given such culture-conflict, tradition/modernity hypothesis, one is bound to commend (d'Almeida, Makward) or berate (Ojo-Ade) the novel, depending on the entity in the pair to which one swears fealty.[4] Ojo-Ade swears fealty to tradition, thus his discomfort with the novel is inevitable. There is more to, or rather a related reason for, this discomfort. Culture-conflict criticism such as his construes Europe and Africa as self-contained, culturally hermetic entities locked, like primeval forces, in eternal combat. If binarism—past/present, tradition/ modernity—is the basic structure of this critical methodology, metonymy is its favorite rhetorical form. Together, structure and rhetoric make for a manichean periodization of African women's writing into a non-feminist "old guard" (Grace Ogot, Efua Sutherland, Ama Ata Aidoo, and Flora Nwapa) and a corps of rebellious young renegades (Mariama Bâ, Buchi Emecheta, and Nafissatou Diallo); the first group is "steeped in the traditions of the land" and finds refuge from women's tribulations "in *a society that has proclaimed woman the mother*," while the second is composed of traitors to eternal motherhood, the calling preordained for women and guaranteed to give them a sense of fulfilment.[5]

Ojo-Ade's culture-conflict criticism has spurred objections, but few of these objections are directed at the premises outlined above. And of those that do, there is a tendency to overlook or minimize the presence of binary thought in the novel and its significance in the narrative. As if traditionalism were unproblematic, critics focus on the more obvious anti-feminism in Ojo-Ade's work. Pauline Nalova Lyonga, for example, rightly rejects his assumption of "a common Afro-centric ground for envisioning the woman's role and condition," insisting that women's "adjustments to their roles" *as women* in African communities "have distinctive 'woman' features."[6] But she remains silent about his traditionalism. For Obioma Nnaemeka, Bâ is to African cultures what Derrida (or Foucault) is to European philosophy. Her texts "question, subvert, and destabilize certain dichotomies rooted in race, age, sex, and culture." They "expose and reestablish the truth by subverting the 'truth' which is established by the 'law.'" Thus Nnaemeka sees Bâ's novel as dismantling the foundation of the repressive logocentric edifice of patriarchy.

On account of her deconstructive explication of the novel it is inevitable that "ways of seeing and ways of knowing . . ." are a component of Nnaemeka's preoccupation as a critic.[7] "Ways of seeing and knowing," or the devices by which texts such as *So Long a Letter* construct knowledge of quotidian events, places, values, is the focus of this essay. Today most critics would agree that literary texts do not just entertain or instruct; they produce, and are often cited as sources of, knowledge. This is especially true when the object domain is the distant or the "different." Texts, in this context, are devices by which we mediate being and meaning in time and space. And they serve this purpose even when, inspired either by modernism's philosophical skepticism toward the authority of the past (Descartes, Bacon) or by professional expectations of criticism, we interpret each text as if it were an isolate, autotelic phenomenon.[8] If texts produce knowledge effects, and these effects contribute to our understanding of the text both as text and as text-in-the-world, then, as critics, we must also inquire into the mechanisms by which these effects are generated.

We cannot be content with the claim that narratives disclose truths "about the human condition," for example, without asking how truth is produced.

My argument is, quite simply, that "Art is a mode of cognition *sui generis* . . .," and how texts produce their knowledge, or the process of "aesthetic cognition," is as much the business of criticism as analyses of form, studies of sources, and the like.[9] In accordance with this argument, I propose a reading of *So Long a Letter* as a text which combines an Afro-Islamic aesthetics of disclosure with a technology of knowledge inherited from the Enlightenment. Thus, I hope to pave the way for "further possibilities of knowledge" about important issues in African cultures.[10]

GENDER, GENRE, AND AUTHORITY: 'MIRASSE' AS NARRATIVE DEVICE

No critic has placed as much value upon *mirasse* as has Mbye B. Cham. *Mirasse* is crucial in his interpretation of *So Long a Letter*. Bâ, he argues, "extends and adapts the notion of disclosure embodied in the concept of 'mirasse'" in such a way as to provide Ramatoulaye

> with the structural and, indeed, cultural framework within which to undertake a comprehensive exposition [*dépouillement*] of intimate secrets of married life with Modou Fall, particularly the latter's weakness as a human being and the effect of this on their relationship . . . 'Mirasse', therefore, becomes the principle that legitimises and regulates Rama's act of systematic personal revelation which simultaneously constitutes a systematic analysis of some of the most pressing socio-economic and cultural issues challenging women and society.[11]

Appropriately, Ramatoulaye's personal disclosures and simultaneous analysis follow the invocation of *mirasse* in the fourth chapter, and the preceding chapters constitute her prologue. (SL 9) It seems, from this, that *mirasse* is primarily a narrative device. But it does more than merely facilitate the narrative. With *mirasse*, Bâ boldly redefines the relationship of (African) women to the secular and the sacred, to European epistolarity and to Afro-Islamic ritual mandated by the Koran.

In "Senegalese Women Writers," a brilliant analysis of the "organization and generic status" of Bâ's novel, Christopher L. Miller observes that *So Long a Letter* slides from "the format of an epistolary novel" to that of a journal. The reason for this slide, he explains, is that "there is no exchange of correspondence." Bâ's generic iconoclasm, Miller adds, doubly marginalized her work, first "in relation to the francophone corpus, which eschews epistolarity" and second "in relation to the European epistolary genre, which normally represents an exchange of letters" (TA 278). Observing that the lack of "a real exchange of letters between Ramatoulaye and Aïssatou compromises . . . 'the epistolary pact,'" and that with the absence of a desire for exchange an epistolary novel is hardly distinguishable from a journal, Miller concludes:

> This is precisely the case with *Une si longue lettre*, although it would not appear to be the desire that is lacking, but the possibility. Ramatoulaye is confined and writes to create a simulacrum of contact with the outside world, with her friend. Exchange is blocked by the Islamic custom of confinement, so Ramatoulaye constructs artificial exchanges, in which others speak and write through her recollections. (TA 281–282)

The conclusion that the "Islamic custom of confinement" blocks exchange is correct. However, it must be noted that if Cham is equally correct about *mirasse*, then what makes even the "artificial exchanges" possible is an Islamic ritual. In other words, Ramatoulaye circumvents the constraint of confinement imposed by Islamic custom with an Islamic ritual. Never an apostate, she works within Islam, finding novel uses for its rules, rituals, and regulations, cross-breeding them with alien generic formats. Miller is therefore quite right in describing *So Long a Letter* "as a peculiar hybrid, representing an original act of literary creativity, a brilliant departure" (TA 283).

Juxtaposing this positive view of the novel as a "hybrid" against Ojo-Ade's disparaging remarks about the rebellious offspring "of tradition and colonialism," one is struck by the fact that issues of cultural reproduction, with their attendant anxieties of paternity, miscarriages, miscegenation, and deformity, are central to contemporary African literary criticism. Masculinist traditionalism, committed to the culture-conflict hypothesis, remains haunted by the spectre of the hybrid text. Ethnocriticism, enthusiastic about bold experiments that transgress generic borders, celebrates the arrival of the new. Ojo-Ade's paternalism has little to recommend it, and as I have already pointed out, valid objections have already been made to his reading of *So Long a Letter*. What intrigues me, then, is neither the text's cultural or symbolic parentage (Ojo-Ade) nor the fact of its transgressive hybridity (Miller). Rather, I am particularly interested in the characterization of the novel's relationship to dominant modes of literary production within a neo-colonialist matrix.

Repeatedly Miller presents the novel as charting a middle, independent course between two restrictive alternatives: a male-dominated francophone African discourse which, in its oral as in its literary form represses women's voices, and a hegemonic Western literary presence. Thus, judging from his commentary on the author's political blueprint for African women, it would appear that in charting "a new relation to the literary mode," Bâ advocates a "militant but non-violent" committment "to difference" (TA 272). However accurate this interpretation might be, it does not vividly characterize the nature of the relationship between this novel and antecedent literary traditions and generic formats. Rather than view her work merely in terms of a committment to difference, it seems more accurate to me to describe it as an instance of "consumer production." Consumer production identifies "the models of action characteristic of users whose status as the dominated element in society" is a form of production in its own right. In this respect, consumption becomes a productive activity, a form of "poaching" which utilizes "the property of others" to manufacture contrary and alternative meanings. *So Long a Letter* exemplifies consumer production because its effect of prior generic and literary norms and traditions is estranging.[12] By combining features of the journal with the epistolary novel, it alienates both from themselves, making possible alternative forms of literary production which point to oft proclaimed but little explored possibilities of material transformation in the realm of economic production.

The theoretical advance the notion of consumer production makes possible is offset by a problem endemic to post-colonial literary theory, namely, a tendency to mortgage the interpretation of subalternist writing to the hegemonic modes of literary production. Is it altogether inconceivable that even in texts such as *So Long a Letter* there exist narrative codes or conventions whose meanings are not altogether taken up in the consumptive transformation of dominant genre and traditions? Perhaps this difficulty can be resolved. What would happen if we stopped thinking of devices such as *mirasse* as belonging to a culturally homogeneous matrix? As far as products go, it is hardly pure. The best analogy for it is the novel itself; *mirasse* is a hybrid product of another process of cultural syncretism, that is, the fusion of Wolof with Islamic ritual. Looking at it in this way allows us a glimpse into the complex configuration of social hierarchies, ethics, rituals, and mores that constitute the fabric of the Afro-Islamic world of the novel. Or, if it does not accomplish that much, then it may indicate the excess of form and meaning which lies over and above the point of engagement at which consumer production occurs.

Without a thorough and rigorous study of *mirasse* we cannot describe this excess with appropriate exactitude. Yet, even with this constraint, the text affords us a glimpse of it, thereby suggesting what significance its appropriation by Ramatoulaye might have for women. Her invocation of *mirasse* indicates that the ritual grants survivors of the deceased the authority of disclosure. However, it does not specify the identity of the survivor to exercise this authority. Is it the son, the daughter, the wife, the parents? Could it even be a friend, a cleric, a *griot*? Who speaks the "intimate secrets" of the dead? On this question the text is silent as, perhaps, befits a text committed to subversion. Uncannily echoing the silence of women, this silence in koranic law reveals a gap or fissure which Ramatoulaye seizes: "With consternation, *I* measure the extent of Modou's betrayal" (SL 9). Thus does she become the subject of a discourse authorized by the Koran, the canonical text of the religion which confines her, making it impossible for her to fulfill the "epistolary pact."

Yet if confinement obstructs the desire to exchange correspondence with Aïssatou, it, on the other hand, provides a context for Ramatoulaye's invocation of *mirasse*. In other words, in foreclosing an avenue of exchange as mandated by Western "norms" of epistolarity, confinement opens up an alternative medium for women's speech by exploiting a fissure in koranic law. To put it in yet another way, the effect of Islamic discourse is not merely repressive; it is also enabling. But what exactly does it enable? In the passage in which she invokes the *mirasse*, Ramatoulaye writes that it "requires that *a dead person* be stripped . . ." (SL 9). Yet, as Cham observes, the disclosures which follow this statement exceed the requirements of the Koran. The object revealed is simultaneously private and public, individual and social. Modou's "secrets" are collective because they encompass the web of reproductive, economic, political, and social relations possible within the community. It is this last fact, repeatedly reinforced by the analogies Ramatoulaye draws between hers and the experiences of other women of her class, which saves her disclosures from becoming anecdotally structured "ornamental, variations on the world."[13] If the world as perceived by Arab Islamic orthodoxy was, indeed, "a plenum," for Ramatoulaye, Aïssatou, and other women in Afro-Islamic cultures, it is less so. Neo-colonial Senegal is a world of incompletion, a world of potentialities which narratives may amplify or diminish.

Obviously, the objective of *So Long a Letter* is to amplify. But how is this objective accomplished, and at what cost? Following Miller we would admit that amplification is accomplished through francophone literacy. Unlike Miller, however, we must insist that even in struggle the source of an "imperative," ethical or technological, is a significant consideration in evaluating its achievement (TA 275–276). For not to rigorously question the source of any imperative is to condemn oneself to mimicry and, as I soon shall demonstrate, to run the risk of retarding the accomplishment of one's objectives by misapplying a technology of domination against the insurrectionary self. This is precisely the point at which the excess of the local forms and meanings mentioned above begin to emerge. For, as we shall see, it is these forms and meanings which she later describes as "moral standards," that constrain her to view "the flow of progress" with some skepticism (SL 77).

The novel makes clear the fact that in her youth "the flow of progress," at that point equivalent to francophone literacy, had been fashioned at Ponty-Ville. Armed with literacy, or the "power of books," Aïssatou finds refuge in "the Senegalese Embassy in the United States" from Mawdo Bâ's betrayal of their marriage. Ironically, however, literacy also provides a self-indulgent male rationalization of polygyny. Mawdo explains his polygynous relationship with the young Nabou by recalling a scene of cannibalism in a film: "'I saw a film in which the survivors of an air crash survived by eating the flesh of the corpses. This fact demonstrates the force of the instincts in man'" (SL 33).

If we overlook the fact that Mawdo's "fact" is a fiction, we still can say that it does not prove that human behaviour is driven solely by instincts. For, at a very practical level, the conditions under which this cannibalism occur are not remotely similar to those under which he seduces and marries Nabou.

Besides, sexual drives and the necessity to satiate hunger are not identical. Ramatoulaye could quite convincingly have rejected his arguments on these grounds. But, rather than do so, she is satisfied with declaring that she "could not be an ally to polygamic instincts" (SL 34). In other words, she accepts Mawdo's explanation. But to describe her response as acceptance is to overlook another possibility: that she accepts his explanation because it is a view she shares with him, differences in the particular institutions in which they received their education notwithstanding. In other words, Ramatoulaye and Mawdo Bâ share a class-oriented view of polygyny.[14]

Now if we are to rid ourselves of views which mystify polygyny and, thereby, facilitate a rigorous examination of the practice, we must seek the source of the view as well as the epistemological machinery which makes its production possible. We must question "the assimilationist dream of the colonist"; but, in addition, we need to interrogate the very technology which make our alternative truths possible (SL 24).

ENLIGHTENMENT EPISTEMOLOGY AND THE INVENTION OF POLYGYNY

In "The Anthropologist's Influence: Ethnography and the Politics of Conversion," V.Y. Mudimbe contends that "missionary accounts and those of anthropologists" during the colonial period "witness to the same *episteme*," adding that, if identification of their discourses is needed, then "it must be with European intellectual signs and not with African cultures."[15] He traces the genealogy of these "intellectual signs" back to European classical texts in history, drama, geography, and poetry, and identifies Herodotus, Pliny, and Diodorus of Sicily as the founts from which modern Europeans such as John Locke derived their descriptions of Africans and African cultural practices. "At the other extreme," he continues, "nineteenth-century anthropologists depict the essential paradigm of the European invention of Africa: Us/Them," which often "express the belief that the African is a negation of all human experience, or is at least an exemplary exception in terms of evolution."[16]

With changing relations between Europe and Africa in the twentieth century, this paradigm has undergone cosmetic, largely terminological, modification, with the result that it lives on in the form of the tradition/modernity opposition still found in various discourses from modernization and culture-conflict theories to conservative nationalism.[17] In dealing with this paradigm, we shall focus on two questions not addressed in Mudimbe's work: first, what was its structure in Enlightenment thought; and, second, in what form has it been translated into nationalist discourse in *So Long a Letter*, and with what consequences?

Answers to the first question are readily available in Johannes Fabian's *Time and the Other*. Fabian describes the epistemology by which the Enlightenment accounted for the diversity of human cultural forms and practices as Time/Space distancing.[18] This paradigm supplanted that of the

Middle Ages in whose model Time/Space were conceived "in terms of a history of salvation" and "the Time of Salvation was conceived as inclusive or incorporative." With the Enlightenment a naturalized, secular Time superseded the Judeo-Christian, sacred Time, and "temporal relations" were redefined "as exclusive and expansive" (TO 26–27; see Figure 5.1). The core of this paradigm, Now/Here, corresponds to Civilization and England. From this temporal and spatial core, "given societies of all times and places may be plotted in terms of relative distance *from* the present." "Savage" Time/Space is thus effectively removed from the anthropologist's Time/Space to a primeval past and ancient place marking the evolutionary beginnings of the human species (TO 26–27).

As for the second question, we must look closely at Bâ's handling of the tradition/modernity paradigm. Perhaps the passage which best exemplifies this handling is Ramatoulaye's recollection of "the aims of our admirable headmistress":

> To *lift* us out of the bog of tradition, superstition and custom, to make us appreciate a multitude of civilizations without renouncing our own, to *raise* our vision of the world, cultivate our personalities, strengthen our qualities, to *make up* for our inadequacies, to *develop* universal moral values in us: these were the aims of our admirable headmistress. (SL 15–16; my emphasis)

In this passage we can hear echoes of Diderot and d'Alembert's *philosophe* (*Encyclopédie*, 1779), trampling "on prejudice, tradition, universal consent, authority, in a word, all that enslaves most minds."[19] Ponty-Ville was, indeed, the training ground for the African *philosophe* and her double, the national bourgeoisie. It is not improbable that at institutions like Ponty-Ville she recited, among others, the line "nos ancêtres, les Gaulois [our ancestors, the Gauls]."[20]

Ponty-Ville then is the crucible in which a new, pliable post-colonial subject, the agent of social transformation, is formed. "Lift," "raise," "make up," "develop": these are stock terms of discourses informed by the evolutionist ethos of the nineteenth century. A sense of teleological motion, of transition, pervades the verbs. Movement from "tradition, superstition and custom" to "a multitude of civilizations" is evolutionary and successive, always tending toward a European norm. "Bog" designates both the place of entrapment and temporal stasis; it is at a distance, removed from the vicinity of civil society. The Time/Space of civil society (England) is now occupied by "a multitude of civilizations" whose "moral values" are "universal"; Savage Society (Figure 5.1) in which subjects are mired in stasis, gives way to Zero Society (Figure 5.2), home of "tradition, superstition and custom."

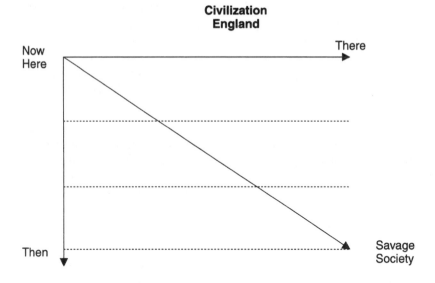

Figure 5.1 Modern Time/Space: distancing

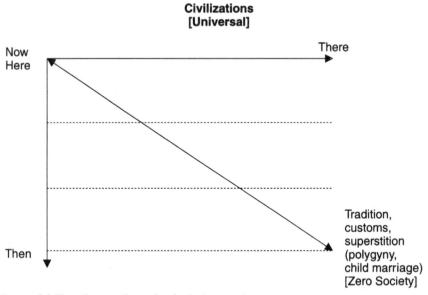

Figure 5.2 Time/Space: distancing in *So Long a Letter*

Just as distance and exclusion make possible the production of the "other" in nineteenth-century anthropology, so would they make possible the production of polygyny in twentieth-century African nationalist discourse. But this is getting ahead of the story. For Ramatoulaye, the route from the passage quoted above to the exclusion of polygyny from the structure and ethos of the nation state passes through a phase of anti-colonialist nationalist consciousness:

> The assimilationist dream of the colonist drew into its crucible our mode of thought and way of life. The sun helmet worn over the natural protection of our kinky hair, smoke-filled pipe in the mouth, white shorts just above the calves, very short dresses displaying shapely legs: a whole generation suddenly became aware of the ridiculous situation festering in our midst. (SL 24)

This passage does not identify "our admirable headmistress" as one of "the colonists." In view of her admiration for her instructor, this is hardly surprising. Quite plainly she is aware that not all French subjects in the colony work as functionaries in the political and economic sectors of the colonial power. Yet it is also obvious that the headmistress is indebted to French colonialism for her mission of salvation as she is indebted to nineteenth-century evolutionism for her instructional "aims." Her labor as a teacher, in other words, cannot be completely detached from the matrix of colonialism. In the rather paradoxical situation in which even well-meaning Europeans find themselves under colonialism, she is at once a source of inspiration and empowerment for the women and, as her "aims" reveal, a purveyor of an evolutionist view of African culture. Thus it is that she becomes the source of Ramatoulaye's disdain for "traditions" which fail to fit into the framework of the discourse of civil society and the bourgeois nation state.

The foregoing argument calls for some clarification. My contention is *not* that Ramatoulaye finds no value whatsoever in "tradition, superstition, and custom." Nor am I claiming that she maintains the tradition/modernity binary in every situation. Indeed, sometimes even her endorsement of the modern wavers. My contention is that she is selective about "tradition" and "modernity," just as a farmer would sort her seeds into viable and non-viable before planting. Aunty Nabou belongs to the latter category. She does not fit into Ramatoulaye's "imagined community" (SL 26).[21] Neither do teenage drinking and smoking and unsupervised contacts between boys and girls, but for a different reason: they belong to the latter category because they are deleterious to "moral values" (SL 77).

As the single parent of young adults in an unstable, rapidly changing world, Ramatoulaye must find new ways of dealing with common problems. Her handling of problems such as Aïssatou's unplanned pregnancy is a case in point. Farmata expects punitive sanctions against the young woman. But realizing the agony of her daughter and reminded of bonds of filial affection between them, Ramatoulaye resolves to forgive, console, support, and assist her: "I took my daughter in my arms. Painfully, I held her tightly, with a force multiplied tenfold by pagan revolt and primitive tenderness" (SL 83). By so doing, she breaks with local expectations, here represented by the *griot* woman, Farmata: "she will never know what to expect from me. To give a sinner so much attention was beyond her" (SL 83–84). The significance of Ramatoulaye's reaction to the crisis in her family thus emerges from the contrast with local norms: wailing, threats, reprimands. As her resolve to pre-empt the recurrence of such crisis by giving her children instructions in sex education shows, her unconventional resolution of Aïssatou's crisis does not constitute an unconditional endorsement of the ethics of the emerging social order. What it does reveal is a willingness to take the measure of events in terms of contingent realities. Thus, she astutely maneuvers around the false dichotomy between modernity and tradition, those shibboleths which for most of this century have cast a long shadow over the analysis of African cultural life.[22]

Ramatoulaye's successful resolution of this domestic crisis becomes even more significant when set against the backdrop of her discussion with Daouda Dieng of the low ratio of women's representation to men's in the National Assembly. Successful as a medical practitioner and politician, grave, gentle, and considerate, Dieng cannot see any justification for Ramatoulaye's protest. He is at first dismissive, arguing that women are disorderly and disruptive. But pressed by Ramatoulaye, and forced to pay attention to her ideas, he becomes stentorian, admonishing women to become involved in national politics and condemning them for being more interested in domestic affairs and class privileges (SL 61–62). In his view, affairs of the state encompass national interests, and these are of greater importance than domestic matters which relate to individual families. Subtending this view is a distinction between the personal and the political, the family and the state, a distinction whose effect on thought is not unlike that of the tradition/modernism binary. Against the backdrop of Dieng's unimaginative response to the political crisis in the National Assembly one cannot but be impressed by Ramatoulaye's insistence on the need for increased women's representation and her creative reaction to Aïssatou's pregnancy. If her deferential yet resolute opposition to his views holds any message, it is that resistance to women's political demands is still firmly entrenched, and even in "the general economy of new African words," in "theories commenting upon the catastrophe" of colonialism and "articulating in new ways other objects of desire," that resistance is hardly diminished.[23]

In view of the foregoing observations, I hope my analysis of the representation of polygyny in *So Long a Letter* would be placed in proper perspective. Bâ is quoted as arguing that, "As women, [we] must work for our own future, [we] must overthrow the status quo which harms [us] and [we] must no longer submit to it."[24] This is certainly a desirable end. However, unless a careful analysis of the role of polygyny in the maintenance of that status quo is undertaken, unless care is taken to distinguish the exploitation of polygyny for selfish ends (Mawdo Bâ) from the supercilious and pejorative view of the practice fostered by European ethnocentrism, African women (and men) run the risk of retarding the process of cultural self-criticism implicit in Bâ's manifesto.

Bâ's deployment of Time/Space distancing (Figure 5.2) has a twofold effect: first, it facilitates the characterization of polygynous forms of reproductive association as instinctual and regressive; and, second, it contrasts these attributes with those supposedly belonging to monogamous associations—love, fidelity, individuality, lifetime commitment to one's mate. Indeed, what makes Mawdo Bâ's decision to marry Nabou odious to Aïssatou is not just the fact of his taking a second wife. Rather, it is the fact that the action betrays a prior commitment made to her during their courtship. At that time, and against his mother's wishes, he, a Toucouleur and son of a princess "from the Sine," had insisted that "Marriage is a personal thing" and "emphasized his total commitment to his choice of life partner by visiting" Aïssatou's goldsmith father (SL 17). Later, confronted by his mother's intransigent disrespect for the integrity of his marriage, he fails to stand firm by this commitment, pleading the need to preserve her life and "fulfill a duty" (SL 31). Aïssatou justifiably rejects his argument. But one of her reasons for doing so, "that there can be no union of bodies without the heart's acceptance," seems to imply that the separation of body from heart is fundamental to the functioning of polygyny. If this deduction is correct, it extends a class-specific problem beyond that class. It may well be true that in the peasantry and other classes polygyny may index inequities in relations of production and reproduction. But Mawdo is a member of both the Wolof nobility for which polygyny is permissible, and the bourgeoisie for which it is not. His failure to sustain his commitment to Aïssatou must, therefore, not be understood as revealing anything about the relationship of body to heart in polygyny as such. Rather, it discloses much about the contradictory tensions in the social and sexual life of African nobility and bourgeoisie in the post-independence era.

If this, indeed, is the case, then we are constrained to read the nationalist manifesto with which Ramatoulaye ends her letter with some skepticism:

> I remain persuaded of the inevitable and necessary complementarity of man and woman . . .
> Love, imperfect as it may be in its content and expression, remains the natural link between these two beings . . .
> The success of the family is born of a couple's harmony, as the harmony of multiple instruments creates a pleasant symphony.
> The nation is made up of all the families, rich or poor, united or separated, aware or unaware. The success of a nation therefore depends inevitably on the family. (SL 88–89)

In the phrase "necessary complementarity of man and woman" Ramatoulaye articulates a primordial ideal of a non-hierarchized social relations of reproduction. But if this ideal is egalitarian, it is, as the passage shows, egalitarian *because* it is monogamous: "these two beings," "each partner," "a couple's harmony." Other forms of reproductive relations are, by implication, non-egalitarian. Organic nature ("love") and musical expression ("the harmony of multiple instruments") provide her with imagery with which to legitimate this view of the ethics and politics of monogamy.

Yet implicit in Ramatoulaye's imagery is a distinction, not between nature and culture, but between harmony and disharmony, order and chaos, consonance and dissonance, *in* nature and culture. The first term in each pair—harmony, order, consonance—represents feelings and institutions whose coherence derive from being associated with the organic: love, monogamous pairs, symphonies, the nation. Here the macrocosm (nation) is the sum of microcosmic reproductive units (couples); within the larger national structure, these then become the only viable subunits. But, for this to be so, it must also be asserted, or at least implied, that other possible units (unpaired or uncoupled) are not viable as constitutive subunits of the nation state. In other words, it must be suggested that the process of national becoming is historical, that this history is diachronic, and that certain forms of reproductive association are incompatible with that process.

To put this in stark terms, it must be implied that the *difference* between the first and second set of terms is a difference in the scale of values associated with nation building, and that the value of each term is determined by *distance from* the nation. In this respect the value of romantic love in monogamous associations, and the value of the latter in nation building, derive from two things. Love is an affect subtending reproductive behavior in Ramatoulaye's Time/Space: the Now/Here of the emergent bourgeois African nation and its subjects; it is also, and maybe for that very reason, a measure of the temporal and spatial distance separating the nation and its subjects from prior forms of reproductive association and subjectification (Figure 5.2). Love, then, is that whose lack sets polygyny apart, rendering it inimical to nation building and national consciousness.

Indeed, Bâ is alleged to have declared polygyny "evil" and an instinctual behavior "innate in every man."[25] If this is correct, then it reveals the ethical scale on which she evaluates this practice. But to declare polygyny innate is counterproductive to the objectives she has outlined for the female writer. Innatism doubles as an effective apologia for that which it supposedly denigrates. After all if I cannot help myself, why hold me responsible for my actions? Neither Mawdo nor Modou are helpless victims of their sexual instincts. Mawdo's failure to keep his commitment to Aïssatou is premeditated. Aunty Nabou and Nabou are mere alibis. Aïssatou understands this, and so leaves him. To attribute polygyny to innatism is to surrender the struggle against "the status quo" to another status quo, namely, biologism. For women whose trust has been betrayed, and for children traumatized by conflicts arising from such betrayals, this is not a satisfactory resolution.

Those still enamored of the tradition/modernity postulate must understand that the objection to it is not that both are illusions, or that any cultural phenomenon is necessarily inferior by virtue of being associated with tradition or modernity.[26] Rather, the objection is to conceptions and uses of each term as the antithesis of the other. Such uses have the effect of compelling us, as Paulin Hountondji argues, to choose between the two in the name of one, and to render absolute "the internal rationality of . . . traditions." Hountondji's solution to this problem is that we "try and know our traditions as they were, beyond any mythology and distortion, not merely for the purpose of self-identification or justification, but in order to help us meet the challenges and problems of today."[27]

It is not clear to me whether, and how, traditions could be known "as they were." However, it is clear that these "challenges and problems" or, as Fabian describing the origins of anthropology puts it, the "dialectic of repression and revolt" (TO 66) constitute the matrix of knowledge about African culture even today. It is this matrix that invests current evaluations of polygyny with social, economic, and political urgency. Under these circumstances, it would not do to dismiss the issue, as eighteenth-century apologetics of slavery did, as "the expression of innate lusts."[28] Nor will it do to declare it, as proper humanists might be tempted to do, a depravation of an otherwise stellar "universal human nature."[29] The problem with notions of universality is not whether or not there is such as thing. It is that whatever is universal in "human nature" (reproduction, for example) does not have a universal *expression*, and that where one is found, its morphology will disclose a repressive will-to-power rather than a transcendental truth.[30]

ACKNOWLEDGMENTS

I am indebted to Susan Z. Andrare, Professor Abiola Irele, and Professor Obioma Nnaemeka for comments on earlier drafts of this chapter.

NOTES

1 The epigraphs are taken, respectively, from Irène Assiba d'Almeida, "The Concept of Choice in Mariama Bâ's Fiction," *Ngambika: Studies of Women in African Literature*, ed. Carole Boyce Davies and Anne Adams Graves, p. 167; and Edris Makward, "Marriage, Tradition and Woman's Pursuit of Happiness in the Novels of Mariama Bâ," *Ngambika*, p. 274, my emphasis.

2 Mariama Bâ, *So Long a Letter*, trans. Modupé Bodé-Thomas; hereafter abbreviated SL.

3 Mineke Schipper, *Beyond the Boundaries*, p. 121; and Christopher L. Miller, "Senegalese Women Writers," *Theories of Africans: Francophone Literature and Anthropology in Africa*, p. 250, respectively. All references to *Theories of Africans* are hereafter abbreviated TA.

4 Femi Ojo-Ade, "Still a Victim? Mariama Bâ's *Une si longue lettre*," p. 72. For comments on elitism in the novel, see Charles Ponnuthurai Sarvan, "Feminism and African Fiction: The Novels of Mariama Bâ," pp. 460–461.

5 Ojo-Ade, "Still a Victim?" p. 72, my emphasis. See also, "Female Writers, Male Critics," p. 179.

6 Pauline Nalova Lyonga, "Uhamiri or a Feminist Approach to African Literature," p. 3. See also p. 176.

7 Obioma Nnaemeka, "Mariama Bâ," pp. 13–16.

8 Theodor W. Adorno, *Negative Dialectics*, pp. 53–54.

9 Thomas Metscher, "Literature and Art as Ideological Form," p. 21. I cite Metscher here for conceptual reasons rather than for reasons of identification with, critique or repudiation of his suggestions concerning the manner in which the epistemological dimension of art discloses itself (pp. 22–25).

10 See Wlad Godzich's foreword to de Centeau's *Heterologies*.

11 Mbye B. Cham, "Contemporary Society and the Female Imagination," pp. 91–92.

12 Michel de Certeau, *The Practice of Everyday Life*, pp. xi–xiv.

13 Edward W. Said, *Beginnings*, pp. 81–82. Said writes: "Islam views the world as a plenum" which prose fiction can neither diminish nor amplify. "Thus even autobiography as a genre scarcely exists in Arabic literature." He attributes to Islam the structural and generic peculiarities of Arabic literature. But Senegalese Muslims are not Arabs. This being the case, it is doubtful that his statement applies to Senegalese writing. See also Said's introduction to Halim Barakat, *Days of Dust*, pp. xiii–xiv.

14 For an autobiographical account of Mariama Bâ's education, see Alioune Touré Dia, "Succès littéraire de Mariama Bâ pour son livre: *Une si longue lettre*," pp. 12–14.

15 V.Y. Mudimbe, *The Invention of Africa*, pp. 71– 77.

16 Mudimbe, *The Invention of Africa*, pp. 71–72.

17 For modernization theory, see James Coleman, *Education and Political Development* and Samuel P. Huntington, *Political Order in Changing Societies*. I am indebted to Janet Afary, "*Grassroots Democracy*" for these references. Frantz Fanon, "The Pitfalls of National Consciousness," in *The Wretched of the Earth* is still the most forceful critical evaluation of conservative nationalism.

18 Johannes Fabian, *Time and the Other*, pp. 3–4; hereafter abbreviated TO. What is presented here is only a brief synopsis of Fabian's argument. Oscar Kenshur ("Demystifying the Demystifiers", p. 336) cautions against criticism which makes direct links between "the epistemological principles and . . . political convictions" of seventeenth-century objectivist philosophy. Taking his comments seriously, I read some of the texts cited by Fabian as well as period studies: John Locke, *Essay Concerning Human Understanding*, vol. 1, pp. 25–118; Joseph-Marie Degerando, *The Observation of Savage Peoples*; and Voltaire, *Candide*; Norman Hampson, *A Cultural History of the Enlightenment*; Roy Porter, *The Enlightenment*; Winthrop D. Jordan, *White Over Black: American Attitudes Toward the Negro, 1550–1812*; Stephen Toulmin and June Goodfield, *The Discovery of Time*; and Max Horkheimer and Theodor W. Adorno, *Dialectic of Enlightenment*. These texts do not contradict Fabian's analysis.

19 Porter, *The Enlightenment*, pp. 3–4.

20 Françoise Lionnet, *Autobiographical Voices*, p. 2. Education in colonial Africa has been the subject of numerous studies and commentaries. See, for example, Charles H. Lyons, "The Educable African: British Thought and Action, 1835–1865," *Essays in the History of African Education*, ed. Vincent M. Battle and Charles H. Lyons; Charles H. Lyons, *To Wash an Aethiop White: British Ideas About Black African Educability 1530–1960*; Ngũgĩ wa Thiong'o, "Education for a National Culture," in *Barrel of a Pen: Resistance to Repression in Neo-colonial Kenya*; Ngugi wa Thiong'o, *Decolonising the Mind: The Politics of Language in African Literature*. In "Functional Co-operation in West Africa: An Introduction," p. 56, Mazi Ray Ofoegbu identifies "Ponty graduates" as elites

prepared to serve the bureaucracy of the French colonial administration. For reflections on a post-colonial education, see Paulin Hountondji, "Scientific Dependence in Africa Today," pp. 5–15

21 *So Long a Letter* is probably one of the most dramatic examples in contemporary African literature of the process of national becoming. For a study of the evolution of nations and national consciousness, see Benedict Anderson, *Imagined Communities*.

22 These comments are crystalized from readings on the notions of "tradition" and "custom": Paulin Hountondji, *African Philosophy: Myth and Reality*, pp. 159–164; Edward Shils, *Tradition*; Ngũgĩ wa Thiong'o, "National Identity and Imperialist Domination: The Crisis of Culture in Africa Today," in *Barrel of a Pen: Resistance to Repression in Neo-Colonial Kenya*; Andrew Spiegel and Emile Boonzaier, "Promoting Tradition: Images of the South African past," in *South African Keywords: The Uses & Abuses of Political Concepts*, ed. Emile Boonzaier and John Sharp, pp. 40–41; Matthew H. Kramer, *Legal Theory, Political Theory, and Deconstruction*, p. 195; Max Weber, *Basic Concepts in Sociology*, pp. 67–81; Llyod I. Rudolph and Susanne Hoeber Rudolph, *The Modernity of Tradition*; and Janice E. Perlman, *The Myth of Marginality: Urban Poverty and Politics in Rio de Janeiro*.

23 V.Y. Mudimbe, "Letters of Reference," p. 64.

24 Bâ, quoted by Mineke Schipper and, subsequently, by Miller (TA 271).

25 Miller, quoting Barbara Arnhold, *Theories of Africans*, p. 280, n. 91.

26 See Oyekan Owomoyela, "African Philosophy," pp. 14–45; and Christopher L. Miller, "Theories of Africans."

27 Paulin Hountondji, "Reason and Tradition," p. 137.

28 Dorothy Hammond and Alta Jablow, *The Africa That Never Was*, p. 23; quoted in Abdul R. JanMohammed, *Manichean Aesthetics*, p. 7. In spite of the vast body of literature on this subject, it is to be noted that the issue is yet to be resolved. See, for example, Elizabeth Joseph's article "My Husband's Nine Wives," *New York Times* (May 23, 1991), p. A15; Anon., *A Dialogue of Polygamy, Written Originally in Italian: Rendered into English by a Person of Quality; and Dedicated to the Author of that well-known Treatise call'd, Advice to a Son* (London, 1657); James Cookson, *Thoughts on Polygamy, Suggested by the Dictates of Scripture, Nature, Reason, and Common-Sense* (Winchester, 1789); Walter M. Gallichan, *Women Under Polygamy* (New York, 1915); John Cairncross, *After Polygamy Was Made a Sin: The Social History of Christian Polygamy*; and Sylvie Fainzang-Odile Journet, *La Femme de mon mari*.

29 Roland Barthes, "The Great Family of Man," in *Mythologies*, p. 101.

30 For a non-ethnocentric methodology for negotiating the shoals of universalism in intercultural literary criticism, see Françoise Lionnet "Dissymmetry Embodied," pp. 2–4.

WORKS CITED

Anon. *A Dialogue of Polygamy, Written Originally in Italian: Rendered into English by a Person of Quality; and Dedicated to the Author of that well-known Treatise call'd, Advice to a Son*. London: 1657.

Adorno, Theodor W. *Negative Dialectics*. Trans. E.B. Ashton. New York: Continuum, 1990.

Afari, Janet. "Grassroots Democracy and Social Democracy in the Iranian Constitutional Revolution, 1906–1911," vol. 1. Ph.D. dissertation. Ann Arbor: The University of Michigan, 1991.

Anderson, Benedict. *Imagined Communities: Reflections on the Origin and Spread of Nationalism*. London and New York: Verso, 1983.

Bâ, Mariama. *So Long a Letter*. Trans. Modupé Bodé-Thomas. London: Heinemann, 1981.

Barthes, Roland. *Mythologies*. Trans. Annette Lavers. London: Jonathan Cape, 1972.

Cairncross, John. *After Polygamy Was Made a Sin: The Social History of Christian Polygamy*. London: Routledge & Kegan Paul, 1974.

Cham, Mbye B. "Contemporary Society and the Female Imagination: A Study of the Novels of Mariama Bâ." *Women in African Literature Today*. Trenton, NJ: Africa World Press, 1987.

Coleman, James. *Education and Political Development*. Princeton: Princeton University Press, 1965.

Cookson, James. *Thoughts on Polygamy, Suggested by the Dictates of Scripture, Nature, Reason, and Common-Sense*. Winchester: 1789.

d'Almeida, Irène Assiba. "The Concept of Choice in Mariama Bâ's Fiction." *Ngambika: Studies of Women in African Literature*. Ed. Carole Boyce Davies and Anne Adams Graves. Trenton, NJ: Africa World Press, 1986.

Davies, Carole Boyce and Anne Adams Graves, eds. *Ngambika: Studies of Women in African Literature*. Trenton, NJ: Africa World Press, 1986.

de Certeau, Michel. *The Practice of Everyday Life*. Trans. Steven Rendall. Berkeley: University of California Press, 1984.

Degerando, Joseph-Marie. *The Observation of Savage Peoples* (1800). Trans. F.C.T. Moore. Preface by E.E. Evans-Pritchard. London: Routledge & Kegan Paul, 1969.

Dia, Alioune Touré. "Succès littéraire de Mariama Bâ pour son livre: *Une si longue lettre*." *Anima* 84 (1979).

Fabian, Johannes. *Time and the Other: How Anthropology Makes its Object*. New York: Columbia University Press, 1983.

Fanon, Frantz. *The Wretched of the Earth*. Trans. Constance Farrington. New York: Grove Press, 1963.

Gallichan, Walter M. *Women Under Polygamy*. New York: Dodd, Mead, 1915.

Godzich, Wlad. "Foreword: The Further Possibility of Knowledge." *Heterologies: Discourse on the Other* by Michel de Certeau. Trans. Brian Massumi. Minneapolis: University of Minnesota Press, 1986.

Hammond, Dorothy and Alta Jablow, *The Africa That Never Was: Four Centuries of British Writing About Africa*. New York: Twayne Publishers, 1970.

Hampson, Norman. *A Cultural History of the Enlightenment*. New York: Pantheon Books, 1968.

Horkheimer, Max, and Theodor W. Adorno. *Dialectic of Enlightenment*. Trans. John Cumming. New York: Continuum, 1988.

Houtondji, Paulin. "Reason and Tradition." *Philosophy and Cultures: Proceedings of the 2nd Afro-Asian Philosophy Conference, Nairobi, October/November 1981*, eds. H. Odera Oruka and D.A. Masolo. Nairobi: Bookwise, 1983.

——. *African Philosophy: Myth and Reality*. Trans. Henri Evans. Intro. Abiola Irele. Bloomington: Indiana University Press, 1983.

——. "Scientific Dependence in Africa Today." *Research in African Literatures* 21. 3 (Fall 1990): 5–15.

Huntington, Samuel P. *Political Order in Changing Societies*. New Haven: Yale University Press, 1968.

JanMohammed, Abdul R. *Manichean Aesthetics: The Politics of Literature in Colonial Africa*. Amherst, MA.: The University of Massachusetts Press, 1983.

Jordan, Winthrop D. *White Over Black: American Attitudes Toward the Negro, 1550–1812*. Chapel Hill, NC: The University of North Carolina Press, 1968.

Joseph, Elizabeth. "My Husband's Nine Wives." *New York Times* (May 23, 1991): 15.

Journet, Sylvie Fainzang-Odile. *La Femme de mon mari*. Paris: L'Harmattan, 1988.

Kenshur, Oscar. "Demystifying the Demystifiers: Metaphysical Snares of Ideological Criticism." *Critical Inquiry* 14. 2 (Winter 1988): 335–353.

Kramer, Matthew H. *Legal Theory, Political Theory, and Deconstruction: Against Rhadamanthus*. Bloomington and Indianapolis: Indiana University Press, 1991.

Lionnet, Françoise. *Autobiographical Voices: Race, Gender, Self-Portraiture*. Ithaca, New York: Cornell University Press, 1989.

——. "Dissymmetry Embodied: Feminism, Universalism and the Practice of Excision." *Passages* 1 (1991): 2–4.

Locke, John. *Essay Concerning Human Understanding*, 2 vols, vol. 1. New York: Dover Publications, 1959.

Lyonga, Pauline Nalova. "Uhamiri or a Feminist Approach to African Literature: An Analysis of Selected Texts by Women in Oral and Written Literature." Ph.D Dissertation. Ann Arbor: The University of Michigan, 1985.

Lyons, Charles H. "The Educable African: British Thought and Action, 1835–1865." *Essays in the History of African Education*. Ed. Vincent M. Battle and Charles H. Lyons. New York: Teachers' College Press, Columbia University, 1970.

——. *To Wash an Aethiop White: British Ideas About Black African Educability, 1530–1960*. New York: Teachers' College Press, Columbia University, 1975.

Makward, Edris. "Marriage, Tradition and Woman's Pursuit of Happiness in the Novels of Mariama Bâ." *Ngambika: Studies of Women in African Literature*. Ed. Carole Boyce Davies and Anne Adams Graves. Trenton, NJ: African World Press, 1986.

Metscher, Thomas. "Literature and Art as Ideological Form." *New Literary History* XI. 1 (1979): 21–39.

Miller, Christopher. *Theories of Africans: Francophone Literature and Anthropology in Africa*. Chicago: The University of Chicago Press, 1990.

Mudimbe, V.Y. *The Invention of Africa: Gnosis, Philosophy, and the Order of Knowledge*. Bloomington and Indianapolis: Indiana University Press, 1988.

——. "Letters of Reference." *Transition* 53: 62–78.

Ngũgĩ wa Thiong'o. *Barrel of a Pen: Resistance to Repression in Neo-Colonial Kenya*. Trenton, NJ: Africa World Press, 1983.

Nnaemeka, Obioma. "Mariama Bâ: Parallels, Convergence, and Interior Space." *Feminist Issues* 10. 1 (1990): 13–35.

Ofoegbu, Mazi Ray. "Functional Co-operation in West Africa: An Introduction." *Ikenga: Journal of African Studies* 1. 2 (July 1972): 56–65.

Ojo-Ade, Femi. "Still a Victim? Mariama Bâ's *Une si Longue Lettre*." *African Literature Today*. Ed. Eldred D. Jones. New York: Africana Publishing, 1982.

——. "Female Writers, Male Critics." *African Literature Today: Recent Trends in the Novel*. Ed. Eldred D. Jones. New York: Africana Publishing, 1983.

Owomoyela, Oyekan. "African Philosophy: The Conditions of Its Possibility." *Sapina Newletter: A Bulletin of the Society for African Philosophy in North America* III: 1 (Jan.–July 1990): 14–45.

Perlman, Janice E. *The Myth of Marginality: Urban Poverty and Politics in Rio de Janeiro*. Berkeley: University of California Press, 1976.

Porter, Roy. *The Enlightenment*. London: Macmillan, 1990.

Rudolph, Lloyd I. and Susanne H. Rudolph. *The Modernity of Tradition*. Chicago and London: The University of Chicago Press, 1967.

Said, Edward W. *Beginnings: Intention and Method*. New York: Columbia University Press, 1975.

——. "Introduction." *Days of Dust* by Halim Barakat. Trans. Trevor Le Gassick. Wilmette, IL: The Medina University Press International, 1974.

Sarvan, Charles Ponnuthurai. "Feminism and African Fiction: The Novels of Mariama Bâ." *Modern Fiction Studies* 34. 3 (August 1988): 453–464.

Schipper, Mineke. *Beyond the Boundaries: African Literature and Literary Theory.* London: Allison & Busby, 1989.

Shils, Edward. *Tradition.* Chicago: The University of Chicago Press, 1981.

Spiegel, Andrew, and Emile Boonzaier. "Promoting tradition: Images of the South African past." *South African Keywords: The Uses & Abuses of Political Concepts.* Ed. Emile Boonzaier and John Sharp. Cape Town and Johannesburg: David Philip, 1988.

Toulmin, Stephen and June Goodfield. *The Discovery of Time.* New York: Harper & Row, 1965.

Voltaire. *Candide.* Ed. Milton P. Foster. Belmont, CA: Wadsworth, 1962.

——. *Decolonising the Mind: The Politics of Language in African Literature.* Portsmouth, NH: Heinemann, 1986.

Weber, Max. *Basic Concepts in Sociology.* Trans. H.P. Secher. London: Peter Owen, 1962.

6   Calixthe Beyala's "femme-fillette"

Womanhood and the politics of (M)Othering[1]

Juliana Makuchi Nfah-Abbenyi

> Donne-moi la main, désormais tu seras moi. Tu auras dix-sept saisons, tu
> seras noire, tu t'appelleras Tanga ... Donne ta main et mon histoire
> naîtra dans tes veines. Tu verras comment dans mon pays, l'enfant naît
> vieux, puisqu'il ne peut porter en lui le bouquet du printemps.[2]

Calixthe Beyala's *Tanga* opens with two women in a prison cell, a seventeen-
year-old African woman, Tanga, and a French-Jewish woman, Anna-Claude.
Tanga is about to die and Anna-Claude cajoles her to tell her story. In the
quotation above, Tanga responds affirmatively to Anna-Claude's request,
agreeing to narrate her story on the condition that Anna-Claude feels and
"becomes" herself, a black seventeen-year-old woman called Tanga. One is
struck by two features of this situation: firstly, a story is being handed down;
secondly, this story is being handed down from one woman to another, a black
woman to a white woman.[3] Black women/feminist critics have in the past
decade sought to posit the problematic of womanhood as seen through their
own "I"/"Eyes" by positioning themselves and the works that are the object
of their critique at the center of their discursive practices.[4] By so doing, they
have brought the lives of black women to the forefront either by rejecting the
position of "Other" ascribed to them by dominant discourses or by claiming
their "Otherness" as a weapon of resistance against those hegemonic
discourses.[5] Trinh Minh-ha aptly states that within the context of such
ideologies of dominance, "a concept of the Other is almost unavoidably
either opposed to the self or submitted to the self's dominance. It is always
condemned to remain its shadow while attempting at being its equal."[6] These
women have sought to lay bridges across such dualistic dichotomies as
male/female, woman/nature, subject/object, self/other given that the very
nature of their own lives does not obtain at the level of these dichotomies as
they simultaneously experience self and other within multiple contradictory
locations and by so doing construct for themselves multiple identities/
subjectivities.

The story that Tanga tells Anna-Claude can be read in different ways. It is
an indictment of human depravity in African urban slums, of patriarchal
society as a whole; one that condones child abuse/slavery/prostitution; a

society in which women and children are the Other, one that is not only oppressive to women but one in which women also act as oppressive agents to other women. My focus here will be on women's bodies and their sexuality with the aim of showing how Calixthe Beyala's novel seeks to subvert and politicize not only "Woman" (Tanga shares her prison and story with a white-Jewish woman) but the woman's body/experiences. In Iningué society, womanhood and motherhood are concepts that are intrinsically linked, but Beyala articulates a liberatory sexual politics, one that need not necessarily define womanhood in relation to motherhood.[7]

Tanga often refers to herself in binary terms, such as "la femme-fillette" (the woman-girlchild)[8] in order to describe the dual faces of a child's lifestyle as she is forced (especially by her mother) to live as a woman and of a woman who dreams of recapturing a lost childhood. This bipolar description of "femme" on the one hand and "fillette" on the other, aptly brings out how an Other is constructed in another position of otherness. One is keenly aware of an "ungraspable middle space"[9] around which childhood and womanhood seem to fluctuate, a space that Trinh Minh-ha theorizes as that of the "inappropriate/d other" when she states that the latter "is never installed within marginality . . . never dwells outside it."[10] This fluctuating subjective marginal space is that which Tanga strives to locate. Womanhood and mothering are closely linked in the story and Tanga seeks to position herself as an Other by rejecting the stereotype of woman/mother while at the same time reclaiming that same position of otherness (on her own terms), that she feels has been attributed to her in this hemisphere of women/mothers. Although she often seems to experience self-ness and other-ness separately (this will constitute the first part of my argument), the underlying struggle in the text is that of striving to experience body/soul, self/other, subject/object, simultaneously. It is this constant clash of Tanga's subjectivities that highlights my reading of the text and captures the problematic of womanhood as it transcends a normative reading that would restrict the woman's body to mothering, to stasis.

Tanga comes from four generations of women who are named in hyphenated terms: "femme-mère" (woman-mother) (wife-mother), "femme-maîtresse" (woman-concubine), "femme-enfant" (woman-child), "pute-enfant" (prostitute-child), "enfant-parent" (child-parent); the text abounds in such hyphenated references. Naming women in binary terms is a discursive act that not only informs of the hyphenated identities of these women and the hierarchical, dominant society in which they live but also of the problematic of womanhood as it relates not only to mothering and reproduction but to sexual pleasure, male sexual pleasure, given that embedded in these dualistic descriptions is the oppression of women and the objectification of their bodies.

Tanga's grandmother, Kadjaba Dongo is raped many times, she gives birth to Tanga's mother whom she rejects, gives the child to her mother and vows against motherhood.

Kadjaba coupa le cordon, cracha trois fois par terre pour tuer sa fertilité, jura qu'aucun cri d'enfant jamais plus ne s'élèverait de ses tripes et retourna chez elle, la vieille la mère dans ses bras. Elle la confia à sa mère. (43)

[Kadjaba cut the umbilical cord, spat three times on the ground to put an end to her fertility, swore that no cry of a baby would ever be heard from her bowels and returned home, my mother in her arms. She entrusted her to her mother.]

Tanga's mother, Taba, grows up a vagabond who also tries to escape brutal treatment from men. She does not want her body to be violated in the same way as her mother's, and consequently rapes herself by forcing palmnuts up her vagina at the age of thirteen. She falls in love with Tanga's father hoping to break the chain of misfortune encountered by her maternal ancestors but her husband turns out to be a womanizer who openly abuses her verbally and physically, a man who rapes and impregnates his own twelve-year-old daughter.

Ainsi de l'homme mon père, qui plus tard, non content de ramener ses maîtresses chez nous, de les tripoter sous l'oeil dégoûté de ma mère, m'écartèlera au printemps de mes douze ans, ainsi de cet homme, mon père qui m'engrossera et empoisonnera l'enfant, notre enfant, son petit-fils, cet homme ne s'apercevra jamais de ma souffrance et pourtant cette souffrance a duré jusqu'au jour de sa mort, jusqu'au jour de ma mort. (50)

[And so about the man called my father, who later on, not content with bringing his mistresses home, of toying with them under the disgusted watch of my mother, will spread out my legs at the spring of my twelve years, and about this man, my father who will impregnate me and will poison the child, our child, his grand-son, this man will never perceive of my pain and yet this pain lasted to the day of his death, and will last till the day of my death.]

The pain ensuing from this incestuous rape that is both physical and psychological, external and internal is what Tanga attempts to confront throughout her life, between the ages of twelve and seventeen. She resolves to redefine different spaces both interior and exterior, spaces that will set her apart from the destiny reserved for Iningué women. She moves from the lack of control of her body which she puts on the market of prostitution, to what Adrienne Rich calls the repossession by women of their bodies.[11] Like all the women in her family, Tanga is subjected to violent verbal and sexual abuse and this physical trauma forces her to treat her own body like an-Other, that is, not-I.

J'amenais mon corps au carrefour des vies. Je le plaçais sous la lumière. Un homme m'abordait. Je souriais. Je suivais. Je défaisais mes vêtements. Je portais mon corps sur le lit, sous ses muscles. Il s'ébrouait. D'autres images m'assaillaient . . . Je ne sentais rien, je n'éprouvais rien. Mon corps à mon insu s'était peu à peu transformé en chair de pierre. (19–20)

[I took my body to the cross-roads of lives. I placed it under the light. A man accosted me. I smiled. I followed. I undid my clothes. I put my body on the bed, beneath his muscles. He snorted. Other images assailed me . . . I sensed nothing, I felt nothing. My body, unknown to me had bit by bit transformed itself into stone.]

Tanga loses total control over her body the moment she is raped by her father and later forced into prostitution by her own mother who expects her daughter to utilize her charms and body for economic benefit. Tanga describes her mother's expectations as the bitter pill that the "enfant-parent" (child-parent) is forced to swallow all her life, given that all s/he represents to her parents is a financial old-age "insurance policy," an insurance policy whose premium is paid for by the child (with her body), one that her mother consolidates by subjecting her daughter to a clitoridectomy that "prepares" Tanga's body for men and the money market. The mutilation of body parts and sexuality can be construed as that which validates the power of males to control women's sexuality and further reinforces woman's otherness, that which is dominated and manipulated:

"Elle est devenue femme, elle est devenue femme. Avec ça, ajoute-t-elle en tapotant ses fesses, elle gardera tous les hommes." Je n'ai pas pleuré, Je n'ai rien dit. J'héritais du sang entre mes jambes. D'un trou entre les cuisses. Seule me restait la loi de l'oubli. (24)

["She has become a woman, she has become a woman. With this," she added patting her buttocks, "she will keep all the men." I did not cry, I did not say anything. I inherited blood between my legs. A hole between my thighs. All that was left for me was the law of forgetting.]

The right to womanhood is here directly associated not only with sexual intercourse but also with institutionalized heterosexuality. Tanga's mother's reaction demonstrates that clitoridectomy does not only define her daughter as a woman, i.e., she has crossed over from childhood to womanhood, but also captures the right that this act gives men to possess Tanga's body. She has no say either in the process or in the resultant objectification of her own body. This is reminiscent of one of the scenes in the prison cell where in order to punish and silence Anna-Claude, one of the prison-guards proposes (to the amusements of his colleagues) that her clitoris be "cut off": "on pourrait peut-être lui couper le clitoris" (69).

Tanga's identity and sexuality are controlled and exploited by men and patriarchy but this control, viewed in terms of gender and power relations, is also compounded by the cooperation of her own mother. Tanga's experience shows how women within patriarchy are built into the ladder of power struggles in such a way that they become accomplices with that very control of power and sexuality that men have claimed for themselves. Tanga's mother quietly looks the other way at her daughter's rape and pregnancy and jubilates at her clitoridectomy. It is a complicity that Tanga finds "shameful." She has been so used to alienating her-self from her-body that she has never been able to feel shame; in short, to feel at all. She feels shame when the first man she falls in love with, the only man that she refuses to regard as a customer, treats her like the "slut" that she represents; and this shame and anger remind her of the only other time she had felt shame in her life, which was when her mother took her to the "arracheuse de clitoris" (the woman responsible for "tearing out" her clitoris). This shame/anger directed towards the mother is indicative of the fact that she believes the latter possessed the power, even though positioned within patriarchy, to protect her from the pain and the loss. Her mother could have prevented the mutilation but she did not.[12] Instead she saw in this ritual the culmination of commercial servitude that she expects and demands of her daughter.

A Iningué, la femme a oublié l'enfant, le geste qui donne l'amour, pour devenir une pondeuse. Elle dit: "L'enfant, c'est la sécurité vieillesse." D'ailleurs le gouverneur en personne médaille les bonnes pondeuses. Service rendu à la patrie. La vieille la mère a essayé de se faire couronner. (89–90)

[At Iningué, the woman has forgotten the child, the gesture that gives love to become a breeder. She said: "The child is old age insurance." By the way, the Governor himself hands out medals to good breeders. Service rendered to the fatherland. My old lady tried to get herself a crown.]

Tanga rightly condemns mothers who deprive their children of a "home," of that private space in which children are loved and nurtured; mothers who instead treat their children as commodities that bring rewards in monetary and material terms. It is interesting to note here how women's work in the home, that traditional Marxists referred to as unremunerated work and having only a use-value, is politicized in a public space of surplus-value, one that recognizes and rewards biological mothers with a social status that is directly linked not only to the womb as agent of reproduction but one that also controls the numbers produced, and the socio-political functions/benefits ascribed to the womb.[13] What this means is that childless women or women who do not produce certain quantities of children are consciously excluded and positioned as inappropriate Others, as women who have no rights within the public sphere. The viciousness of this practice of Othering is seen in Taba's letter to the Governor in which she claims to have been unjustly forgotten just because she lost ten of her twelve babies. She makes her demands on the ontological basis of her womb and body as active participants in the process of reproduction and nation building while the Governor makes epistemological choices based on numbers and surplus-value. Women like

Taba are thus reduced to bodies, objects of production and reproduction and they in turn objectify the bodies of their own daughters.

There is a remarkable difference between the letter written by Taba and that written by her daughter, Tanga. Both letters are written to men, one to an administrative political head and the other to an anonymous man. But the issues addressed by both women, which bring out their innermost yearnings, are divergent. Taba's letter captures the cultural and political construction of a dispossessed body (one that is an object of desire, pleasure, and reproduction) whose material gain is supposedly a medal that is never awarded, a body that conforms to the metaphor of the prison in which Tanga tells her story. Tanga's letter speaks of that same imprisoned body but one that seeks to break out of those prison walls. This section will deal with Tanga's attempt to break away from that physical/psychical prison by building physical, emotional and semiotic walls of resistance through what bell hooks has described as resisting by constantly shifting "from the margin to the center,"[14] a theory that directly correlates with Trinh Minh-ha's notion of appropriating the marginal space by never being installed within it and never dwelling outside of it. Anna Claude's words best describe Tanga's "prison."

> "Tu vas mourir. Je le sens, je le sais. Donne-moi ton histoire. Je suis ta délivrance. Il faut assassiner ce silence que tu traînes comme une peau morte . . . Donne-moi ton histoire et je répandrai ton rêve." (17)

> ["You are dying. I feel it, I know it. Give me your story. I am your release. You must get rid of this silence that you carry around like dead skin . . . Give me your story and I will spread your dream."]

Tanga is a romantic, a dreamer, in spite of the numerous ways in which she has been silenced: rape, incest, prostitution, even the right to speech is taken away from her by a father (who takes her along with him as early as the age of six to his concubine to whom he makes love in front of his own child) who tells her that a child must always keep its eyes on the ground. Consequently, one of her passions growing up is watching people's legs, a vantage point from which she claims to see everything despite her father's injunction. By so doing, she subverts her father's injunction and constructs him as the other by indirectly "seeing" all that goes on around her without his knowledge or awareness of it. Tanga's other passion is to dream about the man that she loves, hoping that he would one day love her back, so much so that she would be able to love freely, own a home, have children, a dog, a garden and be able to enjoy life without restraints. As she puts it herself:

> Je veux les épisodes suivants, ceux qui libéreront la femme et enterreront à jamais l'enfance morte . . . je veux enjamber le malheur, m'embarquer dans le train du devenir. (36)

[I want the following episodes, those that will liberate woman and bury deadened childhood forever . . . I want to stride over misfortune, board the train of becoming.]

The first act of becoming, liberating woman and recapturing the lost childhood, is initiated by Tanga when she personally makes the decision to reject motherhood and give up prostitution against bitter protests from her mother who promptly turns her youngest daughter over to the world's oldest trade. What Tanga always dreamed of when her thoughts drifted away from her body that was being possessed by men is suddenly achieved through one act. She plugs her vagina with a ball of clay which she claims acts as a poison that destroys whatever had or would want to possess it and from that moment she celebrates what she calls her new-found virginity and her right not to bear any child; a virginity that is for her metaphorically mental and physical. It is a symbolic break with the past but a past that then permits her to shape the future, one that actively participates in the process of self-actualization.

The contradictions and ambiguities involved in this process of the re-definition of the self must be stressed because Tanga does not completely quit those margins that define her in binary oppositions like "femme-fillette" or "enfant-parent" but subverts them to her own benefit, in her struggle to build strong, multiple and changing subject positions for herself, similar to what Teresa de Lauretis has described as "the concept of a multiple, shifting, and often self-contradictory identity."[15] Her adoption of the disabled child Mala is a case in point. One wonders why a woman who rejects motherhood would adopt a child. There are many reasons that can account for this identifiable contradiction.

Tanga has experienced sexual pleasure with two men only. The first one, Hassan, she falls in love with. He is the only man or person she loves, and because of him she refuses to be designated as a prostitute, an object. He is the man she had hoped and dreamed would love her and treat her differently from the way her father treated her mother. It does not work out that way because Hassan only wants her body and when she proposes marriage he laughs at her:

Et, pour me décourager, il évoque les femmes-mères, assises sous les vérandas, le ventre flasque. Il dit leurs seins bas, leur voix acide d'épouses déçues et qui peu à peu sombrent dans le mutisme. Même pas de larme pour pleurer le manque de plaisir! (139)

[And in order to dissuade me, he cites the wife-mothers, seated beneath the verandas, with flabby stomachs. He says their breasts are flat, their voices harsh, the voices of embittered wives who gradually fade into silence. Not even have they tears to shed for the lack of pleasure!]

Tanga does not want to become one of these embittered woman/wife/mothers whose sexuality is reduced to reproduction. The other man with whom she experiences sexual pleasure is Cul-de-jatte, a truant who exploits child labour, with the difference that the children share in their earnings and are given a much-needed sense of home and belonging where they are well fed and never physically abused. She enjoys her relationship with Cul-de-jatte but abandons him when he asks her to bear him a child, a son.

Tanga deliberately rejects motherhood when it is imposed on her by the man. She becomes a mother to Mala, also known as Pieds-gâtés, not only out of choice but because of the selflessness of the love involved and the fact that Mala helps her in her healing process. In Mala she seeks that primal, maternal semiotic link (described by Julia Kristeva)[16] repressed in every "femme-fillette" or "enfant-parent". She is both mother to, and child with, Mala. She spends some time with Mala, playing with him and feeling like a child again, while at the same time enacting the role of the mother by breastfeeding him. She initiates a libidinal link with Mala who was never breastfed or taken care of by his own mother who gave him up to his alcoholic grandmother:

> Durant cette période, j'avais la sensation du bonheur. Pieds-gâtés était mon fils. Il se collait à ma poitrine. Il disait: "J'ai faim Mâ." Je sortais un sein. Il tétait. Il s'endormait. Je me souciais de son bonheur dans mon bonheur. (192)

> [During this period, I had the sensation of bliss. Pieds-gâtés was my son. He would glue himself to my chest. He would say: "I am hungry Mâ." I would take out one breast. He would suckle. He would go to sleep. I was concerned about his happiness in my happiness.]

Consequently, Tanga stops thinking of herself as an object, that Other of man's desire, and blossoms in this new-found selfless love and agency, an agency that is however once more threatened by Mala's death and her arrest by the police.

Right up to the moment of her death, Tanga keeps on (re)-constructing her identity. The final straw in this process has to do with her ability to reach out to Anna-Claude through the medium of storytelling. Recounting her story is the final step in her will to break the *silence*. Trinh Minh-ha rightly states that within the context of women's speech, silence has many faces such as, "silence as a will not to say or a will to unsay and as a language of its own."[17] Tanga no longer has to pretend to keep her eyes on the ground as her father ordered but looks another woman in the face and relates to her, tells her a story that the latter promises to perpetuate, asserting that her struggles will not be lost.

Although Tanga has lost Mala, she still constructs that maternal, if not semiotic, link with Anna-Claude. As she weaves in and out of her story, Tanga insists on everything about both women touching: their stories, their minds, their bodies. As we gathered from the quote at the beginning of this chapter, Tanga asks to take Anna-Claude's hand in her own. This act is the beginning of something mental and sensual that ignites the flow of the story. There is a persistent touching of hands/membranes without which she feels no warmth or communication. This mental and physical touching, recaptures for both women what they interpret to be the maternal, as in this instance:

> Leurs corps s'enlacent. Anna-Claude pleure. Tanga trace sur son cou et son flanc des sillons de tendresse. Elle lui dit de ne pas pleurer, qu'elles venaient de connaître le cauchemar mais que le réel était l'étreinte. Elle lui dit qu'elles frotteront leur désespoir et que d'elles jaillira le plus maternel des amours. (72)

> [Their bodies embrace. Anna-Claude cries. Tanga traces on her neck and side fields of tenderness. She tells her not to cry, that they had just known a nightmare but the embrace was reality. She tells her that they will dust off their despair and from them will spring the most maternal of loves.]

Female bonding develops out of this sensuous maternal love (which may or may not be sexual) and paves the way for both women to shift in and out of their marginality, for their stories to be told. Although Tanga speaks most of the time, her story is interwoven with Anna-Claude's, just as in her life she shifts in and out of fantasies, dreams of perfect love and brutal reality. She narrates her story in the same way as she struggles to construct an identity of the self and a subjectivity that are changing. Like a folktale narrator, the story is a performance with movement in and out of the story, intertwined with digressions, flashbacks, Anna-Claude's story.

Anna-Claude's and Tanga's stories are interwoven in such a way that at the end of the story she has totally assumed Tanga's identity and that is the identity she presents to the police officer who interrogates her:

> "Nom, prénom, âge, profession.
> -Femme-fillette, noire, dix-sept ans, pute occasionnelle." (184)

> ["Surname, firstname, age, profession.
> -Woman-girlchild, black, seventeen years old, part-time prostitute."]

Richard Bjornson suggests that:

> The merging of the two women's identities in the face of death, despair, and decay symbolizes the possibility of achieving the ideal love they had formerly associated with their illusory images of Ousmane and Hassan ... the meaning of [Tanga's] life survives in Anna-Claude's conscious-ness, suggesting that the love of women can transcend the ugliness of the prison world into which they have been thrust by the cruelty and indifference of men. (*African Quest* 419)

When Anna-Claude presents herself as Tanga, she is not only making a personal statement for herself but a political statement that includes Tanga and all other marginalized women like herself. She therefore speaks both *for* and *about* herself and the Other.[18] Calixthe Beyala seems to be making a global political statement about the concept of "Woman" (as unified subject) and women's experiences. Many times within the text Anna-Claude's otherness is compared with Tanga's. Even though Anna-Claude is white/French, she is persecuted in France for her Jewishness. She also spends her time fantasizing about love and an ideal African man, Ousmane, crafted in her image. She finds neither of these images of fantasy in France nor in Africa where she comes to find them, but is also persecuted for her femaleness, whiteness, and Jewishness. Beyala, to my mind, is trying to create an essentialist feminist utopia for marginalized women or those Others of society. It is my conjecture that such essentialist attempts at global sisterhood can only be useful in one way, in that they can conveniently pinpoint the broader issues at stake for women and feminism and map out the lines along which political action can take place on a wider scale.

If this is not the case, then it is disturbing to find that Anna-Claude "loses" her own specific identity and claims for herself the identity of an-other Other (what happens at the end of the story is much more than a merging of identities). Anna-Claude presents herself to Tanga's mother (Taba) as Tanga, her daughter. Her last sentence to Taba is, "Vous nous avez tuées, madame" ("Madam, you killed us"). Taba's incapacity to understand this essentialist notion of woman-as-oppressed, of woman-as-oppressor, or "see" Anna-Claude as her daughter, demonstrates the difficulty, if not, impossibility of simply transcending age, race, and class difference. No matter what the similarities are, or where their sympathies lie, women cannot speak for others or the Other at the expense of erasing identity (and, in the process, agency), and difference. "Otherness becomes empowerment, critical difference when it is not given but recreated."[19] Tanga is able to empower herself, to explore many layers of "I", of her subjectivity, by subverting and recreating her own positions of Other. Anna-Claude does empower herself by reconstructing otherness in correlation with Tanga, but in the process of this re-articulation of the self, Calixthe Beyala unfortunately constructs an identity that at the same time erases race, class, and difference. Audre Lorde would describe this as using the Master's tools to dismantle the Master's house.

NOTES

1 Calixthe Beyala is a Cameroonian woman writer. Cameroonian women writers are not as widely known as their male counterparts such as Ferdinand Oyono, Mongo Beti, Guillaume Oyono-Mbia, Francis Bebey, to name a few. Although most of these women published their works in the late 1960s and 1970s (for example, Kuoh-Moukouri Thérèse, Dooh-Bunya Lydie, Assiga-Ahanda Marie Thérèse), two women have distinguished themselves in the 1980s: Werewere Liking and Calixthe Beyala. The latter published her first novel *C'est le soleil qui m'a brûlée* in 1987 followed by *Tu t'appelleras Tanga* in 1988, both with Éditions Stock, and a third novel in 1990 *Seul le diable le savait* with Le Pré aux Clercs, none of which has been translated into English. It is also unfortunate that most

critical works on Cameroon literature usually mention these women writers in passing or simply gloss over their work. See, for example, Josette Ackad (1985), David Ndachi Tagne (1986), Claire Dehon (1989). Richard Bjornson's impressive work *The African Quest for Freedom and Identity: Cameroonian Writing and the National Experience* does pay attention to works by women writers but the author does not allocate a chapter or an in-depth study to any woman writer in the way he does to some male writers.

2 *Tu t'appelleras Tanga*, p. 18. Hereafter cited in the text as *Tanga*. All subsequent translations are mine.

3 The matrilineal tradition of handing down her-stories among black women has been reclaimed by African and African-American writers/feminist literary critics. Abena Busia, for example, states that, "as black women we have recognised the need to rewrite or reclaim our own *her*stories, and to define ourselves" ("Words Whispered over Voids," p. 1). See also, Barbara Christian's *Black Feminist Criticism: Perspectives on Black Women Writers.* Most critical work on the black matrilineal tradition restricts itself to black women and their maternal heritage. *Tanga* provides us with a new perspective, one that is complicated by race, difference, and an essentialist notion of sisterhood/womanhood that will be discussed later.

4 See for example, Alice Walker's *In Search of Our Mothers' Gardens.*

5 See, for example, Valerie Smith, "Black Feminist Theory and the Representation of the "Other"; and Trinh Minh-ha *Woman, Native, Other: Writing Postcoloniality and Feminism.*

6 "Not You/Like You: Post-Colonial Women and the Interlocking Questions of Identity and Difference," p. 71.

7 In her "Introduction" to *Ngambika*, Carol Boyce Davies states that African women writers (unlike most of their male counterparts), strive to present positive images that do not "limit women into postures of dependence or submergence," through potrayals that "suggest the possibility of transcendence" p. 15.

8 I am translating "femme-fillette" as "woman-girlchild" instead of the informal expressions of "fillette" in English such as girlie/lassie or "woman-child" because child in English will not convey the specific feminine gender embedded in "fillette." This also averts confusion with other terms such as "femme-enfant" (woman-child) that occur in the same text and refer to the same individual.

9 This is a phrase used by Donna Haraway to describe Trinh Minh-ha's theory of the "inappropriate/d other." "Reading Buchi Emecheta: Contests for 'Women's Experience' in Women's Studies," in *Simians, Cyborgs, and Women*, p. 239.

10 "Introduction" to *She, the Inappropriate/d Other, Discourse 8* (Fall–Winter 86–87), p. 3. Although Trinh Minh-ha's theory refers specifically to the figure of the post-colonial woman within the larger frameworks of patriarchy and feminist discourse, I am using it here to refer to Tanga who like other women is defined within specific margins but who unlike the others is constantly shifting in and out of that marginal space.

11 In her book, *Of Woman Born: Motherhood as Experience and Institution*, Rich discusses a number of issues relating to the woman's body particularly the relationship of women to their powers of reproduction, and motherhood as an institution laid down by patriarchal order that enables men to control women's bodies. She argues strongly against this oppressive institution which she regards as one that gives women no autonomy over their bodies. I am aware of the fact that many Third World feminists have argued that the major problem for Third World women is not gaining control over their bodies (given that they claim motherhood as empowering), but other interrelated issues such as lack of sex

education, birth control policies, infant mortality, insufficient healthcare facilities (see Patricia Collins, 1990; Chandra Mohanty et al., 1991). Rich's argument that is of interest to me here is the point that women must repossess their bodies and that in this act of repossession, motherhood becomes a free choice and childbirth an experience that enriches a woman's life instead of a formula that prescribes woman's place in the home, bearing/raising children, one that presupposes acts of love and patience as natural.

12 Tanga's younger sister also becomes a prostitute but we are not told that she is also subjected to a clitoridectomy that "makes" her a woman. When Tanga gives up prostitution, she encourages her sister to educate herself in order to escape the same fate but her mother promptly turns her elder daughter's customers to the younger one.

13 Marxist feminists have problematized the body as an instrument of production under the primacy of the sexual division of labor by privileging material bodily experiences of women. But Gayatri Spivak has gone further than the former in her deconstruction of Freud and Marx by specifically describing the womb as a "workshop," as a "place of production [that] is avoided in both Marx and Freud." See *In Other Worlds* (1987), pp. 80–81.

14 See *Feminist Theory: from Margin to Center* (1984). bell hooks argues that marginalized women can fight hegemonic discourses not by staying at the margins but by shuffling between their margins and the center, i.e., the dominant discourses, and that by so doing they bring the margins to the center and vice versa.

15 De Lauretis has described the nature of women's subjectivity as being constantly in flux. See, "Feminist Studies/Critical Studies," p. 9. Chandra Mohanty and Biddy Martin also posit the concept of identity and subjectivity as having a multiple and shifting perspective in their essay, "Feminist Politics: What's Home Got to Do with It?" in De Lauretis, ed. *Feminist Studies/Critical Studies*.

16 See "From One Identity to An Other," in *Desire in Language* (1980).

17 Trinh Minh-ha (1988), pp. 73–74.

18 In her essay, "The Problem of Speaking for Others," Linda Alcoff maintains that, the practice of speaking for others is as problematic as the practice of speaking about others, "since it is difficult to distinguish speaking about from speaking for in all cases" (p. 111). Although she rejects "a general retreat from speaking for, [she does not advocate] a return to an unselfconscious appropriation of the other, but rather that anyone who speaks for others should only do so out of a concrete analysis of the particular power relations and discursive effects involved."

19 Trinh Minh-ha (1988), p. 75.

WORKS CITED

Ackad, Josette. *Le roman camerounais et la critique*. Paris: Éditions Silex, 1985.

Alcoff, Linda. "The Problem of Speaking for Others." *Who Can Speak?* Ed. Judith Roof and Robyn Wiegman. Urbana: University of Illinois Press, 1995: 97–119.

Beyala, Calixthe. *Tu t'appelleras Tanga*. Paris: Éditions Stock, 1988.

Bjornson, Richard. *The African Quest for Freedom and Identity: Cameroonian Writing and the National Experience*. Bloomington: Indiana University Press, 1991.

Busia, P.B. Abena. "Words Whispered over Voids: A Context for Black Women's Rebellious Voices in the Novel of the African Diaspora." *Black Feminist Criticism and Critical Theory*. Ed. Joe Weixlmann and Houston A. Baker, Jr. Greenwood, Florida: Penkevill Publishing Company, 1988.

Christian, Barbara. *Black Feminist Criticism: Perspectives on Black Women Writers*. New York: Pergamon, 1985.

Collins, Patricia H. *Black Feminist Thought: Knowledge, Consciousness and the Politics of Empowerment*. Boston: Unwin Hyman, 1990.

Davies, Carole Boyce. "Introduction: Feminist Consciousness and African Literary Criticism." *Ngambika: Studies of Women in African Literature*. Ed. Carole Boyce Davies and Anne Graves Adams. Trenton, NJ: Africa World Press, 1986.

Dehon, Claire. *Le roman camerounais d'expression française*. Birmingham, Alabama: Summa Publications, 1989.

de Lauretis, Teresa. "Feminist Studies/Critical Studies: Issues, Terms and Contexts." *Feminist Studies/Critical Studies*. Ed. Teresa de Lauretis. Bloomington: Indiana University Press, 1988.

Haraway, Donna J. "Reading Buchi Emecheta: Contests for 'Women's Experience' in Women's Studies." *Simians, Cyborgs, and Women: The Reinvention of Nature*. New York: Routledge, 1991.

hooks, bell. *Feminist Theory: From Margin to Center*. Boston: South End Press, 1984.

Kristeva, Julia. "From One Identity to An Other." *Desire in Language*. Trans. Leon Roudiez. New York: Columbia University Press, 1982.

Lorde, Audre. "The Master's Tools Will Never Dismantle the Master's House." *This Bridge Called My Back: Writings By Radical Women of Color*. Ed. Cherríe Moraga and Gloria Anzaldúa. New York: Kitchen Table: Women of Color Press, 1983.

Mohanty, Chandra and Biddy Martin. "Feminist Politics: What's Home Got to Do With It?" *Feminist Studies/Critical Studies*. Ed. Teresa de Lauretis.

Mohanty, Chandra, Ann Russo and Lourdes Torres, eds. *Third World Women and the Politics of Feminism*. Bloomington: Indiana University Press, 1991.

Rich, Adrienne. *Of Woman Born: Motherhood as Experience and Institution*. New York: W.W. Norton, 1986.

Smith, Valerie. "Black Feminist Theory and the Representation of the 'Other'." *Changing Our Own Words: Essays on Criticism, Theory, and Writing by Black Women*. Ed. Cheryl Wall. New Brunswick: Rutgers University Press, 1989.

Spivak, Gayatri C. "Feminism and Critical Theory." *In Other Worlds: Essays in Cultural Politics*. New York: Routledge, 1987.

Tagne, David. *Roman et réalités camerounaises*. Paris: Éditions l'Harmattan, 1986.

Trinh T. Minh-ha. "Introduction." *She, the Inappropriate/d Other. Discourse 8*, Fall–Winter, 1986–87.

——. "Not You/Like You: Post-Colonial Women and the Interlocking Questions of Identity and Difference." *Inscriptions* 3/4 (1988): 71–77.

——. *Woman, Native, Other: Writing Postcoloniality, and Feminism*. Bloomington: Indiana University Press, 1989.

7 Bound to matter

The father's pen and mother tongues

Cynthia Ward

> We African writers are bound by our calling to do for our languages
> what Spencer, Milton and Shakespeare did for English; what Pushkin and
> Tolstoy did for Russian; indeed what all writers in world history have done
> for their languages by meeting the challenge of creating a literature in
> them, which process later opens the languages for philosophy, science,
> technology and all the other areas of human creative endeavours.
>
> Ngũgĩ wa Thiong'o, Decolonizing the Mind

In analyzing the situation of "the African writer," many literary critics have
found it useful to postulate it as Oedipal in relation to the writer's literary
precursors. This formulation resembles Harold Bloom's psycholiterary theory
of the "anxiety of influence," but with a twist. While Bloom never questions
the authority of the forefathers and the "strong poetic" tradition they have
dialectally constructed, V.Y. Mudimbe asks, "What if the father to which
you have subjected yourself is an imposter; a false father who wrongly
usurped the position of authority? What happens then to the son?" (73). In
his article "Letters of Reference," which uses Christopher Miller's *Theories
of Africans* and Bernadette Cailler's study of Edouard Glissant to explore the
motifs of "an African childhood as metaphor, the French language as a sign
of male power, and the refused voice of African women" (69), Mudimbe
suggests that the crisis of the psychic space created by the confrontation of
the writer with the false fathers—"producers of discourses that have been
coded in advance"—might be productively opened out into the discursive
regime of the mother, or, more precisely, the superlative mother, the "mother
of all mothers":

> daily experience of Caribbean or African speech . . . establishes another
> unique regime: that of the power and the love of the grandparents,
> particularly of the grandmother, often perceived and defined as the
> depository and matrix of the memory of the family, the social group, and
> the community. She would transcend, furthermore, the archetype of the
> mother, according to Jung, since she is of the universe of goddesses and
> gods. She is, in fact, the mother of the mother and, based on that, the
> grandest, that is to say, the *grand* mother who can within herself reunite

positive knowledge (wisdom) and negative knowledge (sorcery). On the one hand, she would incarnate all the formulas of power and their fabulous and mysterious virtues. On the other hand, through the "joke relationship" ... she signifies under the sign of play the materialization of a smooth continuity. Based upon this, the speech of the grandmother is a re-actualization of what was and what will be again ... the reign of the grandmother is the other side of the presence of the father (false or true, it matters little) whose power is questioned in the smile and the memory of the grandmother. (77–78, Mudimbe's emphasis)

Mudimbe concludes his essay without elaborating on how a writer is to submit to the reign of the grandmother, or how readers are to read from within her discursive field. Presumably, despite his acknowledgment of Miller's concern over the "deafening silence" of African women writing in French prior to 1976, Mudimbe is not really insisting on hearing the mother's voice "in her own words" through the works of African women writers—itself a risky project whose pitfalls I will shortly discuss. Rather, Mudimbe seems to imply that the "matrix of memory" is the equivalent of "African orature," which Chinweizu, et al. claim "is important to [the] enterprise of decolon-izing African literature for the important reason that it is the incontestable reservoir of the values, sensibilities, esthetics, and achievements of tradi-tional African thought and imagination" (2). If this matrix is the site of decolonization and liberation from the false father, however, the impassioned call by Kenyan writer Ngũgĩ wa Thiong'o for African writers to write in their own African languages is the most forceful and direct demand made by any critic for the rejection of that putative and punitive father and the em-bracement of the nurturing tones of the mother tongue.

In *Decolonizing the Mind: The Politics of Language in African Literature*, Ngugi raises issues that go beyond the plight of the individualized writer-as-artist-confronting-the-father. He perceives that the obstacles presented by the discursive reign of the "false father" do not merely hinder a writer's ability to establish "his" authority and identity but are deeply rooted in colonial strategies for controlling entire populations: "The domination of a people's language by the languages of the colonising nations was crucial to the domination of the mental universe of the colonised" (16). His advocation of the use of vernacular languages by writers of African literatures reflects an understanding of the role of literature and the educational infrastructure in constructing knowledge about oneself and the world:

So the written language of a child's upbringing in the school became divorced from his spoken language at home. There was often not the slightest relationship between the child's written world, which was also the language of his schooling, and the world of his immediate environment in the family and the community ... This resulted in the disassociation of the sensibility of that child from his natural and social environment, what we might call colonial alienation. (17)

It should also be stressed that Ngũgĩ's demand for the use of African languages as literary languages is not an attempt to return to an imaginarily pure language and time, but recognizes that African nations are deeply implicated in global cultural and economic structures. He is concerned with making literary works directly accessible to the African working class: those whose mental decolonization and subsequent mobilization can contribute the most to effect the political and economic decolonization of African nations. Finally, he recognizes that African languages are not static repositories of ancient and unchanging traditions, but dynamic and fluid media for human communication.

But whether based on an imagined retreat to a notion of an uncorrupted past or an advance into a future shaped by the mobilization of African peasants and workers, a call for the embracement of "the mother" overlooks a hard-learned lesson from those who have also been confronted with a "false father." The reification of the mother tongue or the mother as the "depository and matrix of memory" is not a fond and flattering caress but a deadly act of appropriation.

What I, a feminist, found striking in the passage I use for an epigraph is the absence of women from Ngũgĩ's roster of European writers who have worked to make their languages "matter." While Ngũgĩ may have intended his rhetoric to evoke in his audience a sense of the grandeur and sweep of human agency in the development of "philosophy, science, technology and all the other areas of human creative endeavours," it evokes in me the exclusion of women from such projects. It is not an exclusion that can be rectified by the kind of inclusion—on our own terms in our own language—that Ngũgĩ is arguing is possible for and, indeed, required of African writers. While one may hope that Ngũgĩ's seemingly unconscious reference to "the African child" as male may not be indicative of the future, educational statistics for African nations—where education is seldom compulsory or free and girls are overwhelmingly slighted in the allocation of scarce family resources—it may harbinger a parallel gender gap for the African literary tradition Ngũgĩ seeks to establish. It must not be forgotten that literacy even in one's own language demands formal education.

Even though Ngũgĩ's project of decolonization ultimately seeks to transform the neo-colonial political and economic basis of African nations, the utopian goal of making literature in one's "mother tongue" accessible to everyone through universal literacy nevertheless risks compliance with European epistemological hegemony at an even more profound level of consciousness. The exclusion of women from the project of making their languages matter, which is a historical fact of European literary and philosophical history and which seems to bode ill for the African literary history that Ngugi envisions, is an exclusion inscribed into the very *matrix* [Lat. < breeding-animal < *mater*, mother] of *material* [Lat. *materia* < *mater*, mother], i.e. written, language. The very authority that makes a language "matter" [Lat. *materia* < *mater*, mother] arises from its appropriation of vernacular "mother tongues" for the creation of literary languages. As Sandra M. Gilbert and Susan Gubar note, "European male writers have, since the High Middle Ages, been deeply involved in a struggle into (and with) the vernacular, a project which has continually forced them to usurp and transform the daily speech of women and children so as to make it into a suitable instrument for (cultivated) male art" (252).

Ngũgĩ implies that the replacement of colonial languages with African languages would entail a reenactment of the transformation in Europe of literary media from Learned Latin to vernacular languages. Such a comparison is constructive, because in calling for the technologizing of the African word, Ngũgĩ is advocating a process that will, if effective, alter African vernaculars as radically as the European vernaculars were transformed by their Renaissance reconstruction into literary languages. I would like to look more closely at this process via a narrative that recounts its historical development, while simultaneously retelling the historical narrative, attempting to point to some of its hidden centers.

The role served by European languages today in Africa is very similar to the role served by Learned Latin for over ten centuries in Europe. The language of written discourse—and political and economic power—was completely separate from the everyday vernaculars, while access to it was rigidly controlled by the social and political structures whose interests it served. Latin was the language of the controlling religious institution, of law, and of all textual knowledge. While access was largely determined by membership in hereditary castes, women were categorically prevented from participating in its development and deployment. It was, as oral theorist Walter Ong puts it, a "sex-linked language," chirographically controlled by men, as indeed, were almost all of the great writing systems of roughly the same era: Rabbinic Hebrew, Classical Arabic, Sanskrit, Classical Mandarin, and Byzantine Greek (114). But in its operation as a language of power, the sanctioned barriers were necessarily breached—in both directions—and the interanimation of this dominant, unitary language with the local vernaculars had a variety of effects.

On the one hand, the forms of "objective" knowledge—philosophy, science, and technology—that Ngugi praises were, as Ong points out, in fact made possible by the same kind of disassociation between the languages of school and home that Ngũgĩ terms "colonial alienation":

Learned Latin was a striking exemplification of the power of writing for isolating discourse and of the unparalleled productivity of such isolation. Writing ... has served to separate and distance the knower from the known and thus to establish objectivity. It has been suggested that Learned Latin effects even greater objectivity by establishing knowledge in a medium insulated from the emotion-charged depths of one's mother tongue, thus reducing interference from the human lifeworld and making possible the exquisitely abstract world of medieval scholasticism and of the new mathematical modern science which followed on the scholastic experience. Without Learned Latin, it appears that modern science would have got under way with greater difficulty, if it had got under way at all. (113–114)

Ong thus sees the power of Learned Latin in the objectification made possible by its separation from maternal languages. While Latin gets the credit for its powers of objectivity, *both* languages are needed: the vernacular language for domestic purposes and Learned Latin for the marketplace of commerce and ideas. The history and meaning of the term "vernacular" is, in this regard, significant; as Ivan Illich shows, *vernaculum* was a Roman juridical term that indicated "the inverse of a commodity"; it was used to designate "things not destined for the marketplace, but that are for home use only" (68).

On the other hand, the presence of different languages for different uses created a polyglossia in which a struggle over the power of the word subjected the authority of the unitary—Latin—word to a continual process of deconstructive *de*-objectification. M. M. Bakhtin explores most fully this process. Basing his analysis on the written forms that materially represent this polyglossia, Bakhtin shows how the parodic-travestying forms "liberated the object from the power of language in which it had become entangled as if in a net; they destroyed the homogenizing power of myth over language; they freed consciousness from the power of the direct word, destroyed the thick walls that had imprisoned consciousness . . ." (60). The interanimation between languages is instrumental in liberating the individual consciousness from the tyranny of monoglossia: "Only polyglossia fully frees the consciousness from the tyranny of its own language and its own myth of language" (61).

Though we have no access to the "consciousness" of the women of this time, particularly since they were not among those who committed their polyglossic speech to writing in the early forms of novelistic discourse that are Bakhtin's object of study, we can infer that their documented participation in the parodic and travestying folk and holiday merrymaking as "unruly women" who reversed gender roles, set up "women's courts," and participated in licentious masquerades, while arguably serving to reinforce the dominant structures, at least provided channels for liberation from linguistic impositions dictated by class and gender.[1] While women's behavior during non-holiday times was circumscribed by custom and law, as, indeed, was the behavior of most members of medieval society, their polyglossia, which distinguished between the language of power and their own vernaculars, may have prevented them from internalizing and reifying the structures of power.

The widespread appropriation of vernacular dialects by the emerging middle class throughout European during the Renaissance to create national literary languages instituted a change in this polyglossic consciousness, eventually leading to the monoglossia that Bakhtin contends is characteristic of language today. The shift to national languages was not a smooth one. Entailing a great deal more than a mere alphabetic transcribing of spoken vernaculars, the creation of national languages sought to resolve the multiple and conflicting tensions inherent in the political, economic, and gender stakes that any struggle over language—and identity—entails. These tensions are embodied in a famous narrative related by Caxton in his introduction to the first printed translation of Vergil's *Aeneid*, published in 1490.[2] As the first publisher of texts in English, Caxton was faced most directly with the mundane but crucial decisions to be made in the task of technologizing the word:

> For we englysshe men / ben born vnder the domynacyon of the mone. whiche is neuer stedfaste / but euer wauerynge / wexynge one season / and waneth & dyscreaseth another season / And that comyn englysshe that is spoken in one shyre varyeth from a nother. In so moche that in my dayes happened that certayn marchauntes were in a shippe in tamyse for to haue sayled ouer the see into zelande / and for lacke of wynde thei taryed atte forlond. and wente to lande for to refreshe them And one of theym named sheffelde a mercer cam in to an hows and axed for mete. and specyally he axyd after eggys And the good wyf answerde. that she coule speke no frenshe. And the marchaunt was angry. for he also coude speke no frenshe. but wold haue hadde egges / and she vnderstode hym not / And thenne at last a nother sayd that he wolde haue eyren / then the good wyf sayd that she vnderstod hym wel / Loo what sholde a man in thyse dyes now wryte, egges or eyren / certaynly it is harde to playse euery man / by cause of dyuersite & chaunge of langage.

The first observation that can be made from this narrative highlights the number and fluidity of varieties of English whose "dyuersity & chaunge" dramatically slowed after 1476 with the printing press both inciting and arbitrating a true fight to the finish between dialects that had coexisted as a constant reminder of the arbitrariness of the sign: the "marchaunt" and the "good wyf" did, eventually come to understand each other after an exchange that must have taken place at a metalinguistic level of discourse. But the printing press meant that tension must be resolved by the selection of a particular dialect to be the one that is transformed into a "grapholect"—a transdialectical dialect—to become the universally understood standard.

Less easily perceived is the economic basis underlying the need for such a universal standard. Pointing out that his reading is the first to comment on the economic implications of this passage, Colin MacCabe observes that the "establishment of capitalist forms of production in England at this time is crucially dependent on the dissemination of a national language which is the precondition of a national market, and Caxton's little story eloquently demonstrates how crucial language is to the process of buying and selling" (4). Caxton eventually settled on the southern variety of English used during the fifteenth century in the burgeoning national economic center of London.

Indeed, the replacement of the vernaculars by a "market" national language signaled the rationalization of the market economy as well as the nation as a political unit: a fully rationalized market language best fully rationalizes a market economy, and vice versa. The way these economic and political factors impinge on one another in linguistic power stakes are still reflected in notions of "correct English." To a large extent one's position in the class structure is determined by one's economic wealth and indexed by one's speech, whether it conforms to the "universal" standard of the metropolis or is an "abnormal" localized variant.

Finally, but not least important, gender politics are also embodied in the struggle that takes place in this passage. In the war of words, the man with the name and trade—"sheffelde a mercer"—wins; the anonymous and generic "good wyf" loses. Caxton, apparently, solved his dilemma by deciding to "playse" sheffelde rather than the good wyf, and today we all speak of his "egges" rather than her "eyren."

This narrative, however, also serves to remind us that it is not appropriation of the *language* that women spoke, as if men and women spoke different languages that belonged to them as property—as Ong points out, it was print "that created a new sense of the private ownership of word" (131). Nor should the "mother tongue" or the vernacular domestic space be essentialized as feminine; rather, *the feminization of vernaculars as mother tongues is a radical component in the monolgossic ideological-verbal belief system that emerges with the appropriation of vernaculars to literary languages, a system within which all fields of objectified knowledge are feminized.* The "matrix-as-mother-of-all-mothers" does not appear outside of this monoglossic discourse that has been coded in advance. It is of significance, however, that it is not feminization per se, but motherization—*mater*ialization, the productive and procreative aspect of "woman"—that is appropriated to the service of engendering capital and productive meaning, an appropriation that renders women's procreative powers as "merely" originary, ahistorically trapped within nature, which too is feminized, presented to be acted upon.

It is this procreative aspect engendered from the conceptualization and appropriation of the Mother with a capital "M" that contributes to the objectification of language. Ong uses the subject's relation to the object to distinguish between the oral perception of "Man" as the "navel of the world" and the literate perception of the world as "something laid out before [Man's] eyes . . . ready to be explored" (73). As in the case of such binary dichotomies, the "difference" produced in this comparison is the opposite side of the same coin, for, in the latter instance, Man indeed is at the center, the center of perception: the position that provides the objective perspective by which the object is endowed with meaning. To evoke a "women's perspective" immediately situates perspective as masculine, for the need to evoke a women's—different—perspective signals that women have a "sub-jective"—partial, interested—viewpoint rather than the only authorized viewpoint: the objective one. Objectivity is constituted as precisely that which is not given to those whom it objectifies. The authority, the power, of objectivity finds its basis in the materiality of the thus embodied others who are always subject to their physical condition. Thus the "silencing" of women is not merely a condition of limiting their access to means of education, but central to the giving "voice" to the invisible author.

What makes language a "material" thing is not so much its commitment to print—though clearly the perception that one's spoken word is committed to a visual field is of significance—as the creation of national literatures "dialogically" engendered via the forcible appropriation of the feminized mother tongues by the father's pen. This genderized aspect is repressed by much of masculine literary and linguistic theory even while the theories outline the dynamics by which it operates. Bakhtin writes:

> in the process of literary creation, languages interanimate each other and objectify precisely that side of one's own (and of the other's) language *that pertains to its world view*, its inner form, the axiologically accentuated system inherent in it. For the creating literary consciousness, existing in a field illuminated by another's language ... what stands out is precisely that which makes language concrete and which makes its world view ultimately untranslatable, that is, precisely the *style of the language as totality*. (62, Bakhtin's emphasis)

The "other" to which Bakhtin consciously refers is a *written* body of language that is not one's maternal tongue: his example refers to the production of Roman literary language in the light of Greek literary language. In this sense, the "other" appears to be the "false father" of literary tradition described at the beginning of this essay, leading to the inference that national literatures arise primarily in a context of situations of linguistic imposition. If such is the case, then the false father is even more instrumental than the authentic father in the process of engendering literary language upon mother tongues. However the productive "other" that creates objectivity is not the Greek other (for Romans), or the Latin other (for Europeans), or the European other (for Africans), but the (M)Other tongue itself, which is "othered" at the moment it is seized and made available for use outside the home, in dialectic battle against the father's monoglossic hegemony.

The power of monoglossia is the power of objectivity internalized; it dictates that in order to "speak" productively, with power, one must "assume the position" from which the world-view is comprehensible (graspable, seizable) and before which all fields of knowledge appear prone. While the "objective" position is constructed in European monoglossia as the place of the privileged white male, any individual can take it, even individuals who are categorically silenced by it; yet it compels them to see and speak themselves as other: both women and the neo-colonial writer who use that monoglossic language.

The similarity of their situation does not make them allies, however, for both have something to gain by taking the position that "others" the other.

Euro-American women have been complicitous in their own othering as a result of the benefits gained by objectifying the "ethnic" other. Some of these benefits include the material advantages afforded by colonial exploitation and the power that accrues to women who participate in more subtle neo-colonial practices, such as portraying "Third World" women as suffering from patriarchy and in need of their help to develop educated Western consciousness. And a project of decolonizing of the mind by embracing "the mother" in the creation of national literatures is a trap that will at best ensnare women.

Indeed, the tenuous position of women writers in relation to emerging canons of African literature is instructive. Called upon to represent the African woman's point of view, to "speak" for the silent African woman, African women writers are in effect silenced as being "not representative" when they don't subordinate themselves to the ahistoric, generic models of women dictated by patriarchal images inscribed within national languages and literatures. Femi Ojo-Ade advocates that readers turn to women writers because "only women can best represent their interests in society. Only a mother knows what it is to bear a child" yet simultaneously excuses writers like Buchi Emecheta (who had, incidentally, borne five children prior to writing her many novels) "from the list of African authors," declaring that "her viewpoint ought not to be turned into a war cry for every African woman" (21) because it is formed from painful personal—and therefore non-representative—experience with patriarchy. It is the impossibility of charting a course for women's self-representation through this Scylla and Charybdis of appropriation and silencing that leads Gayatri Chakravorty Spivak to declare that "the subaltern cannot speak."

This is an inescapable trap *if* this monoglossic world-view has in fact permeated every aspect of modern life. Bakhtin clearly concludes that it has:

> In modern times the functions of parody are narrow and unproductive. We live, write and speak today in a world of free and democratized language, the complex and multi-leveled hierarchy of discourses, form, images, styles that used to permeate the entire system of official language and linguistic consciousness was swept away by the linguistic revolutions of the Renaissance. European literary languages—French, German, English—came into being while this hierarchy was in the process of being destroyed. (71)

This perspective of language and history, however, contains another repressed "other," for obviously not *all* of "us" live, write, and speak in a world of democratized language; the imperialist formations that emerged in relation to European economic, cultural, and literary developments in the Renaissance and post-Renaissance period seem to continue the dialect Bakhtin describes, with the "colonized" responding to the centrifugal unitary languages of power with their own deconstructive, polyglossic linguistic practices. Many of these practices take the form of writing. One early, non-African, example is the twelve-hundred-page "letter" to King Philip III of Spain written in a mixture of Quechua and non-standard Spanish by Felipe Guaman Poma de Ayala in 1613. Entitled *The First New Chronicle and Good Government*, the manuscript, consisting of almost eight hundred pages of written text and four hundred drawings, combines European pictorial representation with Andean spatial symbolism as well as the two languages to create what Mary Louise Pratt calls an "extraordinary intercultural tour de force" that argued powerfully against Spanish colonial practices in the Andes (34). Examined from the Bakhtinian perspective that considers the "other" to be no more than the culturally different monologic precursor, such a document can be considered as a continuation rather than a disruption of the dialectic of the European dialogic imagination. And from this perspective African novels written in African languages as well as African novels written in English but which appropriate vernacular idioms can both be contained in single historical narrative.

In fact, Ngũgĩ's insistence that African writers are bound by their calling to create literary languages is based on the assumption that Africa is historically bound to recapitulate European material and philosophical development. This can only be the case, however, if "Africa" as a place and an idea were not already profoundly implicated in European material and philosophical history in the way that Woman—or Mother—is implicated in the notion of Man. Since the first European ship rounded Cape Bojador in 1434, Africa has been the repressed center of Europe both in "body" and "mind." The centuries of economic exploitation of Africa and Africans for labor, resources, and land that followed were instrumental to the "development" of European economic institutions and material culture. As European languages materialized through their literatures, they inscribed into their very matrices a virulent sexism and racism which worked to consolidate and rationalize the economic gains of colonialism and which provided the other to the European self.

Similarly, as Africa supplied the image of European civilized identity via what Michelle Rosaldo calls "the image of ourselves undressed," so too it supplied the logocentric notion of the "other" language behind its own language-identity: orality. Postulated as *the* monoglossic, originary (feminized, mater-ized) presence standing prior to and in opposition to writing, this notion of primitive orality instead reflects the dream of wholeness behind written languages. Such a notion of original linguistic presence lurks behind Bakhtin's concept of monoglossia, which he attributes to both pre- and post-polyglossic historic periods. Jacques Derrida has deconstructed this logo-centric notion of orality as, to paraphrase Rosaldo, the image of our language undressed. But, while the Derridean conclusion announces not that the emperor—speech—has no clothes but rather that every language is always already dressed—is always already written (perhaps an even more deeply Eurocentric claim than the difference postulated between orality and literacy)—another approach to take might consider what the consequences of this insight mean for speakers of vernacular languages that have not been deeply committed to writing.

The theoretical critique of logocentrism is in fact confirmed by cultural critics: the concept of a pure orality that encloses its speakers in an envelope of mother-tongue monoglossia, while based on models of small-scale, "primitive" societies that share a fixed language and identity, has never been descriptive of such societies but was constructed on paper and in the Euro-American imagination as part of the combined civilizing/domesticizing mission. In relation to African languages and ethnicity, Robert Thornton shows how first missionaries then anthropologists ignored widespread poly-lingualism and fluid networks of identity in their consolidation of multiple dialects into unified languages/ethnic groups such as "the Zulu" in order to facilitate first religious proselytizing—enabling missionaries to standardize grapholects into which the Bible could be translated—and later ethno-graphical objectification—establishing a fixed object of study that could be described, "known," and thus controlled. Such representations of "primit-ive" nationalism were in turn consumed by readers at home, facilitating the reification of the emerging bourgeois national formations in a process of imaginary community building described by Benedict Anderson in *Imagined Communities*. Anderson demonstrates the degree to which print capitalism has been instrumental in the construction of boundaries of national and linguistic identity and the ideology of monolingualism itself.

Even today in West Africa, multilingualism in indigenous vernaculars as well as in European languages remains overwhelmingly the norm. Studies of African multilingualism are few, but in 1966 a linguistic survey of a Ghanaian village with a population just over two thousand found that over 70 percent of the inhabitants reported competency in three or more languages, less than 4 percent were monolingual, and over 80 different mother tongues were spoken in the one village (Berry 324–325). The multilingualism of Buchi Emecheta, who says she chose to write in a language "that is not my first nor my second or third but my fourth" (*Head* 2), is fairly typical.

Vernaculars do not, like languages, denote a fixed national or even ethnic identity—unless they are called upon to do so.[3] Contrary to monoglossic ideology, oral vernaculars do not encapsulate their speakers in a monoglossic envelope of pure presence: vernaculars are more susceptible, not less, to subtle and profound fluidity across time, space, and speaker, with speakers understanding a variety of vernaculars and having the ability, indeed, the responsibility, to keep their vernaculars alive by subjecting them to constant change. Vernaculars are a dynamic medium of communication in which speakers of different varieties, like "sheffelde the mercer" and the "good wyf", are required to constantly negotiate meaning at the metalinguistic level. While oral speakers do perhaps exhibit, as Ong argues, a consciousness that is "different" from the literate consciousness, their "failure" to objectify themselves and their insistence instead on making the object "speak" to them can be perceived as a refusal rather than a lack. Monoglossia, like logocentrism, is a product of the union of the father's pen and the mother's tongue. It is "our" burden. To project it onto "prehistoric"—"African"—times is to naturalize it as primitive, natural, other: as (M)Other.

While Africa was central to European history, however, in many ways Europe was marginal to Africa; Europe's foibles were observed and learned from, and the persistent orality of African vernaculars could conceivably be a rejection of the technology of writing, which, despite being a part of the consciousness of African people since the eras of Egyptian kingdoms and Islamic empires, has only been voluntarily adapted in sub-Saharan Africa in localized instances and for limited purposes.[4] European languages have not exerted the same kind of power over African vernaculars—or in the same kinds of ways—that Learned Latin exerted over European vernaculars; on the one hand, in the African context such control was and is perceived as externally imposed onto a self-sustaining social order rather than a part of an indigenous hierarchical social structure, and, on the other hand, Learned Latin was at the time no one's maternal language.

The polyglossia that exists in Africa today, which is polyglossic across vernaculars as well as between vernaculars and European languages, is an extremely complex one whose implications are not easily determined by comparison with European experience, so it is difficult to predict to what extent the process of appropriation of vernacular languages to literary languages will recapitulate European experience. Already it is apparent that similar struggles over the selection of particular vernaculars or dialects to become national languages are taking place; Christopher Miller notes that Ngũgĩ's goal of making African vernaculars into literary languages will not free the linguistic problem from other legacies of colonial practice: "Ngũgĩ's Gikuyu, as it happens, is the language of the dominant group in Kenya; his choice of Gikuyu may represent liberation in a Gikuyu context, but to others it may have a different implication" (83). The technologizing of the African word is subject to the same political conflicts that Caxton agonized over, but the decisions left to the owner of a printing press are in the context of today's world fraught with greater stakes: Senegalese writer Ousmane Sembene turned to film to make his work more accessible to a non-reading audience, yet his film *Ceddo* was banned in Senegal because the spelling of the title did not conform to the nationally standardized Wolof orthography. It is not within the scope of this chapter to cover all of the possible economic and political ramifications that may come to bear on the project of creating a literature in African languages, but one area to consider is whether or not such a task can be accomplished without another "other" to materially exploit.

Even if the material hindrances to widespread literacy are overcome, however, success in transforming African vernaculars into literary languages risks institutionalizing a monoglossia that will not decolonize the mind so much as patriarchize it. Nnu Ego, a character in Buchi Emecheta's *The Joys of Motherhood* makes a polyglossic distinction between vernacular speech and unitary language, calling English the language that "only pen and not mouth could really talk" (179). Nnu Ego is in this context swearing that *all* her children, "even the girls," will go to school to learn to read that language, but as the narrative continues it becomes apparent that financial constraints and day-to-day realities dim that resolve and only the boys are actually sent to school; they learn to speak the language that only pen can talk, a language that honors the Mother only as an idea—only in death. Because her sons speak a language that postulates her maternal value as generic and that does not recognize her voice, Nnu Ego suffers a devastating silencing that is repeated thematically in other works by women writers of African descent and put into practice by masculinist critics who would deny them the right to speak "as an African." Nnu Ego's formula, however, also evinces an awareness that it is possible for the mouth, and not just the pen, to "talk"—to speak in a way that frees the mind from the authoritarian pen of both the European and the African fathers (and sons): *all* such Fathers are, as are all Mothers, false.

Constrained by the conventions of the essay form which demand I take and argue a position, I may be assumed in this chapter to be advocating against the use of African languages to write African literature; however any kind of dictation of writing practices—proscriptive or prescriptive—is not only abhorrent but useless. My agenda for positive action is rather to attend to polyglossic practices informed by vernaculars, which only tongue can speak and which emphasize the importance of the audience and reception practices over the object, the "text." Guaman Poma was in effect silent for three and a half centuries because his letter, addressed and delivered to a monoglossic court, was never "received": there was no one on the other side of the Atlantic to hear him "polyaurally." Pratt points out that "it was not till the late 1970's as positivist reading habits gave way to interpretive studies and colonial elitisms to postcolonial pluralism, that Western scholars found ways of reading Guaman Poma's *New Chronicle and Good Government*" (34). African texts, especially those by women, are also beginning to be heard in a polyaural way that challenges appropriative practices—whether in the interests of African nationalism or in the interests of feminism—because these "hearings" cannot resolve into a single, objective, perspective. Though Emecheta may write in English, her other languages can be heard as well in her texts by those who read them "polyaurally." Certainly Emecheta's works have spoken to women in a way that is silent to men such as Ojo-Ade, who can only monologically "hear" the universal, naturalized experience of women. Perhaps, most of all it is an audience who refuses to consume a work as a univocal cultural artefact that keeps alive polyglossia and its ongoing deconstruction of the power of unitary language.

Finally and importantly, this audience need not be "literate," nor does the "text" need to be written. To believe that creative human endeavors—or deconstructive practices—become fully realized only in the context of widespread literacy and the market-based national economy needed to finance it is to be complicitous with the monoglossic assumption that one only "speaks" if one writes, is published, distributed, and read. Writing is only one, though highly privileged, scene of transcultural encounter, of polyglossic and deconstructive practice. This is especially true today in an era of an increasingly globalized culture that is technologically informed by "secondarily oral" media. The difficulties that Guaman Poma encountered in finding an audience for his text have been more successfully overcome by Amerindians in Brazil who have begun using video technology to record oral treaties as well as evidence of those treaties' violations.

In addition, reception practices in relation to these new technologies may be very different from the "norms" established by Euro-American reading practice. For example, audience interaction during a movie—talking out loud to the screen and to other audience members, which parallels the interactive context of oral storytelling, can be very disturbing to moviegoers used to "reading" a film like a book in a private, individualized act of cultural consumption, and the threat the experience poses to such consumers' way of knowing—to their very identity—is often defused by attributing it to the unsophisticated behavior of people for whom the medium is "still" a novelty. However, such radical "non-reading" practices, which shift attention from a text-based to an audience-based experience, in fact demand new categories of understanding and interpretation—or even shatter such categories altogether. As our mass culture becomes increasingly secondarily oral as well as "multicultural," these contestatory, non-reading practices may play a part in more localized vernacular struggles over the meaning of cultural objects closer to home.

But even beyond video and audio technologies, which, like the printing press, produce material artefacts, we can also look to more ephemeral popular cultural practices for avenues of decolonization *and* depatriarchization. One may consider polyglossic many practices that do not contribute to the creation of a written literary tradition, for example "traditional" festivals, such as the Yoruba *Gèlèdé*, with its parodies of notebook-bearing anthropologists; cloth designs that incorporate spark plugs and electric fans; and hairstyles named after NASA's most recent space shot. Idioms, practices, and performances that depend more directly on interaction with their polyglot audience resist capture and containment by the centrifugal factors that seek to bind national literatures to a monologic viewpoint. Just as much as these polyglossic vernacular practices continue to deconstruct such a mindset, African "mother tongues" are *not* bound to matter.

NOTES

1 See Natalie Zemon Davis for a discussion of these practices.
2 This text is a fortuitous one as well, for it was commissioned by Augustus and written as a conscious literary appropriation of Greek originary oral epics in the services of creating a Roman national epic and identity. Its "august" orderliness

was satirized in Ovid's *Metamorphosis*, which contrasts images of change, fluidity, and divine fallibility with the political and social stability Vergil was seeking to effect through literary representation.

3   Warfare, for example, provides a compelling motivation for ethnic identification. The ethnic categories created by anthropologists take on a life of their own in the context of modern African politics: Ayodele Ogundipe observes that during the Nigerian civil war, speaking a language was not enough to identify someone as belonging to that group; Yoruba soldiers at roadblocks required people to recite Yoruba tongue twisters to demonstrate native linguistic ability. Thornton notes that early anthropological studies often focused on groups whose identity was temporarily consolidated by the stress of warfare – circumstances which were decontextualized in the studies so as to render the findings "timeless."

4   see Emmanuel N. Obiechina for a discussion of a variety of writing systems adapted by both pre- and post-colonial African societies.

WORKS CITED

Anderson, Benedict. *Imagined Communities: Reflections on the Origins and Spread of Nationalism*. London: Verso, 1984.

Bakhtin, M. M. *The Dialogic Imagination*. Ed. Michael Holquist. Trans. Caryl Emerson and Michael Holquist. Austin: University of Texas Press, 1981.

Berry, Jack. "The Madina Project, Ghana (Language Attitudes in Madina)." *Language Use and Social Change*. Ed. W. H. Whitely. London: Oxford University Press, 1971, 318–333.

Chinweizu, Onwuchekwa Jemie, and Ihechukwu Madubuike. *Toward the Decolonization of African Literature*. Washington, DC: Howard University Press, 1983.

Davis, Natalie Zemon. *Society and Culture in Early Modern France*. Stanford: Stanford University Press, 1975.

Emecheta, Buchi. *Head Above Water*. London: Fontana, 1986.

——. *The Joys of Motherhood*. New York: Braziller, 1979.

Gilbert, Sandra M. and Susan Gubar. *No Man's Land: The Place of the Woman Writer in the Twentieth Century. Volume 1: The War of the Words*. New Haven: Yale University Press, 1987.

Illich, Ivan. *Gender*. New York: Pantheon, 1982.

MacCabe, Colin. "Righting English or Does Spelling Matter?" Collins English Dictionary Annual Lecture, December 5, 1984.

Miller, Christopher. "Ethnicity and Ethics in the Criticism of Black African Literature." *South Atlantic Quarterly* 87.1 (Winter 1988): 75–108.

Mudimbe, V. Y. "Letters of Reference." *Transition* 53 (1991): 62–78.

Ngũgĩ wa Thiong'o. *Decolonizing the Mind: The Politics of Language in African Literature*. London: James Currey, 1986.

Obiechina, Emmanuel N. *Language and Theme: Essays on African Literature*. Washington, DC: Howard University Press, 1990.

Ogundipe, Ayodele. "Yoruba Tongue Twisters." *African Folklore*. Ed. Richard Dorson. Bloomington: Indiana University Press, 1979, 211–220.

Ojo-Ade, Femi. "Of Culture, Commitment, and Construction: Reflections on African Literature." *Transition* 53 (1991): 4–24.

Ong, Walter. *Orality and Literacy: The Technologizing of the Word*. London: Methuen, 1982.

Pratt, Mary Louise. "Arts of the Contact Zone." *Profession* 91: 33–40.

Rosaldo, Michelle, Z. "The Use and Abuse of Anthropology: Reflections on Feminism and Cross-Cultural Understanding." *Signs* 5. 3 (Spring 1980): 389–417.

Spivak, Gayatri Chakravorty. "Can the Subaltern Speak?" *Marxism and the*

Interpretation of Culture. Ed. Cary Nelson and Lawrence Grossberg. Urbana: University of Illinois Press, 1988. 271–313.

Thornton, Robert. "Narrative Ethnology in Africa, 1850–1920: The Creation and Capture of an Appropriate Domain for Anthropology." *Man* 18 (1983): 502–520.

8   MotherTongues and childless women

The construction of "Kenyan" "womanhood"

Celeste Fraser Delgado

Two years ago few people—either African, Asian, or European inside Kenya, or any race outside it—thought that the new nation could be successfully born in 1963; and many others who supposed that its birth soon afterwards was inevitable assumed it would be still-born, or that within a few months of its emergence from the womb of Mother Africa it would die from chronic internal disorders. Now this book is being published on Independent Kenya's first birthday; and the infant nation is hale and hearty, with every prospect of many happy returns of the day.[1]

The Right Honorable Malcolm MacDonald, former colonial official, gave this dubious welcome to the "infant" independent Kenya in 1964, in his introduction to the collected speeches of the new Prime Minister, Jomo Kenyatta. The health of the newly decolonized nation seems to take the Right Honorable observer from the first world by uneasy surprise, but he comes to good humor at last, noting that Kenya is, after all, if not exactly "still born," still only a child. MacDonald's wishes mark a transition in Kenya not so much from subjugated colony to sovereign state, as from direct colonial rule to indirect and often competing international influences manipulating and manipulated by the post-colonial regimes of Kenyatta and his successor, Daniel Arap Moi. MacDonald's benevolent infantilization of the newly independent nation stands in tension with the images of the "Motherland" used by Kenyatta and Moi in an attempt to legitimate their authoritarian regimes. Substituting "Mother Kenya" for "Mother Africa," Kenyatta and Moi positioned themselves as "father" presiding over a nation of "children."[2] Despite their paternal position, Kenyatta and Moi's efforts at control of the Kenyan populace coincided with one instrument of international influence. We hear echoes of that instrument in MacDonald's lengthy digression into a metaphoric progress through miscarriage, stillbirth, and infant mortality: population control.

The technology of population control, promoted by the governments of both Kenyatta and Moi, limits the resonance of fertility associated with the image of the Motherland. Indeed, motherhood as metaphor and practice in Kenya serves as a site of cultural contestation for a number of actors:

international donors who promote population planning; the political regimes who mandate an officially delimited Motherland; revolutionaries who recur to the Motherland as a point of origin before colonial and post-colonial domination; women for whom these preceding discourses, whether or not they participate in them, will reverberate against their own practice either in mothering children or in attempting to control their own fertility so as to delay or defer childbirth. Using a modified version of Homi K. Bhabha's concept of "dissemiNation" as a tool, I will attempt to wedge apart the conflicting discourses of Kenya as nation condensed into the concept of Motherhood. Departing from the official and technologically supported delineations of Kenya, I will consider *Maitu Njugira (Mother, Sing for Me)* produced by Ngũgĩ wa Thiong'o and the Kamiriithu Community Center in 1982 as a counternarrative of the conflation of Motherhood and the nation. This analysis will serve as a grid, allowing me to move back in time to produce a reading of the contradictions transversing Rebeka Njau's 1975 novel *Ripples in the Pool* as a narration of the nation that, written from the positionality of post-colonial Kenyan womanhood, cannot cohere.

This is not a story of Kenya. This is the story of the stories of Kenya, as I have heard them from the outside, from the so called "developed" world. This is not a story of Kenyan womanhood. This is an interrogation of the categories "woman" and "nation" as produced crossculturally by international development agencies, feminist discourse, and anti-colonial struggles.

In his article "DissemiNation: Time, Narrative, and the Margins of the Modern Nation," Homi K. Bhabha redefines the modern nation as a construction premised not on the existence and exclusion of an Other as in Enlightenment thinking, but rather as a "narrative strategy—and an apparatus of power—that ... produces a continual slippage into analogous, even metonymic, categories, like the people, minorities, or 'cultural difference' that continually overlap in the act of writing the nation."[3] If we take "Kenya" as both a narrative strategy and an apparatus of power, what role do women play in that "dissemiNation"? One chilling suggestion comes from the 1982 parliamentary debate over the legal responsibility of men for their children conceived with women other than their wives. In support of the final resolution stating that parents should "bring up daughters to be more chaste," one MP stated: "It is the woman who makes the decision. My work, as a man, is to plant the seed and quit" (Björkman 36). If men "plant the seed" that grows into the nation, then women would seem to serve as the ground upon which this writing of the nation grows.

Bhabha highlights the grounding of the concept of nation in motherhood in his modification of Derrida's deconstruction of the present as a "mother-form": "the present is no longer a mother form [read mother-tongue or mother-land] around which are gathered and differentiated the future (present) and the past (present) ... [as] a present of which the past and the future would be but modifications."[4] The dislodging of the present time of the nation from the position of "motherland" or "mothertongue" disrupts a notion of "Tradition" as a unified historical movement gathering together one people into one nation. The recurrence of "mother" in the "form," "land," and "tongue" of the one nation, suggests an operation that takes place as much within the concept of Motherhood as within Tradition or Time. Motherhood, in which the seeds of dissemiNation are sown, grounds the narrative of Tradition. Recognition of the gendered construction of the ground of Tradition/Nation permits us to substitute "Kenyan women" for "the people" as a category metonymic for Kenya as nation. Square brackets indicate this substitution into Bhabha's explication of the performative and the pedagogical strategies engaged in writing Kenya:

> [Kenyan women] must be thought in a double-time; [Kenyan women] are the historical "objects" of a nationalist pedagogy, giving the discourse an authority that is based on the pre-given or constituted historical origin or event; [Kenyan women] are also the 'subjects' of a process of signification that must erase any prior or originary presence of the nation-[Kenya-women] to demonstrate the prodigious, living principle of [Kenyan women] as that continual process by which the national life is redeemed and signified as a repeating and reproductive process.[5]

The metonomy of Motherhood has its stake in the bodies of Kenyan women. A nationalist pedagogy that posits the Motherland as origin always threatens slippage into the reproductive practices of women in Kenya. This pedagogy overlays the bodies of Kenyan women with a fiction of motherhood: a fiction of full presence, a virginal mother-form, or what the Kenyan parliament may have termed a "chaste" receptacle of seeds. At the same (in double-) time, women in Kenya must "erase" that pedagogy, performing the nation in a process of daily living that must negotiate the fictions of the nationalist pedagogy according to their own desires, the exigencies of the economy, and the conditions of reproduction in the nation.

A negotiation of the nationalist pedagogy requires a refraction of the fiction of full presence that Derrida designates as "the hymen." The hymen serves as "the false appearance of a present," "a pure medium of fiction," a "mirror" that will "of course break, but it will reflect that breaking in a fiction that remains intact."[6] We see such a break within the parliamentary resolution encouraging chastity, which relies upon a fictional Kenya in which economic constraints do not require young women to rely upon men outside their families for support. The erasure of this fiction will require a refraction of the mirror, in which Kenyan women write their own nations, redeeming and signifying national life in a plot that repositions the stake of the nation in their bodies.

These new plots will require the rewriting of not one, but at least two competing nationalist pedagogies that currently write Kenya. The concept of national pedagogy in post-colonial Kenya requires a more complicated configuration than those developed by Derrida and Bhabha in relation to the West. Far from deriving authority "based on the pre-given or constituted historical event," the nationalist pedagogy of the post-colonial regimes can only recur to the originary events of the stealing of land and the massacre of the ethnic peoples who would be called Kenyans, the imposition of colonial rule, and the ultimate betrayal of the attempted Mau Mau revolution. The "Motherland" here functions as an empty term, a screen covering a colonial past, a post-colonial present, and an uncertain future. A counterpedagogy promoted by revolutionaries recalls these events in remembrance of a prior origin, another Motherland, violated by colonial penetration. This pedagogy relies not upon the "ficiton of a pure present," but a fiction of a purified future: an imaginary of fertility. Both pedagogies come into conflict with the performance of Kenyan women as mothers, non-mothers, government officials, and revolutionaries.

The introduction of a feminist discourse of reproductive control at this juncture might be dismissed by many across the masculinist political spectrum as, in Kamari Jayawardena's words, "alienat[ing] [women] from their culture, religion and family responsibilities, on the one hand, and from the revolutionary struggles for nationalism and socialism on the other."[7] However, the politics of population/reproductive control comprise one instance of the concept of "fighting against two colonialisms" develcped in the socialist/nationalist revolution in Guinea-Bissau that "emphasizes the need for women to play an equal political, economic, and social role in both the armed struggle and the construction of the new society."[8] The fight against foreign domination depends upon a recognition of concerns often dismissed as "feminist" and therefore not indigenous to Africa, precisely because the hierarchical organization of international power works through and in the bodies of women.

As Jacqui Alexander points out, whether nationalist governments promote pronatalist policies in reaction against or population control in conjunction with international agencies, "women's wombs become the conduit of 'development.'"[9] Official policies compound difficulties women experience in asserting reproductive control within the performative context of sexual relationships with men. In the context of promoting AIDS prevention, Caroline Bledsoe provides an important study of resistance within Africa, particularly within Kenya, to condom use in particular and birth control in general. This resistance takes root in the high value placed on fertility in many African cultures, including many cultures within Kenya. Further complications arise from the economic dependency that frequently characterizes heterosexual relations. Many women have difficulty convincing male partners to use condoms "because fertility is expected, even demanded, of a viable relationship . . . Denying a man children risks a number of things, among them, that he will stop supporting her and find another woman."[10] A conflict exists between cultural expectations of fertility, the alternating political promotion of fertility or family planning, and individual desires for fertility control whether motivated economically or otherwise.[11]

Cooperation with international agencies earned the government of Kenya praise in a 1978 study sponsored by the Development Center and World Bank. Despite the Kenyan government's commitment to population control, the rate of population growth remains the highest in the world. Having dismissed the calls for a wider conception of development voiced by other nations, successive governments seem not to have quieted the protest within Kenya manifested in the resistance to the practice of population planning. This resistance stems in part from suspicions regarding the motives of international organizations in promoting population planning. As reported by David Fanthorpe, an analyst of political risk in Africa south of the Sahara for the London-based Control Risk, Ltd., suggests the structure of power that gives rise to such suspicions. Addressing an international audience of police, military, and highly placed business executives in 1983, Fanthorpe classes "a rapid rate of population growth" with the uncertain succession of a second generation of post-colonial rule and tribal antagonisms as three of "the threats to their operations which businesses face." Fanthorpe's use of metaphors, such as "Nairobi's shanty towns are becoming breeding grounds for violent crime," indicates the concern over population growth seems to have more to do with control of the populace than with development.[12] As suggested by the title of the collection featuring that warning, *The Future of Political Violence*, the danger to investment posed by population growth, tribal antagonisms, and the tenuous hold of the post-colonial status quo rests in the potential rupture of the violently contained official meaning of Kenyan national life.

Behind the multinational efforts to contain the fertility of women in Kenya lurks an impulse to "fix" the nation itself; to contain the multiple potentialities of national meanings in one easy-to-manage state open to penetration without consequence by international interests. A February 21, 1987 editorial in the *Kenya Times*, the organ of the only legal political party in Kenya, demonstrates how controlling the conception of nation as mother can facilitate the control of political opposition, calling the foundation of Ukenya (Movement for Unity and Democracy in Kenya) "yet another campaign of blatant lies aimed at besmirching their motherland's good image."[13] The push for family planning not only literally eases the repressive management of a people by limiting their numbers, but reinforces the effective delimiting of the politically available image of the "Motherland." Fanthorpe's relatively mild diagnosis of the risk of investment in Kenya recognizes the redoubled efforts by the Kenyan government at the containment of proliferation on four levels: (1) *reproductive potential* through population control; (2) *military potential* through the bolstering of Kenyan forces by the US military support in exchange for the positioning of US bases in Kenya; (3) *political potential* through the constitutional change of June 10, 1982 that made Kenya officially a one-party state; and (4) *cultural potential* through censorship, particularly the banning of all Kenyan theater and the consequent exile of playwright and novelist, Ngugi wa Thiong'o.

Maitu, Njugira (Mother, Sing for Me), a collaborative work by the villagers of the Kamiriithu Community Center and Ngũgĩ wa Thiong'o, literally staged the "performative" in a counternarration of the state's nationalist pedagogy in a production perceived as a direct threat to the Moi government. Imprisoned by Kenyatta after the production of his first collaboration with Kamiriithu, Ngũgĩ scripted their second play after his release in a symbolic gesture by Moi at his accession to the presidency. As Ingrid Björkman, a former student of Ngũgĩ's who conducted a study of the effect of this production by interviewing thirty-seven audience members of various ethnic groups and educational levels, notes:

> Manifestations of a national culture in Kenya are stifled because they would relate to a reality in which the government development policies make conditions increasingly desperate for the poor majority. Any cultural expression which can be understood by the illiterate masses is banned and its creator punished because it might motivate the people to mobilize in revolt. (48)

While both the official and the outlaw narrations figure motherhood as metonymic for the nation, *Maitu, Njugira* intends "motherland" in a very different sense than that intended by the government and its supporters.

One of the songs banned by the British in colonial times because sung by workers in preparation for rebellion, *Maitu, Njugira* inscribes within the very title the potential reproductive, military, political, and cultural proliferation that the Kenyan government would check. Literally translated as "Mother, trill *ngemi* for me," the song brings joy because the trilling of *ngemi* means welcome. At the birth of a child, five trills welcome a boy and four trills a girl. Here again Kenya as "motherland" stands in for the "infant" Kenya over whom the colonial powers attempted to retain control. However, rather than appealing to the officially delimited mother whom the post-colonial government co-opted as a check to the coming to power of the majority of Kenyans, the singers position themselves as children calling to a mother who will deliver them through revolution.

Representing their contestation of the regime's nationalist pedagogy in a play, the villagers provide an alternative pedagogy. Thus, as Björkman observes, the "characters are not individuals with psychological depth but representations of corporate social groups, such as women, collaborators, patriots, foreign rulers, workers, and peasants" (76). In making up this list, Björkman neglects the mobility of "women" across all of the former categories, collapsing the potential of "women" into their gender. The text authorizes this collapse as the women on stage represent two specific fictions of the manifestation of power in both colonial and post-colonial rule. Nyathira represents the prostitution forced upon the nation by colonialism.

In the drama, first the colonial plantation owner, then his neo-colonial African replacement, rape her. After the first rape, and according to the original draft written by Ngũgĩ after the second rape as well, Nyathira "becomes a prostitute, begins to use cosmetics, and wear western clothes" (67). The physical invasion of Nyathira's body leaves her marked with the symbols of the West. The sexual violence inflicted upon Nyathira localizes an international struggle for power. The other figure, referred to simply as "the woman" or "the pregnant woman," localizes the politics of population planning as perceived by Alexander and Fanthrope. The police brutality that meets the workers' attempt to rebel focuses particularly on the pregnant woman's capacity for reproduction, forcing her to miscarry as the police step on her stomach. The prostitute and the bereft mother form two poles of womanhood metonymic for the subjugated nation.

The action of the play transforms the dirge of the bereft mother into a cry for liberation, transforming the symbolic content of motherhood as metonym for the nation from sterility to fertility. As Ngũgĩ described the scene of mourning:

> Thunder, lightning, wind, rain. The sound of a child crying. Enter the woman who had a miscarriage. She is looking for her child, for she imagines that she delivered properly and that the child is only missing. She hears the cry of the missing child everywhere. At times she imagines she has found him. At such a moment the cry of the child ceases. The mother picks up the child. She sings one, two, or three songs. Then she realizes she is not holding the baby. She hears another cry. She rushes here and there. Finds the baby. Holds it. Sings. (66)

The bereft mother's song connects her to the motherland of *Maitu, Njugira*; the transformation of her song takes place when she delivers a new generation.

Ngũgĩ embodies the new generation in the character Kariuki, "the appointed saviour of his people" (68). Kariuki recalls the political activist J.M. Kariuki who was murdered in 1975. Ngũgĩ recalls he heard student protests at the death of organizer J.M. Kariuki:

> youthful voices, shouting defiance, denouncing the lies, and singing poems to the struggle, voicing their determination to take up the fallen sword of J.M. and continue the struggle against inequalities in our land. British Imperialist Forces Out! I remember they were shouting. I remembered that Mwangi [J.M.] is the name of a generation; and Kariuki means born again, or the resurrected. Mwangi Kariuki. A generation resurrected. (70)

Both a play on his name and a tribute to his politics, Kariuki becomes the figure for the generation that will deliver Kenya from neo-colonialism.

The play marks this deliverance with a traditional ritual of rebirth. As Björkman transcribes the scene:

Kariuki: *I am Kariuki.*
Woman: *Kariuki? Kariuki!*
Woman touches him on head with trembling hands.
She sits down behind Kariuki, legs spread in
    such a way that Kariuki sits between them.
And now the ceremony of second
    birth is enacted.
Kariuki folds legs and hands and falls asleep
on one side, in the shape of a foetus. Nyathira
stands behind the woman and provides support.
Woman undergoes motions of birth pains.
Suddenly a baby's cry is heard.
Women say the five ululuations of a boy child. (69)

Significantly, while the bereft mother and the prostitute work together to bring about the new generation, that new generation is represented by a "boy child." While the female figures stand for the *concept* of Kenya—as utterly oppressed in the case of the prostitute and as endlessly fertile in the case of the liberated "Motherland," Kariuki represents the *people* of Kenya who will take action against the government. This gendered distinction entails a difference in relation to men and women as material referents; the symbolic function of "woman" as the ground for revolution threatens to overshadow the active role of women in struggle.

Rather than position the Prositute as the ultimate victim of imperialist aggression and the Mother as an idealized inspiration to revolution, the Kamiriithu villagers supplied an alternative ending that places women as active nation builders. In Ngũgĩ's original draft, Mwendanda, the post-colonial ruler, rapes Nyathira forcing her back into prostitution. In the collaborative version reworked by the women of the village, Mwendanda rapes but does not break Nyathira. She throws back his money and the pregnant woman embraces her. A third woman lifts a bundle of sticks to a song proclaiming unity as a revolutionary force. She points the sticks like a rifle, taking on the role of revolutionary actor. No longer do the women wait as mothers and victims for deliverance of and by a boy child. The alternative ending enacts a slippage between women and the reproductive function. Motherhood remains as one role available to women, in addition to the prostitute who resists victimization, and the revolutionary who takes arms in her own defense. The reworked version by the villagers underscores the issue of sisterhood in a combined feminist/ national struggle.

The cast finished the alternative ending with a recap of the duet sung by Kariuki and Nyathira immediately after Kariuki's rebirth: "The Decider." "Decider" means "rifle" in Kikuyu. Initiated in the final version by the third woman—the active revolutionary—the chorus runs:

> If you ever hear *tu tu tu*
> Don't think it's rain or thunder
> It's the blood of the workers
> Crying *for* Kenya our motherland [first verse]
> Crying *to* Kenya our motherland [last verse]

The sound of the rifle becomes the cry and blood of the newborn child/ generation. The mother finds her child in gunfire—the "birth pains" acted out in the ritual rebirth do not serve a merely mimetic function, but incorporate the armed struggle necessitated by the new generation's birth. The alternate ending reinforces the shift in the preposition from "for Kenya our Motherland" to "to Kenya"; the revolutionaries of Kenya do not merely cry for the plight of the "Motherland," but cry to her, entreating her as an actor to join in the struggle. In the performance of the play, women actively participated in the violent struggle that led to the nation's rebirth. The ending of the play arrests the violence that will lead to the re-birth of the nation at the moment of inception. Given the figurative nature of the play, the ending assumes but does not enact, the utopic moment of the coming of age of the new generation.

The play must end on an assumption, a projection of imagined fertility, because the wild applause of the audiences of thousands that crowded into rehearsals did not form the ultimate frame for this performance. Arrested at the rehearsal stage, *Maitu Njugira* never appeared as scheduled at the Kenyan National Theatre. The government exiled Ngũgĩ, razed the community center, and assured the usual progress in the National Theatre of British actors presenting Shakespeare and Shaw. Despite the MP's claim that "it is the woman who makes the decision," the Motherland's lullaby of the "decider" performed by the Kamiriithu Community Center could not drown out the "decider" maintained by the Kenyan Armed Forces, supported by the US military. Military control, converging at certain points with the technology of population planning, acts as a prophylactic on the imaginary of fertility. Arresting the Motherland in the dramatic moment of re-birth resolves the dialectic of proliferation and prophylactic for a revolutionary nationalist pedagogy. Voiding the Motherland of indigenous content after penetration and withdrawal by international forces, effects that resolution for the Kenyan government. Rebeka Njau's rooting of that dialectic in the body of a Kenyan woman negotiating the post-colonial constraints and expectations of fertility, makes any such resolution implausible.

Ripples in the Pool incorporates the interpenetration of the "developed" and the "developing world" in the transgressive body of the protagonist Selina: "For Selina was no ordinary girl: she was arrogant, self-centered, highly expensive and feared no man. Once every year she visited the village of her birth like a tourist who goes sight-seeing in underdeveloped lands."[14] Through a complicated series of events, the novel recounts Selina's disastrous final return to her native village. "Self-centered," she moves from the center of the Nairobi social scene to the center of village gossip and intrigue. Over the course of the novel, the narration attributes to Selina her mother-in-law's desertion; her husband, Gikere's, dissolution; the downfall of Kefa Munene, a revolutionary turned corrupt MP; and the murder of two young lovers: her sister-in-law Gaciru and her cousin Karuga. At the same time the narrator reverses these accusations, providing extensive rationalization for Selina's actions. We might investigate these contradictions by considering Trinh T. Minh-ha's discussion of the post-colonial female subject in her work *Woman, Native, Other: Writing Postcoloniality and Feminism*. As her title suggests, Minh-ha, like Bhabha, draws from the Derridean concept of writing, discussing the subject from the perspective of "the differences grasped both *within* and *between* entitites, each of these being understood as multiple presence." This multiplicity occurs because "the line dividing *I* and *not-I*, *us* and *them*, or *him* and *her* is not (cannot) always (be) as clear as we would like it to be. Despite our eternal attempt to separate, contain, and mend, categories always leak."[15] Where the narration of the nation enacts a "slippage ... into metonymic categories," that slippage further manifests itself within the subject because any momentary representation of "I" "does not (cannot) coincide with the lived or performed."[16] Selina's "self-center" cannot hold, as the "leakage" within "categories" allows for the "multiple presence" within Selina of mother/prostitute, woman/man, victim/oppressor, and developing/developed world. The novel positions Selina within and between the structures of power and powerlessness, an ambiguous space that guarantees the empowerment of the oppressed, particularly women. With Selina as the shifting center, *Ripples in the Pool* ultimately construes a narration of the nation only by destroying narration itself.

The centering of the novel around Selina deviates from the plotting of what Obioma Nnaemeka calls the "second generation" of African women writers. Nnaemeka examines the circumscription of the narrative domain of many African women writers by "domestic" or "motherhood" literature asserting: "the issue at stake here is to understand why the centrality of the representative of *tradition* ... is always guaranteed while the 'deviant,' less conformist characters remain marginal figures." Concentrating on Buchi Emecheta and Mariama Bâ, Nnaemeka does not mention *Ripples in the Pool*, an omission not surprising, since probably no other novel exhibits to such a bewildering degree "the ambivalence, contradictions, and ambiguities of the works of African women writers [that Nnaemeka] views as indicative of the attempts to explain or come to terms with the complexities of the positionality of these women writers." Selina marks the site of convergence of post-colonial political relations onto "motherhood" and the "domestic," as the contending discourses of development, revolution, and feminism become inscribed on her body.[17]

The opening of the novel constructs a problematic of womanhood premised on the opposition between Selina, the woman of the city, and her mother-in-law, the "representative of *tradition*." "No one could explain why Gikere married Selina even in the face of the protests of his own mother" (1). Selina displaces her husband's mother to the margin, placing herself in his village after leaving a successful career of modeling and prostitution in Nairobi. In an attempt to convince her son to leave Selina for a village woman, Gikere's mother links her life in the city to sterility:

"She just had a miscarriage, didn't she?"

"That was bad luck."

"Women like her are sterile."

"You do not like her I know."

"She will never keep a baby in her womb."

"How can you be so sure of that, mother?"

"I know her. I know what she has been through. If you do not believe me, wait and see." (12)

While the novel never fully communicates what Gikere's mother knew about Selina, her adamance about Selina's sterility suggests she knew that Selina had "been through" Nairobi. The capital and locus of modernization, Nairobi also served as the national site of contraception. Private physicians began to make contraception available in Nairobi and Mombasa as early as 1950. In 1961, Kenya became the first African member of International Planned Parenthood. By 1974, the time of Njau's writing, the City Council of Nairobi alone had established forty-three dispensaries, serving 20 percent of the country's acceptors of contraceptive devices.[18] Speaking as the voice of Tradition, Gikere's mother values women only for their fertility. In an argument with Selina, Gikere's mother broadens her critique of Selina's personal life in the city to encompass the new post-colonial generation Selina represents. Fertility not only becomes a determinant of value, but a determinant of the ontology of womanhood: "You are not a woman. That is what is wrong with you . . . Your whole generation is sterile" (36).

The action of the novel undercuts the assertion of the sterility or non-womanhood of the generation of "development" made in the name of "tradition," both by dramatizing the fertility of the women of that generation and exposing the social system that relieves men from responsibility for the children these women bear. The novel opens with a conversation between Selina and her modeling colleague, Sophia, who has just delivered a baby. Berating the government official who deserted her with the child, Sophia lists a number of friends in a similar predicament: "Look at Mary. Look at Ciku! They were all decent girls, but where are they now?" (3). The length of the list indicates the economic exigency that young women attempting to make careers or attend school rely upon better-off men to make up for scant income: "because no one man is likely to help them consistently, some schoolgirls who need support turn to different partners and try, often by abortion, to avoid pregnancy long enough to complete their schooling."[19] According to the 1969 census, few women had the means to support themselves independently as only 16 percent of the women working in Kenya held positions in the mid- to high-level manpower categories—with the majority of these working as tele-typists, shorthand secretaries, nurses, midwives, and teachers.[20] Selina herself supplemented her income as a nurse through modeling and casual acquaintance with city men. According to her own narrative, she came to Nairobi to escape beating at the hands of her father. She survived on the streets committing petty crime as a child, then turned to prostitution in order to finance nursing school. Because few women have the economic clout to oppose their partners' wish for children, Selina must have asserted herself aggressively to achieve the success in controlling her fertility that eluded her friends.

The novel supports this reading, as the plot attributes Selina's failure to give birth to a cause other than sterility. The miscarriage noted by Gikere's mother follows directly upon a severe beating Gikere gives Selina. Nevertheless, Selina attributes the miscarriage to her traditional mother-in-law: "She makes me sick . . . She gives me nightmares. That's why I can't keep a baby in my womb" (42). A second miscarriage follows another severe beating: "So he kicked her right in the belly. She was four months pregnant so she could not steady herself. She fell on the ground. Gikere was not satisfied that she had had enough punishment. So he looked for a strong rope and tied her hands and feet against one of the posts on the verandah and left" (137). Njau shifts the blame from Selina as an individual actor partaking in the corrupt values of the city, to a system of violence enacted by Selina's husband and supported by her mother-in-law.

Gikere anticipates the action of the police in *Maitu, Njugira* as he kicks Selina in the belly, directing his violence at her womb. The violence that maintained the authority of the colonialists and post-colonial rulers also maintains the authority of man over woman, husband over wife. Like the post-colonial rulers, certain women comply with the dominating forces for their own gain. Gikere's mother and Maria, the village woman she had hoped her son would marry, join in a chorus urging Gikere to establish his manhood by beating Selina: "You must make her realize that you are a man" (41); "You must hit and hit her hard until she realizes that you are a man" (135). These cries and the miscarriages they occasion ironically premise manhood on physical violence which ultimately undoes the motherhood that purportedly serves as the ontological basis for womanhood. In response to the observation that "Selina feared no man" (1), Gikere attempts to pound into her a realization of her powerlessness. He attempts to force her to categorize herself as dangerously deviant with his rallying cry before a severe beating that sent her to the hospital: "You selfish and mad woman!" (44). This epithet consists of three intended pejoratives: "selfish" (self-centered?), "mad," and "woman." These beatings repeat and effectively reinforce the beatings Selina suffered as a child at the hands of her father. Selina refuses to have the message of her madness—or in her father's words, her status as "Good for nothing" (52)—beaten into her. She explains her rebellion by asserting an alternate subject-position premised not on her fertility but on her desires: "I'm a human being who wants to be loved" (52).

Where the subjugation of a mythical womanhood by a paternalistic colonial figure symbolized the subjugation of the Kenyan nation to First World powers, domestic violence literally localizes patriarchal domination as an instance of the international system of oppression. Through the parable of Njeru the goat, Njau situates domestic violence within a global paradigm. Njeru also garners the epithets "mad" and "selfish" as his caretaker, Selina's young cousin Karuga, notes: "nothing would ever satisfy this wild beast . . . Everyone in the village knew the madness of this creature" (56). Karuga also refers to Njeru as "you good-for-nothing beast" (56), further establishing a connection between the goat and Selina. In a scene immediately following Selina's narrative of the beatings she received as a child, Karuga sets out in a mood of "frustrated violence" (55) that he displaces onto an "unusual hatred for Njeru" (55). As with Gikere, well-wishers warn Karuga that his manhood depends upon violent subjugation of this creature; his employer Maina announces: "He will be a man when he learns how to curb Njeru's tricks" (57). The "wildness" of the "beast" reflects back on Selina, posing violence as the weapon of the domestication of women.

Karuga's foster-father, Muthee, referred to as "the old man," counters the "tradition" voiced by Maina, Maria, and the old woman. He rescued Selina from her father's violence when he found her hiding by the sacred pool that provides the novel's title (53). He pleas for Karuga to restrain himself in punishing the goat: "Where is our strength if we fail to control one helpless little creature? If we destroy Njeru, is that the end of pain? What shall we do with all the other Njerus among us?" (68). As Karuga does not heed the old man's warning he brings violence upon himself; when he tries to poison the goat, the goat pierces him, almost removing an eye (72). Recalling another biblical parable, "one helpless little creature" becomes the "scapegoat" of an endless proliferation of violence.

This parable extends to Selina, the prostitute, as a scapegoat for the violent system of imperialist domination. Karuga's bus ride from Itukurua to Kantukwa, the village home of Selina and Gikere, provides the occasion for a discussion among rural folk of the prostitute as corruptor of society. The conversation begins as the bus driver puts an alleged thief off the bus. The argument slides from a recognition of the thief to a generalized discussion in which "the bus teemed with stories of robberies, bag snatchings, drinking, and prostitution in the dark lanes and lodges of the city" (94). Prostitution becomes the origin of the evils of the city, as one man asked: "Who will destroy these whores?" (94). Selina herself, "that notorious woman at Kantukwa" (94), becomes the topic of discussion. A scapegoat for post-colonial crime, the people on the bus position Selina as the origin of the very violence her own narrative poses as determining her position.

Selina rationalizes her prostitution to her husband as both a means of escaping the violent power structure of her home life and a means of survival in the post-colonial world: "White men used my body and paid highly for it. I tell you these things so that you may understand my sickness. I wanted to use your innocence and be born again, but you have failed to understand me" (66). Selina married Gikere because she believed she had found a man who "would take me for what I am" (3), but the narrative erodes the possibility of that ontology. When, in the first of the arguments that would lead to the breakdown of their marriage, Gikere asked: "what are you?" (11), Selina answered tautologically: "I am your wife who needs you, who needs your love and sympathy" (11). Later she would modify her answer according the perceptions of the villagers: "I *am* strange . . . Everyone says so. They say I'm mad. They say I'm a witch. I've been called all the filthy names in this village. Men look at me as though I'm dung itself. Women spit when they see me" (67—68).

Selina anchors her hopes for rebirth not in a purified Motherland, but in giving birth to a child through the "innocence" of her husband assured by his village upbringing. Encountering instead violence sanctioned by his village mother, she exchanges the role of dominated woman/wife for a relationship in which she attempts to "possess" the innocence of her husband's sister: "your hand soothes me because it has the warmth and the innocence of a world which has not been confused; a world which has not been littered with dirt and filth" (111). Taking Gikere's sister Gaciru as her lover, Selina consciously transgresses the relations that would subjugate her as a woman: "they want to show you a woman is nothing. But I have money . . . I am your mother, your sister, your friend, your everything" (111). Money, not fertility, becomes the currency of womanhood, purchasing for Selina at last the position of "mother" as, able to "be" "everything," she eludes any single ontology. Despite the mobility of her own identity, Selina hopes to anchor herself in "innocence," finding in Gaciru's body a purified world.

Selina's efforts to purify herself through rebirth parallel the quest of her cousin Karuga to discover the mystery of his mother's death in the sacred pool: "one day he might discover the mystery for himself; he might even discover the unseen thing that had killed his mother" (25). Karuga's search for his origins alternates in the narration with his struggle against the goat:

At such moments [when the goat survived his assaults], his mind was thrown back to the story of his mother. A desire to see her and talk to her overwhelmed him, and he found himself groping into darkness trying to form a clear image of her. But the more he tried to shape the picture, the hazier the whole thing became, until in the end all he was left with was just a formless mass that brought into his mind fearful illusions which made him feel tormented and pursued by evil. (73)

Karuga's attempt to "form a clear image" of his mother fails, resulting only in a feeling of "torment." Njau's intercalation of the plot of the goat with

Karuga's search for his mother suggests a reciprocal relationship between his misdirected violence and his thwarted desire to fix a picture of his origins.

Minh-ha's treatment of the concept "authenticity" suggests a further relationship between Karuga and Selina's separate quests for origins and the form of *Ripples in the Pool*:

> *Authenticity* as a need to rely on an "undisputed origin," is prey to an obsessive fear; that of losing a connection. Everything must hold together. In my craving for a logic of being, I cannot help but loathe the threats of interruptions, disseminations, and suspensions. To begin, to develop to a climax, then to end . . . Thus, a clear origin will give me a connection back through time . . . to abolish it in such a perspective is to remove the basis, the prop, the overture, or the finale—giving thereby free rein to indeterminacy: the result, forefeared, is either an anarchic succession of climaxes or a de(inex)pressive uninterrupted monotony—and to enter into the limitless process of interactions and changes that nothing will stop, not even death.[21]

We might consider the plot—already developing in a number of directions: the stealing of deeds, the betrayal of independence, descent into alcoholism, seduction, impregnation and abandonment, embezzlement, wife murder, and witchcraft—"an anarchic succession of climaxes." Alternatively, we might consider the conjuncture of the quests of Karuga and Selina a climactic moment punctuating the "de(inex)pressive uninterrupted monotony" with which the novel characterizes the post-colonial scene that even the death of nearly all of the characters cannot stop.

Unable to grasp an image of his mother, Karuga travels to the village of Selina's husband, hoping to help his last surviving relative. He too falls in love with Gaciru, proposing to rescue her from an affair he claims "is not the normal type of love" (118). This return to normalcy through the mating of innocents fails as innocence collapses as a category. The justification of Karuga's love for Gaciru as normative indicts the union in the system of compulsory heterosexuality that insures manhood only through a violent imposition of womanhood. Crazed with jealousy, Selina strangles Gaciru. Both Selina and Karuga return separately to the pool in their native village. Where Karuga had once hoped to find his mother, he discovers Selina, mistaking her at first for "the spirits of the pool cry[ing] out for vengeance" (150). In that moment, Njau collapses the figure of the mother, the childless prostitute, and the sacred grounding of tradition. This collapse provides a fatal end to a quest for a pure origin, as Selina stabs Karuga in the moment that he recognizes in her "the face of a murderer, the face of the only blood relation he knew" (151).

Like *Maitu, Njugira, Ripples in the Pool* closes with an unseen utopia: "Suddenly a light shone upon [the old man's] face as he stared at it and he realized that that fig tree would survive the generations and generations to come like the light, spirit, and truth that live on for ever" (152). In contrast to Karuga who sought an origin in the fixed image of his mother, to Selina who sought purification through a return to innocence, and to the old woman who posited a tradition that can only take root in an oppressive ontology of womanhood, the power of tradition for the old man takes the form of the living presence of the unseen. The form of *Ripples in the Pool* dissolves into indeterminacy after a series of catastrophic climaxes undercut every attempt by characters to establish a pure origin or true self.

The narrative strategies of Ngũgĩ, the government, and the international aid agencies all variously and in different registers constructed women as metonymic for the nation in a manner that positions women according to their reproductive function as the objects of a pedagogy of revolution, development, and technological control. The intervention of the third woman in *Maitu, Njugira* positions women as the potential narrators of the nation. When Rebeka Njau plays out that potential in a plotting of womanhood not contained in any monolithic imaginary of Motherhood, her narration stakes the nation on unstable ground. Njau refracts the nationalist pedagogies through the body of Selina, exposing not only the official fictions of womanhood, but the ruptures those fictions sustain. While the continued control of the Kenyan populace by the current regime and international influences requires a fixing of both identity and reproductive potential, the utopian hopes articulated in *Maitu, Njugira* and *Ripples in the Pool* depend upon an unknown, unfixable identity of Kenya and Kenyan womanhood.

NOTES

1 Malcolm MacDonald, quoted in Jomo Kenyatta, *Harambee*, ix.
2 See particularly the song written for Kenyan schoolchildren, "Moi, Our Father, Guardian of Children," in which the chorus portends an eternal childhood for citizens: "Oh, our father, rule us." Quoted in Ingrid Björkman, *Mother Sing for Me*, p. 49. Subsequent references noted parenthetically in text.
3 Homi K. Bhabha, "DissemiNation: Time, Narrative, and the Margins of the Modern Nation," *Nation and Narration*, p. 297.
4 Bhabha, p. 293. Square brackets in Bhabha's text.
5 Bhabha, p. 292.
6 Jacques Derrida, *Dissemination*, pp. 294–295.
7 Kumari Jayawardena, *Feminism and Nationalism in the Third World*, p. 2.
8 Stephanie Urdang, *Fighting Two Colonialisms*, p. 15.
9 Jacqui Alexander, "Mobilizing against the State and International 'Aid' Agencies," p. 53.
10 Caroline Bledsoe, "The Politics of AIDS, Condoms, and Heterosexual Relations in Africa," p. 219.
11 According to Rosalind Petchesky Pollack: "while population control and sexual control over women are coexistent strategies in state societies (which are also male-dominated societies), at various historical junctures they come into serious conflict. The role of the state is to mediate this conflict by developing fertility policies that authorize population control measures and set limits on the legitimate boundaries of women's control over their fertility and sexuality, especially women who are the concern of patriarchal authrorities: wives and unmarried dependent daughters." *Abortion and Woman's Choice*, p. 50.
12 David Fanthorpe, "Violence South of the Sahara," p. 116.

13 Carol Sicherman, *Ngũgĩ wa Thiong'o*, p. 96.
14 Rebeka Njau, *Ripples in the Pool*, 1. Subsequent references noted parenthetically in the text.
15 Trinh T. Minh-ha, *Woman, Native, Other*, p. 94.
16 Bhabha, Minh-ha, p. 94.
17 Obioma Nnaemeka, "From Orality to Writing," p. 151.
18 Margaret Wolfson, *Changing Approaches to Population Problems.* p. 141.
19 Bledsoe, p. 205.
20 Karibu Kinyanjui, "Educational and Formal Employment Opportunities for Women in Kenya," p. 7.
21 Trinh T. Minh-ha, p. 94.

WORKS CITED

Alexander, Jacqui. "Mobilizing against the State and International 'Aid' Agencies: 'Third World Women Define Reproductive Freedom.'" *From Abortion to Reproductive Freedrom: Transforming a Movement.* Ed. Marlene Gerber Fried. Boston: South End Press, 1990.

Bhabha, Homi K. "DissemiNation: Time, Narrative, and the Margins of the Modern Nation." *Nation and Narration* . Ed. Homi K. Bhabha. New York: Routledge, 1990.

Björkman, Ingrid. *Mother Sing for Me.* London: Zed Press, 1989.

Bledsoe, Caroline. "The Politics of AIDS, Condoms, and Heterosexual Relations in Africa: Recent Evidence from the Local Print Media." *Births and Power: Social Change and the Poliftics of Reproduction.* Ed. W. Penn Handwerker. Boulder: Westview Press, 1990.

Derrida, Jacques. *Dissemination.* Trans. Barbara Johnson. Chicago: University of Chicago Press, 1981.

Fanthorpe, David, "Violence South of the Sahara." *The Future of Political Violence.* Ed. Richard Clutterbuck. New York: Royal United Services Institute, 1986.

Jayawardena, Kumari. *Feminism and Nationalism in the Third World.* London: Zed Press, 1986).

Kenyatta, Jomo. *Harambee: Speeches 1962–1963.* Nairobi: Oxford University Press, 1964.

Kinyanjui, Karibu. "Educational and Formal Employment Opportunities for Women in Kenya." *Participation of Women in Kenyan Society,* conference held in Nairobi, August 11–15, 1978 . Nairobi: Kenyan Literature Bureau, 1974.

Njau, Rebeka. *Ripples in the Pool.* Nairobi, Heinemann: 1975.

Nnaemeka, Obioma. "From Orality to Writing: African Women Writers and the (Re)Inscription of Womanhood." *Research in African Literatures* 25.4 (1994): 137–157.

Pollack, Rosalind Petchesky. *Abortion and Women's Choice: The State, Sexuality, and Reproductive Freedom.* Boston: Northeastern University Press, 1984, rev. edn 1990.

Sichermann, Carol. *Ngũgĩ wa Thiong'o, the Making of a Rebel: A Source Book of Kenyan Literature and Resistance.* London: H. Zell Publications, 1990.

Trinh T. Minh-ha. *Woman, Native, Other: Writing Postcoloniality and Feminism.* Bloomington, University of Indiana Press, 1990.

Urdang, Stephanie. *Fighting Two Colonialisms: Women in Guinea-Bissau.* New York: Monthly Review Press, 1979.

Wolfson, Margaret. *Changing Approaches to Population Problems.* Paris: Development Centre of the Organisation for Economic Co-operation and Development; Washington, DC: Publications and Information Center, 1978.

9 Ontological victimhood

"Other" bodies in madness and exile—toward a Third World feminist epistemology

Huma Ibrahim

Audre Lorde's essay, "The Master's Tools Will Never Dismantle the Master's House,"[1] indirectly reaffirms what has been integral to that aspect of colonial discourse which addresses the split between Third World and white feminisms. This split had been intellectually, and in terms of group-action or global feminism, profoundly shocking to those of us who did not wish to privilege women's differences in colonial hierarchical terms but rather to understand the complexity of subject/object distinctions in the post-colonial milieu by utilizing a universal value system. Here, I am referring to the kind of "universalism" problematized by Bessie Head in *A Question of Power*[2] as well as in her collected letters, *A Gesture of Belonging*.[3]

Hazel Carby, as early as 1982, in an important, ground-breaking book about racism in Britain, *The Empire Strikes Back*, made it very clear in her essay titled "White Woman Listen! Black Feminism and the Boundaries of Sisterhood"[4] that unless there was an understanding of a separate *her*story of black women by white and black feminists scholars, the old racially determined hierarchical dialectic would continue to be preeminent. Jill Lewis and Gloria Joseph's *Common Differences*[5] predates Carby by one year and outlines specific dialogic problematics between the white Western and the Third World feminists.[6] In response to a marginalized historical consciousness within the larger feminist context, Alice Walker even proposed a different word, womanist, for our feminism in her book of essays, *In Search of My Mother's Garden*.[7] This term later came under considerable attack from Third World feminists themselves, but it had a certain history in the African American context and at the level of "nomenclature" it certainly was a step in the right direction. Even though any attempt at naming/renaming is inclusive of some and exclusive of other experiences, the process is valuable as additive to a feminist dialectic and the term "womanist" was no exception. The fundamental distinction that Third World feminists went on to make between themselves and white/Western, middle-class, liberal feminists was that the latter did not take into full account the complexities and intersections of race, class, and gender.[8]

Several problems were raised through this initial split. But as we move along in defining ourselves and elaborating our discourse as it is separate from as well as coincides with white feminist discourse, we discover that what JanMohammed and others have called "generic" concepts have become incorporated so far as to be inseparable from an understanding of Third World feminist/womanist dialogue in the last decade. These generic concepts tend to define what has not yet been examined with rigorous attention directed at real historical and political differences. These concepts represent an ideology that presents a problem and culminates in an ontology which falsifies spaces of resistance carved by Third World and lesbian feminist scholars as well as activists within and outside the academy.

In the following, I wish to extend the notion of an existent structural hierarchy of class and race within feminist discourse as it views the idea or status of "victims," which has become a "generic" idea suggesting a specific ideology rooted entirely in white feminist/colonialist discourse. Essentially, there are three varieties of victim that I am going to analyze. One kind of victimization is connected to women's sexuality as it is separate from motherhood and another to her gender as it is integral to motherhood. The last is the variety related to the dialogic clash between a woman and her society and how it affects her as perceived in the case of Head's protagonist in *A Question of Power*. In the 1980s, in the United States, one perceived a kind of women's studies scholarship in anthropological, literary, and sociological studies, coming from both Third World and white feminists *on* Third World women, which implied an unexamined disenfranchisement of the latter. *This Bridge Called My Back*, among others, were anthologies exploring a problematic based *on* the victimhood of Third World women. Part of the ideology of "sisterhood" was structured into the way it would take the Western feminist's discursive practice to eliminate social ills, like the practice of clitoridectomy, existing "out there." As Third World feminists living in the West, we could either condemn all Western interference as uncomprehending of social customs or say, again categorically, that we in the West have somehow to save our "victimized" sisters in the Third World. At such times the discursive discomfort of the Third World feminist teaching in institutions in the West becomes apparent.

This essentially hierarchical discourse automatically sets up yet another subject/object dialectic with attending problems of definition particular to the white/Third, World feminist/womanist split. The racial/dialectical innocence with which we Third World women scholars have incorporated the "victim" in our discourse is well worth looking into. Our complicity is problematic at several levels. As a friend recently asked, Why is it that "I feel like a fraud when I take on the Third World women as victim voice?" Gayatri Spivak, in her book, *In Other Worlds*,[9] lends a valuable dimension to the "victim's" discourse. In translating Mahasweta Devi's deconstructed rendition of the Draupadi story originally recorded in the *Mahabharata*, Spivak introduces several extremely important facets to the notion and reality of the victim, particularly the active resistance within a specified socio/sexual context. I shall, in this essay, examine how the idea for the classical Draupadi's unending *saree* in the Mahabharata story gradually becomes the trope for the victim, systematically deconstructed by the very resistance which is inherent in any victim's condition and quite obviously in her reponse to victimization.

Let me elaborate the specifics of the concept of "victim" given certain ideological biases that I wish to deal with here. I will elaborate two problems connected to the concept of "victim": the first constitutes the ideology of colonialism, which creates a very specific sense of the viewed victim's object space, and the second, the "victim's" varied response to, first, that treatment which victimizes her and, secondly, the process of internalizing what then becomes a given part of the same ideology. Here, the question of women's "subversive identities" becomes part of the larger problematics of the issue of victimhood. Why does my Third World academic feminist colleague feel like such a fake, albeit enmeshed in varying degrees of complicity with social and educational privilege? Trinh Minh-ha writes informatively:

> Identity ... supposes that a clear dividing line can be made between I and not-I, he and she; between depth and surface, or vertical and horizontal identity; between us here and them over there. The further one moves from the core the less likely one is thought to be capable of fulfilling one's role as the real self, the real Black, Indian or Asian, the real woman. The search for an identity is, therefore, usually a search for that lost, pure, true, real, genuine, original, authentic self, often situated within a process of elimination of all that is considered other, superfluous, fake, corrupted, or Westernized.[10]

How does this relate to that part of the identity that constitutes the victim self? In Spivak's translation, Dopdi, radical peasant leader, after being tortured and sexually brutalized by her captors, can only tear the cloth they give her to cover their victimization of her. With an eloquent and vital gesture she tears off the label of "victim," as she tears off the covering her victimizers throw at her in order to cover not her, but their own handiwork. When she is brought to their boss she chooses to be naked and unveiled. It is their act of victimization that she throws back into their face. As one of the leaders of the revolution, she refuses to passively accept her victimhood. Spivak translates:

> Draupadi wipes the blood on her palm and says in a voice that is as terrifying, sky splitting, and sharp as her ululation, What's the use of clothes? You can strip me, but how can you clothe me again? Are you a man?
>
> She looks around and chooses the front of Senanayak's white bush shirt to spit a bloody gob at and says, There isn't a man here that I should be ashamed. I will not let you put my cloth on me ...
>
> Draupadi pushes Senanayak with her two mangled breasts, and for the first time he is afraid to stand before an unarmed target, terribly afraid.[11]

Like the classical Draupadi, only a god can "clothe"/veil, not men, not even men to whom the dis/honor of women is bequeathed. The victim throws her victimization into the lap of the victimizer and refuses to be "ashamed" of her humiliation because she did not perpetrate it and will not take responsibility for it. Dopdi's act becomes a radical departure from her brutalizers' gender expectations. Dopdi's discomfort with victimhood is echoed by Third World feminist discourse.

The generic notion of "victim" indirectly perpetuates the subject/object dialectic in a new and perhaps disarmingly acceptable way. It is disarming precisely because it refuses to take questions of class and race into account. Draupadi refuses to let herself be the silent suffering deity, remaining the resistant fighter to the end. Whereas the subject/object notion of victimization deifies the "victim" with all the fervor reserved for an ancient and capricious goddess, freezing the "victim" in an immovable object space determined by the dominant discursive desire of the subject identity. Draupadi refuses to recede from that subject identity to which the dominant discourse wants to exile her. And yet, any other way of looking is easily silenced especially since the term "victim" comes out of a specific evocation of the Third World ridden with real post-colonial, socio-economic devastation. It is a definitional understanding imposed on the post-colonial world by friends in the "same movement," who have enjoyed our collaboration and are loath to lose it. However, the price for the continuance of this collaboration is very high, for alliances can only be made with "friends" who wish to be absolved through their white feminist discourse because that discourse has allowed room for a very spatially limited and far too well-defined monologue in which Third World feminist discourse must learn to have a precarious residence. There is no room for the Draupadis in that dominant discourse. I may add that, even though real alliances are being sought, feminist discourse still resides positionally at the juncture of the non/exchange that occurred between Audre Lorde and Mary Daly in 1979 and recorded in Lorde's collection of essays, *Sister Outsider.*[12]

Trinh T. Minh-ha writes in *Woman, Native, Other*:

> You who understand the dehumanization of forced removal-relocation-reeducation-redefinition, the humiliation of having to falsify your own reality, your voice—you know. And often cannot *say* it. You try and keep on trying to unsay it, for if you don't, they will not fail to fill in the blanks on your behalf, and you will be said . . . they work toward your erasure while urging you to keep your way of life and ethnic values *within the borders of your homelands.*[13] (emphasis in the original)

It is only within the borders of our homelands that we can accept this, for wont of a better term, intellectual pity, which "generously" dismisses real difference and in fact helps maintain our silence. This is when it becomes imperative for us to seize the precarious positionality of our own strategies and discourse.

Unsaying an already-said concept is obviously not the same as the actual saying and defining of the same concept. Through this false dialectic of naming, it becomes clear that Third World feminists have to seize their own spatially defined areas in order to commence the task of defining our discourse, which has so often got waylaid in arbitrary dialogue. Trinh Minh-ha notes that "Stolen language will always remain that other's language." And I would add, that stealthily stolen, impositional definitions and the consciousness arising out of it will always remain, in large part, that other's discourse. The importance of defining-the-self consists of entering the calamitous process of looking for identity in that place which Susan Griffin calls "the place in myself where words have authority, some true and untouched place that does not matter what has been said before . . . and make in the very telling a proof of authenticity."[14]

I believe anecdotes like the following abound in the American academy and their telling in this context is still useful. In 1989 while I was teaching in the University of Hawaii, an institution still actively suffering from its colonial legacy, my white feminist colleagues, to say nothing about the male colleagues, found it disconcertingly painful, both intellectually and socially, to be left outside the formation of a Women of Color group which came into existence to address our socio/political needs in that academy. It is true that some of us had been victimized by the colonial academy and did not want to perpetuate the silence, the maintenance of which some of our white feminist colleagues went to great pains and lengths to effect, often as we collaborated to fight other battles in the same academy. However, after several meetings between Third World and white feminists where the later accused the former of not speaking up and the former of not being heard, the project was abandoned and animosities continued in silence.

In this regard, does the task of definition lie in the lap of the usually silent/silenced "victim?" Often silence is perceived as complicitous in the definition that has already been named. And yet, we have recourse to other interpretations of that very same silence. Mahasweta Devi's Dopdi does not remain silent and her victimhood un/defines her. As Trinh Minh-ha affirms,

> Silence as a refusal to partake in the story does sometimes provide us with a means to gain a hearing. It is voice, a mode of uttering, and a response in its own right. Without other silences, however, my silence goes unheard, unnoticed; it is simply one voice less, or more point given to the silencers.[15]

She is right in cautioning us about the silence. The victim's silence is no less valuable. The victim's silence is also a "voice," and a "mode of uttering" to which we as Third World feminist scholars must add our silence rather than be compelled very quickly to take up the empty spaces we imagine are left by it. Even among ourselves, we must learn to listen to the silences of silenced "victims" in order to direct our discourse which is so often captioned by voices that do not and should not belong to us and often create discomfort in us because of their unfamiliarity. The voices which do not belong to us must learn, especially in the academy, to perceive commonality in the distinctions that our discourse produces. Dopdi's torturers are terrified of the emergence of her discursive victimhood, and are silenced by it. Out of that silence emerges their victim's discourse, which is one of total liberation after going through extreme pain at the hands of patriarchal relational systems of dominant discourse.

In nearly all the literatures of the world there abound many female victims who are perceived to be so by the author, by the reader, and also by themselves in the textual framework. I am going to examine several such victims, for the notion of "victim" is stealthily pervasive in feminist discourse. One of the characters I shall discuss is Bessie Head's protagonist, Elizabeth, in *A Question of Power*, and it is fairly clear that she is very different from Emecheta's characters, Nnu Ego in *Joys of Motherhood*[16] and Adah in *In the Ditch*,[17] whose victimhood is tied to motherhood. Another character which has received real currency in women's studies classes in the United States and therefore warrants a special place is, Nawal El Saadawi's Firdaus, in *Woman at Point Zero*,[18] who is victimized by her class and gender. I shall, in addition, and whenever useful, refer to some other "victims" created by African women writers as well as some South Asian writers, particularly Mira Masi in Anita Desai's *A Clear Light of Day*,[19] who is in fact liberated by her "demented jouissance," as Kristeva calls motherhood.[20]

The reason I begin with Firdaus is that she, most of all, falls into the fabulously complex and continuous folds of the victim's *saree*. She is, in many ways, the Darupadi of the Mahabaharata. Each bit of victimization she receives finds her womanhood/sexuality barricaded in yet another fold, protected from the male gaze. Tarabishi has suggested that in Firdaus's case her extreme sexual "passivity" is the only way she can humiliate the male. However, it is her numbness that allows her to resist sexo/social onslaughts. I believe her aim is to protect herself while she is being regaled and repelled by various forms of male sexuality.[21] Mahasweta Devi's Dopdi, too, becomes folded in the trope of a "victimhood." Like Firdaus, the condition of this victimhood which she resists, "liberates" her.

Saadawi's valorization of Firdaus's victimhood is extremely problematic because its subject space is privileged in Third World feminist discourse. Can we be allowed to speak authoritatively about our experience if the suffering that attended it is excruciating? I would argue along with Spivak's translation that in certain extreme conditions it is the trope of inflicted suffering which makes us define our discourse, much as the experience of colonialism did. Knowledge, somehow liberates the marginalized victim or the disenfranchised madman, as Foucault would argue. Does Saadawi's Firdaus negotiate the same space out of the tropes of her victimhood as Devi's Dopdi does after "their/her humiliation?" *The Woman at Point Zero*, Firdaus, enjoys the admiration of her biographer. She is mythologized to the extent where the writer is convinced that the woman who "rejected her" was "a much better person than I." This feeling of rejection reminds her of the time when she "had fallen in love with a man who did not love her. I felt rejected . . . by every living being or thing on earth, by the vast world itself."[22] Georges Tarabishi, in his recent critique of Saadawi, wrongly considers this mythologizing of the "murderess" as comprising a set of divisive "clichés," used in order to get the readers "wholeheartedly [to] empathize" with the protagonist. I believe the obvious explanation for Saadawi's fascination is the attraction between the two women—an attraction which is complicated and determined by the consideration of where one wishes theoretically to push feminist discourse and where the other, the narrator or Saadawi, in her capacity as a middle-class doctor, has been in terms of practical life experiences.

At the beginning of the novel, Firdaus seems like a capricious lover/ goddess who has risen above everyone because she is surrounded by this aura of remarkability. Tarabishi is right in saying that Saadawi wants us to "emulate" Firdaus. But it is not Firdaus's actions, as Tarabishi suggests, that Saadawi wants us to emulate but rather her discourse—her analysis of the patriarchal society where she lives—which attracts the author/biographer. The codes of this society are totally unfamiliar to Firdaus at first, and are used to suppress and brutalize not only her sexuality, but every aspect of her socio/economic life.

The simultaneous unveiling/veiling constitutes the liberatory force in a victim's life. Trinh Minh-ha, as a post-dated Heideggerian, astutely writes: "If the act of unveiling has a liberating potential, so does the act of veiling. It all depends on the context in which such an act is carried out, or more precisely, on how and where women see dominance."[23] Firdaus puts on the veil as well as unveils herself through every episode of victimization that she goes through. It gives her power, power to control the resources available to her in order to set herself free, through a minimal dependence on the rules of patriarchy. However, the question of whether the context of her discourse is rooted firmly in patriarchal discourse, remains unanswered and perhaps needs to remain so, because her sphere of specific problematics would certainly not exist except in conjunction with the patriarchy.

Firdaus flees various situations. First she leaves her father's house, then her uncle's, then her husband's, later Bayoumi's imprisonment. Her journey unended, she leaves Sharifa's "protection" and lastly she leaves her own house which has been taken over by the pimp. Each episode is a signification of a simultaneous veiling and unveiling of her discourse till the final liberation. When she leaves her father's house, the experience leaves her wondering whether one can be "born twice." Each of these veilings/ unveilings is revelatory for her at several levels and each time she experiences a "second birth." Each time an opportunity for freedom presents itself to Firdaus, a closer look shows that there is nothing but another form of bondage. At a certain level she is happy at the home of her uncle who does not continue to molest her, but rather provides opportunities for her to study.

But it is also her uncle who sells her into the marital arms of an old and completely repulsive man.

Firdaus's bondage continues, but each time she is able indeed to be "born again" protected by the simultaneous veiling/unveiling folds of her fore-mother Draupadi's *saree*. Like Draupadi, Firdaus's liberation comes to her only through her analysis, even though her motivations remain veiled to the systems of dominance which imprison her. In the final analysis, she tells her biographer:

> I only arrived at the savage, primitive truths of life after years of struggle ... And to have arrived at the truth means one no longer fears death. For death and truth are similar in that they both require a great courage if one wishes to face them.[24]

Mahasweta Devi's Dopdi, like Firdaus, is no longer afraid of death or punishment or her torturers, who cower in fear in front of her fearless unveiling/veiling, just as Firdaus's persecutors do.

Victimhood takes on a different aspect when we examine Mira Masi in Anita Desai's *A Clear Light of Day*, or the protagonists in Buchi Emecheta's, *The Joys of Motherhood* or even her first novel, *In the Ditch*. Here victimhood is tied to motherhood. Desai's Mira Masi, resists in the only way she can; she escapes being sexually exploited. In a different way from Firdaus, she passively resists the advances of the younger men in the family by making herself totally "unappetizing." Feminists, in turn, must respect that silent resistance without valorizing it. Even given general criteria for productive work, we know that Mira Masi gets herself out of her husband's family's house albeit into a situation in which she is no longer needed and lives to "become herself." She becomes the mother of four children whom she does not birth but is "mother" to, and who end up being very devoted to her in different ways. It is out of this power that she has never had before that she lives out her thus far veiled inner life of fears. It is true that her resistance has been bare, generally against silence/death and alienation from love and human interaction.

But if we are to regard childrearing/childcreating as a supremely productive and fulfilling activity, then even given the narrow confines of social perception, Mira Masi's is a useful life. She is able to, not allowed to, live a life in which she does not just scrape by but survives; to "live" (*vivre*) "above" (*sur*), which represents the deepest heritage of this term's emancipatory significance. Traditionally, childrearing is just that place where the split between Third World and white feminist discourses takes place but if we are to take Kristeva's lingual lyricism about motherhood/tongue at all in its context, then Mira has succeeded in liberating a dementing/"demented jouissance" within her subject existence.

Even though aspects of patriarchal discourse sanction motherhood and indeed often protect women who have children rather than mothers from being overtly victimized the underlying commitments are not toward women/

humans but rather as they symbolize patriarchal control at individual, societal, or national levels. Mira Masi's motherhood comes out of her own nature but it is also part of the patterns of resistance she successfully develops against the life which had wrenched motherhood away from her. It is not that Mira Masi is manufacturing a false sense of motherhood for her immediate survival, but rather, with her capacity to release that creativity in herself, she is simultaneously able to resist the world that alienates her. Third World women writers have often asserted that women are not victimized by motherhood but motherhood provides a tenacious resistance against the victimizing world. This is certainly the case for Emecheta's two mothers who give up everything in order to become mothers, even though in these cases the same motherhood is used to victimize them.

In *In the Ditch*, Adah, with her five children, is left to the racist/classist mercy of the dole system in England. Although Adah's husband abandons her contrary to African family context, she never sees herself as completely victimized. One of the strongest narratological defenses Emecheta uses is Adah's capacity to laugh at her situation and the project houses she lives in, as well as her desire to "survive." She does. In spite of every conceivable problem thrown at her, which would ordinarily not let her get out of the quagmire of poverty, she emerges, with all five children, and "lives to tell the tale." The only reason that this journey is extremely difficult for her is because she has the sole responsibility for those five children.

Mira Masi and Adah are made "whole" by their contribution to and reception of the children's love, though it is not always displayed in appropriate or welcome ways, thus forming the fundamental elements of human dialectic through which they can begin to understand themselves and others. Here, the term "whole" has to be used guardedly and perhaps in the context of Kristeva's concern regarding mothers, particularly the issue of "demented jouissance." However, in this madness there is power, as Foucault would argue about other sorts of madness, and this power is manifested socio-personally. It is this small power, as bell hooks would say, of "talking back" with legitimate tools of resistance that gives mothers, even as victims, their survival credence. It is through this talking back that language has the potential, as Cixous tells us, to be "born over and over again," that even a "victim" like Mira Masi or Adah can "give birth" to the hidden self in her. At the end of her life, Mira Masi, like Dopdi, Firdaus and Nnu Ego, becomes Hélène Cixous's "sorceress . . . and hysteric, whose body is transformed into a theater for forgotten scenes, relives the past, bearing witness to a lost childhood that survives in suffering."[25]

After the children in her charge no longer need her directly, Mira Masi becomes the sorceress and hysteric at first almost in spite of herself in a celebratory gesture of completed motherhood. At the end, her body does become a theater for forgotten scenes from the past. Perhaps it is the past which she has been able to take charge of only through this reliving of her suffering. Her suffering allows her to shed her constraints in an attempt to be free. Even the few clothes she is wearing seem to choke her and she tears them off, much like Sojourner Truth baring her breast in a simultaneous act of freedom and proof. Through her veiling/unveiling, she proves to be the direct descendant of Dopdi and Firdaus. Thus, the journey of that life, the process of that "victimization" becomes in and of itself valuable, because through that very experience and through that resistance, she is able to be "born again."

In Emecheta's *The Joys of Motherhood* and *In the Ditch*, childlessness as well as abundance of progeny seem to be the root cause of the suffering woman victim. In *In the Ditch*, motherhood shields Adah from racism. It is the reality that she is able to form with her children which facilitates her survival in a potentially eroding and alien situation. However, in *The Joys of Motherhood*, Nnu Ego is victimized first by her inability to become a mother and later, because she is a mother. Lack or abundance of children suggests several ways in which the dominant power structure first tantalizes and then victimizes women.

In her first marriage, Nnu Ego is told in no uncertain terms that her husband cannot be expected to waste his "precious seed" on a barren woman. She is led to believe it is all her fault, especially when the second wife conceives. She is further humiliated and reminded of her childlessness, for she nurses the second wife's child as the latter is kept sexually busy by a young husband who disregards tradition, as well as the comfort of his new wife and her baby. This act gets her a terrible beating from her husband who is relieved of Nnu Ego once her bride price is returned to him. The cat-and-mouse game she is forced to play with motherhood ends when she becomes a prolific producer of children and becomes the envy of Adaku, her junior wife, who can only produce girls. Her husband taunts her "What type of *chi* have you got, eh? When you were desperate for children she would not give you any; now that we cannot afford them, she gives them to you."[26] However, he cannot criticize too much because she is able to produce sons. Adaku, who is unable to have a son, is not protected by patriarchy and leaves the charade of a marriage that provides no protection in order to live a better, more comfortable life for her daughters and herself.

Nnu Ego's entire life is taken up by a life-and-death struggle to feed and educate her children because patriarchal systems of powers tell her that her children are her only value and that they will take good care of her when she is old. This becomes the ultimate irony, because she dies alone out of the sight of her children or the man who fathered them. Her victimization and loneliness are complete. The only consideration her heir, Oshia, shows her is to give her a fabulous funeral. In death, when a shrine is made to the glory of her victimized motherhood, she rebels: "however many people appealed to her to make women fertile, she never did."[27] Emecheta is taking a very risky position in regard to motherhood and the travails connected with the bearing and raising of children in poverty, scarcity, and loneliness. The dementia of Nnu Ego as mother, that is, her "jouissance," compels her to risk her personhood and like Mira Masi, she has to seize power—some power—, through the process of suffering itself, and she does that by not granting children to women who appealed to her.

Nnu Ego's posthumous rebellion is symbolic of the slight power/madness that mothers are allowed, but at the same time, in not granting other women children, she manifests the ambiguity of the same "demented jouissance," that is also responsible for her desire for them. Emecheta's sarcasm at the end is well placed, "The joy of being a mother was the joy of giving all to your children, *they said* . . . Did she not have the greatest funeral . . . That was why people failed to understand . . . for *what else* could a woman want but to have sons who would give her a decent burial?" (emphasis mine).[28] Madness, like motherhood, in most cases, and certainly so in Mira Masi's and Nnu Ego's, is a space into which the woman allows no one but herself to enter. For the mother, this private sphere always provides joy, suffering, and power. For Mira Masi, madness becomes the space in which she remains supreme and through that process she enacts her journey past, present, and what is yet to come. This has repercussions for the already defined/named victim of social, economic, political, and sexual institutions. Under such circumstances is it enough merely to glamorize the victim by calling her so? I, white academic feminist, claim you, Third World woman, not being able or desiring to carry the class label of feminist, as victim. I, white feminist, name you victim in defining/calling you victim. I call you thus, often with complicitious silence from Third World academic feminists. I, Third World feminist, subject, look at you often with varying degrees of "critically conscious"[29] discomfort. How do I find room for defining this discomfort? I, Third World feminist, who often share with you the questionable title of "victim" often at the cost of feeling like a "fraud." When Trinh Minh-ha talks about the "inappropriate other in every I,"[30] is she recommending Emecheta's subject-position which is considerably more privileged than Nnu Ego's or Firdaus's or Adah's?

Upon turning to Bessie Head's protagonist, Elizabeth, the issue of "victim" becomes vastly more complex. Elizabeth is an actual exile from apartheid South Africa. Unlike Mira Masi, who is in exile from and exiled by her own society, Elizabeth leaves her country of birth and "chooses" to live in neighboring Botswana. She can no longer function with the apartheid rules of destructive hate imposed on every aspect of her life and chooses the only course open to her.

However, this is not where the novel ends. This is where it begins. Here I am going to simplify the textual analysis of *A Question of Power*, having done this elsewhere at greater length (*Bessie Head*), in order to talk about how the madness and exile of the protagonist, Elizabeth, are the resistance/ space created by her so that she can understand larger implications of Good and Evil. This resistance/space is directly created out of her "madness," much like Dopdi's or Firdaus's. The madness and exile are often manifested by silence. She is able to block out the tasks of mundane survival by something that she seems to have no control over, yet in so doing, she is able to understand the potential good that has the capacity to transform itself into evil in human beings.

Out of the deliberate formation of this resistance/space emerges a previously deadened sphere for understanding the self/body, in this case, through writing. In *A Question of Power*, Elizabeth even though she is victimized sexo/socially by apartheid, does not have any space to understand the condition of her birth. When she becomes "mad," it is through her created nightmare of Medusa that she and other victims like her can begin to understand their victimhood. As Trinh Minh-ha writes:

> "Women must write through their bodies." Must not let themselves be driven away from their bodies. Must thoroughly rethink the body to re-appropriate femininity. Must not however exalt the body, not favor any of its parts formerly forbidden. Must perceive in its integrity. Must and must-nots, their absolution and power. When armors and defense mechanisms are removed, when new awareness of life is brought into previously deadened areas of the body, women begin to experience writing/the world differently. This is exciting and also very scary. For it takes time to be able to tolerate great aliveness.[31]

Emecheta, Mahasweta Devi, Saadawi, Desai, and Head are writing through their mother's bodies in order to create definitions and strategies of feminist discourse which emerges from the tropes of their characters' victimization and which addresses the negotiations of resistance, ignored thus far.

Even though, in Elizabeth's case, it is much harder to see her as a victim simply because she has physically escaped the madness of apartheid, there are expectations placed on her by her new community which are just as silencing as apartheid. This silence is what victimizes her, and later it is through the process of madness that she is liberated. The silence is connected with her relationship to exile and apartheid South Africa. While at first, in her homeland, she is numb and unable to produce any thing meaningful, later it is through the process of creating (growing living things in her garden) that she is able to break the spell of silent psychological inertia that she experienced in transition.

However, she is plagued by various aspects of exile–which I argue is a perpetual women's exile. Her sexuality is plagued by Medusa, one of the deliberately female personifications of exile, as well as her inability to belong to M/Other Africa. During one of her mad spells she is accused of not knowing any African languages by Medusa, one of her tormentors. I would argue that in spite of these physical and sexual attacks on her it is clear that through her carefully timed madness, she breaks the defenses that alienate her from herself even as they protect her from external onslaught.

Femi Ojo-Ade suggests in his article "Bessie Head's Alienated Heroine: Victim or Villain?" that Elizabeth is indeed a victim and Head, like many other writers, "resorted to the secondary resistance of the written word."[32]

The distinction that Ojo-Ade is making between "armed struggle" and writing is unclear to me. For a South African refugee, writing in exile in a neighboring country does not spell safety. But as the Angolan and Mozambican situation indicates, this is a potentially life-threatening situation. There is a distinct similarity in the victimhood and later liberation of both Dopdi and Elizabeth. Dopdi can no longer be unveiled or tortured and Elizabeth after a series of unveilings can finally "belong" to her community in exile.

What brings about the complete sense of belonging at the end of the novel is the actuality of the madness, mentioned earlier. The madness facilitates the dispensation of what Trinh Minh-ha calls "the absolution of must and must-nots." And further it is through this "re-appropriation," without the banishment of the "inappropriate in every I," of her femininity that Elizabeth sees herself as one with the land of her exile. Life comes to the "previously deadened areas of the body" and, I add, to the previously deadened areas of her and other consciousnesses.

In her letter of criticism to Mary Daly, Audre Lorde says:

Then I came to the first three chapters of your Second Passage, and it was obvious that you were dealing with noneuropean women, but only as victims and preyers-upon each other. I began to feel my history and my mythic background distorted by the absence of any images of my fore-mothers in power.[33]

Here she is un-appropriating the same victimhood which had been frozen in a spatially defined discourse.

NOTES

1 Cherríe Moraga and Gloria Anzaldúa, *This Bridge Called My Back*, p. 98.
2 Bessie Head, *A Question of Power*.
3 Robert Vigne, *A Gesture of Belonging: Letters from Bessie Head, 1965–1979*.
4 Centre for Contemporary Cultural Studies, *The Empire Strikes Back*.
5 Gloria Joseph and Jill Lewis, *Common Differences*.
6 Here, I am using Mohanty's loose definition of the term "Third World" to be found in her Introduction to *Third World Women and the Politics of Feminism*, p. 2.
7 Alice Walker, *In Search of Our Mother's Gardens* pp. xi–xii.
8 These categories are not intended to be exhaustive but for the purposes of this essay are documented by Toril Moi in *Sexual/Textual Politics* and by Barbara Christian in *Black Feminist Criticism*.
9 Gayatri Spivak, *In Other Worlds*.
10 Trinh T. Minh-ha, "Not You/Like You," p. 71.
11 Spivak, p. 196.
12 Audre Lorde, *Sister Outsider*, pp. 66–71.
13 Trinh T. Minh-ha, *Woman, Native, Other*, p. 80.
14 Susan Griffin, "Thoughts on Writing," p. 110.
15 Trinh T. Minh-ha, *Women, Negative, Other*, p. 83.
16 Buchi Emecheta, *The Joys of Motherhood*.
17 Buchi Emecheta, *In the Ditch*.
18 Nawal El Saadawi, *Woman at Point Zero*.

19 Anita Desai, *A Clear Light of Day.*
20 Toril Moi, ed., "Stabat Mater," in *The Kristeva Reader*, pp. 160–185.
21 Georges Tarabishi, *Woman Against Her Sex.*
22 Saadawi, *Women at Point Zero*, p. 4.
23 Trinh Minh-ha, *Inscriptions*, p. 73.
24 Saadawi, *Women at Point Zero*, p. 102.
25 Cixous and Clément, *The Newly Born Woman*, p. 5.
26 Emecheta, *The Joys of Motherhood*, p. 91.
27 Emecheta, *The Joys of Motherhood*, p. 224.
28 Emecheta, *The Joys of Motherhood*, p. 224.
29 Paulo Freire uses this term throughout in his *Pedagogy of the Oppressed.*
30 Trinh Minh-ha, *Inscriptions*, p. 77.
31 Trinh Minh-ha, *Woman, Native, Other*, p. 36.
32 Femi Ojo-Ade, "Bessie Head's Alienated Heroine," p. 14.
33 Lorde, *Sister Outsider*, p. 67.

WORKS CITED

Centre for Contemporary Cultural Studies. *The Empire Strikes Back: Race and Racism in 70s Britain.* London: Hutchison, 1982.

Christian, Barbara. *Black Feminist Criticism.* New York: Pergamon, 1986.

Cixous, Hélène and Catherine Clément. *The Newly Born Woman.* Trans. B. Wing. Minneapolis: University of Minnesota Press, 1986.

Desai, Anita. *Clear Light of Day.* New York: Harper & Row, 1980.

Emecheta, Buchi. *In the Ditch.* London: Barrie & Jenkins, 1972.

——. *The Joys of Motherhood.* New York: George Braziller, 1979.

Foucault, Michel. *Madness and Civilization.* New York: Vintage Books, 1988.

Freire, Paulo. *Pedagogy of the Oppressed.* New York: Seabury Press, 1968.

Griffin, Susan. "Thoughts on Writing: A Diary." In Janet Sternburg. *The Writer on Her Work.* New York: W.W. Norton, 1980.

Head, Bessie. *A Question of Power.* London: Heinemann, 1973.

Ibrahim, Huma. *Bessie Head: Subversive Identities in Exile.* University of Virginia Press (forthcoming).

Joseph, Gloria and Jill Lewis, eds. *Common Differences.* New York: Doubleday, 1981.

Lorde, Audre. *Sister Outsider.* Tramansburg, NY: Crossing Press, 1984.

Mohanty, Chandra, Ann Russo, and Lourdes Torres, eds. *Third World Women and the Politics of Feminism.* Bloomington: Indiana University Press, 1991.

Moi, Toril. *The Kristeva Reader.* New York: Columbia University Press, 1986.

——. *Sexual/Textual Politics.* New York: Routledge, 1988.

Moraga, Cherríe and Gloria Anzaldúa, eds. *This Bridge Called My Back: Writings by Radical Women of Color.* Watertown, MA: Persephone Press, 1981.

Ojo-Ade, Femi. "Bessie Head's Alienated Heroine: Victim or Villain?" *Ba Shiru: African Women and Literature* 8.2 (1977): 13–21.

Saadawi, Nawal El. *Woman at Point Zero.* London: Zed Books, 1983.

Spivak, Gayatri. *In Other Worlds: Essays in Cultural Politics.* New York: Routledge, 1987.

Tarabishi, Georges. *Woman Against Her Sex: A Critique of Nawal El-Saadawi.* London: Saqi Books, 1988.

Trinh T, Minh-ha. *Woman, Native, Other.* Bloomington: Indiana University Press, 1989.

——. "Not You/Like You: Post-Colonial Women and the Interlocking Questions of Identity and Difference," *Inscriptions* 3/4 (1988): 71–77.

Vigne, Robert. *A Gesture of Belonging: Letters from Bessie Head, 1965–1979.* London: Heinemann, 1991.

Walker, Alice. *In Search of Our Mother's Gardens.* New York: Harcourt, Brace, Jovanovich, 1983.

10 Urban spaces, women's places

Polygamy as sign in Mariama Bâ's novels

Obioma Nnaemeka

While the prerogative of speaking for others remains unquestioned in the citadel of colonial administration, among activists and in the academy it elicits a growing unease and, in some communities of discourse, it is being rejected. There is a strong, albeit contested, current within feminism which holds that speaking for others—even for other women—is arrogant, vain, unethical, and politically illegitimate.

Linda Alcoff, "The Problem of Speaking for Others" (97–98)

J'était offusquée. Il me demandait compréhension. Mais comprendre quoi? La suprématie de *l'instinct*? Le droit à *la trahison*? La justification du désir de *changement*? Je ne pouvais être l'alliée *des instincts polygamiques*. Alors, comprendre quoi?

[I was irritated. He was asking me to understand. But understand what? The supremacy of *instinct*? The right to *betray*? The justification of the desire for *variety*? I could not be an ally to *polygamic instincts*. What, then, was I to understand?]

Mariama Bâ, *Une si longue lettre/So Long a Letter* 53/34, my emphasis[1]

FEMINISM, SPEECH, AND SILENCE(D)

Linda Alcoff's article, "The Problem of Speaking for Others," wrestles with the dilemma and discomfort facing feminists as they debate the issue of involvement or non-involvement in speaking "other people's business." As an African woman (a. k. a. "Third World"[2] woman as a member of the global community, and "minority" as a member of the citadel of learning), I must admit that I find the distinction Alcoff makes between "the citadel of colonial administration" and "activists and the academy" problematic. In fact, the "unease" that speaking for others elicits "among activists and in the academy" is precisely due to the fact that, although it pretends not to, the academy actually operates like "the citadel of colonial administration" in its full regalia of arrogance and hierarchy of district officers, court clerks, and "natives." Both "the citadel of colonial administration" and the citadel of learning are mired in power politics; the only difference is that "the citadel of colonial administration" is *always* comfortable with *showing off* its hierarchy and hegemony but the citadel of learning is *sometimes* uncomfortable. It seems to me that the problem in this feminist debate about intervention or non-intervention is that of extremes: total involvement or complete withdrawal. Feminist discourse and activism have not quite figured out how to bridge the gulf between this purported irreconcilable difference. We must look for ways in which involvement (proximity) and withdrawal (distance) can evolve into a workable symbiosis that is fashioned in the crucible of mutually determined temperance.

The feminist dilemma would not be that daunting if only feminist praxis could allow itself to be guided by its own ideals: as a pedagogy and a philosophy of social change, feminism mandates involvement, and as an ethics of fair share and live and let live, it advocates moderation and negotiation and counsels against extremes and winner-take-all mentality. Furthermore, I believe that this debate should focus more on issues; we can *lend our voices to* or *speak up against* problems facing others without necessarily *speaking for* them. We should aim at *speaking up with* them *against* the problems and *speaking up with* them *for* solutions without *speaking for/against* them. As feminists, speaking for others requires our carefully walking the fine line between participation and usurpation. It entails our figuring out how to share the site of affliction with the "afflicted" and as defined by them without claiming the whole territory in order to articulate it *for* and *on behalf of* them. *Speaking for* others (in the sense of *speaking with*) does not create absence and exclusion; rather, it ensures presence and participation. In Western-generated controversies about African customs in which the West is talking to the West, Africans are silenced by those who have usurped their discursive territory just as their physical territory became a West-to-West *palaver* in Berlin in the last quarter of the nineteenth century. The inscription of polygamy in Mariama Bâ's works provides the site to (re)tell the story from the inside (to see it with the "other" eye), revisit its articulation in the criticism of Bâ's work, map its relevance to the feminist debate about speaking for others, and reexamine how it is impacted by global, historical, and ideological shifts. In my view, polygamy, as it is elaborated in Bâ's works stands as a sign of cultural hemorrhage and societal rearticulations, and also as a sign of disciplinary failure in African literary criticism. It is puzzling that a book, *Une si longue lettre/So Long a Letter*, in which the word "*la polygamie*/polygamy" *never* appears and polygamy (the institution) *never* functions—Aïssatou leaves immediately her husband marries la petite Nabou; Modou abandons Ramatoulaye for Binetou in spite of the latter's willingness to stay in a polygamous marriage—has been debated and analyzed *ad nauseam* in literary criticism (feminist criticism, in particular) as a book *about the institution of polygamy* (derided as one of Africa's chronic ailments). This chapter reexamines Bâ's work in light of the cultural hemorrhage, societal rearticulations, and disciplinary failure noted above.

In its engagement with the "Third World," Western feminism operates on a system of indirect rule in which a group of "Third World" women (either studying or working in the West or operating from the "Third World" countries) are *authenticated*, naturalized, and installed as mediating forces. The feminist dilemma noted above is complicated for the legitimized *authentic* voice/woman from the "Third World" by the angst she feels for doing what she is called upon to do—that is, speak for the rest of "Third World" women victims. The *authentic* voice is faced with the dilemma of figuring out how to produce a counterdiscourse to the discursive territorial usurpation of Eurocentric discourse without monopolizing her own sisters' discursive field. Peter Hitchcock notes that this "reobjectification" of the African women is an epistemological one: "[t]he epistemological question here is how to counteract the 'all-seeing I' of Eurocentric discourse without assuming the position, as guarantor, of the alternative knowledge that may be at issue."[3] The *authentic* voice from the "Third World" feels uneasy as she executes her assignment. In this regard, Huma Ibrahim notes: she feels "like such a fake, albeit enmeshed in varying degrees of complicity with social and educational privilege."[4] Not only that, the *authentic* "Third World" feminist finds herself paradoxically sandwiched between speech and silence; she speaks for her victimized sisters but at the same time, she is silenced and spoken for by her Western feminist collaborators. As Huma Ibrahim concludes from Audre Lorde's May 6, 1979 letter to Mary Daly that Lorde turned into an open letter "to the community of women" after four months of no response from Ms Daly,

> [T]he price for the continuance of this collaboration is very high, for alliances can only be made with "friends" who wish to be absolved through their white feminist discourse because that discourse has allowed room for a very spatially limited and far too well defined monologue in which Third World feminist discourse must learn to have a precarious residence. There is no room for the Draupadis in that dominant discourse. I may add that, even though real alliances are being sought, feminist discourse still resides positionally at the juncture of the non/exchange that occurred between Audre Lorde and Mary Daly in 1979 and recorded in Lorde's collection of essays, *Sister Outsider*.(150)[5]

Western feminism's search for and legitimation of *authentic* feminist voices from the "Third World" set these voices up for attack and ridicule from all fronts. Installed as the voices that speak for the rest of their downtrodden sisters, and expected to testify against their society by condemning all that is "wrong" with it, these *authentic* feminist voices face resistance no matter what position they take *vis-à-vis* their culture: if they accord their traditional culture some modicum of respect, they are dismissed by feminists as apologists for oppressive and outdated customs; if they critique their culture, they are faced with put-downs and ridicule from the members of their own society for having sold out. In both instances, they are marked as *speakers for*, on the one hand, feminism, and, on the other hand, indigenous cultures.

Femi Ojo-Ade, a Nigerian literary critic, reserves his harshest criticism for these incorporated, *authentic* African feminist voices:

> Grace Ogot, Efua Sutherland, Ama Ata Adioo, Flora Nwapa, women writers all, constitute the "old guard", steeped in the traditions of the land, complaining of their sufferings as subjects of the male master, but seeking solace in a society that has proclaimed woman the mother. That group's conciliatory position has been superseded by a current of revolt. Compromise is replaced by criticism and condemnation. Respect turns into repudiation. Devotion is buried in divorce. Buchi Emecheta, Nafissatou Diallo, Mariama Bâ, those are the voices currently crying out for the liberation of woman, the second-class citizen . . . Feminism, an occidental phenomenon like many others, has spread ever so slowly but steadily to the forbidden land of Africa . . . Such "aberrations" as feminism are abhorred by many who are, however, the very purveyors of the bastardization of that culture whose contents remain confusing to the civilized minds . . . The war between male and female is now a contemporary constant, and new literary voices from among the once silent minority cry out to be heard, even if there is reason to doubt on whose behalf the revolt is being declared. ("Still a Victim" 72)

Ojo-Ade's strident remarks should not be a deterrent to African feminists who are genuinely committed to effecting necessary changes in their cultures. Rather, such voices must be engaged critically. "Feminism" is an English (Western) word but the feminist spirit and ideals are indigenous to the African environment; we do not need to look too far into the annals of African history to see the inscription of feminist engagements.

Recently in the United States, the private life of a polygamous family has been the subject of bemused public discussions. My reading of polygamy in Mariama Bâ's work against a backdrop of these public discussions unfolds into the arguments in the feminist debate about voice (*speaking for*) that is elaborated above. In an article, titled "I Share My Husband with Seven Other Wives," that details the life of the Josephs, Ross Laver and Paula Kaihla claim that "[h]appily married with children, these eight *well-adjusted* American women insist their one man is more than enough. We visited their Utah-based commune and are surprised to report that this unorthodox family is a living arrangement *that—believe it or not—works*" (45, my emphasis). Alexander Joseph, 59, "a businessman and former mayor of the dusty town of Big Water, Utah, 375 miles south of Salt Lake City," is now married to eight wives—Diane, 48 (store manager), Margaret, 45 (sales consultant), Leslie, 47 (factory worker), Joanna, 42 (tour supervisor), Boudicca, 42 (real estate broker), Elizabeth, 42 (lawyer, journalist), Delina, 32 (municipal clerk), and Dawn, 25 (secretary)—although he has married about twenty women in the past two decades claiming, as he does, that "I guess you could say that I'm the overachiever type" (48). The reasons Alex's wives give for marrying him range from falling in love with him to seeing polygamy as an act of defiance against their family and society. Although money is the greatest source of conflict, sex and privacy are sometimes concerns: "[i]n the early years, Alex had the luxury of deciding whom to sleep with on any given night. But soon the women rebelled against that system ... Now each woman books a night with Alex when she wants to have sex. The only problem, they say, is that sometimes Alex loses track, accidentally scheduling two women for the same night. When that happens, one wife is forced to retreat, silently cursing Alex" (48).

Unanimously, the wives assert that the benefits, ranging from freedom and bonding with other women to childcare and stability, far outweigh the disadvantages. All the wives agree that "their decision to enter a 'plural marriage' means they can each truly have it all—security, independence, children, and a career" (46). According to Elizabeth Joseph, "[y]ou would think that polygamy by definition would be oppressive to women ... in fact, a plural marriage is actually empowering. This way, I can have the freedom to explore my own potential without worrying about having to tend to my husband's every need" (46). What do the neighbors think? "To most of the people who live in and near Big Water, Alex and his wives are merely eccentrics—good for a bit of gossip, but otherwise harmless. But others find much praise about this arrangement. 'The argument that it is a feminist lifestyle makes a lot of sense to me,' says Beth Russler, an announcer at the radio station" (50). And what does Alex think? "When I first got into this, I thought the most difficult part would be to find a woman who would do it ... Hell, that was the easy part. The minute I made it known that I was available for this lifestyle, I got more marriage proposals than I could possibly accept" (46). Meanwhile, Alex is in a hiatus because, in spite of his wives' attempts to recruit more candidates, he is not ready to pop the question *for now*: "Elizabeth, in fact, has not given up trying to recruit more eligible bachelorettes into the Joseph clan. She currently has a list of three or four candidates—'including one of my bosses, a real quality person.' So far, though, Alex has shown no interest in popping the question—this time" (50).

This report is pertinent to the questions I raise about voice and agency primarily due to the *manner of its telling*. I have written at length on the report in order to tease out the different categories of speaking subjects—the wives spoke, Alex spoke, the neighbors spoke, and the reporters "reported" without any noticeable insertion of the reportorial voice. The reporters did *not speak for* the Josephs. They treated with respect these "well-adjusted" women who "are virtually indistinguishable from typical, modern American women"; they visited the Joseph wives, saw them as reasonable adults who are capable of making personal decisions and choices, *talked with* them, and walked away convinced that the "living arrangement works." On the contrary, in the narration of African traditional cultures and the ways in which they are "oppressive" for women, African women are not accorded the same respect and subjectivity as Alex Joseph's wives; African women are *spoken for, about, and against*. Alex *chooses* to marry many wives, his wives *choose* to be married to him and the neighbors *choose* not to bother them since they are "harmless." In Western/feminist discourses, African traditional practices are reified and cast as impositions on women. It is unthinkable in such imperialist discourses that African women actually *choose* to have co-wives and some *choose* to be circumcised. African women who are in polygamous marriages are not morons or powerless, exploited, downtrodden victims. Many of these women are intelligent, highly educated, successful, independent women who *choose* polygynous marriage as what is good for them. Rama-toulaye, the protagonist in Mariama Bâ's *Une si longue lettre* chose to stay in a polygamous marriage against the advice of everyone around her: "Et, au grand étonnement de ma famille, désapprouvée unanimement par mes enfants influencés par Daba, je *choisis* de rester." [And to my family's great surprise, unanimously disapproved of by my children, who were under Daba's influence, I *chose* to remain] (69/45, my emphasis).

It is troubling, but understandable, that feminism which has made the issue of "choice" the centerpiece of its theorizing and activism is reluctant to factor the same issue in its analysis of African women's lives. The un-fortunate persistence of feminist arguments premised on the assumption that African women are too downtrodden to be capable of making their own choices and decisions constitutes a stumbling block to genuine engagement and meaningful collaboration. This casting of African women is not sur-prising in view of the fact that imperialist discourses invent targets and causes without which their *raison d'être* will be in jeopardy. If it is recognized and accepted that African women can choose and speak for themselves, the intervention of those who have arrogated to themselves the right to speak and choose for African women will be unnecessary. The construction of the voiceless African woman is, therefore, a necessity. My earlier objection to Linda Alcoff's demarcation of "the citadel of colonial administration" and "activists and the academy" should be understood in the context of the provenance of these "interventionists" on behalf of African women. In their state of (re)objectification, African women do not speak but are spoken for, they do not choose but are chosen for. The objectification of the African woman renders existing feminist criticism of Mariama Bâ's *Une si longue lettre (So Long a Letter)*[6]incapable of capturing Ramatoulaye's different "voices" on polygamy.

MODERNITY AS SUBVERSION

Culturally and epistemologically, *Une si longue lettre* is sandwiched between two interpenetrating contexts (African-Islamic), on the one hand, and what Uzo Esonwanne calls Enlightenment epistemology, on the other hand.[7] Ramatoulaye's power lies in her ability to maintain balance in the difficult task of reworking different cultural and epistemological imperatives while

still mired in them. In my view, in *Une si longue lettre*, polygamy is inscribed
as a sign of the rupture that emanates from these competing forces and their
continuous reworkings. A good understanding of the cultural articulations of
the novel requires that one listen more attentively to and read more carefully
Ramatoulaye's complaints. Her complaints against the so-called oppressive
cultural institutions and practices are framed in the context of her profound
awareness of the subversions of the institutions themselves. A critique of the
institution, say polygamy, serves also as a critique of its subversion and
recoding. More importantly, Ramatoulaye's complaint is less about polygamy as an institution and more about what she calls men's *instincts
polygamiques* (polygamous instincts)—instincts that are found in polygam-
ists as well as among monogamists. It is instructive to note that the word, *la
polygamie* (polygamy), is not even in the book. In the three instances where
Ramatoulaye makes references to polygamy, she does not use the noun (*la
polygamie*) but uses instead the adjective (*polygamique*) —*instincts polygamiques* (53/34), *domaine polygamique* (69/46) and *problème polygamique*
(100/68), usage that absorbs polygamy both as a propensity and as an
institutional question. This nuance is lost in the translation (*So Long a Letter*)
where "le problème polygamique" is translated as "the problem of polygamy," which is similar to translating *le problème politique* (political
problem) as "the problem of politics" (*le problème de la politique*).

Two of the three instances where *polygamique*/polygamous are mentioned
relate to the two letters that are embedded in Ramatoulaye's long letter; the
first instance is immediately after the presentation of the letter Aïssatou wrote
to Mawdo, and the second is in Ramatoulaye's letter of rejection to Daouda
Dieng. Both instances are replete with words—such as *abandonnée* (abandoned), *trahison* (betrayal), *joie éphémère* (ephemeral joy), *changement*
(change/variety)—that have more to do with philandering than with polygamy as an institution. Even on the two occasions that Ramatoulaye makes
references to the institution, *la polygamie* is not used; she chooses instead to
speak about the modalities of its operation as she accepts Modou, "J'étais
préparée à un partage équitable selon l'Islam." [I had prepared myself for
equal sharing, according to the precepts of Islam] (69/46), and rejects Tamsir,
"Ma maison ne sera jamais pour toi l'oasis convoitée . . . tous les jours,
je serai de 'tour'" [My house shall never be for you the coveted oasis . . .
my "turn" every day] (85/58). The acceptance and rejection underscore
Ramatoulaye's ambivalence *vis-à-vis* polygamy as an institution. Ramatoulaye's ambivalence will be discussed later in this chapter. These observations are very important particularly in view of the fact that some of the
criticisms of Bâ's works are imperial fictions which distort and undermine
the works themselves by making them referendums on African customs.
Imperial (re)inventions of African customs as stigma and dilemma will not
let African customs die because if they do, the basis for the insidious
"othering" of Africa will be further eroded. In this regard, I see the
pertinence in rephrasing Jean-Paul Sartre's famous remark on anti-Semitism:

"If polygamy did not exist, Western imperialism would invent it."[8] Or, "If circumcision did not exist, Western feminism would have invented it." Mariama Bâ's most important legacy to the literary world is her extraordinary gift as a *writer*.[9] She wrote with the ease and elegance that make even pain and the ugly sound like a beautiful poem, a view that is confirmed by *West Africa*'s assessment of Bâ's work on the dustcover of *So Long a Letter*: "its undoubted literary qualities, which seem to place it among the best novels that have come out of our continent"; qualities that earned *Une si longue lettre* the Noma award. I have yet to see an analysis of Bâ as a *writer* pursued with the same enthusiasm and vigor shown in knocking down polygamy. Bâ's work is not primarily about the institution of polygamy, although literary criticism has catapulted it to a treatise on polygamy as "part of a scarlet badge on the African face, preserved there for the imperial gaze."[10]

For Ramatoulaye, subversion functions on two levels: the subversion of traditional institutions in an urban milieu ("modernity"), and her own subversion of traditional practices. For example, she appropriates a space of silence (confinement) to break her silence. Through the Islamic ritual of *mirasse*, confinement draws the line between speakers and listeners/observers. It simultaneously inscribes speech and its containment. Ramatoulaye speaks by navigating the boundaries of silence and containment. Culturally marked as listener and observer—"[l]e dos calé par des coussin, les jambes tendues, je suis les allées et venues, la tête recourverte d'un pagne noir." [my back propped up by cushions, legs outstretched, my head covered with a black wrapper, I follow the comings and goings of people] (10/3)—she listens to her husband's *mirasse* during a family meeting held in her living room: "[l]e mirasse, ordonné par le Coran nécessite le dépouillement d'un individu mort de ses secrets les plus intimes. Il livre à autrui ce qui fut soigneusement dissimulé" [the *mirasse* commanded by the Koran requires that a dead person be stripped of his most intimate secrets; thus is exposed to others what was carefully concealed] (19/9). Listening to her husband's *mirasse* provides the impetus for her to (re)strip not only the dead but also strip the living. With outrage in her voice, Ramatoulaye collapses the telling of individual and collective histories. In one narrative gesture, she renames her husband's life of deception and betrayal as she had heard it in her living room, and narrates her own story as well as Aïssatou's and Jacqueline's in the context of the collective national history with its gender politics and economic, class, and ideological conflicts. Ramatoulaye's success at re-inventing herself lies in her ability to rework a religious practice by possessing it, not rejecting it; in other words, she rejects the practice by possessing and subverting it. As Uzo Esonwanne rightly notes, "Ramatoulaye circumvents the constraint of confinement imposed by Islamic custom with an Islamic ritual. Never an apostate, she works within Islam, finding novel uses for its rules, rituals, and regulations, cross-breeding them with alien generic formats."[11]

African women writers often make a clear distinction between love and friendship—on the one hand, the painfully debilitating love and sexual relationship between men and women in marriage and outside of it, and on the other hand, the affirming and empowering friendship between women inside and outside of marriage. Nowhere is the line as clearly drawn as in Mariama Bâ's novel, *Une si longue lettre*: "L'amitié a des grandeurs inconnues de l'amour. Elle se fortifie dans les difficultés, alors que les contraintes massacrent l'amour. Elle résiste au temps qui lasse et désunit les couples. Elle a des élévations inconnues de l'amour." [Friendship has splendours that love knows not. It grows stronger when crossed, whereas obstacles kill love. Friendship resists time, which wearies and severs couples. It has heights unknown to love] (79/54). I argue that what is at issue in Bâ's novels, particularly *Une si longue lettre*, is the transformation of traditional African institutions by "modernity" and the manipulation of these trans-formatory stages by men to their own advantage thereby creating the pain of their female partners. I shall examine polygamy as it is inscribed in both African tradition and Islamic culture, explore its operation in the novels and use my findings as a context for interpreting Ramatoulaye's complaints and pain. It is not sufficient to assert that *Une si longue lettre* is a battle cry against polygamy. It is true that polygamy is at issue here but so is the author's invitation to the reader to come and see what has happened to the institution of polygamy. In its inscription of polygamy, Bâ's novel interrogates both the institution and its subversion in contemporary, urban Senegal.

Like most readers of Bâ, Femi Ojo-Ade centers the issue of polygamy in his analysis:

> Man's basic guilt, the root cause for his vilification, the main element of his vicious behavior, is polygamy. Polygamy, the estate revered by traditionalists as a function of Africanity. Polygamy, once supported and even suggested by African women as a socio-economic expediency. That, vows Aïssatou, is a thing of the past. Polygamy is now the bane of society. Polygamy is a vice to be dealt with not by procrastination but by divorce. So, Aïssatou Bâ leaves the beast called Mawdo. ("Still a Victim" 76)

Ojo-Ade's justification and praise of polygamy as "a function of Africanity" mimics the all too familiar excuse given by Mawdo Bâ (*Un si longue lettre*) and Ousmane (*Un chant écarlate*) to justify their infidelity and philandering. By delineating the distinction between polygamy as an institution and its practice in post-independence urban Senegal, Bâ details how the subversion of the institution further complicates women's lives. Words, such as deception, betrayal, and abandonment, that punctuate the complaints of the female characters are not necessarily synonymous with the institution of polygamy in Islamic or African culture. Mariama Bâ's work brings under the microscope "polygamy" as it is practiced in African urban areas particularly by affluent, middle and upper-middle classes.

I agree with Femi Ojo-Ade that there exists some confusion in some "civilized minds" (72) and also that *"Une si longue lettre* is a study of these contradictions." However, we differ in our naming of the confused minds and our interpretations of the origin and content of the confusion and contradictions. While Femi Ojo-Ade ascribes the contradictions to cultural conflict between Africa and the West, I see them at a deeper and more complex level than the tradition/modernity binary, particularly in light of the gender politics that (re)structures and intensifies the confusion and contradictions. In order to fully account for the ways in which these contradictions are complicated and exacerbated by the dissonances in the African environment itself, one must examine critically the ways in which the "modern," urban (but not so urbane!), African man juggles and manipulates different, sometimes conflicting, systems in an attempt to enjoy the best of all possible worlds. In many ways, the so-called modernity has intensified the masculinization of the African tradition, thereby deepening the marginalization of women and creating instances (for the women in particular) where tradition is progressive and modernity reactionary. If Mariama Bâ's work speaks about aberrations, it is not against "such 'aberrations' as feminism" that it speaks; the voice of outrage in the work is screaming high and far against aberrant behaviors and practices of *specific* men. The issue of specificity is extremely important because criticism of African literature has the tendency to naturalize, "normativize," and generalize the behaviors, inclinations, and actions of the characters in the literary works. In this regard, Okonkwo in *Things Fall Apart* is installed in criticism as the norm and as a paragon of Igbo virtue when the author, Chinua Achebe, has taken pains to cast him as an embodiment of what his people value (hard work and responsibility) and what they condemn (excess, intolerance, arrogance, and violence), through the simultaneous inscription in this one man the normative and the marginal, the acceptable and the aberrant. Unidimensional analyses of *Things Fall Apart* fail to factor in the repeated condemnations and sanctions Okonkwo receives from his people for his excesses. Mariama Bâ's *exposé* of aberrant behaviors are generalized and etched in literary criticism as a critique of an "aberrant institution" (polygamy) with its *natural, inherent,* and *essential* propensity toward misogyny.

If the women are confused, as Ojo-Ade claims, it is precisely because they are living with contradictions and enigmas in the form of husbands. If the woman is "still a victim,"[12] it is to these confused minds that she remains so! I will examine the contradictions and discrepancies which exist between theory and praxis as they relate to the institution of polygamy in modern, urban Africa. How does polygamy as an institution and as an experience affect the lives of women in Mariama Bâ's novels? In examining the practices which distort and even vulgarize the institution thereby leading to the excruciating pain of the women, I will focus not only on the exegesis of the tenets of the institution of marriage in Islam and the African traditional culture but also on the transformations the institution has undergone in modern times.

In his study of the rights of women in Islamic Sharia, Rafi Ullah Shehab notes that according to the Holy Koran, polygamy was initially introduced as a means of rehabilitating widows and orphans: "And if you fear that ye will not deal fairly with orphans, marry of the women, who seem good to you, two two or three three or four four; and *if ye fear that you cannot do justice (to many wives) then one only*" (AL Quaran, Surah Al-Nisa-3, my emphasis). Furthermore, Islam allows polygamy but with certain restrictions and conditions. A man should marry only when he can afford it: "And let those who cannot afford marriage keep themselves chaste until Allah provides them with means" (AL Quaran-Surah Al-Noor-33). Shehab explains that under Islamic law, the would-be husband is responsible for all marriage expenses. The custom of dowry (especially as practiced in India and Pakistan) is foreign to Islam as evidenced by the non-existence of the word "dowry" in the Arabic language. Islam considers love as an essential ingredient in marriage; consequently, a man should not compel a woman who does not like him to marry him.[13] Marriage is thus a life-long contract requiring a firm agreement, *Messaqan Ghaleezan*, between a man and a woman. Although, in principle, Islamic laws grant equal rights of separation to both spouses, in practice these rights are only enjoyed by men. Shehab explains that the three important conditions in the Islamic marriage institution are the following:

> The main condition mentioned in the Holy Quaran for allowing polygamy is to solve the problems of orphans and widows but it also mentioned three conditions such as justice between wives, sexual capability and equality in meeting expenses. *It may be mentioned here that if a person is not in a position to meet the expenses of one wife, he, according to Islamic law, is not allowed to marry.* (*Rights* 43, my emphasis)

Shehab concludes by noting that the Islamic marriage institution has undergone changes due to contact with other systems with the result that certain rights which the institution guarantees women are denied them in practice.

It will also be helpful to examine what Ojo-Ade calls "polygamy, the estate revered by traditionalists as a function of Africanity" (76). Patrick Merand notes that the reasons for contracting a polygamous marriage in the traditional African society range from the superior numerical strength of women, to female infertility, to the acquisition of prestige.[14] Another form of polygamy is the leviratical marriage which aims at caring for and protecting women and their children. In the polygamous family in indigenous African society, a particular living arrangement is observed and respected. The man lives in the *same compound* with *all* his wives and children. Usually, boundaries of marked spaces are respected; the man has his own house and each wife lives in her own house with her children; the man is responsible for the general welfare, maintenance, and operation of his compound while each wife is directly responsible for her children. Sexually and materially, the man seeks to maintain fairness, equity, and justice among the wives. The children all grow up together and the man is *always there* for his family. Arthur Phillips and Henry Morris note that "the normal position is therefore that, among Africans who are living under their tribal law, polygamy is permitted, and the rights and obligations arising therefrom are legally recognized" (88).[15] The man, or the woman, does not only enjoy the rights and privileges of the arrangement but must also execute his/her obligations. Peace and harmony are maintained through the observance of not only equity but also hierarchy—between the man and his wives and children on the one hand and between co-wives on the other hand. As Patrick Merand rightly observes,

> [L]'importance du rang parmi les coépouses, appelées aussi, "veudieux," joue un grand rôle. La première femme bénéficie d'une autorité indéniable sur ses collègues: c'est par définition la plus agée; elle seule n'a pas été choisie en "remplacement". (*Vie* 89)

> [The importance of rank among co-wives is emphasized. The first wife, usually the oldest, enjoys undisputed authority over her co-wives; she is the only wife not chosen as "replacement."]

Just as in the Islamic institution of marriage, the traditional African polygamous marriage aims at the maintenance of equity, justice, harmony, and sharing of responsibility. More importantly, the man is *physically there* for his entire family.

Let us revisit the Josephs in Big Water, Utah. "Alex takes care of the major expenses of the compound with the money he earns running a dry-dock business for boaters ... Each of the wives, meanwhile, is responsible for her own children's clothing and groceries expenses, as well as phone bills and other minor charges" (50). Alex's wives point out that "countless 'monogamous' men have multiple relationships—everything from one-night stands to long-term affairs—they just don't tell their wives. 'Our family life is a lot more honest,' says Dawn Joseph, a petite 25-year-old with curly blond hair. 'I can't imagine a more satisfying and fulfilling relationship than the one I have with my husband'" (46). Finally, let us go back to the African village of Umuofia and visit the Nwakibies and the Okonkwos (*Things Fall Apart*). Modou (Ramatoulaye's husband in *Une si long lettre*) is no Okonkwo. Although Okonkwo has his own problems of arrogance, impatience, and intolerance, he is a decent, honest, responsible family man who fully executes his obligations to his wives and children, who is no absentee landlord but lives in the *same* compound with his family and is *always there* for them, who maintains harmony in his household through fairness, justice, and equity, who is no philanderer (like Modou) that abandons his family. Like Okonkwo and the other polygamous men in Umuofia, Nwakibie respects the space each wife occupies:

> Nwakibie calls in his wives: Anasi was a middle-aged woman, tall and strongly built. There was authority in her bearing and she looked every inch the ruler of the womenfolk in a large and prosperous family. She wore

the anklet of her husband's titles, which the first wife alone could wear. She walked up to her husband and accepted the horn from him. She then went down on one knee, drank a little, and handed back the horn. She rose, called him by his name and went back to her hut. The other wives drank in the same way, in their proper order, and went away. (*Things Fall Apart* 18–19)

"Proper order," rank and superior position of the first wife are respected and maintained. Usually, the senior wife reciprocates the respect through friendship and bonding. Of course like in all other types of marriage, some polygamous marriages are good and others bad. The polygamous arrangements mentioned above capture in essence the following notions: harmony, responsibility, fairness, honesty, equity, order, friendship, respect, satisfaction, sharing, bonding, etc.

However, the "polygamous" arrangements that operate in Mariama Bâ's novels are a far cry from what I have noted above. Patrick Merand observes that:

Dans les villages et dans les milieux urbains modestes, le mari vit avec ses coépouses dans une concession regroupant toute la famille. Chaque femme dispose d'une ou plusieurs pièces, la cour demeurant une partie commune. Les enfants logent avec leur mère respective, mais passent toute la journée ensemble. *Dans les milieux riches des grandes villes,* il s'agit d'une "polygamie géographique." (*Vie* 88, my emphasis)

[*In the villages and poor urban milieus,* the husband, his wives, and children live in the same family compound. Each woman has a room or more and everyone has equal access to the courtyard. Children live with their respective mothers but spend the day together. *In rich urban milieus,* "geographic polygamy" prevails.]

In my view, "la polygamie géographique" is nothing but a euphemism for formalized concubinage. Vincent Monteil in his study of the practice of Islam in Dakar,[16] identifies an extreme and more disruptive variant of polygamy:

La polygamie est, bien entendu, en baisse, dans une grande ville comme Dakar, où il est bien difficile à un fontionnaire d'entretenir deux ou trois foyers. En pratique, ce qui se passe, c'est plutôt une polygamie "successive," facilitée par les divorces hâtifs et l'instabilité conjugale. ("L'Islam" 82)

[Certainly, polygamy is in the decline in a big city like Dakar where it is difficult for a civil servant to maintain two or three homes. In practice, what obtains is a "serial" polygamy facilitated by quick divorces and conjugal instability.]

Monteil makes a clear distinction between polygamy (the institution), which is on the decline, and its vulgarization in practice, which is on the upsurge. For the women in Bâ's work, it is the vulgarization of the institution of polygamy that constitutes the scandal. Ousmane Sembène lends his voice to the *exposé* of these urbanized variants of polygamy through his depiction of the irresponsible, vagrant, urban polygamist:

> *En ville*, les familles étant dispersées, les gosses ont peu de contacts avec leur père. Ce dernier, par son mode d'existence, navigue de maison en maison, de villa en villa, n'est présent que le soir pour le lit. Il n'est donc qu'une source de financement quand il a du travail. Quant à l'éducation des enfants, la mère s'encharge. (*Xala* 104, my emphasis)

> [*In the urban milieu*, because each wife and her children live in a separate location, the children have little contact with their father, whose vagrant lifestyle allows him during the day to move from house to house, villa to villa, and come home at night to sleep. He is, therefore, only a source of financial support when he has a job. Each woman is responsible for the education of her children.]

What emerges from the foregoing is an extreme systemic contradiction that I call "monogamized polygamy." In this strange marriage of two completely different systems (which goes to support my earlier assertion that the modern, urban African man juggles different systems to his advantage), the man avails himself of the companionship and services of one wife at a time and totally ignores the existence of, and his responsibility to, the other wife/wives. What the women find psychologically and emotionally disturbing is the confusion resulting from this oxymoron of monogamy in polygamy. As critics, let us keep in mind the salient issues raised above as we engage in our analysis of "polygamy" in Bâ's works: (1) Rafi Ullah Shehab credits the Holy Koran for stipulating that if a man is not sure of being fair to many wives, he should have only one; the man must be guided by these three most important factors—justice between wives, sexual capability and meeting expenses. (2) Patrick Merand indicates that in polygamy, as an indigenous African institution, rank between co-wives is important and maintained. This fact is also obvious in the above brief quote on Nwakibie and his wives in *Things Fall Apart*. (3) Patrick Merand makes an important distinction in the practice of polygamy in *African villages and among the urban poor*, on the one hand, and among *affluent urbanites* on the other hand; the former shows cohesion and shared responsibility, the latter arcs towards anarchy and irresponsibility.

LIVING WITH CONTRADICTIONS: DIFFERENT LIVES, SAME STORY

I shall examine the lives of three victims of these variants of *de jure* and *de facto* urbanized polygamy—"polygamie géographique," "polygamie successive," "monogamized polygamy," "polygamized monogamy"— Ramatoulaye and Aïssatou (*Une si longue lettre*), and Mireille (*Un chant écarlate*). An important common denominator in the lives of these three women is the fact that their husbands kept them in the dark as they contracted a second marriage in spite of the fact that they married their respective husbands at great personal risk by alienating themselves, temporarily or permanently, from their families. When Ramatoulaye met and fell in love with Modou, she had a string of suitors but still preferred her "homme à l'éternel complet kaki" [man in eternal khaki suit] (28/16). She waits for him while he studies in France during which period he writes her eloquently reassuring letters: "C'est toi que je porte en moi. Tu es ma négresse protectrice. Vite te retrouver rien que pour une pression de mains qui me fera oublier faim et soif et solitude" [It's you whom I carry within me. You are my protecting black angel. Would I could quickly find you, if only to hold your hand tightly so that I may forget hunger and thirst and loneliness] (25/14). When Modou returns to Senegal, Ramatoulaye secretly marries him in spite of her other suitors and strong opposition from her family, especially her mother:

> Daouda Dieng savait aussi forcer les coeurs. Cadeaux utiles pour ma mère, allant du sac de riz, appréciable en cette période de pénurie de guerre, jusqu'au don futile pour moi, enveloppé avec préciosité, dans du papier enrubanné . . . Notre mariage se fit sans dot, sans faste, sous les regards désapprobateurs de mon père, devant l'indignation douloureuse de ma mère frustrée, sous les sarcasmes de mes soeurs surprises, dans notre ville muette d'étonnement. (28)

> [Daouda Dieng also knew how to win hearts. Useful presents for my mother, ranging from a sack of rice, appreciated in that period of war penury, to the frivolous gift for me, daintily wrapped in paper and tied with ribbons . . . Our marriage was celebrated without dowry, without pomp, under the disapproving looks of my father, before the painful indignation of my frustrated mother, under the sarcasm of my surprised sisters, in our town struck dumb with astonishment.] (16)

After twenty-five years of marriage and twelve childbirths, after a lifetime of hard work to raise a family and amass some appreciable wealth, Ramatoulaye discovers that her husband has abandoned her for her daughter's adolescent classmate, Binetou, thereby making himself a hopeless case of what Nigerians call *sugar daddy*.[17] Despite the hurt and humiliation, Ramatoulaye accepts to stay in the marriage but Modou leaves her and her children anyway. The book opens at Modou's death when Ramatoulaye is in seclusion as mandated by Islamic law. During the Islamic ritual of *mirasse* in which the dead (Modou) is stripped of his most intimate secrets, Ramatoulaye is outraged to discover her husband's deception and betrayal during their married life.

Let me isolate some of Ramatoulaye's most bitter complaints to see if and how they relate to polygamy. Her first complaint is leveled against her sisters-in-law who do not respect her status as the senior wife by treating her and Binetou similarly: "Nos belles-sœurs traitent avec la même égalité trente et cinq ans de vie conjugale. Elles célèbrent, avec la même aisance et les mêmes mots, douze et trois maternités. J'enregistre, courroucée, cette volonté de nivellement qui réjouit la nouvelle belle-mère de Modou" [Our sisters-in-law give equal consideration to thirty years and five years of married life. With the same ease and the same words, they celebrate twelve maternities and three. I note with outrage this desire to level out, in which Modou's new mother-in-law rejoices] (11/4). As I noted above, through a structural observation and preservation of hierarchy, polygamy aims at order and fairness. Ramatoulaye is aware of the hierarchy that prevails in the system and it is against the subversive non-observance of the hierarchy that she complains.

Secondly, Ramatoulaye complains about Modou's secret marriage to Binetou because of whom he marries (her daughter's friend and family friend) and, more importantly, how he marries her (secretly, without consulting with his wife). More than anything else, it is Modou's deception/betrayal with its concomitant humiliation that causes Ramatoulaye the most pain:

Et, au crépuscule de ce même dimanche où l'on mariait Binetou, je vis venir dans ma maison, en tenue d'apparat et solennels, Tamsir, le frère de Modou, entre Mawdo Bâ et l'Imam de son quartier . . . Je m'assis devant eux en riant aussi. L'Imam attaqua: "Quand Allah tout puissant met côte à côte deux êtres, personne n'y peut rien . . . Dans ce monde, rien n'est nouveau" . . . Je pensais à l'absent. J'interrogeai dans un cri fauve traqué: "Modou?" "Oui, Modou Fall, mais heureusement vivant pour toi, pour nous tous, Dieu merci. Il n'a fait qu'épouser une deuxième femme, ce jour. Nous venons de la Mosquée du Grand-Dakar où a eu lieu le mariage." (55–56)

[And in the evening of the same Sunday on which Binetou was being married off I saw come into my house, all dressed up and solemn, Tamsir, Modou's brother, with Mawdo Bâ and his local Imam . . . I sat in front of them, laughing with them. The Imam attacked: "There is nothing one can do when Allah the almighty puts two people side by side . . . There is nothing new in this world" . . . I thought of the absent one. I asked with the cry of a hunted beast: "Modou?" . . . "Yes, Modou Fall, but happily, he is alive for you, for all of us, thanks to God. All he has done is to marry a second wife today. We have just come from the mosque in Grand Dakar where the marriage took place."] (36–37)

There is *nowhere* in Islamic or African polygamous practice that an irresponsibility of this magnitude is inscribed as either legal or acceptable. Modou's action is the foolish act of an irresponsible, wayward spouse and *sugar daddy* that has absolutely nothing to do with the institution of polygamy as it is inscribed both in Islamic law and African culture. The polygamous institution in traditional African society is not designed to spring such devastating, lunch-hour surprises. Usually, the first wife participates in marriage ceremonies performed on behalf of her co-wife. Modou's unspeakable act of betrayal is inconceivable in the world of the Okonkwos and Nwakibies of Umuofia (*Thing Fall Apart*); or even in the case of Alex Joseph of Big Water, Utah, whose wives actually recruit co-wives.

Ramatoulaye now knows the reason for her dishonest husband's numerous absences which he explained away as job-related and she, the trusting wife that she is, believed him. Despite her initial shock in learning about this new marriage, Ramatoulaye shows dignity, restraint and maturity in her comportment:

> Je pensais à son absence, toute la journée. Il avait simplement dit: "Ne m'attendez pas à déjeuner." Je pensais à d'autres absences, fréquentes ces temps-ci, crûment éclairées aujourd'hui et habilement dissimulées hier sous la couverture de réunions syndicales . . . Je m'appliquais à endiguer mon remous intérieur. Surtout, ne pas donner à mes visiteurs la satisfaction de raconter mon désarroi. . . . Enfin seule, pour donner libre cours à ma surprise et jauger ma détresse. Ah! Oui, j'ai oublié de demander le nom de ma rivale et de pouvoir ainsi donner une forme humaine à mon mal. (57–59)

> [I thought of his absence, all day long. He had simply said: "Don't expect me for lunch." I thought of other absences, quite frequent these days, crudely clarified today yet well hidden yesterday under the guise of trade union meetings . . . I forced myself to check my inner agitation. Above all, I must not give my visitors the pleasure of relating my distress . . . Alone at last, able to give free rein to my surprise and to gauge my distress. Ah! yes, I forgot to ask for my rival's name so that I might give human form to my pain.] (37–38)

This omission marks both her disarray and the secondary importance of her rival, or even of polygamy *per se*. What is at issue is the deception and humiliation she has come to know. In spite of her pain and humiliation, Ramatoulaye decides to stay in the marriage with young Binetou *according to Islamic law*: "Je pleurais tous les jours. Dès lors, ma vie changea. Je m'étais préparée à un *partage équitable selon l'Islam*, dans le domaine polygamique. Je n'eus rien entre les mains" [I cried every day. From then on, my life changed. I had prepared myself for *equal sharing, according to the precepts of Islam* concerning polygamic life. I was left with empty hands] (69/46, my emphasis). Unfortunately, Ramatoulaye does not get the equity and justice that are mandated for a polygamous marriage in Islam. In fact, at this point, she is not even in a *de facto* marriage (polygamous or not). Modou has abandoned her and her children.

Thirdly, like the shortest verse in the Bible that carries in its brevity an event of tragic proportions, "Jesus wept," Ramatoulaye's most serious complaint is devastatingly encoded in one of the shortest sentences in the book and strategically inscribed at the very end of chapter fourteen of the twenty-eight-chapter book: "Il nous oublia" [He forgot about us] (69/46). The insertion of this most painful sentence exactly at the halfway mark (center) emphasizes its centrality, pertinence, and importance. Ramatoulaye chooses to stay in a polygamous marriage but, unfortunately, her husband abandons her: "Le vide m'entourait. Et Modou me fuyait. Les tentatives amicales ou familiales, pour le ramener au bercail, furent vaines ... Il ne vint jamais plus; son nouveau bonheur recouvrit petit à petit notre souvenir. Il nous oublia" [I lived in a vacuum. And Modou avoided me. Attempts by friends and family to bring him back to the fold proved futile ... He never came back again; his new found happiness gradually swallowed up his memory of us. He forgot us] (69/46). Modou's evasiveness has absolutely nothing to do with polygamy. We must also not forget that the fear of abandonment is at the root of Ramatoulaye's rejection of Daouda Dieng's marriage proposal: "*Abandonnée* hier, par le fait d'une femme, je ne peux allègrement m'introduire entre toi et ta famille." [*Abandoned* yesterday because of a woman, I cannot lightly bring myself between you and your family] (100/68, my emphasis). Obviously, the issue here is not polygamy; it is abandonment. A polygamist is one that has more than one spouse but at the point that Modou leaves, he is no longer a functional polygamist. What he does, in effect, is to leave one woman for another, thus making himself a *de jure* polygamist (he does not divorce Ramatoulaye) and a *de facto* monogamist. Affluence in an urban milieu makes such relocations and dislocations possible; it makes it possible for rich urbanites to purchase or rent homes for their women in different parts of the city (although in the case of Modou, he mortgages his home with Ramatoulaye in order to finance Binetou's villa). Obviously, Modou fails to heed the Islamic injunction that stipulates the following: "And let those who cannot afford marriage keep themselves chaste until Allah provides them with means" (Al Quaran-Surah Al-Noor 33). Ramatoulaye makes the connection between affluence/materialism and "polygamy géographique" in her assessment of Binetou and the other young women like her: "Binetou est un agneau immolé comme beaucoup d'autres sur l'autel du 'matériel'" [Binetou, like many others, is a lamb slaughtered on the altar of affluence] (60/39).

Ramatoulaye is confused and troubled by the apparent enigmas and contradictions in her married life. The first is her husband whose unexplained radical change she tries but fails to understand: "L'adjonction d'une rivale à ma vie ne lui a pas suffi. En aimant une autre, il a brûlé son passé *moralement et matériellement*. Il a osé pareil reniement pourtant. Et pourant, que n'a-t-il fait pour que je devienne sa femme!" [The addition of a rival to my life was not enough for him. In loving someone else, he burned his past, both *morally and materially*. He dared to commit such an act of disavowal. And yet, what didn't he do to make me his wife!] (23/12, my emphasis). Secondly, she is troubled by the discrepancies which exist between the institution of polygamy in Islamic and traditional African cultures on the one hand, and its practice, especially in her own marriage, on the other hand. She is guaranteed neither the justice and equity mandated in Islam nor is she the beneficiary of the *moral and material* support of her husband as well as the superior position which the ranking of wives in the African traditional marriage guarantees.

Ramatoulaye remains ambivalent about polygamy. She does not walk away from it like Aïssatou did; even as she accepts to remain in it, she is aware of and deeply concerned about its subversion (conjugal responsibility, respect for hierarchy among wives, etc.). Even her position *vis-à-vis* polygamy/monogamy at the end of her letter is not as clear as Esonwanne's essay claims.[18] Esonwanne argues that Ramatoulaye's implied preference for monogamy is driven by her captivity to Enlightenment epistemology as learned from Ponty-Ville. Now, let us look at some of Ramatoulaye's utterances on which Esonwanne's argument hinges:

> Je reste persuadée de l'inévitable et nécessaire complémentarité de l'homme et de la femme. L'amour, si imparfait soit-il dans son contenu et son expression, demeure le joint naturel entre ces deux êtres. S'aimer! Si chaque partenaire pouvait rendre sincèrement vers l'autre! S'il essayait de se fondre dans l'autre! . . . C'est de l'harmonie du couple que nâit la réussite familiale, comme l'accord de multiples instruments crée la symphonie agréable. Ce sont toutes les familles, riches ou pauvres, unies ou déchirés, conscientes ou irréfléchies qui constituent la Nation. La réussite d'une nation passe donc irrémédiablement par la famille. (129–130)

> [I remain persuaded of the inevitable and necessary complementarity of man and woman. Love, as imperfect as it may be in its content and expression, remains the natural link between these two beings. To love one another! If only each partner could move sincerely towards the other! If each could only melt into the other! . . . The success of the family is born of a couple's harmony, as the harmony of multiple instruments creates a pleasant symphony. The nation is made up of all the families, rich or poor, united or separated, aware or unaware. The success of a nation therefore depends inevitably on the family.] (89)

One can call this an endorsement of monogamy based on the following assumptions: (1) complementarity of man and woman functions only in monogamy; (2) two beings can love each other and "melt into the other" only in monogamy; (3) partners exist only in monogamy; (4) partners can sincerely move toward one another only in monogamy; (5) successful families and harmonious couples are prerogatives of monogamy; (6) couples exist only in monogamy. Will a polygamist and one of his wives walking down the street not be called a couple (meaning two)? I wonder. In my view, these assumptions on which rests Esonwanne's forceful argument have more to do with Enlightenment epistemology than Ramatoulaye's ambivalence. If the case for monogamy is made because of Bâ's use of "couple," we must not forget that in the same breath, Bâ talks of the harmony of a *couple* and the harmony of *multiple* instruments (my italics). Bâ sees the family as the building-block of the nation but her emphasis is more on the recogniton of different types of families than an endorsement of a particular type. We must not also forget that in *So Long a Letter*, Ramatoulaye had three chances to be in a polygamous marriage; she accepted one (with Modou) and rejected two (with Tamsir and Daouda Dieng).

Aïssatou's marital woes came to a head three years before Ramatoulaye's crisis. Faced with similar crisis, each woman takes a different path to a solution: Ramatoulaye remains in her marriage but Aïssatou seeks divorce. Aïssatou's marriage to Mawdo is as controversial as Ramatoulaye's: "Puis, ce fut ton mariage avec Mawdo Bâ, fraîchement sorti de l'Ecole Africaine de Médecine et de Pharmacie. Un mariage controversé. J'entends encore les rumeurs coléreuses de la ville" [Then came your marriage with Mawdo Bâ, recently graduated from the African School of Medicine and Pharmacy. A controversial marriage. I can still hear the angry rumours in town] (30/17). After several years of a happy marriage and four sons, Aïssatou walks out on her marriage when she discovers, again *after the fact*, that her husband has married another wife, a blue blood and a much younger woman handpicked and indoctrinated by his mother, while claiming that he became a polygamist to avert the untimely demise of his implacable mother. It is true that Mawdo's mother, perched on her inflexible aristocratic arrogance, never forgave Mawdo for contracting a misalliance with a jeweler's daughter and consequently vowed to have her only son properly married to a true blue blood. However, the narrator, Ramatoulaye, provides the crucial subtext: "La petite Nabou était si tentante" [Young Nabou was so tempting] (48/30)! Like Ramatoulaye, Aïssatou is kept in the dark, and like Ramatoulaye, she is devastated by the humiliation and betrayal. Everyone, expect Aïssatou, knew that a co-wife was in the works: "Je savais, Modou savait. La ville savait. Toi, Aïssatou, tu ne soupçonnais rien et rayonnais toujours. Et parce que sa mère avait pris date pour la nuit nuptiale, Mawdo eut enfin le courage de te dire ce que chaque femme chuchotait: tu avais une co-épouse" [I knew about it. Modou knew about it. The whole town knew about it. You, Aïssatou, suspected nothing and continued to be radiant. And because his mother had fixed a date for the wedding night, Mawdo finally had the courage to tell you what every woman was whispering: you had a co-wife] (48/30). Aïssatou divorces her cheating and conniving husband, leaves with her four boys and settles into a good job in Washington, DC. However, her departure is dramatized by a symbolic gesture; she writes her husband a scathing letter of loss of confidence and leaves it on their *matrimonial bed*:

> Au bonheur qui fut nôtre, je ne peux substituer celui que tu me proposes aujourd'hui. Tu veux dissocier l'amour tout court et l'amour physique. Je te retorque que la communion charnelle ne peut être sans l'acceptation du cœur, si minime soit-elle. Si tu peux procréer sans aimer, rien que pour assouvir l'orgueil d'une mère déclinante, je te trouve vil. Dès lors, tu

dégringoles de l'échelon supérieur, de la respectabilité où je t'ai toujours hissé . . . Ton raisonnement qui scinde est inadmissible: d'un côté, moi, "la vie, ton amour, ton choix", de l'autre, "la petite Nabou, à supporter par devoir". Je me dépouille de ton amour, de ton nom. Vêtue du seul habit valable de la dignité, je poursuis ma route. (50)

[I cannot accept what you are offering to me today in place of the happiness we once had. You want to draw a line between heartfelt love and physical love. I say that there can be no union of bodies without the heart's acceptance, however little that may be. If you can procreate without loving, merely to satisfy the pride of your declining mother, then I find you despicable . . . Your reasoning, which makes a distinction, is unacceptable to me: on one side, me, "your life, your love, your choice", on the other, "young Nabou, to be tolerated for reasons of duty" . . . I am stripping myself of your love, your name. Clothed in my dignity, the only worthy garment, I go my way.] (31–32)

Aïssatou's letter is very illuminating. Jealousy of her rival is really not the issue. In fact, she expresses concerns for her rival, "la petite Nabou," who, according to Mawdo, is brought in not to be loved but as a breeder of children and a mark of filial loyalty. Aïssatou takes issue with every single one of Mawdo's weak arguments; she finds, in particular, his separation of carnal and romantic love abhorrent and unacceptable. Furthermore, it is important to note that Aïssatou's *first* complaint in her letter is a brief but virulent attack on classism, particularly in view of Mawdo's mother who is eminently "déclinante"/condescending: "Les princes dominent leurs sentiments, pour honorer leurs devoirs. Les 'autres' courbent leur nuque et acceptent en silence un sort qui les brime. Voilà, schématiquement, le règlement intérieur de notre société avec ses clivages insensés. Je ne m'y soumettrai point." [Princes master their feelings to fulfill their duties. "Others" bend their heads and, in silence, accept a destiny that oppresses them. That briefly put, is the internal ordering of our society, with its absurd divisions. I will not yield to it] (50/31). In fact, more than a novel about polygamy and gender relations, *Une si longue lettre* examines specifically how class stratification and conflicts are implicated in, complicate, and determine gender relations, between genders and within gender. The fact that Ramatoulaye lives in a very class-conscious culture is evidenced in the many vernacular words in the text that refer to class distinctions based on birth, economic status, and proximity to "civilization": *ngac* (bush [unsophisticated, uncivilized] woman), *ndol* (the poor), *Guélewar* (Princess), *guer* (statutory nobleman). In addition to Mawdo's mother who in her aristocratic arrogance treats Aïssatou condescendingly because she comes from the class of craftsmen (*artisanat*), the novel is replete with articulations of class consciousness, one of which shows that Ramatoulaye herself is equally guilty of class arrogance: "Je ne comprends pas . . . l'entrée de Modou, une 'personalité' dans cette famille de 'ndol', d'une extrême pauvreté." [I don't understand . . . the entrance of Modou, a 'personality', into this extremely poor family] (59/39). The society's profound class consciousness is certainly "un aspect important" with its "soubassements culturels" that the blurb on the dustjacket of *Une si longue lettre* claims the novel unearths: "Chaque page, chaque paragraphe, chaque phrase presque, mettent l'accent sur un aspect important de la société sénégalaise, dont les soubassements culturels se trouvent exhumés, expliquant conduites et attitudes" [Every page, every paragraph and almost every sentence emphasize an important aspect of Senegalese society whose cultural underpinnings are exposed in order to explain behavior and attitudes].

After the second marriage of Mawdo, "fils de princess" [son of a princess] (33/19), Aïssatou, "enfant des forges" [child from the forges] (33/19), nurses her humiliation in the context of the troubling ambiguity and incomprehensibility of human nature which is flawed even as it arcs toward the ideal: "Mawdo, l'homme est un: grandeur et animalité confondues. Aucun geste de sa part n'est de pur idéal. Aucun geste de sa part n'est de pure bestialité." [Mawdo, man is one: greatness and animal fused together. None of his acts is pure charity. None is pure bestiality] (50/32).[19] The question of bestiality raised here will be resurrected later by Ramatoulaye's use of "instincts" (in the sense of irrational and out of control) in her assessment of Mawdo's betrayal (53/34). Mawdo is a seriously flawed, "vil/despicable" man; his fatal (meaning "deadly," and not in the sense of "controlled by fate") flaw brings him crashing down from the pedestal where Aïssatou had placed him: "Dès lors, tu dégringoles de l'échelon supérieur, de la respectabilité où je t'ai hissé" [At that moment you tumbled from the highest rung of respect on which I have placed you] (50/32). Aïssatou is a respectable woman with a tremendous sense of direction, but more importantly, she has the courage and will—"tu eus le surprenant courage de t'assumer" [you had the surprising courage to take your life into your own hands] (50/32)—to follow with dignity the direction which she has carved out for herself.

In recounting Aïssatou's failed marriage, Ramatoulaye pinpoints the issues at stake—infidelity, betrayal, and lack of trust—as she addresses Mawdo:

Ainsi, pour se justifier, il ravalait la petite Nabou au rang de "mets". Ainsi, pour changer de "saveur", *les hommes trompent leurs épouses.* J'était offusquée. Il me demandait compréhension. Mais comprendre quoi? La suprématie de l'instinct? *Le droit à la trahison?* La justification du désir de changement? Je ne pouvais être l'alliée *des instincts polygamiques.* Alors, comprendre quoi? (53, my emphasis)

[Thus to satisfy himself, he reduced young Nabou to a "plate of food". Thus, for the sake of "variety", *men are unfaithful to their wives.* I was irritated. He was asking me to understand. But understand what? The supremacy of instinct? *The right to betray?* The justification of the desire for variety? I could not be an ally to *polygamic instincts.* What, then, was I to understand.] (34, my emphasis)

In actuality, much of the argument about polygamy in *Une si longue lettre* rests on this statement by Ramatoulaye. What is at issue is not polygamy as an institution but men's *polygamous instincts* that inaugurate philandering, betrayal, infidelity, lack of trust, and abandonment. One does not need to be a *de jure* polygamist to have *polygamous instincts*; monogamists are equally prone to such maladies. The issue here is less about Islamic or African culture and more about men's inability to control their roving eyes. Dawn Joseph of Big Water, Utah, rightly notes that "countless 'monogamous' men have multiple relationships—everything from one-night stands to long-term affairs—they just don't tell their wives" (46). This observation is equally applicable to Modou, Mawdo, and Ousmane (as we shall see later) who do not tell their wives until it becomes inevitable. Mariama Bâ puts on stage a bunch of irresponsible philanderers who use the institution of polygamy as an alibi, whose wealth and easy mobility in an urban setting make it possible for them to manipulate the system to their own advantage. I have raised elsewhere a definitional question about polygyny: "*Polygyny* comes from two Greek words: *poly* (many) and *gyne* (woman or wife). *Polygyny* has, therefore, two possible meanings—'many women,' or 'many wives' [just like the French *femme*—woman/wife]. The English dictionary sanctifies only one of the two possibilities, 'many wives,' a limitation to which no one seems to object. I remember that the first English dictionary I used in the colonial school was written by one Michael West, *a man*. I gather that men still write dictionaries—English dictionaries! *Polygyny* as 'many women' places the Western man with one wife and one or more mistresses in the same category as the African man who legitimizes his relationship with more than one woman" ("Bringing" 315). The difference here is that the African man (*de jure* polygamist) is up front and decent about it, or as Dawn Joseph says of her polygamous marriage: "Our family life is a lot more honest" (46). The *polygamous instincts* that are at the heart of *Une si longue lettre* are of a global nature, and have more to do with polygyny as "having many women" than polygyny as "having many wives."

In Mariama Bâ's second and posthumous work, Mireille's encounter with Ousmane is an extreme and complex case in view of the fact that the marital problems noted in the cases of Ramatoulaye and Aïssatou are further complicated by race conflicts. Mireille de la Vallée is a young, white woman from France, and Ousmane is a young, black man from Senegal. When Mireille's father, a French diplomat working in Dakar, finds out that his daughter is dating a black man, he puts her on the next available flight back to France. From France, Mireille keeps in touch with Ousmane who eventually goes to study there. In spite of the vehement opposition to her relationship with Ousmane, Mireille chooses to marry him at the risk of alienating her family—sounds familiar. In his letter to his father after their wedding, Ousmane admits the immense positive contribution Mireille has made to his life—sounds familiar:

Si j'ai réussi, si je suis ta fierté comme tu dis, si j'ai comblé tes désirs, si tu es loin de la poussière d'Usine Niari-Talli, si tu vois d'un oeil plus calme les trimestres s'étirer, c'est à elle que tu le dois. Entreprendre est difficile pour un homme seul ... Mireille m'a permis, par un soutien moral constant, de me réaliser. Elle était devant moi, comme un flambeau, illuminant mon chemin. Elle n'est pas l'une de ces vulgaires aventurières qui s'accrochent aux Nègres pour ne pas sombrer. Mireille est une fille d'ancienne noblesse. (99)

[If I have made a success of my life, if I am, as you say, your pride and joy, if I have fulfilled all your wishes, if you have left the dust of Usine Niari Talli behind you, if you can contemplate serenely the months and years stretching out before you, it is all thanks to her. It is difficult for a man to undertake anything alone ... Mireille has helped me, by her unflagging moral support, to realise my potential. She was always before me, like a flaming torch, lighting up my path. She is not one of those common women, on the lookout for the main chance, who use black men to get themselves out of deep water. Mireille comes from a noble family that goes back in time.] (64)

The couple returns to Senegal to settle. Mireille gives birth to a son and soon discovers that contrary to Ousmane's earlier assertion: "Entreprendre est difficile pour un homme seul" [It is difficult for a man to undertake anything alone] (99/64), it is not "difficult for a man [Ousmane] to undertake [things] alone"; Ousmane starts cheating on her (a *major* undertaking without the knowledge, approval, and support of Mireille). Like the Ivoirienne, Jacqueline (*Une si longue lettre*), who becomes a "gnac" (bush girl) when her Senegalese husband, Samba Diack, starts flirting with Senegalese girls, Mireille is now "une Toubab" (white woman) and marked for exclusion. Kept in the dark, Mireille does all she can to familiarize herself with her new environment and establish close ties with her husband's family without the encouragement and support of her husband, Ousmane. Unknown to Mireille, Ousmane starts dating a Senegalese girl, Ouleymatou, whom he eventually marries. Another home is rented for Ouleymatou, and Ousmane is now the privileged master of two homes! Like the other men who abandon their wives, Ousmane claims that the devil made him do it—it is destined to be! He suddenly discovers his *négritude* (or "Africanity" according to Ojo-Ade)!:

"Ma rencontre avec la Blanche relève du destin car plus que jamais, je me veux Nègre" ... "Ouleymatou, symbole double dans ma vie!" "Symbole de la femme noire" ... "Symbole de l'Afrique" dont il était l'un des "fils éclairés". Ouleymatou se confondait dans son esprit avec l'Afrique, "une Afrique à réinstaller dans ses prérogatives, une Afrique à promouvoir!" ... Reculer à cause des fureurs de ma Blanche qui clame sa colère dans la violence? Reculer à cause de ma conscience

quotidiennent alertée? Reculer à cause du code universel de l'honneur et
de la dignité? Impossible! (225)

["My meeting with the white girl was determined by Fate; my will,
more than ever, influences me to retain my identity as a black man."
"Ouleymatou, the symbol of my double life!" Symbol of the black woman,
whom he had to emancipate; symbol of Africa, one of whose "enlightened
sons" he was. In his mind he confused Ouleymatou with Africa, "an
Africa which has to be restored to its prerogatives, to be helped to
evolve!" . . . "Must I back down because of my white wife's anger?
Because she may get violent in her fury? Because, every day, my
conscience hears a warning bell? Back down because of the universal code
of honour and dignity? Impossible!"] (149–150)

Oh Mother Africa, one of thy "enlightened sons" taketh thy name in vain!
This deceit wrapped up in naturalized, originary, feminized, idealized, and
"motherized" Africa and sung in poetry will be met with poetic justice at
the end on the novel. Ousmane is not in the least confused, he knows what
he is doing; he is only battling his demons. Mariama Bâ's sarcasm is
disarmingly apparent here.

The shock of the discovery of this immense deception drives Mireille
crazy. In a fit of anger and confusion, she pastes Ousmane's love letters to
her all over their home, kills their only child and stabs Ousmane when he
comes home, as usual, in the early hours of the morning. The contradictions
of Mireille's married life take a human form in her mulatto son whom she
kills as a rejection and possible resolution of those contradictions. Her letters
feverishly pasted all over the house contain sentiments—*"Je n'aimerai que
toi, la vie . . . Toi ma blanche! Toi ma blonde, comme tu me manques!
. . . Sans toi, la vie n'a pas de sel"* ["I shall never love anyone but you,
as long as I live" . . . "You, my 'Blanche', you my 'Blond', how I miss
you! . . . Without you, life has no relish."] (244/163, emphasis
in the original)—that contradict Ousmane's current attitude towards her.
Ousmane's bravado—"[r]eculer à cause des fureurs de ma Blanche qui clame
sa colère dans violence" [Must I back down because of my white wife's
anger? Because she may get violent in her fury?] (225/150)—is not a smart
move, after all. Mireille stabs him. Fortunately for Ousmane, he is left
bleeding but not declared dead; fortunately for Mireille, the plea of insanity
remains a legal recourse.

Mariama Bâ's novels show the extent to which religious and traditional
institutions are subverted by "modernity" in Africa's urban areas, particularly among the more affluent middle and upper-middle classes. A.B. Diop,
in his study of the organization of the African family in Dakar, also makes
the connection between affluence and "polygamie géographique."[20] It is
ironic that the wealth which the first wife helps to acquire is eventually used
against her. Furthermore, there is the related issue of responsibility; particularly the ways in which the abandonment of responsibility is at the core

of the manipulation and distortion, as well as the dubious, selective, and misleading exegesis of religious canonical texts. Oftentimes, the privileges are appropriated without the responsibility. For example, one of the epigraphs to Femi Ojo-Ade's articles is taken from the Bible: "The head of every man is Christ, the head of every woman is man." This is one line of a longer quote from St Paul's epistle to the Ephesians, chapter five. Read alone (as contained in Ojo-Ade's text), it unequivocally establishes male power, authority, and privilege, but if read together with the part omitted in Ojo-Ade's text, we see that the Bible is less strident and more benevolent; it stipulates that male authority must be tempered by love and responsibility. The following is the part not incorporated in Ojo-Ade's epigraph:

> Husbands, love your wives as Christ loved the church and gave himself up for her . . . Even so husbands should love their wives as their bodies. He who loves his wife loves himself. For no man ever hates his own flesh, but nourishes and cherishes it, as Christ does to the church, because we are members of his body. For this reason a man shall leave his father and mother and be joined to his wife, and the two shall become one flesh. (1421)

The omission, intentional or non-intentional, in Ojo-Ade's text guarantees a misleading interpretation. The distortion that emanates from this and similar acts of omission sustains the oppressor/oppressed dialectic in which the oppressor, as interpreter of the canon, reigns supreme.

REVENONS A NOS MOUTONS![21]

These remarks are presented not as an apologia for polygamy but as an appeal to critics of African literature to dismantle the unidimensional, simplistic paradigms that oversimplify and distort African literary texts by their failure to absorb the complex nature of the issues presented therein. Or, as Uzo Esonwanne states more elegantly in his study of Mariama Bâ, "[t]he theoretical advance the notion of consumer production makes possible is offset by a problem endemic to post-colonial literary theory, namely, a tendency to mortgage the interpretation of subalternist writing to the hegemonic modes of literary production."[22] In her work, Mariama Bâ shows how personal traumas and disorders are symptomatic microcosms of broader issues of post-colonial dislocations and cultural hemorrhage in an environment where internal systems are undergoing self-induced and externally enforced rearticulation. On another level, this essay interrogates the articulation of polygamy as the centerpiece of Bâ's work. As I discussed above, a distinction must be made between polygamy as an institution and the way it functions in Bâ's novels, particularly in view of the fact that what obtains in some of the relationships is not even polygamy but the men's inability to hold in check their *polygamous instincts*.

Furthermore, the reification and demonization of polygamy as an institution short-circuits a serious engagement with its internal dynamics. Apart from the usual charge of unorthodoxy leveled against polygamy in the West (as in the article on the Josephs), a major problem with some analyses of polygamy is that they overinvest the husband by the inordinate focus on him as the main, if not the only, beneficiary of the system, in the same way that Peter Hitchcock's study[23] of the gaze/look in Egyptian women's fiction argues against Malek Alloula's analytical strategy in *The Colonial Harem* on the ground that "it places too much emphasis on the 'eye of the beholder' rather than the looking of the seen" (70). With regard to the analysis of polygamy, the overinvestment in the man is due primarily to the fact that sexuality is inscribed as the criterion for measuring benefit with the result that the husband is cast as the major beneficiary because he gets more sex than each wife. As we heard from the Josephs, polygamy is not just about sex, it is about human relations.

In addition, polygamy has the potential of decentering male power due to the fact that it inaugurates potential points of insurrection that, if well organized, can dilute male authority (like the rebellion led against Alex Joseph by his wives), although the points of insurrection can remain fragmented and ineffective if male authority succeeds in maintaining a strong and consistent divide-and-conquer strategy. The objectification of women in polygamous marriages in these analyses invests all power on the man and, consequently, distorts, dislocates, and mis(un)articulates locations of power. The major argument against polygamy is that it dehumanizes women who are compelled "to share" one man (a word that is visibly inscribed in the title of the article on the Josephs). What such an argument ignores is that much more is shared—friendship, companionship, expertise, time, childcare, loss, misery, happiness, etc. Above all, there is the central question of *choice* (sometimes, women *choose* to have co-wives), an issue that is at the core of feminist theorizing and activism.

Let me end with another look at Ojo-Ade's reading of African women writers, those he designates as "the voices currently crying out for the liberation of woman." The women in the literary works are not declaring war on men as Ojo-Ade claims: "the war between male and female is now a contemporary constant" (72); they are only pursuing happiness,[24] which is normal and should be encouraged. The women are demanding respect and honesty from their spouses, and that is not asking too much. The women are rejecting deception, humiliation, and betrayal from their spouses, and that is not a bad idea after all. The women are not enthused about living with enigmas—"Car Mawdo demeurait pour moi une enigme et à travers lui, tous les hommes" [For Mawdo, and through him all men, remained an enigma for me] (52/33)—and that is quite understandable.

In my many years of researching this extraordinarily gifted Senegalese writer, Mariama Bâ, I have come in contact with people who knew her very well and their unanimity on two scores is encoded in the two phrases that I have heard repeatedly: (1) "Elle savait écrire" [She knew how to write]; and (2) "Elle savait aimer" [She knew how to love]. This beautiful woman with great love in her heart saw deception and wrote a masterpiece against it. Mariama Bâ's works stand as an eloquent psychology of deception/deceivers (those captives of the devil-made-me-do-it syndrome that pervades the works). The women have no illusions about the proliferation of such "captives"; they can literally read deceit on a man's face. For example, Ramatoulaye's mother sees Modou's gapped teeth and sees trouble; she warns her daughter but she is too much in love to heed the warning: "Elle parlait souvent de la séparation voyante de tes deux premières incisives supérieures" [She often spoke of the wide gap between your two upper incisors] (26/14). Ramatoulaye learned the hard way; she sees the absence of the gapped teeth in Ibrahima Sall's face as a good indication of his trustworthiness: "Mon regard s'attarda sur la dentition. Pas de séparation traitresse." [I let my gaze rest on the set of his teeth. No treacherous gaps] (123/84). Nonetheless, like Mariama Bâ herself, some of her protagonists still have faith in the cooperation between man and woman. Ramatoulaye ends her long letter on a hopeful note: "Je reste persuadée de l'inévitable et nécessaire complémentarité de l'homme et de la femme" [I remain persuaded of the inevitable and necessary complementarity of man and woman] (129/89). Didn't Mariama Bâ, after all, also dedicate Ramatoulaye's long letter, *Une si longue lettre*, to men (qualified, however!): "aux hommes de bonne volonté" [to men of goodwill]. Are Modou Fall, Mawdo Bâ, Samba Diack, and Ousmane among these honorable men? I wonder.

NOTES

1 Although "polygamic" appears in Modupé Bodé-Thomas's translation of *Une si longue lettre*, I use "polygamous" in my chapter.
2 The expression, *Third World* (*Tiers Monde*, *Tercer Mundo*, etc.), is so inappropriate in a *civilized* world that I strongly recommend it be banned. In fact, a starving American once called a meal I prepared "Third World food" after gulping down every bit of it. Well, what can I say?—just a *small* price a *Third World* woman has to pay for hobnobbing with *civilization*! At any rate, I use *Third World* guardedly and parenthetically.
3 See Hitchcock in this volume, p. 79.
4 See Ibrahim in this volume, p. 149.
5 Audre Lorde, *Sister Outsider*, pp. 66–71.
6 All English translations of *Une si longue lettre* are from Mariama Bâ, *So Long a Letter*, Trans. Modupé Bodé-Thomas, 1981. Translations of *Un chant écarlate* are from Mariama Bâ, *Scarlet Song*, Trans. Dorothy S. Blair, 1985. All other translations are mine.
7 See Uzo Esonwanne in this volume.
8 In his book, *Anti-Semite and Jew*, Jean-Paul Sartre notes that "if the Jew did not exist, the anti-Semite would invent him" (p. 13).
9 In fact, a test of the power and beauty of Mariama Bâ's writing is that, to a great extent, it survived Modupé Bodé-Thomas's sometimes inelegant *mot-à-mot* (word-for-word) rendition of *Une si longue lettre*.
10 From Chimalum Nwankwo's abstract of his essay on polygamy and imperial refractions.

11 Esonwanne, this volume, p. 85.

12 Part of the title of Femi Ojo-Ade's article.

13 Rafi Ullah Shehab cites the example of Jamila, wife of Sabit bin Qais. Jamila, dissatisfied with the ugliness of her husband, decided to separate from him. She approached the Holy Prophet who granted the separation without hesitancy but on condition that Jamila returned the Orchard which Sabit gave her in lieu of dowry money.

14 See Patrick Merand, *La vie quotidienne en Afrique noire à travers la littérature africaine.*

15 See Arthur Phillips and Henry Morris, *Marriage Laws in Africa.*

16 See Vincent Monteil, "L'Islam."

17 A rich, flirtatious, married old man who preys on girls young enough to be his daughters.

18 Esonwanne, this volume.

19 This and the next quote from Aïssatou's letter are instances of Bodé-Thomas's *mot-à-mot* translation that undermines Bâ's poetic rendition.

20 A. B. Diop's research shows that polygamy in the urban areas increases as one goes up the economic ladder: "D'autre part, on constate l'augmentation du taux de polygamie avec la montée des chefs de menage dans la hiéarchie des professions ... Ce taux passe de 8, 2% chez les domestiques à 10, 8% chez les ouvriers, employes, artisans, 17, 5% chez les commerçants; elle atteint 19, 5% chez les fonctionnaries ... La polygamie ... ne devient frequénte que dans les catégories qui ont les moyens économiques les plus importants" "L'Organisation de la famille africaine," p. 309). [On the other hand, there is an increase in the rate of polygamy for male heads of household as one goes up the professional ladder. The rate increases from 8.2% for houseworkers to 10.8% for workmen and craftsmen, to 17.5 for tradesmen and reaches 19.5% for senior civil servants ... Polygamy ... becomes rampant only among the very affluent.]

21 This phrase which literally means "let's return to the sheep" is taken from a medieval French farce, *La Farce de Maître Pathelin*, and is used to bring people back to the issue at hand if they start wandering away from it. I find this expression appropriate for my repeated calls to all of us as critics of African literature not to wander too far afield into all brands of epistemologies, theories, and methodologies that have little or no relevance to African literary texts as *cultural* productions. Although the African texts are written in languages with which we are familiar— English, French, Portuguese, and Spanish—they are all encoded in the *language of culture (in all its specificity)* that demands other levels of understanding and other manners of "speaking." These are not easy, superficial texts, although sometimes our readings of them make them look that way. They are complex texts whose decoding requires a firm grasp of the *language of culture*. Our interest in and commitment to African literature, particularly for those not born in that environment or without formal training in the field of African literature, is a laudable one that can be sustained only by a serious engagement in/with the *language of culture*. Cultural illiteracy engenders paralysis, and African literature is too effervescent to be mired in paralysis. A very good understanding of the texts and the environment from which they evolved must be the engine that drives the car of African literary criticism. Any epistemology or theory that is alien to that environment must be used guardedly as a frame of reference, at best, and not as a substitute for the literary texts themselves; to do otherwise is suicidal. As my people say, *okenye adi ano nuno ewu anwuo nogbili* (an adult cannot be home and a goat dies at the tether). We, as critics, are the adults who must not watch the goat (African literature) strangle to death or, worse still, participate in its strangulation.

22 Esonwanne, this volume.

23 Hitchcock, this volume.

24 In his article which appears in *Ngambika: Studies of Women in African* Literature, Edris Markward examines the quest for happiness in Bâ's novels.

WORKS CITED

Alcoff, Linda. "The Problem of Speaking for Others." *Who Can Speak? Authority and Critical Identity.* Ed. Judith Roof and Robyn Wiegman. Urbana: University of Illinois Press, 1995, 97–119.

Bâ, Mariama. *Une si longue lettre.* Dakar: Nouvelles Éditions Africaines, 1980.

——. *So Long a Letter.* Trans. Modupé Bodé-Thomas. London: Heinemann, 1981.

——. *Un Chant écarlate.* Dakar: Nouvelles Éditions Africaines, 1981.

——. *Scarlet Song.* Trans. Dorothy S. Blair. New York: Longman, 1985.

Diop, A. B. "L'Organisation de la famille africaine." *Dakar en devenir.* Ed. M. Sankale, L. V. Thomas, and P. Fougeyrollas. Paris: Présence africaine, 1968, 299–313.

Laver, Ross, and Paula Kaihla. "I Share My Husband With Seven Other Wives." *Marie Claire* (November 1995): 44–50.

Lorde, Audre. *Sister Outsider.* Trumansburg, NY: The Crossing Press, 1984.

Makward, Edris. "Marriage, Tradition and Woman's Pursuit of Happiness in the Novels of Mariama Bâ." *Ngambika: Studies of Women in African Literature.* Ed. Carole Boyce Davies and Anne Adams Graves. Trenton: Africa World Press, 1986.

Merand, Patrick. *La Vie quotidienne en Afrique noire à travers la littérature africaine.* Paris: Harmattan, 1980.

Monteil, Vincent. "L'Islam," *Dakar en devenir.* Ed. M. Sankale, L.V. Thomas, and P. Fougeyrollas. Paris: Présence africaine, 1968, 199–210.

The New Oxford Annotated Bible. Ed. Herbert G. Mazy and Bruce M. Metzger. New York: Oxford University Press, 1973.

Nnaemeka, Obioma. "Bringing African Women into the Classroom: Rethinking Pedagogy and Epistemology." *Borderwork: Feminist Engagements with Comparative Literature.* Ed. Margaret R. Higgonet. Ithaca: Cornell University Press, 1994, 301–318.

Ojo-Ade, Femi. "Still a Victim? Mariama Bâ's *Une si longue lettre.*" *African Literature Today* 12 (1982): 71–87.

Phillips, Arthur and Henry F. Morris. *Marriage Laws in Africa.* London: Oxford University Press, 1971.

Sartre, Jean-Paul. *Réflexions sur la question juive.* 1946. *Anti-Semite and Jew.* Trans. George J. Becker. New York: Grove Press, 1960.

Sembène, Ousmane. *Xala.* Paris: Présence africaine, 1973.

Shehab, Rafi Ullah. *Rights of Women in Islamic Sharia.* Lahore: Indus Publishing House, 1986.

11 Reconstructing motherhood
Francophone African women autobiographers

Renée Larrier

La mère de famille n'a pas du temps pour voyager. Mais elle a du temps pour mourir.

[The mother of a family has no time to travel. But she has time to die.]
Mariama Bâ, *Une si longue lettre/So Long A Letter* (110/75)

As a young girl, Ramatoulaye in *Une si longue lettre* (1980) expresses misconceptions about motherhood: "Je croyais qu'un enfant naissait et grandissait sans problème. Je croyais qu'on traçait une voie droite et qu'il l'emprunterait allègrement" [I thought a child was born and grew up without any problem. I thought one mapped out a straight path and that he would step lightly down it] (110/75). Experience with her own children, however, proved otherwise: "Or, je vérifiais, à mes dépens les prophéties de ma grand-mère" [I saw, at first hand, the truth of my grandmother's prophecies"] (110/75). The narrator is alluding to the wide gap between the institution of motherhood, a concept, and the experience of mothering, an activity.[1] This gap or space can best be studied in African women's autobiography.

African autobiography in general aims to "set the record straight," to document history for future generations, a history that has been distorted by the West. Consequently, it emphasizes lived experience in order to counteract racist stereotypes.[2] Nafissatou Diallo, for example, writes in the preface to *De Tilène au Plateau* (1975): "Le Sénégal a changé en une génération. Peut-être valait-il la peine de rappeler aux nouvelles pousses CE" [Senegal has changed a lot in one generation. Perhaps it is worthwhile to remind the youth what we were]. John Blassingame comes to a similar conclusion about African-American autobiography when he says it provides another source of historical information (2–9). African and African-American autobiography also share a concern for the group rather than the individual experience.[3] Recent work on women's autobiography reveals that contemporary women's self-stories address gender issues.[4] In addition, Françoise Lionnet concludes that women's autobiographies are structured by relationships with family and loved ones,[5] as are African-American women's autobiographies, according to Joanne Braxton.[6] African women's autobiography intersects with black as well as women's autobiography. It reveals concerns with documenting history, the collective experience, and family and gender issues. At the same time, however, as Carole Boyce Davies points out, there are certain specificities found in African women's autobiography due to the public silencing and voicelessness of women (268).

But how do francophone African women autobiographers represent motherhood? Do they idealize the status or do they marginalize it? Is childlessness a punishment? Is motherhood at the center of their works? Do these writers address the dichotomy between motherhood and mothering? How does their representation differ from that of male writers? As we shall see, sex, gender, and experience make a world of difference.

MOTHER=MOTHER AFRICA IN "MASTER TEXTS"

In African societies being a mother is a cultural mandate and a privilege. According to Ifi Amadiume in *Male Daughters, Female Husbands*:

> Maternity is viewed as sacred in the traditions of all African societies. And in all of them, the earth's fertility is traditionally linked to women's maternal powers. Hence the centrality of women as producers and providers and the reverence in which they are held. (191)

Sociologist Fatou Sow, like Amadiume, notes:

> "La terre, porteuse de vie, est symbolisée de manière variée selon les ethnies et les terroirs, mais elle est partout symbole de féminité". (107)

> [The earth, giver of life, is symbolized in various ways by ethnic groups and areas, but it is a symbol of femininity everywhere.]

This explains Léopold Sédar Senghor's use of the mère/terre trope in "Femme noire" published in *Chants d'ombre* (1945).[7] In the poem's first stanza the adult narrator recalls his *mother's* role as a protector: "J'ai grandi à ton ombre, la douceur de tes mains bandait mes yeux" [I grew up in your shadow, the sweetness of your hands shielded my eyes]. Camara Laye followed Senghor's model in the dedication to *L'Enfant noir* (1953). In the form of a prose poem, it reads:

> Femme noire, femme africaine, ô toi je pense à toi ... O Dâman, ô ma mère, toi qui me porta sur le dos, toi qui m'allaitas, toi qui gouvernas mes premiers pas, toi qui la première m'ouvris les yeux aux prodiges de la terre, je pense à toi ...[8]

> [Black woman, African woman, Oh, I think of you ... O my mother, you who carried me on her back, you who nursed me, you who guided my first steps, you who first opened my eyes to the wonders of the earth, I think of you ...]

Both writers, far away from home, associated the body of "mère" (mother) with "terre" (Africa). The female body—the hands, specifically—protected Senghor from the sun;[9] Camara Laye recalls her back, breasts, and hands. The sons' memory and representation of the mother as "corporeally scattered", to borrow Nancy Vickers's term, accentuates metonymically the physical, and temporal distance. This fetishization, idealization of the body, of the "mère/terre," is one characteristic of négritude whose writers were responding to the negative images of Africa that were prevalent at the time.[10] It is ironic, however, that these same writers do not eulogize their own wives who are also mothers in the same manner.

In male texts like the ones cited above, being a mother often means having sons who will offer their praise. The absence of children—read sons—however, brings emptiness and suffering. Ferdinand Oyono offers this less romanticized vision of motherhood in the fictional *Le Vieux nègre et la médaille* (1956). In a very short scene, Kelara comes to realize the folly of sacrificing her two sons to war in exchange for a medal, when she overhears a sarcastic remark during the ceremony: "Il a bien perdu ses terres et ses fils pour ça" (105) [To think he lost his land and his sons just for that] (94). Kelara, overcome with grief, weeps. Her tears express more than the sorrow of a mother who has lost two sons to war. She realizes for the first time the true cost of the medal: "Mes enfants, mes pauvres enfants, on vous a vendus comme Judas a vendu le Seigneur" (112) [My children, my poor children—sold like the lord who was sold by Judas] (99). She angrily curses Meka for allowing it to happen.

Although this is a short episode, it serves to reinforce Oyono's intention, that is, the denunciation of the patriarchal colonial system and the complicity of the villagers in their own oppression. Kelara was partly responsible for the loss of her sons who died without leaving any offspring. She, therefore, has no heirs. The lesson is that collaborators not only will be deprived of descendants, but will lose a part of themselves in the process. This episode, although gender-specific, summarizes the intention of the entire text.

Salimata in *Les Soleils des indépendances* (1968) embodies the subversion of the "mère/terre" trope as Kelara does in Oyono. Salimata with "le destin d'une femme stérile comme l'harmattan et la cendre" (30) [the destiny of a woman sterile like the dry African wind and ashes] will not produce anything. She represents, along with her husband Fama, the broken promises of African independence.[11]

In *Les Bouts de bois de Dieu*, a text that has many important women characters, there is a more balanced treatment of motherhood. While in *Le Vieux nègre et la médaille* we saw Kelara only after the death of her children, in *Les Bouts* we see constant interaction between mothers and children, and even between grandmothers and grandchildren. There are also a mother of grown children, of twins, and a blind mother. While motherhood is represented in its many aspects in *Les Bouts*, overall motherhood is still a marginalized activity in "master texts."

WOMEN WRITING THEMSELVES

When francophone women writers began to publish novels in the 1970s, women were no longer reduced to body parts, but were represented as whole persons who played several roles in the home and wider community. Women writers also offered a more realistic and varied perspective on motherhood (and mothering), showing that it is not limited to caring for a child, but is a lifetime commitment that involves many stages from pregnancy to old age. Several essays in Susheila Nasta's *Motherlands: Black Women's Writing from Africa, the Caribbean and South Asia* (1991) explore women's attempts to demythologize the link between "motherland, motherculture, and mothertongue" (xix). According to Patricia Hill Collins, African American feminists question the contradiction between the stereotyped image of the black mammy, matriarch, and welfare mother and the actual experience of mothers and "othermothers."[12] Mariama Bâ's novel *Une si longue lettre* (1980) provides the best example of the rewriting of "master texts" in francophone Africa.

Ramatoulaye is only one of many mothers in *Une si longue lettre*; she and Aïssatou, Tante Nabou, Dame Belle-Mère, Binetou, all have children, but they also function outside of that role. In addition, different kinds of relationships are represented: between sons and mothers (Mawdo and Tante Nabou), daughters and mothers (Daba and Ramatoulaye, Aïssatou and Ramatoulaye, Binetou and Dame Belle-mère), mothers-in-law and daughters-in-law (Dame Belle-mère and Ramatoulaye, Tante Nabou and Aïssatou), mother-in-law and son-in-law (Ramatoulaye and Abou and, soon to be, Ibrahima Sall), granddaughter and grandmother (Ramatoulaye and her grandmother), substitute mother and daughter (Tante Nabou and Petite Nabou). These relationships are distinguished by generation, class, and gender. Some are central to the narrative: Rama and her children; Tante Nabou, Mawdo and Petite Nabou; Dame Belle-Mère and Binetou. Others are marginalized—Binetou and her children. In no way are these relationships romanticized.

Through Ramatoulaye, Bâ also touches on other aspects of mothering: the differences between raising boys and girls, the exploitation of daughters by their mothers through forced marriage to older men for material gain, the unpleasant physical aspects of pregnancy, miscarriage, the difficult decisions confronting the mother of a pregnant unwed daughter who is still a student. While Bâ acknowledges the hardships of mothering, she does not ignore its rewards: the comfort children's presence provides and the pride a mother feels when her children excel in school and succeed in life. That Rama prepares her daughter, Aïssatou, for motherhood and marriage illustrates what is addressed in the introduction to *Ties That Bind—Essays on Mothering and Patriarchy*:

Yet no woman comes to motherhood in a vacuum. From her earliest years, she has been the recipient of a continuous stream of dictates, determinations, representations, and symbols emanating from her culture, and instructing her in the norms of femininity—a condition exemplified by heterosexual marriage and motherhood. (1)

In addition, Bâ does not condemn a young couple—Daba and Abou—for being childless. For all the reasons mentioned above, we can conclude that Bâ provides a different perspective on motherhood in francophone African literature.

Not all women fiction writers, however, question the perceptions of motherhood in male texts. Diattou in Aminata Sow Fall's *L'Appel des arènes* (1982) is made to suffer because she cannot have more than one child. On a symbolic level, she is being penalized for substituting Western values for traditional ones. In this way Sow Fall links the inability to have several children, an expectation in African societies, with punishment.

While many Western critics and writers privilege the mother–daughter relationship in life as well as in literature,[13] African, African-American, and Caribbean women writers give special attention to the grandmother in the development of female identity.[14] Simone Schwarz-Bart's *Pluie et vent sur Télumée Miracle* is a hymn to such a relationship; Toussine Lougandor not only raises granddaughter Télumée, but is a pivotal presence in her life, providing guidance and protection against the storms of life alluded to in the title.[15] While Ramatoulaye's relationship with her grandmother is not at the center of *Une si longue lettre*, it is from that bond that Rama derives strength at moments of crisis involving her own children. At one particularly trying moment, Rama remembers her grandmother's remarks about the burdens of motherhood: "la mère de famille n'a pas du temps pour voyager. Mais elle a du temps pour mourir" and "Ah! que n'ai-je un lit pour me coucher" [The mother of a family has no time to travel. But she has time to die . . . Ah, if only I had a bed on which to lie down] (110/75). Young Rama did not understand the meaning of those statements at the time, until she experiences them first hand as an adult.

Her grandmother's teachings in the form of maxims provide an explanation for the differences in personality among her children and how to cope with them:

"Naître des mêmes parents ne crée pas des ressemblements, forcément chez les enfants. Leurs caractères et leurs traits physiques peuvent différer. Ils diffèrent souvent d'ailleurs." "Naître des mêmes parents, c'est comme passer la nuit dans une même chambre" . . . "Des caractères différents requièrent des méthodes de redressement différentes. De la rudesse ici, de la compréhension là. Les talouches qui réussissent aux tout petits, vexent les aînés. Les nerfs sont soumis quotidiennement à dure épreuve! Mais c'est le lot de la mère." (110–111)

["The fact that children are born of the same parents does not necessarily mean that they will ressemble each other." "Being born of the same parents is just like spending the night in the same bedroom." Different personalities require different forms of discipline. Strictness here, comprehension there. Smacking, which is successful with the very young ones, annoys the older ones. The nerves daily undergo severe trials! But that is the mother's lot." (75–76)]

In narratives by women, the lessons that grandmothers offer do not romanticize motherhood, but rather present the various aspects of mothering: its trials and pains as well as its privileges and rewards.

WOMEN'S AUTOBIOGRAPHY AND MOTHERING

What is most remarkable about the mothers of francophone women autobiographers is their virtual absence—be it voluntary or involuntary—from their daughters lives and consequently from the text. Nafissatou Diallo's mother died when she was still very young (*De Tilène au Plateau*); Ken Bugul (*Le Baobab fou*) was abandoned by her mother at an early age; Andrée Blouin (*My Country, Africa*[16]) was placed in an orphanage at the age of three by her father over her mother's objections; Aoua Kéita (*Femme d'Afrique: la vie d'Aoua Kéita racontée par elle-même*) and Kesso Barry (*Kesso, princesse peuhle*) distanced themselves from their mothers' traditional lives. What these daughters had in common was the construction of an identity not based on their mothers, but informed by changing societies that witnessed women challenging ways of life that their mothers had accepted. Often that involved a conscious effort to be unlike their mothers.

This rejection of the mother's life is first seen in *La Vie d'Aoua Kéita racontée par elle-même* (1975). Her mother is a traditional wife who wants her daughter, born in 1913 in Mali, the former French Sudan, to follow her lead; that is, marry, manage a house, and raise children. The stories her mother tells her—the foundation of a girl's traditional education—define gender roles and reinforce these values. But Aoua's father has other plans for her. Because there are no sons—who would ordinarily assume the responsibility for the mother after the father's death—he breaks with tradition by making the practical decision to send her to the French public school in Bamako. The mother's role as the primary educator of her daughter is thus usurped. She sabotages the project by keeping Aoua at home:

Pour ma mère, c'était un scandale d'envoyer une fille en classe. Aussi était-ce avec peine qu'elle me voyait quitter la maison deux fois par jour, surtout en compagnie de garçons, alors que toutes les filles de la famille étaient occupées aux travaux ménagers. Ne pouvant manifester son mécontentement à mon père, toute sa colère retombait sur moi. Pour me retenir à la maison, de menus travaux domestiques m'étaient confiés. (24)

[For my mother it was a scandal to send her daughter to school. Also it was painful for her to see me leave the house twice a day, especially in the company of boys, while all the girls in the family were doing housework. Unable to show her discontent to my father, all of her anger fell on me. In order to keep me at home, she gave me small chores to do.] (*My translation*)

When the authorities inform her father that Aoua has missed classes, he becomes angry. Powerless in front of this authority, her mother responds by purposely ignoring Aoua, and favoring her sisters.

This incident underscores the complicity of the mother in domesticating her female children. Aoua, who enjoys school, however, does not hold a grudge. She seeks her mother's comfort after her father gives away their beloved horse, knowing that only she will share and understand her pain. After graduation from the École des médecins in Dakar as a midwife, she is sent to Gao to work. Again her mother is not happy and wants her father to marry Aoua to a relative who is a tailor. Although Kéita cannot have children of her own (she marries M. Diawara in 1935—not her parents' choice—and later divorced) being a midwife put her in that milieu. She links motherhood and politics by recruiting new members for the independence group—the Union Soudanaise du Rassemblement Démocratique Africain. In fact, she holds secret meetings in the maternity hospital in Niono to explain voting procedures; forms a women's section of the local USRDA in Gao; organizes unions of working women in Nara. Through her work as a midwife, she assists in a symbolic way in the birth of activism among women in Mali. Her "offspring" are the women who vote for the first time and thus obtain a voice in their political life.

Andrée Blouin, a contemporary of and an activist like Aoua Kéita, also combines motherhood and politics. It is her real-life offspring, however, who spark her activism. When son René is stricken with malaria, she fights the law that restricts quinine treatment to whites. This is the first step in her awakening to the injustices of colonialism. She will go on to become an activist in the independence movements in Guinea and the Belgian Congo. Blouin's representation of mothering in *My Country, Africa* is highly problematic. Born in 1921 in the Central African Republic (Oubangui-Chari at the time), she is placed at the age of three in an orphanage for "métisses" by her father, Pierre Gerbillat, a French trader, over her mother, Joséphine Wouassimba's, objections, when he moves away to marry a European woman. Colonial patriarchy is thus replaced by Christian patriarchy, ironically represented in the text by women—nuns. Another view of "motherhood" is illustrated as Mother Thérèse, Mother Germaine, and Mother Superior teach the girls "an abiding sense of shame and guilt for our parentage. All of us had been born out of wedlock" (3). Physical and emotional cruelty are substituted for nurturing as the girls are primed to serve whites and the church.

To young Andrée her mother simply disappeared "before I was old enough to store away the memory of her face. I was too young, then, to keep the sweet warmth of her tenderness for later comfort" (13). This forced separation is the cause of numerous difficulties. Under Gerbillat's orders Joséphine is barred from visiting Andrée. She manages to visit the orphanage only twice: when Andrée is nine and then again when she is fifteen. Andrée speaks French, Joséphine speaks Lingala and Sango, thus communication is a serious problem. The deliberate erasure of Andrée's African identity by the nuns' teaching of racial inferiority and submissiveness coupled with her mother's example—Joséphine does not criticize Pierre's actions—lead Andrée to become attracted to and involved with white men who mistreat her. Her education and experience have taught her that this is normal behavior.

Kesso Barry has a role model in her mother, but it is one that she chooses to reject. The cover of the autobiography *Kesso: princesse peuhle* (1988) calls attention to this choice by juxtaposing the old and the new, the traditional and the modern, the African and the European: Kesso in a studio photograph with straightened hair, makeup, nail polish, and a white floor-length wedding dress faces her mother, Diello, seen head only in profile, wearing the elaborate hairstyle of a Peul princess.[17] The wedding dress is doubly significant. Kesso has literally and figuratively married the West. As she writes in the text: "J'ai tourné le dos à cette vie . . . J'ai brisé la coquille, je suis partie. J'ai voulu m'échapper et je l'ai fait" (11) [I turned my back on that life . . . I broke the mold, I left. I wanted to escape and I did.] *Kesso* is the story of an individual famous not for her political activism like Aoua Kéita or Andrée Blouin, but for her ancestry. Kesso Barry is the daughter of L'Almamy Ibrahima Sory Barry of Dara, king of the the Peuls of Fouta-Djalon in Guinea. Being a member of a longstanding royal family brings power and privilege to Kesso. As an adult, she becomes a celebrity as an international fashion model based in France.

The text, addressed to her ten-year-old daughter Sandra, resembles an oral story, but differs markedly from those told by Aoua Kéita's mother. She wants Sandra to "écouter" and "entendre" the story of her life that was "un combat que la femme en toi comprendra" (9) [a fight that the woman in you will understand]. She goes on to explain that as a princess she was expected to marry a chief and become an obedient, discreet, and submissive wife, but after witnessing on several occasions her mother accept humiliation and victimization from her father, Barry distances herself from those traditions that keep a woman silent and passive. She chooses instead to enroll in French school, play with boys, secretly watch the boys' initiation ceremony, and drive a car:

> Je défiais les interdits et bousculais les vieux principes. J'avais tellement peur de tomber dans le piège de la femme traditionnelle, de devenir comme ma mère ou ma soeur, une épouse cloîtrée et soumise! J'étais capable de faire n'importe quoi pour bien montrer que je n'étais pas de celles-là. (122)

> [I defied the taboos and the old principles. I was so afraid of falling in the trap of the traditional woman, of becoming a cloistered and submissive

wife like my mother or my sister! I was capable of doing anything to show that I was not one of them.] (*My translation*)

Words like "struggle," "escape," "defiance," taboos," and "trap" indicate Kesso Barry's determination to flee a restricted space delimited by the Muslim religion and African custom. Andrée Blouin was similarly trapped in a prison, one created by Christianity's collaboration with colonialism or as Blouin writes: "As punishment for the crime of being born of a white father and a black mother" (3).[18]

Like Kesso Barry, Ken Bugul also struggles to escape from the post-colonial condition, a situation rendered more intense by the disappearance of her mother from her life at an early age. *Le Baobab fou* (1982) recounts its profoundly detrimental effect on her. The narrator associates absence and silence with her mother who used to leave her playing alone under the baobab tree when she was only two years old, and then leave by train—two scenes that would haunt her throughout her life. Mother and daughter would later be reunited when Ken is seven, but "Le vide laissé par le départ de ma mère ne se comblait pas" (130) [The void left by my mother's departure would not be filled] (112). Ken Bugul never felt the mother–daughter bond: "Nous ne nous sentions point mère et fille. Je m'enfermais plus en moi-même depuis ma première menstrue" (129) [We didn't feel at all like mother and daughter. At my first period, I closed more into myself] (111).

Ken was also estranged from her maternal grandmother: "Elle non plus ne me parlait pas, elle me regardait avec mépris, elle n'avait jamais été d'accord pour que j'aille à l'école française (130) [She didn't talk to me either; she looked at me with scorn; she had never agreed to my going to the French school] (112). I agree with Mildred Mortimer that the French school where Ken Bugul learned about her "ancêtres les Gaulois" contributed to her alienation (171–173). Her total identification with the West is transformed into a literal exile as she eagerly leaves Senegal for Belgium on a scholarship. The Europe she had read about in magazines does not exist. Moreover, she is treated like an "exotic object." Feeling abandoned and rootless, she eventually drops out of school, drifts, and experiments with drugs. Ken Bugul searches for an identity that she was denied growing up, a symptom of the post-colonial condition. She must return to Senegal in order to construct her identity as an African woman and to reestablish roots, or she would suffer the same fate as the abandoned baobab she left behind that died without the proper attention, care, and nurturing—activities associated with mothering.

As we mentioned above, in works by black women, when a mother is not available, a grandmother often takes her place. Nafissatou Diallo's grandmother's importance in her life is reflected in her place in the text—her voice frames *De Tilène au Plateau* (1975); it is the first and last one the narrator quotes. Her earliest memory is of Mame's oral stories at night to the assembled children. As the narrative closes, Diallo, preparing to leave for France, hesitates in the doorway until Mame frees her to embark on a new stage in her life with a simple "va avec la paix" (133) [go in peace]. Safi, who had slept by her side for eighteen years, is thus able to accept the separation.

Mame, originally from Gorée, exerts great influence over other areas of Safi's life. She is responsible for convincing her husband to allow Safi to attend public school after she finished Koranic School. Her grandfather had had a successful life without French diplomas and believed "l'homme en avant, la femme au foyer" (42) [the man in front, the woman at home]. Consequently, in 1948 Safi became the first female in the family to be sent to public school. Mame, who cured mumps and parasites, and whom Safi watched massage newborn babies, was not only admired by Nafissatou, but was the most influential woman in her life. Her chosen profession—midwifery—is an extension of Mame's.

When it is a question of representing motherhood and mothering francophone African women autobiographers have a unique perspective. Although they come from different countries—Kéita, Mali; Diallo, Bugul, Senegal; Blouin, Central African Republic; Barry, Guinea—and different generations—they were born between 1913 and 1948—their experience as daughters of traditional mothers, whether absent or present, affected their lives. As Ellen Bayuk Rosenman has written:

> mother continues to create her daughter long after she actually gives birth. Not only gender identity, but a more general sense of self in relation to other people and the outside world originate in this attachment. It is a source of both coherence and conflict, of stability and threat as, paradoxically, the daughter must define herself both with and against the mother to achieve selfhood. (ix)

Sidonie Smith writes that the woman autobiographer represses the mother in her; "she turns away from the locus of all that is domesticated and disempowered culturally" (53). This is partly true in the case of the lives we have just considered. Although they do not choose the life of a traditional wife and mother who does not enter the public arena, they do not reject everything their mothers represent. They have retained from their mothers the desire to teach the young about the past.

Both Kesso Barry and Andrée Blouin have children themselves (Nafissatou Diallo, a midwife, is pregnant at the close of *De Tilène au Plateau*; Aoua Kéita, also a midwife, observes her mother giving birth as a child). As we have seen, all present different models for their daughters than their mothers had. In these autobiographies we are far from the mère/terre trope, the narrow often romanticized version of motherhood as depicted by male writers who were looking nostalgically toward the past. Although male writers and autobiographers represent mothers as nurturers, caretakers, and educators,[19] and eulogize their mothers,[20] the male perspective is limited. Mariama Bâ alludes to this situation when she calls on women to write their own stories: "les chants nostalgiques dédiés à la mère africaine confondue dans les angoisses à la Mère Afrique ne nous suffisent plus"[21] [the nostaligic songs dedicated to the African Mother which express men's anxieties about Mother Africa are no longer sufficient]. By relating their lived experiences, franco-phone African women autobiographers rewrite the conventional expectations for women and thus reconstruct motherhood.

ACKNOWLEDGMENTS

I am grateful to Jerry Aline Flieger and Obioma Nnaemeka who read a draft of this chapter and offered valuable suggestions.

NOTES

1 See Adrienne Rich *Of Woman Born: Motherhood as Experience and Institution.* New York: Norton, 1976.

2 See this author's "Autobiographical Authority and the Politics of Narrative." *Studies in Twentieth Century Literature* 15.1 (Winter 1991): 77–86. For a more general study of African autobiography see: E. Kwadwo Opoku-Agyemang, "The Wisdom of the Eye: A Theory of African Autobiography," diss. York University, Toronto, 1986.

3 See note 1 for African autobiography. For a discussion of group identity in African-American autobiography, see Nellie McKay, "Race, Gender, and Cultural Context in Zora Neale Hurston's *Dust Tracks on a Road*," in *Life/Lines: Theorizing Women's Autobiography*, ed. Bella Brodzki and Celeste Schenck (Ithaca: Cornell University Press, 1988), 179.

4 Sidonie Smith, *A Poetics of Women's Autobiography: Marginality and the Fictions of Self-Representation* (Bloomington: Indiana University Press, 1987), 56. See also Susan Groag Bell and Marilyn Yalom, eds, *Revealing Lives: Autobiography, Biography, and Gender* (Albany: SUNY, 1990).

5 Françoise Lionnet, *Autobiographical Voices: Race, Gender, Self-Portraiture* (Ithaca: Cornell University Press, 1989), 94. Her study examples are Zora Neale Hurston, *Dust Tracks on a Road*; Maya Angelou, *I Know Why the Caged Bird Sings*; Maryse Condé, *Hérémakhonon*; Marie-Thérèse Humbert, *A l'autre bout de moi*; Marie Cardinal, *Les Mots pour le dire*.

6 Joanne M. Braxton, *Black Women Writing Autobiography: A Tradition Within A Tradition* (Philadelphia: Temple University Press, 1989), 184.

7 Florence Stratton traces the figure of woman as a represention of Africa in texts by Ayi Kwei Armah, Okot p'Bitek, Ousmane Sembène, Nuruddin Farah, Mongo Beti, Wole Soyinka, and Ngugi wa Thiongo in "'Periodic Embodiments': A Ubiquitous Trope in African Men's Writing." *Research in African Literatures* 21.1 (Spring 1990): 111–126.

8 For a discussion on the mother/son relationship see also Fritz H. Pointer, "Laye, Lamming and Wright: Mother and Son." *African Literature Today* 14. London: Heinemann, 1984. For a discussion of the mother figure in twenty novels by male writers see Alphamoye Sonfo, "La Mère dans la littérature romanesque de la Guinée, du Mali et du Sénégal." *Revue ouest africaine des langues vivantes* 2 (1976): 95–107.

9 According to Serer belief, the moon does not shine as brightly as the sun because "the moon muted her own light so that her daughter might watch, without being blinded, her mother the moon bathing naked." Robin Morgan, ed., *Sisterhood is Global* (Garden City: Anchor Books/Doubleday, 1984), 593.

10 See Anne-Claude Lelieur and Bernard Mirabel, eds, *Negripub–L'Image des noirs dans la société depuis un siècle* (Paris: Bibliothèque Forney, Les Presses Artistiques, 1987); V.Y. Mudimbe, *The Invention of Africa: Gnosis, Philosophy, and the Order of Knowledge* (Bloomington: Indiana University Press, 1988); Christopher L. Miller, *Blank Darkness: Africanist Discourse in French* (Chicago: University of Chicago Press, 1985).

11 It is ironic that later on it is revealed that it is not Salimata, but Fama who is sterile.

12 See especially chs 4 and 6 of *Black Feminist Thought: Knowledge, Consciousness, and the Politics of Empowerment.*

13 See Ellen Bayuk Roseman, *The Invisible Presence* (Baton Rouge: Louisiana State University Press, 1986); Mickey Pearlman, ed., *Mother Puzzles: Daughters and Mothers in Contemporary American Literature* (Westport: Greenwood Press, 1989).

14 See Mildred A. Hill-Lubin, "The Grandmother in African and African-American Literature: A Survivor of the African Extended Family," *Ngambika: Studies of Women in African Literature*, ed. Carole Boyce Davies and Anne Adams Graves (Trenton: Africa World Press, 1986), 257–270. Her study examples are Maya Angelou's *I Know Why The Caged Bird Sings*, Ama Ata Aidoo's *No Sweetness Here*, along with Frederick Douglass's *My Bondage and My Freedom*, and Ezekiel Mphahlele's *Down Second Avenue.*

15 For an excellent discussion of this relationship see Ronnie Scharfman, "Mirroring and Mothering in Simone Schwarz-Bart's *Pluie et vent sur Télumée Miracle* and Jean Rhys's *Wide Sargasso Sea*," *Yale French Studies* 62 (1981): 88–106.

16 Although the Blouin autobiography was published in English, I have included it here because Andrée Blouin was born in Central Africa, the former colony Oubangui-Chari and grew up in the Congo. In addition, *My Country, Africa* carries on its title page "In collaboration with Jean MacKellar" which indicates that it could have been transmitted orally in French and then translated into English. My inquiries to the publisher concerning the nature of the collaboration have not been answered.

17 Diello's portrait appeared on Guinean stamps and postcards.

18 For an excellent discussion of the alliance between missionaries and colonialism, see V.Y. Mudimbe, *The Invention of Africa: Gnosis, Philosophy, and the Order of Knowledge* (Bloomington: Indiana University Press, 1988), 45–54.

19 The role of the African woman as an educator has been studied extensively. In *La Civilisation de la femme dans la tradition africaine* (Paris: Présence africaine, 1975), there are six articles alone on women and education.

20 See especially Wilfred Cartey's opening chapter, "Autobiography . . . Mother and Child", in *Whispers from a Continent.*

21 Mariama Bâ, "La Fonction politique des littératures africaines écrites," *Ecriture française* 3.5 (1981): 7.

WORKS CITED

Amadiume, Ifi. *Male Daughters, Female Husbands.* London: Zed Books, 1987.

Bâ, Mariama. "La Fonction politique des littératures africaines écrites." *Ecriture française* 3.5 (1981): 4–7.

——. *So Long A Letter.* Trans. Modupé Bodé-Thomas. London: Heinemann, 1989.

——. *Une si longue lettre.* Dakar: Nouvelles Éditions Africaines, 1986.

Barry, Kesso. *Kesso, princesse peuhle.* Paris: Seghers, 1988.

Blassingame, John. "Black Autobiographies as Histories and Literature." *Black Scholar* 5.4 (1973–74): 2–9.

Blouin, Andrée. *My Country, Africa*. With Jean MacKellar. New York: Praeger, 1983.

Braxton, Joanne M. *Black Women Writing Autobiography: A Tradition within a tradition*. Philadelphia: Temple University Press, 1989.

Bugul, Ken. *The Abandoned Baobab*. Trans. Marjolijn deJager. New York: Lawrence Hill, 1991.

———. *Le Baobab fou*. Dakar: Nouvelles Éditions Africaines, 1984.

Cantey, Wilfred. *Whispers from a Continent*. New York: Random House, 1969.

Collins, Patricia Hill. *Black Feminist Thought: Knowledge, Consciousness, and the Politics of Empowerment*. Perspectives on Gender. Vol. 2. Boston: Unwin Hyman, 1990.

Davies, Carole Boyce. "Private Selves and Public Spaces: Autobiography and the African Woman Writer." *CLA Journal* 34.3 (March 1991): 267–289.

Diallo, Nafissatou. *De Tilène au Plateau*. Dakar: Nouvelles Éditions Africaines, 1975.

Keita, Aoua. *Femme D'Afrique: La vie d'Aoua Kéita racontée par elle-même*. Paris: Présence africaine, 1975.

Kourouma, Ahmadou. *Les Soleils des indépendances*. Paris: Seuil, 1970.

Laye, Camara. *L'Enfant noir*. Paris: Presses Pocket, 1976.

Lionnet, Françoise. *Autobiographical Voices: Race, Gender, Self-Portraiture*. Ithaca: Cornell University Press, 1989.

Morgan, Robin, ed. *Sisterhood is Global*. Garden City: Anchor Books/Doubleday, 1984.

Mortimer, Mildred. *Journeys Through the French African Novel*. Portsmouth: Heinemann, 1990.

Nasta, Susheila. *Motherlands: Black Women's Writings from Africa, the Caribbean, and South Asia*. New Brunswick: Rutgers University Press, 1991.

O'Barr, Jean F., Deborah Pope, and Mary Wyer. Introduction. *Ties That Bind–Essays on Mothering and Patriarchy*. Chicago: University of Chicago Press, 1990: 1–14.

Oyono, Ferdinand. *The Old Man and the Medal*. Trans. John Reed. African Writers Series. London: Heinemann, 1969.

———. *Le Vieux nègre et la médaille*. Paris: 10/18, 1986.

Rich, Adrienne. *Of Woman Born: Motherhood as Experience and Insitution*. New York: Norton, 1976.

Roseman, Ellen Bayuk. *The Invisible Presence*. Baton Rouge: Louisiana State University Press, 1986.

Sembène, Ousmane. *Les Bouts de bois de Dieu*. Paris: Presses Pocket, 1988.

Senghor, Léopold Sédar. *Poèmes*. Paris: Seuil, 1973.

Smith, Sidonie. *A Poetics of Women's Autobiography: Marginality and the Fictions of Self-Representation*. Bloomington: Indiana University Press, 1987.

Sow, Fatou. "Femmes, socialité et valeurs africaines." *Notes Africaines* 168 (octobre 1980): 105–112.

Sow Fall, Aminata. *L'Appel des arènes*. Dakar: Nouvelles Éditions Africaines, 1982.

Vickers, Nancy. "Diana Described: Scattered Woman and Scattered Rhyme. *Critical Inquiry* 8 (1981): 265–279.

12 Geographies of pain

Captive bodies and violent acts in the fictions of Gayl Jones, Bessie Head, and Myriam Warner-Vieyra

Françoise Lionnet

I am
the sun and moon and forever hungry
the sharpened edge
where day and night shall meet
and not be
one.

Audre Lorde, "From the House of Yemanjá"

I do not come like a secret warrior
with an unsheathed sword in my mouth . . .
I come like a woman . . .
warming whatever I touch
that is living
consuming
only what is already dead.

Audre Lorde, "The Women of Dan Dance With Swords in Their
Hands To Mark the Time When They Were Warriors"

Literature, as a discursive practice that encodes and transmits as well as creates ideology, is a mediating force in society: it structures our sense of the world since narrative or stylistic conventions and plot resolutions serve to either sanction and perpetuate cultural myths, or to create new mythologies that allow the writer and the reader to engage in a constructive re-writing of their social contexts. Women writers are often especially aware of their task as producers of images that both participate in the dominant representations of their culture and simultaneously undermine and subvert those images by offering a re-vision of familiar scripts. Thus, Harriet Jacobs, the nineteenth-century African-American writer, uses the conventions of the seduction novel as well as the Victorian ideology of "true womanhood" in order to attract readership for her *Incidents in the Life of a Slave Girl*. But she transforms those conventions by concluding her autobiographical tale with the statement "Reader, my story ends with freedom; not in the usual way, with marriage" (201), thus placing a high value on a woman's need for independence and self-expression—a radical stance in 1861. Jacobs also stresses the right of her character, Linda Brent, to choose to act in a deliberately calculated way with a single purpose in mind: freedom, even if some of Linda's actions (sexual activity outside of marriage) are socially unacceptable, and morally reprehensible to her readers. Here, for the female slave, the end clearly justifies the means, even if the means are morally suspect. As Jean Fagan Yellin has said: "Instead of coupling unsanctioned female sexual activity with self-destruction and death, *Incidents* presents it as a mistaken tactic in the struggle for freedom. Jacobs's narrator does not characterize herself conventionally as a passive female victim, but asserts that—even when young and a slave—she was an effective moral agent" (xxx). Harriet Jacobs redefines morality by reframing the subject of woman's sexual oppression. She addresses the issue of feminine desire and sexual agency in a way that helps to demystify the ideology of feminine virtue as it was previously constructed in the mid-nineteenth century.

As heirs to the tradition—exemplified by Jacobs—that recasts female subjectivity and agency by allowing women to name structures of oppression, and to resist their debilitating effects, many twentieth-century black women writers in Africa and the diaspora have, since the 1970s, been equating marriage itself (or other forms of heterosexual alliances) with confinement and captivity, denouncing their culture's failure to offer models of sexual partnership that are not demeaning or degrading to women, *and* that allow for the mutual recognition of differences. These African and African-American writers generally place the burden of responsibility for the insidious and gradual deterioration of gender relations on male characters whose indifference and/or aggression serve to perpetuate the structures of authority that contain, confine, and silence women within the domestic domain.[1] Though victimized by patriarchal social structures that perpetuate their invisibility and dehumanization, black female characters actively resist their objectification, to the point of committing murder. This extreme step is often taken after years of attempting to survive in an environment where they are, at best, the victims of sheer neglect, and, at worst, the object of violent abuse. Three contemporary writers, Gayl Jones, Bessie Head, and Myriam Warner-Vieyra, use female murderers as main protagonists, and the themes of disfiguration, castration, and imprisonment feature prominently in their texts. In this essay, I shall attempt to delineate the similarities among the fictions of these authors in order to come to some theoretical conclusions about the symbolic meaning of their choice of motifs, and the cultural anxieties it seems to reveal.

For these writers too the end justifies the means, when the end is freedom from sexual oppression. Unlike Harriet Jacobs, however, Jones, Head, and Warner-Vieyra have no illusions about the fate of women who take action to save themselves: Jones's Eva and Head's Dikeledi are incarcerated; Head's Life and Warner-Vieyra's Juletane and Sidonie die. But whereas Jones and Head suggest that a certain utopian female community is to be found in the "other spaces," the heterotopias of their protagonists' world (among other female inmates victim like them of criminal procedures that attribute guilt unjustly), Warner-Vieyra's is a bleaker vision, anchored in the grim cultural realities of a post-colonial world that links three different countries: Guadeloupe, Senegal, and France. In the texts of Jones and Head, re-visions of the cultural script are mediated by a fantasmatic resolution of differences, a retreat into the imaginary. For Warner-Vieyra, however, madness and death seem to underscore the triumphant reinscription of the symbolic order since the heroine's rebellion fails to dismantle or transpose the patriarchal narrative: Juletane never actually loses the desire to please her husband, Mamadou; and it is Sidonie's brother, Septime, who provides narrative closure after her death. Warner-Vieyra virtually reasserts and reinforces the traditional romantic ideology that revolves around the death of a heroine; by contrast, Jones and Head succeed in constructing an alternative space, a parallel world with utopian possibilities despite the restriction of movement that prison imposes.

Although the wide-ranging psychological and political problems resulting from colonialism or the slave trade are also invoked by these writers, the principal focus remains on sexual, familial, and domestic structures that uphold a particularly coercive order. As Bessie Head has pointed out, "Black women have a certain history of oppression within African culture ... women's problems are rooted in custom and tradition. What is certainly very dominant here is that the male had a superior position to the female ... [and] the disregard of Garesego Mokopi [the husband in 'The Collector of Treasures'] for his wife is based on the fact that he regards her as an inferior form of human life" (Interview 15). Bessie Head's stories—like those of fellow Africans, Buchi Emecheta, Ama Ata Aidoo, Mariama Bâ, Ken Bugul or Assia Djebar and, on this side of the Atlantic, Zora Neale Hurston, Gayl Jones, Maya Angelou, Alice Walker, Gloria Naylor, Toni Morrison, Audre Lorde, Paule Marshall, Simone Schwarz-Bart or Maryse Condé—dramatize deep-seated cultural misogyny and the potentially fatal consequences of practices (such as *de jure* or *de facto* polygamy and/or quotidian forms of sexual slavery) that construct women as objects of exchange within the male economy. As Head likes to stress, the problem is not simply of a "political" nature, that is, linked to the history of colonialism, and to post-independence corruption, even though these aggravate economic conditions. The problem, she implies, is rooted in ancient customs and traditions, for as Paul Thebolo in "The Collector of Treasures" is fond of saying, "The British only ruled us for eighty years" (96), and only a lucid and self-reflexive critique of tradition carried out from within the culture by those best acquainted with it will illuminate the "structural dissymmetry that runs all through and conditions the entire fabric of social and individual life" (Mernissi ix).[2]

The general human malaise stemming from dissymmetrical sexual arrangements has recently been superbly dissected, and denounced, by Paule Marshall in her new book, *Daughters* (1991).[3] *Daughters* is the latest contribution to this rich tradition of feminist writing in Africa and the diaspora, which continues to be extremely controversial because of its frank, and to some, biased, depiction of gender conflicts.[4] Marshall's heroine, Ursa Mackenzie, is the textual daughter of Gayl Jones's Ursa and Eva, Bessie Head's Dikeledi, Mariama Bâ's Ramatoulaye, and Myriam Warner-Vieyra's Juletane and Sidonie, among others—all characters who struggle within the sexual and racial constraints of their post- or neo-colonial societies to achieve—often unsuccessfully—a sense of dignity and freedom against great and painful odds.

But, it is important to stress that they are not meant to be in any way "representative" of a particular cross-section of "real" women. Rather, they are intended to function as *literary* figures (intertextually related to Jacob's Linda Brent or Zora Neale Hurston's Janie) whose extreme predicaments haunt the reader's imagination, and help to crystallize awareness of gender oppression while problematizing these issues in reference to a specific cultural context. My purpose, then, will be to focus on the *literarity* of a group of works whose thematic similarities are uncanny, although their narrative strategies differ considerably. What I am suggesting is that we should be wary of too literal or sociological an interpretation of these texts that would lead us to infer from them a complete breakdown of communication between the sexes, although the recent Thomas hearings in this country would tend to confirm the insights of women writers regarding the continued, and outright dismissal of black women's point of view in sexual matters. Nonetheless, I tend to agree with Deborah McDowell that "feminist critics run the risk of plunging their work into cliché and triviality if they continue merely to focus on how Black men treat Black women in literature" ("New" 196). Literary works, as the Russian Formalists have shown, produce an effect of estrangement and defamiliarization based on the application or subversion of particular literary conventions, as well as on the exaggeration of familiar scenarios that can produce in readers the shock of recognition. Knowledge of these conventions is central to the exchange of meaning between writers and readers, and by using formal methods of comparative analysis, we can perhaps elucidate certain crucial aspects of the cultural schema that subtends the works of these women writers. As Mineke Schipper states: "In studying African literature, one might certainly profit from the substantial progress and the refinement of tools by literary theorists" (*Beyond* 7). Rigorous textual analysis can help us trace the somewhat puzzling, and disturbing, commonalities among these writers, analyze the differences, and outline the ways in which their narrative strategies deconstruct and/or reinforce existing symbolic frameworks.

At the risk of collapsing together vastly different cultural arenas, I am comparing a novel by an African-American from Kentucky (Jones), two short stories by a South African exiled to Botswana (Head), and a novel and a short story by a Guadeloupean living in Senegal (Warner-Vieyra). But, I believe that the task of finding transatlantic connections is rendered all the more important by the fact that these works exemplify a pattern of influence and cross-fertilization evident in their use of themes, in their concern for the negative mythic images of women—such as Medusa, Jezebel, Salome, the Furies, the Amazon, the mad woman, the hysteric, etc.—which they exploit and translate into powerfully subversive fictions. For whereas murder is generally considered to be a crime of the individual against society, in these texts, it is present as a symptom of society's crime against the female individual. Struggle for the control of their own bodies determines the ultimate act of resistance and survival performed by Eva, Juletane, Dikeledi, and Sidonie. The narratives thus construct each of them as a heroine who takes justice into her own hands, revealing a profound conflict of values between the dominant culture and its "weaker" members. The women's subjection to forms of social control that further marginalizes them does not, however, succeed in annihilating their need for recognition and personal agency, even if this only manifests itself in dramatically violent acts. The narrative representation of these acts provokes a reexamination of the doxa—the acceptable norms or moral codes—of their respective cultures, inviting the reader to rethink the role and the definition of "woman." The women writers thus succeed in demystifying age-old traditions, providing a textual space where silence speaks, and reveals a much more complex perspective on what constitutes criminality in both the private and the public domains. For as Foucault has pointed out, "murder establishes the ambiguity of the lawful and the unlawful," and can serve, as a narrative catalyst, to reorganize our cultural experiences, and to blur cultural distinctions between arbitrary or relativistic norms of conduct and a truly ethical or universal moral code (cf. Black 18).

In its singularity, each of the sets of texts I examine refigures a cultural specificity (Kentucky, Botswana, Guadeloupe, Senegal). But taken together, they create a series of *lieux de mémoire* (Nora), that guide the reader through some of the most sordid places in the labyrinth of post/colonial human sexual relationships. These sites record testimonies that memorialize the experiences of a gendered cultural "minority"[5] bringing to representation the calcul-ated—either subdued or explosive—violence that has been the mark of domestic life. These sites, because they evoke the dystopian potential of oppressive and coercive gender arrangements, also "anchor, condense, and express the exhausted capital of our collective memory" (Nora 24), thus suggesting that on the local as well as well as the global level some hypothesis about reciprocal meanings and dialogical encounters can be elaborated on the basis of such a comparison among different cultural contexts. As Nora goes on to say, "contrary to historical objects, *lieux de mémoire* have no referent in reality; or, rather, they are their own referent: pure, exclusive, self-referential signs" (23). As such, then, narratives of murder by female characters open up a wide range of possible meanings: they are rhetorical resources, and offer a "grammar of fictional situations" that can help us explore what Hortense Spillers has called "the politics of intimacy," that is, the myriad ways in which language and literature can "create an attitude of containment or liberation" (89).

It is important to deal with crosscultural comparisons without falling into the trap of essentialism or that of false universalism. To state that comparisons are warranted on the theoretical basis of a certain understanding of *sites* of literarity and textuality is to bypass the culturalist/essentialist approach that tends to naively assume that a common ground necessarily exists among these various fictions simply because their authors share some common "African" origin—which they all do, of course. But, what I want to stress here, is that the similarities of theme in the works of Jones, Head, and Warner-Vieyra are not just the consequence of their shared "Africanness," but of a performative intertextuality which is a function of the ideological and cultural matrix that generates the works.[6] This dialectic of the particular and the universal which exists within the interpretive space of textuality has been understood as the foundation of literariness in the Western context. Now that the definition of literature is finally expanding to include the contributions of women and colonized peoples, it is becoming increasingly clear that this inclusion will inflect the accepted meaning of universality: since literature and literary criticism "[give] us a clue to the text of our own experience" (Spillers 88), it also broadens this experience in light of the alternative models and strategies proposed by heretofore "muted" groups. By focusing on such an extreme issue as murder, Jones, Head, and Warner-Vieyra refuse to be relegated to a relativistic theory of literature and culture: they demand to be taken seriously on the grounds that their concerns are universal ones, and that the issues raised by their fictions are the same that have compelled the human imagination since Sophocles and Euripides entertained fellow Athenians with tragic tales of murder and suicide. These writers make it obvious that Africans and African-Americans have their own particular perspective to add to the concert of voices that have dealt with such issues. As Africanist critic Bernard Mouralis has stated,

A partir du moment où les peuples de l'Afrique et de la Diaspora s'engageaient dans la voie de la création littéraire et assignaient à celle-ci une fonction de dévoilement et de démystification, l'Occident, confronté à ces textes intempestifs et, de surcroît, écrits dans des langues qui étaient les siennes, découvrait du même coup qu'il ne lui était plus possible de continuer à parler à la place de ceux qui les avaient produits. ("Réflexions" 10)

[As soon as the peoples of Africa and the Diaspora started to engage in literary creation, and to use literature as a means of revelation and demystification, the West found itself confronted with these unexpected texts written, furthermore, in its own languages. Westerners simultaneously discovered that it would no longer be possible to continue speaking for those who had produced such texts.]

Indeed, to read these narratives is to be provided with the woman's own perspective on gender dissymmetry within African and diasporic contexts. Furthermore, it is the intertextual references among their texts that underscore their status as literature. As Mouralis adds:

> La littérature est à la fois un objet social—repérable dans sa configuration institutionnelle—et un objet autre qui ne se réduit ni à un reflet du réel ni aux discours que l'idéologie tient sur le réel. (12)

> [Literature is both a social object—with a specific institutional configuration—and an other object which can be reduced neither to a reflection of reality, nor to the discourses on reality that ideology constructs.]

A commonality of theme—what I would like to call a geography of pain—and the production of a specifically female literary vision unite the works of Jones, Head, and Warner-Vieyra. All three write with meticulous attention to realistic detail, and the paradoxical desire to communicate, in the most honest way possible, the radically subjective, and thus generally incommunicable, experience of pain. Elaine Scarry has studied the "language-destroying" attribute of physical pain and torture (19), and its political consequences, namely, that it makes "overt precisely what is at stake in 'inexpressibility'" and thus "begin[s] to expose by inversion the essential character of 'expressibility,' whether verbal or material" (19). Scarry's project, which intersects with that of the women writers under study here, is a phenomenology of pain, it is "about the way other persons become visible to us, or cease to be visible to us. It is about the way we make ourselves (and the originally interior facts of sentience) available to one another through verbal and material artifacts" (22). Eva, Dikeledi, Juletane, and Sidonie (much like Firdaus in Nawal el Saadawi's *Woman at Point Zero*) are characters who come to feel that they are being denied the most elementary form of recognition and visibility, and are thus driven to murder as a result of the "inexpressibility," and cultural invisibility of their pain and dehumanization.

Jones, Head, and Warner-Vieyra are adept at representing the containment and imprisonment of their female characters within a social and textual space that stiffles and silences them. Restricted movement and confined locales are the principal *topoi* of these narratives, whether it be the hotel room where Davis keeps Eva, the village compound that circumscribes Dikeledi's life, the bedroom and then the hospital room where Juletane's madness develops, or the small Paris apartment where Sidonie, the invalid, witnesses her husband's infidelities. In this carceral world, the women's activities as well as their thought processes are controlled and policed by structures of domination that involve complex networks of power vested primarily in the male characters, but at times reinforced by other female characters, such as Juletane's co-wife Ndèye.

DISFIGURATION AND CASTRATION: JULETANE AND SIDONIE

> She did not know what essential parts of you stayed behind no matter how
> violently you tried to dislodge them in order to take them with you.
>
> Tsitsi Dangarembga, *Nervous Conditions* (173)

Published in 1982 and 1988 respectively, *Juletane* and *Femmes échouées*
(which includes "Sidonie") are the most recent of these stories of murder.
It is not clear whether Myriam Warner-Vieyra had read Gayl Jones's *Eva*
(1976), or Bessie Head's *The Collector of Treasures* (1977) before or while
she was writing her own. Warner-Vieyra does not seem to know English—her
only interview, conducted by Anne Adams in 1988, is in French, and does
not refer to any specific literary influences on her creative choices. Bessie
Head's stories have not been translated into French, but a translation of *Eva*
was published under the title *Meurtrière* by the Éditions des Femmes in Paris
in 1977. Whether Warner-Vieyra was influenced by Jones and Head is
impossible to determine at this point. But these works all belong to a period
marked by intense feminist questionings around the world, and which
culminated in the United Nations Decade for Women Conference in Nairobi
in 1985. By translating these international concerns into very private and
personal narratives that reflect her own experience as a displaced Guadeloupean woman, Warner-Vieyra looks at culture from a dual perspective: that
of the Western-educated woman (she has lived and worked as a hospital
librarian in Senegal for more than thirty years, after studying in Paris for a
brief period), who then marries an African intellectual (filmmaker Paulin
Vieyra) and follows him "home." She is thus acutely aware of the difficulties
faced by Antillean women like Juletane who experience culture shock in an
African milieu that is overwhelmingly Muslim.

   Juletane relies heavily on the principle of doubling, on both the levels of
theme and structure. The text constructs a dialogue between Juletane's diary
and Hélène's reading: it is thanks to the personal narrative of a fellow
Guadeloupean that Hélène recognizes her own "face," and her own predicament in the mirror of the story.[7] Doubling also occurs among the three co-
wives, Juletane, Ndèye, and Awa, in a way that is suggestive of the echoing
patterns of disfiguration, death, and castration that are at the center of Warner-
Vieyra's works.

   Feeling exiled in an inhospitable land, Juletane progressively loses her
ability to function in the family compound that she shares with Awa and
Ndèye, and literally shuts herself off from the community, depriving herself
of food, and gradually sinking into mental illness: "Je restai enfermée dans
notre chambre, sans boire ni manger" [I remained locked in our room without
eating or drinking](50/24). After a nervous breakdown and a violent outburst
caused by her inability to adapt to her husband's polygamous culture, she
spends time in a mental hospital, then has a miscarriage as a consequence of

an accident, becomes sterile, and thus alienates herself completely from the household: "J'ai définitivement enterré tout ce qui se passe en dehors de cette maison. Ma vie se déroule dans une chambre de cinq pas sur quatre et sous le manguier de la cour où je prends mes repas"[I have buried once and for all everything that goes on outside this house. My life unfolds in a room five paces by four and under the mango tree in the yard where I eat my meals] (54/26–27). This "manguier stérile" [barren tree] (134/74) is significant: it does not bear any fruit, and planted in the middle of the courtyard, it is a nagging reminder of Juletane's own "shortcomings" as a sterile wife. She begins to think of suicide (70/36), goes for days without food (69/36), shaves her head (72/37), begins to see Mamadou as a "monstre" (73/39), and displaces her fears onto every other human face she sees: "Je regardais les êtres humains qui m'entouraient; c'étaient des géants terrifiants, au visage monstrueux" [I looked at the people who surrounded me; they were frightful giants with monstrous faces] (74/39). She even harbors thoughts of murder against Mamadou: "Pour me venger, je l'imaginais mort, une belle dépouille de crapule puante sur laquelle je crachais" [To get revenge, I imagined him dead, nothing but a fine stinking corpse, on which I spat] (75/39). Her conflicts with Ndèye escalate to the point where the latter, calling her a "toubabesse" denies her the very identity she had come to Africa to claim: that of a black woman (79/42). Ndèye destroys Juletane's recording of Beethoven's Ninth Symphony, and violently slaps her face, propelling Juletane on a violent course of her own: "Cette gifle n'est que la goutte d'eau qui fait déborder ma coupe de passivité et transforme ma patience en torrent impétueux" [That slap in the face was the last drop that made my cup of passivity overflow and transformed my patience into a raging torrent] (93/50). Awa's children are found dead the following morning, and a week later, she literally disfigures Ndèye by pouring hot oil on her face (131/73), an incident that occurs after she had spent some time imagining herself sharpening the long kitchen knife, stabbing Ndèye to death, and watching her face become "un masque hideux aux yeux vitreux" [a hideous death mask, her eyes . . . glassy] (124/69). After being confined to a mental hospital, she dreams of visiting a cemetery with her father, and seeing her own grave stone, with no name on it. Feeling ever more like a "zombi" (74/39) from the Caribbean, she has the impression "d'être à la fois au-dessus et en dessous" [of being inside and outside the grave] (139/77), of being a traveler between the world of the living and that of the dead. Narrative closure is finally provided by her actual death three months later in the hospital, a death that appears to redeem Hélène, the reader in the text, from her own coldness and unfeeling existence as a displaced Guadeloupean.

If, as Paul de Man has written, "The autobiographical moment happens as an alignment between the two subjects involved in the process of reading in which they determine each other by mutual reflexive substitution" (921), then the death of the displaced post-colonial female subject is emblematic here of a much broader cultural phenomenon. Juletane's loss of identity and effective disfiguration and un-naming are a function of her own liminal positionality as both active and passive agent in the text. Clearly, there is a certain "mutual reflexive substitution" between Hélène and Juletane, since reading Juletane's diary transforms Hélène's life. More importantly, though, it is among the three co-wives that textual specularity is established in a non-binary fashion: for if Ndèye and Awa are each other's opposites—the modern, superficially educated, vulgar, spendthrift, urbanized wife, and the illiterate, but refined traditional African rural wife—they are also two figures whose fates incorporate elements of Juletane's own predicament: Awa commits suicide by jumping into a well, while Juletane keeps feeling trapped in a well of loneliness and despair, "ce puits de misère, où git mon corps depuis quelques années" [this well of misery where my body has been lying for years] (18/5); and Juletane appears to enact her own anxieties about her loss of self by disfiguring Ndèye. Juletane's diary thus constructs each of her co-wives as a "substitutive exchange that constitute [her as] subject" (De Man 921), since the specular structure of their relationships points to Juletane's implicit recognition of their shared predicament as faceless/nameless women occupying the position "wife," and hence easily substitutable or permutable within the familial economy. Self-writing or autobiography for Juletane thus serves to reinforce her sense of defacement, and confirms De Man's view that "death is a displaced name for a linguistic predicament, and the restoration of mortality by autobiography . . . deprives and disfigures to the precise extent that it restores. Autobiography veils a defacement of the mind of which it is itself the cause" (930). Indeed, the loss of self experienced by Juletane is reinforced by the writing of the diary: although writing does allow her to take stock of her situation—"écrire me fait du bien" [writing does me good] (87/46); "c'est . . . peut-être une bonne thérapeutique pour mes angoisses" [perhaps it is good therapy for my anxieties] (93/51)—it also participates in the process of un-naming, since the attribution of "monstrosity" slides from Mamadou (73) to Juletane herself as the narrative progresses: "Etais-je ce monstre de douleur?" [Was I this monster of pain?] (135/75), just as the death of Awa and disfiguration of Ndèye prefigure Juletane's own predicament in the end.

Furthermore, Juletane's madness, her feminine disorder, the fact that she ostensibly goes crazy and "loses her head" could be seen as a form of effective decapitation brought about by the patriarchal system up against which she finds herself, but that her transgressive behavior threatens. Her resounding, hysterical laughter, "the laugh of the Medusa" (Cixous), marks two crucial moments in the story. The first is when she imagines Mamadou dead: "Cette vision me fit éclater de rire, un rire absurde et démentiel, jusqu'à perdre le souffle" [this image made me burst out laughing, a ridiculous, demented, laugh which left me breathless] (75/39), and the second, when she fantasizes killing Ndèye: "J'éclate de rire en pensant à tout ce beau sang rouge qui s'échappe de la poitrine de Ndèye . . . Quelle belle farce, la préférée de Mamadou hors du circuit!" [I burst out laughing at the thought of all that beautiful red blood flowing from Ndèye's side ... What a lovely joke, Mamadou's favorite out of the running!] (125/69). Her laughter momentarily liberates her from Mamadou's hold on her. As Hélène Cixous knows so well, it is *laughter* that allows women to function outside of the male economy, and that is why it needs to be contained. In her essay on "Castration or Decapitation," Cixous relates a story about unruly Chinese women who literally have to choose between a beheading or keeping absolutely quiet. She writes:

> It's a question of submitting feminine disorder, its laughter ... to the threat of decapitation. If man operates under the threat of castration, if masculinity is culturally ordered by the castration complex, it might be said that the backlash, the return, on women of this castration anxiety is its displacement as decapitation, execution, of woman, as loss of her head. ("Castration" 346)

Driven to madness by the circumstances surrounding her induction into the economy of polygamy, Juletane, like the women in Cixous's story, does not actually lose her head by the sword. The women only keep their head "*on condition that they lose them* ... to complete silence" (346). Thus, "having lost her head" to what is labeled "madness," Juletane is committed to the psychiatric hospital, but there she refuses to say anything to the doctor who questions her (137): silence is her retreat, her escape, as it will be for Gayl Jones's Eva. Although imposed upon them, silence becomes, for these protagonists, their "loophole of retreat," as Linda Brent would put it about her life in the garret (Jacobs 114).

If, as Cixous argues, the disfiguration and decapitation to which patriarchy subjects women is a displacement of male castration anxiety, then Myriam Warner-Vieyra's works constitute an interesting attempt to work out this problematic in structural as well as thematic terms. In her short story "Sidonie" there is a double crime which links both castration and disfiguration. The castrated husband musters enough strength to strangle his invalid wife who is confined to a wheelchair. Here, it is Sidonie's brother, Septime, whose perspective dominates the third-person narrative. Warner-Vieyra uses free indirect discourse to enter into the minds of all the protagonists. But it is Septime's interior monologue that frames the beginning and the end of the tale. His self-centered concerns for his personal loss at the death of his sister reveals a shallowness, and a callousness which are damming. There is an unequal and dissymmetrical presentation of perspectives which mirrors the relative power of the characters. Each character's interior monologue allows the reader some insight into Sidonie's life and feelings, into her reasons for writing, her jealous nature, her relationship with Bernard, the car accident that paralyzed her, and her feelings toward the young woman her husband has gotten pregnant. But we are never allowed into her own consciousness, and it is truly her silence that is resounding here. No one really knows her. She writes but the reader does not have access to her notebooks. Yolène "croyait bien connaître Sidonie et ne l'aurait jamais crue capable de tant de determination, de violence barbare" (144). Bernard sees "son visage luisant de sueur, déformé par un rictus démentiel," and hears her "fou rire hystérique" just before he strangles her. His hands around her neck, below the mad, angry, and deformed face suggests a metaphoric beheading, actually confirming Cixous's suspicion about decapitation: the text clearly uses it as a form of punishment or retaliation for Bernard's castration.

Furthermore, there is no interpretation of Bernard's own actions and reactions: only Sidonie's unruly behavior gets the benefit of each characters' speculations and judgment. If the surface coherence of the texts thus strongly implies that Sidonie has gone mad, there is however an equally powerful countercoherence that emerges from the radical and disruptive force of the uninterpreted events of the story: it is up to the reader to examine these structural dissymmetries, and to understand the unstated social inequalities in the vision of each character. Sidonie is perhaps a "victim" gone mad, but, as with Juletane whose delusions make it hard to determine what degree of agency she is capable of having, it becomes clear that the very notion of agency needs to be redefined to accommodate those situations where extreme pain is *the* condition of subjectivity, of a "radical subjectivity" (Scarry 50) that imprisons humans in an utterly incommunicable experience. Juletane and Sidonie are locked in a private and painful world that remains largely inarticulate, and eruptions of violence are their only means of acting out their pain.

Thematically and textually, narrative closure is reached in death: the death of the title character. This is a very traditional way to provide closure and to restore order to the community. One might argue, then, that Warner-Vieyra's texts equivocate, that is, that they disown on a constructional level what they embrace on an ideological one.[8] Since Juletane regrets that Mamadou has died before being able to read her journal (140–141), she appears to have reached a state of "rationality" and accommodation that allows her final reentry into the symbolic realm of patriarchal culture. She no longer wants to live: *"Hélène avait appris ensuite que Juletane ne réagissait plus depuis la mort de son mari"* [*Hélène had consequently learned that since her husband's death, Juletane had ceased to react*] (142/79), and it is suggested that Hélène becomes a more gentle, accommodating, and "feminine" woman after reading the diary. (142) In effect, the structure of the work reinforces traditional notions of femininity in the end, despite the strong ideological critique of female alienation that it contains. Warner-Vieyra seems to want to do an about-face that will not antagonize traditional readers who constitute the majority of literate Africans capable of reading her works. This, of course, is a familiar tactic since Harriet Jacobs's *Incidents*. It is even clearer in "Sidonie" since Septime's point of view is more sympathetic to Bernard's awful "mutilation" (146) than to his sister's crippled body and death. Male solidarity triumphs over female hysteria, and the social order remains intact.

MEDUSA'S SILENCE: EVA

> Out of the ash
> I rise with my red hair
> And I eat men like air.

> Sylvia Plath, "Lady Lazarus"

> Your hair fallen on your cheek, no longer in the semblance of serpents,
> Lifted in the gale; your mouth, that shrieked so, silent.
> You, my scourge, my sister, lie asleep, like a child,
> Who, after rage, for an hour quiet, sleeps out its tears.

> Louise Bogan, "The Sleeping Fury"

Castration and hysteria are central to the narrative of *Eva's Man*. Unlike the two previous texts, Gayl Jones's title seems to focus on the man in/of the story. It is after all Davis's death that the story attempts to explain without however requiring that the murderess have a believable rational motive. Eva's subjectivity is filled with the voices of others, it is a kind of echo chamber in which her self-representations are always mediated by the words and actions of others,[9] by the cultural discourses that attribute certain nominative properties to women.[10] Although *Eva's Man* is a first-person narrative, it does not present a coherent perspective. Much like Condé's Veronica who embraces the epithet "Marilisse" despite its negative connotations (*Heremakhonon* 130), Eva interrogates the terms of address that construct women as "Eve," "Medusa," "Salome" or "Queen Bee" by pushing these representations to their logical extreme.

Her story begins at the end: "The police came and found arsenic in the glass" (3). A crime has been committed, but the arsenic does not yet explain why "a lot of people like to go ... and see where the crime happened." The reader's first impression of Eva is mediated by her cell mate Elvira's reported speech: "Elvira said they had my picture [in the paper] and my hair was all uncombed and they had me looking like a wild woman." The figure of Medusa looms behind our initial encounter with Eva, and the impression is confirmed as the story progresses: her lover, Davis "wouldn't let [her] comb [her] hair" (10), and he is explicit about her appearance: "You look like a lion, all that hair ... a male lion ... Eva Medusa's a lion" (16). To which Eva replies that her name is Eva Medina. Later on, he calls her "Eve" (44), and again she angrily corrects him, but he continues to associate her with women who are fatal to men, women whose gaze is a lethal lure: "There was something in your eyes" (46); "Don't look at me that way" (47). Elvira, on the other hand, sarcastically brings up the image of Salomé: "Just like in that Bible story, ain't it? Except got his *dick* on a platter" (47). And finally, Eva herself brings the point home when she says to the prison psychiatrist who questions her about her motives for killing Davis, and the reasons that made her castrate him after his death: "My hair looks like snakes, doesn't it?" (77). This echoes Elvira's intial question, "Do you kill every man you go with?" (17), which overdetermines the reader's understanding of Eva from the beginning. When Eva bites off Davis's penis after having poisoned him, she explicitly relates the event to Eve's biting into the apple of knowledge: "I got back on the bed and squeezed his dick hard in my teeth. I bit down hard. My teeth in an apple" (128). All the cultural symbols that construct woman as a dangerous temptress, a bewitching snare, are brought together at the scene of Davis's castration.

Thus, Eva's self-representation as well as the way she feels about herself and her actions cannot be separated from the cultural images of women that are common currency around her. Consequently, when the psychiatrist who tries to "help" her asks her how she feels, she can only recall other instances of people asking her and other women how "it feels" (77), for how is a woman supposed to feel about her own sexuality when its value is repeatedly denied, when she knows nothing about her own desires, and when male sexuality expresses itself in the form of sexual harassment? The doctor is an obvious composite of the male protagonists who have used her in the past: his name is David Smoot, recalling young Freddy Smoot as well as Davis Carter himself. In fact, just as Eva is made to represent a certain stereotype of fatal woman, all the men eventually merge into one single paradigm of male dominance, the voice of "all them Dr. Frauds" (148) that, since Freud, keeps on interrogating femininity: "Why won't you talk about yourself?" (67); "Why did you kill him?" (167); "What did he do?"(169); "What happened?" (170); "Did you want to do anything you did?" (173). This is the same voice that has always puzzled over "what a woman wants." Like Juletane or Saadawi's Firdaus, Eva refuses to explain herself: "I don't like to talk about myself" (73), and this is the only way she has of resisting the dominant discourses that emprison her inside certain labels: "Her silences are . . . ways of maintaining . . . autonomy," Gayl Jones has said (Interview 97). Her seemingly passive compliance is a way of resisting the double-bind, what Cixous has called the "phallocentric representationalism" ("The Laugh" 254) that distorts and objectifies: "You keep all your secrets, don't you?" (101), Davis says, when there are in fact no "secrets" to keep, only the impossibility for the woman to acceed to the symbolic realm of language without simultaneously putting herself under erasure, risking misunderstanding, or confirming the patriarchal representations that preexist her speech: "A motive was never given. She never said anything. She just took the sentence" (153). It is this apparent "serenity" that leads to the insanity plea: "When a woman done something like you done and serene like that, no wonder they think you crazy" (155), as Elvira explains. Eva instinctively knows what the entire United States would be forced to watch during Anita Hill's testimony before the United States Senate in September 1991: that what a black woman might feel, and what she might want, are so inconceivable to the imagination of a patriarchal nation, so threatening, that she must be neutralized by stereotypical accusations of feminine instability and unreliability.

If Eva conforms to the damaging stereotypes, and plays the part with a vengeance, it is in large measure her way of escaping behind the negative images, of protecting her own autonomy as Jones suggests, of accepting the defacement of those names in order to better subvert the system: she does not attempt to rename or refigure herself. She remains silent, and refuses the psychiatrist's representations: "Don't you explain me" (173; 174). Unlike Eva, however, Elvira's "madness" is the madness of feminine excess: her "problem" is "hysteria" (45), and she is defined by her laughter (10, 16, 45), by the fact that she is allowed to travel between the inside (jail) and the outside (society), and to return with stories of what is being said in the papers about Eva (3). Elvira stands outside of the symbolic framework, can retreat into the imaginary by letting her body talk, and can relate to Eva on the intersubjective level that remakes them both into a new image of femininity, one no longer implicated into the morbid erotic economy of masculine desire triggered by fear. Previously silenced by the (male) other's presence: "I wanted to tell him how I was feeling. But I never would tell him" (158), Eva is now able to recognize her own desire, to "speak her pleasure" ("Castration" 353), and to accept Elvira's offer of lesbian sexuality (177). Her sexual desire is no longer desire-for-the-other; rather, it is desire-in-itself, and it does not need to be verbalized since it is in stillness and secrecy that it can manifest itself without being recuperated by patriarchy. As Cixous explains,

> silence is the mark of hysteria. The great hysterics have lost speech, they are aphonic, and at times have lost more than speech: they are pushed to the point of choking, nothing gets through. They are decapitated, their tongues are cut off and what talks isn't heard because it is the body that talks, and man doesn't hear the body. In the end, the woman pushed to hysteria is the woman who disturbs and is nothing but disturbance. ("Castration" 352)

Eva's disturbance, like Juletane's, is her way of eluding power by means of violent acts that inscribe female agency on the interpretive text of patriarchy, resisting her construction as a "zombi," as one of the "demon women" whose trance-like passivity belies a deep determination to escape from the stereotype (148).

On a structural level, Jones makes no attempt to placate her readers: *Eva's Man* is a difficult book, a tale of great intensity that resists closure. As I suggested above, it is a story about men, about their obsessive sexuality and exploitative relationships. Eva's own personal story is not really told, since most of what we know of her is what the men in her life (Freddy, Mr. Logan, John Canada, Tyrone, Davis, Alfonso, Moses Tripp, James Hunn, and finally David Smoot) have done to the women she knows. The narrative shows how they have made Eva herself into a "little evil devil bitch" (35), a "sweet [castrating] bitch" (see 64, 127, 138, 139, 173). The narrative fragments do not add up to a coherent picture of the past, and the novel thematizes its structural discontinuities by stressing the gaps and the fissures in Eva's memory, by suggesting that it is thanks to those gaps that she can manage to slip out of the symbolic domain, and disrupt the culture's master narrative.

It is interesting to note that the name Eva is contained within the name *Elvira*. This would seem to suggest that Eva is meant to be reincorporated into a different economy, that of a woman-identified sexuality, into which Elvira will finally initiate her. If Elvira can absorb and contain Eva, this icon of all the negative representations of women, then perhaps she can also reengender her as a new female subject: Eva finds in her emprisonment the key to her liberation, since it allows her to discover a female community in the transitional space of the psychiatric ward, in the "in-between" where "different subjects knowing one another and beginning one another anew only form the living boundaries of the other" ("The Laugh" 254). It is in this process of exchange that, according to Cixous, the "newly born woman" can begin to reject the demeaning cultural values she has internalized. It is in that space that she can envisage a world where a "lesbian continuum," as defined by Adrienne Rich, can replace the violence of compulsory hetero-sexuality and female sexual slavery (Rich 51, 43). In the end, Eva realizes that what she wants is "nothing [he] can give" (176). She displaces her focus to a space outside of the politics of (male) aggression and power, offering passive resistance to the cultural scenarios that frame her as a *femme fatale*. Thus, the "Now" (177) she utters as she surrenders to Elvira brings her into a present that suggests an alternative to her passive submission to, and acceptance of, the other's will to pleasure.

FINDING "GOLD AMIDST THE ASH": LIFE AND DIKELEDI

> Where the storyteller is loyal, eternally and unswervingly loyal to the story, there, in the end, silence will speak.
>
> Isak Dinesen, "The Blank Page" in *Last Tales* (100)

Like Warner-Vieyra, Bessie Head is an exile who willingly talks about her personal experiences and how they have affected her creative choices. In this, they differ considerably from Jones who prefers to retain a degree of anonymity and distance from her reading public. Head's works explore the question of marginality from the perspective of a stateless person. Born in an asylum and forced to live as a stateless exiled person in Botswana for many years, Head, who died in 1986, was the mixed-race daughter of a wealthy South African woman of Scottish descent and a black stable boy. Her mother had been committed to the asylum because of the interracial love affair, and, at her death, she left money to be used for Bessie's education. Bessie was first cared for by a foster family who soon rejected her, and she ended up in a mission school where she became very close to one of her teachers.

This aspect of her personal life forms the basis of her novel *Maru*, as well as *A Question of Power*, another autobiographical novel which was written during a period of great stress and depression experienced in the late 1960s, after an unhappy marriage and divorce. But, with the short stories in *The Collector of Treasures*, published after the novels, she writes about village life in Botswana in a clear prose rich in evocative and realistic details, and full of humor and tenderness. It is with those tales that Bessie Head has truly acquired the "cool stance" and "detachment" that she considers her goals as a writer. Her tragic tales of domestic horror focus attention on the mental and physical plight of women who find themselves trapped in the very institution which is supposed to protect and nurture them and their children. She "[leads] us to realize how deeply violence is anchored in the domestic domain" (Bal 231). But her characters, male and female, are depicted with a great deal of affection and concern. She avoids any simplistic polarization of the issues: for her it is not just the advent of modernity or the aftermath of colonialism that causes the breakdown of the family, but deep and specific cultural realities that must be correctly "read," interpreted, and understood before one can propose to act on them.

Indeed, if Head is clearly sympathetic to her women protagonists, one cannot say that she offers a one-sided view of the social picture: her male characters are not uniformly evil, far from it. As she has said, "as a storyteller [you can] shape the future," and she asserts that although she borrows her "basic plot" from life, she likes to add positive male figures that she hopes can act as role models for other young men. Paul Thebolo in "The Collector of Treasures" is such a man, this "*huge* majestic man [who] moves into the story [and is] going to solve all the problems of family life" (14). As Head insists, "there's a kind of coolness and detachment in my work . . . The cool stance means: you are up on a horizon, you have the biggest view possible. The storyteller has to have that. It's not so much a question of being black as of having got control of life's learning . . . I shape the future with this cool stance, the view that's above everything" (Interview 12–13). Her strong belief in the performative powers of narrative places her among those African writers for whom writing is "an essential gesture" (Gordimer) that helps to break the longstanding silence of, and about, women, and to expose oppressive cultural taboos and archaic customs.

Beyond the simple suggestion that murder is an inevitable act of resistance for the female protagonist who has reached the end of her rope and can no longer endure her condition of overt and/or subtle oppression, Head also raises the issue of agency: she is well aware of the all too easy cop-out of representing the Third World Woman as the monolithic "victim" of both *universal* patriarchy, and *specific* black male exploitation. She prefers, instead, to give us some insights into the social configurations of power that drive women to make desperate decisions when they are trapped in dead-end situations. As outsider to the culture of Botswana, she has the kind of freedom from her immediate environment that allows her to apprehend individual pain and suffering without feeling hemmed in by customs and traditions that might be used to justify or defend the status quo. This allows her to play the role of social satirist, to write stories that place her within the European narrative tradition of a seventeenth-century "moralist."

Two of the stories, "Life" and "The Collector of Treasures," offer interesting contrasts: they both deal with the changing village economy, and with domestic conflicts that are resolved violently, the murder weapon being a kitchen knife used, in one case, by Lesego to stab his wife, Life, and in the other, by Dikeledi to castrate her husband. The events that lead to this calmly premeditated act suggest that it is the supportive community that women build around themselves that gives them the courage to oppose the male social order, and to jeopardize their own life and freedom. These communities function on a principle of exchange and barter which gives women a great deal of independence that is gradually undermined by the advent of capitalism.

In "Life," the "beer-brewing women were a gay and lovable crowd who had emancipated themselves some time ago" (39). Much like Cixous's transgressive figures, they "talked and laughed loudly and slapped each other on the back and *had developed a language all their own*" (my emphasis). Men, in this context, are parasites who "[hang] around, [live] on the resources of the women." It is they who become objects of exchange, shared by the women: "Many men passed through their lives." Life introduces prostitution in the village, bringing a more mercenary approach to a system that functioned on the principle of the friendly trade of goods and services. This causes her eventual downfall, as she is too "bold," too "free," and too indifferent to rural "social taboos" (40) to put up with a traditional married life in which "she found no one with whom she could communicate what had become an actual physical pain" (44). Her fun-loving urban ways introduce dissymmetry in her relationships with the people of the village. As the omniscient narrator suggests: "Village people reacted in their own way; what they liked, and what was beneficial to them, they absorbed . . . what was harmful to them, they rejected. The murder of Life had this complicated undertone of rejection" (37). By coming back to the village after ten years in the city and marrying a "dull" shepherd, Life puts herself in a situation where she ostensibly acquires unacceptable power due to her ability to make money by using her body. Money becomes the sign of a disturbing independence for the villagers, it is a destabilizing force which undermines the order of things, and she has to be neutralized. Like the money she makes, she becomes a sign that severely disrupts both the gender economy and the system of barter particular to that village.

After her death, enter the justice system and the courts: Lesego who is apparently a "straightforward, uncomplicated" man proves to be a master of signs as well: "The judge who was a white man, and therefore not involved in Twsana customs and its debates, was as much impressed by Lesego's manner as all the village men had been" (46). He thus gives Lesego a much-reduced sentence (five years) because "this is a crime of passion" (46). Lesego's authoritative "manner," his ability to pass judgment, and to interpret reality, has the desired effect on the white judge. Here, it seems to me, Head underscores universal male solidarity against irrational female behavior: indeed, the text suggests that "*wild anger* was driving [Life] to break out of a way of life that was like death to her" (44). But this contrasts sharply with Lesego's "logical" and "rational" explanation of his own behavior, an explanation that convinces all men present. This is "the fundamental struggle to enforce and strengthen dissymmetrical (unequal) power relations" (18) that Mieke Bal has analyzed in another context: Lesego knows how to use language as an instrument of power, how to put the judge on his side. He "interprets" Life's lived reality the better to reduce her to silence.

By contrast, in "The Collector of Treasures," Dikeledi gets a life sentence. No one argues in her favor for a reduced sentence based on self-defense or a "crime of passion." The workings of the legal system are not made visible in this story. It is as though the female defendant is completely invisible to the justice system. The story begins with the image of the "crumpled" heap, "oblivious to everything but her pain" during the long journey in the police truck to "the long-term central state prison in the south" (87). If the text later makes clear that Dikeledi is a brave and innocent woman, a patient and methodical worker who accomplishes her crime in her own conscienscious way ("With the precision and skill of her hard-working hands, she grasped hold of his genitals and cut them off with one stroke" 103), thus putting the reader's sympathies on her side, it also suggests that she has no means of access to the interpretive system that grants power to those who can manipulate it. She is a socially silenced subject whose ability to act as an effective moral agent to protect herself and her children recalls Linda Brent's familiar predicament in the American slave-owning South.

Dikeledi has a community of supportive women friends with whom she exchanges goods and services. Kenalepe, with whom she has "one of those deep, affectionate, sharing-everything kind of friendships that only women know how to have" (94) even offers her husband because Dikeledi's husband has left her: "I can loan Paul to you if you like" (96). The text suggests that this generous and sharing attitude contrasts with that of the misguided women who, allowing themselves to be divided by the men who use them, chase their unfaithful husbands "from one hut to another [in order to] beat up the girlfriends" (95). "We must help each other" (91) is the message Bessie Head's women give to other women, and Dikeledi can count on Paul and Kenalepe to take care of her children after she is sent to jail. As in "Life," it is interesting to note that money is the primary cause of social disturbance: it is because Dikeledi is "short on R20.00 to cover the fees" (99) for her son's school that she appeals to Garesego for help. It is because he expects her to be sexually available to him if he is going to help financially that she finally rebels against "defilement by an evil man" (101), and castrates him.

What is most significant about these female characters is the degree of independence and agency that they succeed in maintaining throughout the narratives. Unlike Warner-Vieyra and Gayl Jones, Head shows a certain indomitable optimism. To be sure, Life dies and Dikeledi is serving a life-sentence, but Head trusts her reader to share her views about the fundamental inequities that she dramatizes in those stories. She believes that, like Dikeledi, our task as human beings is to attempt to find "gold amidst the ash" (91), to rise above the arbitrary moral codes of a given culture, and to exonerate the victims for whom the end must justify the means. She appeals to a form of classical humanism based on moral standards that transcend cultural epiphenomena. Dikeledi finds a community in jail, she puts ner numerous skills to good use, building friendships behind bars as she had in the village, believing in female solidarity, and finding "deep loves that had joined her heart to the heart of others" (91).

If this is an idealized picture of prison life, it nonetheless suggests the possibility that the role of literature is to reinforce the belief in the "universal" qualities of creativity and generosity that Dikeledi demonstrates. It is thus fair to say that Head would probably subscribe to a recent statement made by critic Guy Ossito Midiohouan about African literature:

> As the expression of a creativity that ceaselessly strives to reinvent society, culture and history in an impulse that renders us more conscious of ourselves and of the world around us, ... modern African literature collectively profiles our identity and helps make us into peoples who, while being carried along by the currents of history and attending to the life of the world, are not assimilated into an impoverishing, planet-wide uniformity but, on the contrary, contribute to the Universal, which can only be rich by virtue of the variety that different peoples bring to it. (96)

However encouraging such a view might be, the question remains of what degree of specificity can be translated into a universal language when the specificity in question is that of the grave physical and emotional pain that generally remains invisible—"planet-wide"—because its victims are only women (again, witness Anita Hill's fate).

As a privileged symbolic space, the "body in pain" translates cultural conflicts into a visible representational frame: the words that describe Dikeledi as she is being carried away to the state prison underscore the extent to which she has been dehumanized, "crawl[ing] painfully forward in silence" (88), "more like a skeleton than a human being" (89). But if women's pain and suffering remain marginal in most cultures, then Dikeledi, like Life, Juletane, and Eva, is locked into a form of subjectivity that annuls our interpretive possibilities *vis-à-vis* these texts. If women's pain cannot be articulated, verbalized, interpreted, and communicated in a language that makes it visible to "universal" patriarchy, then the women protagonists of these stories are in a position of radical dissymmetry as regards the rest of us, writers and critics, who are in command of the interpretative means that can give larger significance to their lives. This is the contradiction inherent in the relationship between textuality and reality: it emphasizes that the problematics of universalism in the context of women's literatures remains a dead letter so long as women's silences and body languages continue to be ignored or recuperated by the symbolic order, thus becoming the "black holes" (so to speak) within and against which all interpretive discourses can only come to a halting stop.

NOTES

1 I am foregrounding the gender issue and working under the well-understood assumption that (post/neo)colonialism is the immediate historical context within which these issues emerge. I do want to stress, however, that my purpose here is not to do a critique of colonialism but of gender dissymmetry. Colonialism has had its share of by now "canonical" critics, from Nkrumah to Cabral, from C.L.R. James to Césaire and Fanon. The position taken by a few radical critics of black sexism is more specifically my focus here.

2 I am not suggesting—and neither is Bessie Head—that the impact of British colonialism on the fact of women's oppression is negligible. Rather, I see Head as stressing the larger historical context, the total cultural picture, instead of simply opposing in binary fashion the indigenous traditions to the colonizer's values.

3 Marshall suggests that Ursa's father, the powerful Primus Mackenzie was born on the wrong side of the Atlantic: that he has, in other words, retained the polygamous customs of his African ancestors (cf. p. 407).

4 The review by Sven Birkerts states "Marshall has written a powerful novel . . . [but] she has impaled the black man in the process" (76). He echoes all the other critics who believe, like him, that "Black women writers appear to have declared open season on black men. In best-selling novels by Alice Walker, Toni Morrrison, Gloria Naylor, and others, I hunt in vain to find males as strong, as honorable or as emotionally mature as their female counterparts" p. 78.

5 Not a numerical minority, but a cultural one: that is, one whose point of view is not part of the "majority" culture.

6 As Jean Bessière puts it in his recent *Dire le littéraire*:

> La validité parfaite du discours serait dans un *universel singulier* . . . La validité du littéraire est par la série de ses phrases qui sont des univers spécifiques et autant de notations de la différence idiomatique . . . Le discours littéraire . . . est l'interprétant de tout discours suivant la pluralité des langages. Il n'éclaire pas mais il dispose les lieux de la parole. Il est inévitablemant un fictif parce qu'il est cette reprise interprétative qui, au moyen de la "textualité", préfigure de façon variable les témoins, les moments, les espaces de la parole. Le littéraire importe ici par ce qu'il suppose d'une *intelligibilité commune*. (310–311)

> [The perfect validity of discourse would seem to reside in the fact that it is a *singular universal*. The validity of the literary stems from its series of sentences which are specific universes, and as many marks of idiomatic difference . . . Literary discourse . . . does not clarify, but it maps out the places of speech. It is necessarily fictive because it is this interpretative repetition, which prefigures, by means of 'textuality,' and in a variable way, the witnesses, the moments, the spaces of speech. The literary matters here because it presupposes a *common understanding*.] (All translations are mine unless otherwise noted.)

7 Jonathan Ngaté's careful study of the *mise-en-abyme* of the effect of reading has stressed this dialogical encounter.

8 See D.A. Miller's discussion of this phenomenon as regards the works of Jane Austen (pp. 48ff).
9 This recalls Maryse Condé's handling of Véronica, the main protagonist in *Heremakhonon*. See Lionnet, *Autobiographical Voices*, ch. 5.
10 See Spillers's discussion of what she calls "overdetermined nominative properties" in "Mama's Baby," p. 65.

WORKS CITED

Bal, Mieke. *Death and Dissymmetry: The Politics of Coherence in the Book of Judges.* Chicago: The University of Chicago Press, 1988.
Bessière, Jean. *Dire le littéraire: points de vue théoriques.* Liège and Bruxelles: Pierre Mardaga Éd., 1990.
Birkerts, Sven. "The Black Woman's Burden." *Mirabella* (October 1991): 76–78.
Black, Joel. *The Aesthetics of Murder: A Study in Romantic Literature and Contemporary Culture.* Baltimore: The Johns Hopkins University Press, 1991.
Cixous, Hélène. "The Laugh of the Medusa." *New French Feminisms: An Anthology.* Ed. Elaine Marks and Isabelle de Courtivron. Amherst: The University of Massachusetts Press, 1980: 245–264.
——. "Castration or Decapitation." *Out There: Marginalization and Contemporary Cultures.* Ed. Russell Ferguson et al. Cambridge, MA: The New Museum of Contemporary Art and MIT Press, 1990: 345–356.
Condé, Maryse. *Heremakhonon.* Paris: UGE, 1976.
Dangarembga, Tsitsi. *Nervous Conditions.* Seattle: The Seal Press, 1988.
De Man, Paul. "Autobiography as De-Facement." *Modern Language Notes* 94 (1979): 919–930.
Foucault, Michel, ed. *I, Pierre Rivière, Having Slaughtered My Mother, My Sister, and My Brother . . .: A Case of Parricide in the Nineteenth Century.* Trans. Frank Jellinek. New York: Pantheon Books, 1975.
Gilbert, Sandra, M. and Susan Gubar, eds. *The Norton Anthology of Literature by Women.* New York: W.W. Norton, 1985. (For poems by Audre Lorde, Louise Bogan and Sylvia Plath.)
Gordimer, Nadine. *The Essential Gesture: Writing, Politics and Places.* Ed. Stephen Clingman. New York: Knopf, 1988.
Head, Bessie. *The Collector of Treasures.* London: Heinemann, 1977.
——. Interview in *Between The Lines.* Ed. Craig Mackenzie and Cherry Clayton. Grahamstown, South Africa: National English Literary Museum, 1989.
Jacobs, Harriet. *Incidents in the Life of a Slave Girl.* Ed. Jean Fagan Yellin. Cambridge: Harvard University Press, 1987.
Jones, Gayl. *Eva's Man.* Boston: Beacon Press, 1977.
——. Interview with Claudia Tate. *Black Women Writers at Work.* New York: Continuum, 1983. 89–99.
Lionnet, Françoise. "Dissymmetry Embodied: Feminism, Universalism and The Practice of Excision." *Passages: A Chronicle of the Humanities* 1 (1991): 2–4.
——. *Autobiographical Voices: Race, Gender, Self-Portraiture.* Ithaca: Cornell University Press, 1989.
Marshall, Paule. *Daughters.* New York: Atheneum, 1991.
McDowell, Deborah. "New Directions for Black Feminist Criticism." *The New Feminist Criticism: Essays on Women, Literature, and Theory.* Ed. Elaine Showalter. New York: Pantheon, 1985. 186–199.
Mernissi, Fatima. *Beyond the Veil: Male–Female Dynamics in Modern Muslim Society.* Bloomington: Indiana University Press, 1987.

Midiohouan, Guy Ossito. "Modern Literature and the Flourishing of Culture in Black Africa." *Research in African Literatures* 22.1 (Spring 1991): 93–99.

Miller, D. A. *Narrative and its Discontents: Problems of Closure in the Traditional Novel.* Princeton: Princeton University Press, 1981.

Mouralis, Bernard. "Réflexions sur l'enseignement des littératures africaines." *Nouvelles du Sud* (Août–Septembre–Octobre 1985): 7–13.

Ngaté, Jonathan. "Reading Warner-Vieyra's *Juletane.*" *Callaloo* 9 (1986): 553–563.

Nora, Pierre. "Between Memory and History: *Les Lieux de mémoire.*" *Representations* 26 (Spring 1989): 7–25.

Rich, Adrienne. "Compulsory Heterosexuality and Lesbian Existence." *Blood, Bread, and Poetry: Selected Prose 1979–1985.* New York: W.W. Norton, 1986. 23–75.

Saadawi, Nawal el. *Woman at Point Zero.* London: Zed Press, 1983.

Scarry, Elaine. *The Body in Pain: The Making and Unmaking of the World.* New York: Oxford University Press, 1985.

Schipper, Mineke. *Beyond The Boundaries: Text and Context in African Literature.* Chicago: Ivan R. Dee, 1989.

Spillers, Hortense. "The Politics of Intimacy: A Discussion." *Sturdy Black Bridges: Visions of Black Women in Literature.* Ed. Roseann P. Bell et al. Garden City, NY: Anchor Books, 1979. 87–106.

——. "Mama's Baby, Papa's Maybe: An American Grammar Book" *Diacritics* 17: 2 (Spring 1987): 65–81.

Warner-Vieyra, Myriam. *Juletane.* Paris: Présence africaine, 1982.

——. *Juletane.* Trans. Betty Wilson. Oxford: Heinemann, 1987.

——. *Femmes échouées.* Paris: Présence africaine, 1987.

Index

Page numbers in bold denote major section/chapter devoted to subject, n denotes note